The President's Kill List

Intelligence, Surveillance and Secret Warfare

Series Editors: Richard J. Aldrich, Rory Cormac, Michael S. Goodman, Hugh Wilford and Daniela Richterova

This series explores the full spectrum of spying and secret warfare in a globalised world

Intelligence has changed. Secret service is no longer just about spying or passively watching a target. Espionage chiefs now command secret armies and legions of cyber warriors who can quietly shape international relations itself. Intelligence actively supports diplomacy, peacekeeping and warfare: the entire spectrum of security activities. As traditional interstate wars become more costly, covert action, black propaganda and other forms of secret interventionism become more important. This ranges from proxy warfare to covert action; from targeted killing to disruption activity. Meanwhile, surveillance permeates communications to the point where many feel there is little privacy. Intelligence, and the accelerating technology that surrounds it, has never been more important for the citizen and the state.

Titles in the *Intelligence, Surveillance and Secret Warfare* series include:

Published:
The Arab World and Western Intelligence: Analysing the Middle East, 1956–1981
Dina Rezk

The Twilight of the British Empire: British Intelligence and Counter-Subversion in the Middle East, 1948–63
Chikara Hashimoto

Chile, the CIA and the Cold War: A Transatlantic Perspective
James Lockhart

The Clandestine Lives of Colonel David Smiley: Code Name 'Grin'
Clive Jones

The Problem of Secret Intelligence
Kjetil Anders Hatlebrekke

Outsourcing US Intelligence: Private Contractors and Government Accountability
Damien Van Puyvelde

The CIA and the Pursuit of Security: History, Documents and Contexts
Huw Dylan, David Gioe and Michael S. Goodman

Cognitive Bias in Intelligence Analysis: Testing the Analysis of Competing Hypotheses Method
Martha Whitesmith

Defector: Revelations of Renegade Intelligence Officers, 1924–1954
Kevin Riehle

Intelligence Power in Practice
Michael Herman with David Schaefer

Estimative Intelligence in European Foreign Policymaking: Learning Lessons from an Era of Surprise
Christoph Meyer, Michael S. Goodman, Aviva Guttmann, Nikki Ikani and Eva Michaels

The President's Kill List: Assassination and US Foreign Policy since 1945
Luca Trenta

Forthcoming:
The Snowden Era on Screen: Signals Intelligence and Digital Surveillance
James Smith

Intelligence, Security and the State: Reviewing the British Intelligence Community in the Twentieth Century
Christopher Murphy and Dan Lomas

British Security Intelligence in Singapore: Counter-Subversion for Southeast Asia, 1939–1963
Alexander Nicholas Shaw

Canada's Secret Cold War History: Learning to Spy as a Middle Power
Wesley Wark

https://edinburghuniversitypress.com/series-intelligence-surveillance-and-secret-warfare.html

The President's Kill List

Assassination and US Foreign Policy since 1945

Luca Trenta

EDINBURGH
University Press

Edinburgh University Press is one of the leading university presses in the UK. We publish academic books and journals in our selected subject areas across the humanities and social sciences, combining cutting-edge scholarship with high editorial and production values to produce academic works of lasting importance. For more information visit our website: edinburghuniversitypress.com

© Luca Trenta, 2024

Edinburgh University Press Ltd
13 Infirmary Street
Edinburgh EH1 1LT

Typeset in 11/13 Adobe Sabon by
IDSUK (Dataconnection) Ltd, and
printed and bound in Great Britain.

A CIP record for this book is available from the British Library

ISBN 978-1-3995-1949-6 (hardback)
ISBN 978-1-3995-1951-9 (webready PDF)
ISBN 978-1-3995-1952-6 (epub)

The right of Luca Trenta to be identified as the author of this work has been asserted in accordance with the Copyright, Designs and Patents Act 1988, and the Copyright and Related Rights Regulations 2003 (SI No. 2498).

Contents

Acknowledgements vii
List of Abbreviations ix

Introduction: The US Government and the Assassination of Foreign Officials 1

1. Experimenting with Assassination: Brainwashing, Poison and Early Cold War Plots 24
2. Patrice Lumumba: Eisenhower's Order to Kill 45
3. Fidel Castro: The US Government's Assassination Campaign against Cuba 75
4. Rafael Trujillo: Assassination and the US Role in Covert Regime Change 110
5. Ngo Dinh Diem: Preparing the Ground for Assassination 133
6. René Schneider: Removing the Main Obstacle to a Coup in Chile 154
7. The 'Season of Inquiry' and the Fight over the Ban on Assassination 180
8. Muhammar Qaddafi: The Return of Assassination during the Reagan Years 213
9. Manuel Noriega: Coups, Failed Coups and the Ban on Assassination 250
10. Saddam Hussein: Assassination and the Long Confrontation between the US Government and Iraq 271

Contents

11. Osama Bin Laden: Assassination and Counterterrorism on the Road to 9/11   301

Conclusion: Assassination, 'Targeted Killings' and the Ban since 9/11   341

Resources   367
Index   370

Acknowledgements

I started researching the US government's involvement in assassination in 2016, when the British Academy took a chance on my project on the re-emergence of assassination in the Reagan era. I am grateful for their support then and since. In the intervening years, several categories of people have helped with the writing of this book. Due to the COVID-19 pandemic and travel restrictions, research assistants helped with the collection of primary sources. These include Max Wright, Michael Callahan, Kellie Solomon and Pauline Kulstad.

Most of the book was written during a sabbatical granted by Swansea University. At Swansea, my thanks go to Dawn Bolger, Dion Curry and Matt Wall who read and provided feedback on various chapters. Jack Tudor helped in the first round of editing, when the manuscript was still an unruly beast.

I am indebted to all the interviewees – listed at the end of the book – who took time to discuss such a controversial topic with me. Many of the interviewees were generous with their time and helped by providing comments, feedback and archival material. A necessarily partial list includes Thomas Tunstall Allcock, James Siekmeier, Thomas Field, Susan Williams, Bernardo Vega, Sarah-Jane Corke and Arturo Jimenez-Bacardi.

I am forever grateful to Edinburgh University Press, to the patient commissioning editor Ersev Ersoy, and to the series editors. Special thanks to Rory Cormac who supported me throughout the project and attentively read – and made more readable – the whole manuscript. In the final stretch, the detailed comments and supportive feedback of Hugh Wilford helped in raising my spirits and in making the manuscript what it is. Any mistakes that remain in the book are mine.

Acknowledgements

On the topic of raising spirits, the process of writing a book has proven much harder than I imagined. The task was made easier by the support, patience and love of my wife Cristina Magro. Finally, my grandfather, whose passion for politics inspired mine, passed away as I was completing the manuscript. This book is in part dedicated to him, as well as to my parents.

Abbreviations

AUMF	Authorization for the Use of Military Force
BNDD	Bureau of Narcotics and Dangerous Drugs
FBI	Federal Bureau of Investigation
CAT	Civil Air Transport
CDF	Chile Declassification Files
CDPL	Clinton Digital Presidential Library
CIA	Central Intelligence Agency
CORDS	Civil Operations and Rural Development
CSG	Counter-terrorist Security Group
CTC	Counter-Terrorism Center
CTG	Counter-Terrorism Group
DCI	Director of Central Intelligence
DDP	Deputy Director for Plans
DEA	Drug Enforcement Administration
DNSA	Digital National Security Archives
EO	Executive Order
FOIA	Freedom of Information Act
FRUS	Foreign Relations of the United States
GFPL	Gerald Ford Presidential Library
GHWBPL	George H. W. Bush Presidential Library
HAC	Health Alteration Committee
HQ	Headquarters
HSCA	House Select Committee on Assassination
IAD	International Activities Division
ILA	Iraq Liberation Act
INA	Iraqi National Accord
INC	Iraqi National Congress
IR	International Relations
ISA	Intelligence Support Activity (Task Force Orange)

Abbreviations

ISI	Inter-Services Intelligence (Pakistan)
ITT	International Telephone & Telegraph Corporation
JCS	Joint Chiefs of Staff
KDP	Kurdish Democratic Party
JFKAR	JFK Assassination Records
JSOC	Joint Special Operation Command
MFF	Mary Ferrell Foundation
MNC	Mouvement National Congolais
MON	Memorandum of Notification
NARA	National Archives and Records Administration
NATO	North Atlantic Treaty Organization
NFSL	National Front for the Salvation of Libya
NIE	National Intelligence Estimate
NPIC	National Photographic Interpretation Center
NSA	National Security Agency
NSAr	National Security Archive
NSC	National Security Council
NSDD	National Security Decision Directive
OAS	Organization of American States
OLC	Office of Legal Counsel
ONI	Office of Naval Intelligence
OPC	Office of Policy Coordination
OSS	Office of Strategic Services
PDD	Presidential Decision Directive
PDF	Panamanian Defence Forces
PUK	Patriotic Union of Kurdistan
RFK	Robert Kennedy
RRPL	Ronald Reagan Presidential Library
SGA	Special Group Augmented
SOD	Special Operations Division
SOUTHCOM	Southern Command
SSCIA	Senate Select Committee to Study Governmental Operations with Respect to Intelligence Activities
TSD	Technical Services Division
UN	United Nations
USG	United States Government
VCI	Viet Cong Infrastructure
WMD	Weapon of Mass Destruction
WPR	War Powers Resolution

Introduction: The US Government and the Assassination of Foreign Officials

After midnight on 3 January 2020, a flight from Damascus, Syria, touched down at Baghdad International Airport. The flight, a few hours behind schedule, landed in a secluded area of the airport. Travelling on the flight to Baghdad was General Qassem Soleimani, the head of Iran's Islamic Revolutionary Guard Corps-Quds Force and the second highest ranking official in the Iranian government, behind Ayatollah Ali Khamenei.

Soleimani was being watched. Three drones armed with Hellfire missiles were hovering above the airport. Three teams of Delta Force operators, special forces under the control of the Joint Special Operation Command, hiding in old buildings and cars around the airport, were peering through their scopes. One member of the team had a camera which livestreamed images to the US Embassy in Baghdad. Next to the airplane, personnel from the Counter-Terrorism Group (CTG), an elite US-trained Kurdish unit, were disguised as airport operators. Their role was to help Delta snipers with wind calls and to provide final identity confirmation. The secretive military intelligence organisation Intelligence Support Activity (ISA), also known as Task Force Orange, was also on the ground for close-range tactical signal intelligence. In Tel Aviv, the US Joint Special Operation Command (JSOC) worked with its Israeli counterpart to track signals from Soleimani's ever-changing cell phones.[1]

After landing, Soleimani and his entourage boarded two vehicles and moved towards the exit. From the White House, President Donald Trump was monitoring the situation. As he recalled, a drone operator told him: 'Two minutes and 11 seconds to live, sir. They're in the car, they're in an armored vehicle. Sir, they have approximately one minute to live, sir. Thirty seconds. Ten, 9, 8 . . .'[2] Two Hellfire missiles destroyed Soleimani's vehicle. As the driver of the second vehicle accelerated and tried to escape, a sniper fired on it, and the vehicle was obliterated by another Hellfire missile.[3]

* * *

'At the direction of the President', read a Pentagon statement late on 2 January 2020, 'the U.S. military has taken decisive defensive action to protect U.S. personnel abroad by killing Qassem Soleimani, the head of the Islamic Revolutionary Guard Corps-Quds Force, a U.S.-designated Foreign Terrorist Organization.' The Pentagon also listed a series of attacks against American and coalition targets that Soleimani had allegedly orchestrated. 'General Soleimani,' the statement continued, 'was actively developing plans to attack American diplomats and service members in Iraq and throughout the region.' The strike on Soleimani aimed at deterring future attacks.[4] President Trump – in a celebratory mood – tweeted a badly pixelated American flag.

Beyond the tweet, as news of the strike spread US officials engaged in a public campaign to justify the decision. Two main arguments quickly emerged. First, as already clear in the Pentagon's statement, the Administration tried to downplay Soleimani's status as a government official. Instead, officials aimed at presenting him as a terrorist. The Trump Administration had declared the Iranian Revolutionary Guards a terrorist organisation in April 2019.[5] Soleimani, though, was a government official.[6]

Second, the Administration argued that Soleimani posed an imminent threat. While several Administration officials repeated this argument in the days following the strike, under scrutiny, it proved unpersuasive[7] – so much so that the Administration ultimately abandoned any pretence.[8]

An attack was not imminent, and the US government knew it. An anonymous US official claimed that the intelligence was 'thin'. More importantly, the United States was in possession of communications between Iran's Supreme Leader Khamenei and Soleimani showing that the former had not yet approved any attack plans and had requested Soleimani's return to Tehran for discussions.[9]

Introduction

And yet, the Administration's early insistence on the imminence of the threat Soleimani posed and on his status as a terrorist played an important role. Certainly, the two arguments had to do with international[10] and domestic law, including self-defence and Article 51 of the UN Charter, Article II of the US Constitution, and the politics and legalities of Congressional notification.[11] But there was more.

The argument built upon and revealed the evolution of US politics, rhetoric and practice surrounding assassination. At least since the 1970s, when a ban on assassination first appeared in Executive Order 11905, the US government has professed its opposition to assassination. The ban was still on the books at the time of Soleimani's killing. In a call with reporters, a US State Department official claimed that this was not an assassination, because 'Assassinations are not allowed under law.'[12] How did we get here? How could the US government kill a foreign official while maintaining that it did not engage in assassination? What has been the role of assassination in US foreign policy?

Argument and Structure

Investigative reporter Bob Woodward once noted that assassination is 'the Scarlet A of American politics', a practice the US government and the US public find repulsive.[13] Assassination challenges the moral standing of the United States. It undermines its self-image as a liberal democracy and as the driving force behind a liberal, rules-based international order. *The President's Kill List* challenges this (self)image. It is the first book to trace the history and politics of the US government's involvement in the assassination of foreign officials.[14] This book finds that assassination has proven to be a persistent feature in US foreign policy, one that has withstood changes in international contexts, in institutional and personal preferences, as well as in ethical and legal constraints.

The history of assassination in US foreign policy offers a window onto the US government's shifting global priorities. The United States deployed assassination in the early Cold War and to

3

counter the emergence of the non-aligned movement. It became involved in assassination during the global Cold War of the 1960s and 1970s. Assassination re-emerged as a policy option in the first 'war on terrorism' of the early 1980s, and in the 'war on drugs' at the end of the same decade. Assassination was considered and – in a few cases – implemented against 'rogue' leaders in the 1990s, and against terrorists before and after 9/11. Finally, assassination was used in the US government's confrontation with Iran.

Tracing this history, the book posits that assassination emerged as a policy option in the confrontation between the US government and leaders and officials of weak(er) states, primarily from the Third World/Global South. Several conditions made assassination more likely. First, the nature and character of the leader/official targeted played a part. Assassination plots tended to target leaders and officials who were perceived as 'irrational', too stubborn, impossible to deal with. At times, these leaders (or officials) did not pose a direct threat but were understood as an unmoving obstacle to the US government's preferred policy. Second, while some assassination plots – for example, that against Raul Castro – emerged as a matter of contingency, more often the targeting of a foreign leader/official represented one option in the context of broader policies of (covert) regime change.[15] In these cases, assassination often became the preferred policy option, especially if other – more constitutional and less controversial – options had proven (or were deemed) impractical. Third, the extent of the US government's reliance on assassination also depended on domestic and international factors, from the attitudes and approaches of US policymakers to the permissiveness of the domestic political environment, and the level of international tension. The higher the (perceived) tension and the more permissive the environment, the higher the likelihood of assassination plots. Finally, assassination was considered more acceptable if a veneer of plausible deniability could be maintained. Over time, plausible deniability worked to protect the reputation and hide the role of both the US government and the president, and eventually, as in the Soleimani case, to deny that US actions amounted to assassination.

* * *

Introduction

Tracing the history of assassination, then, is not always and not solely a matter of investigating who 'pulled the trigger' – or who concocted and delivered the poison, for that matter. The US government's involvement in assassination is more complex, more often a matter of shades of grey than of unequivocal black-and-white decision. For this reason, three main threads run through this book. First, the book explores the nature and extent of US government involvement in assassination. Second, it examines the political context and the decision-making processes in which assassination plots took shape, as well as the degree of presidential control over them. Finally, the book analyses the language used to describe and justify assassination plots. To paraphrase Fitzhugh Brundage, the study of assassination 'necessarily catalogs not only acts of violence but also the explanations, justifications, and denunciations of them'.[16]

As to the first thread, the US government's involvement in assassination can be understood along a continuum from more direct to less direct. At one extreme, the government directly tried to assassinate foreign leaders and officials. For this, it relied on US officials and/or military forces. In the early Cold War, for example, it delivered poison and weapons to its officials in the field, such as the Central Intelligence Agency's (CIA) chiefs of station, who in turn delivered them to agents and/or contractors paid by Langley (the CIA). More recently, it has deployed its own military forces, taking advantage of superior US technology like precision bombing and drones. Instead of relying on single agents, at times the US government has sponsored small groups – such as Cuban exiles – in their missions to assassinate foreign officials.

More often, though, the US government's involvement has been indirect. It has relied on local actors, fostering, nurturing, building upon and – at times – redirecting the existing grievances of political dissidents, liberation movements and disgruntled military officials.[17] In these more indirect approaches, the relevant dimensions are the types (political, ideological, material, financial) and degree of support provided by US government agencies (primarily the CIA), as well as the degree of intentionality.[18] Was assassination an explicit and agreed-upon objective of such support? Was it an expected outcome of US involvement? Or was it unexpected, more the result of loss of control than of premeditated planning? Here the picture gets even murkier since denying intention has long formed part of the US government's effort to distance itself from assassination.

In some cases the US government provided extensive support, including weapons, materiel, money and training. It assessed and reviewed assassination plots and discussed optimal assassination methods with the local plotters. At the indirect extreme of this continuum, the US government's role has been more diffuse. It set the political and ideological stage.[19] It worked to create favourable conditions, eventually letting the plotters take over. In this process, US officials often provided local actors with a system of incentives and sanctions that made assassination, if not inevitable, certainly more likely. Having created favourable conditions, the US government often refused opportunities to save the targeted official.

Furthermore, for some of these operations, the US government did not act alone. It could rely on (covert) cooperation with regional actors – governments who helped US operations by financing and training groups, by sharing intelligence, or by collaborating in the plots themselves. The role of these regional intermediaries added a further layer of deniability permitting the US government to distance itself politically and financially from the assassination plots, but in some cases it made US policy dependent on these allies' political fortunes.

As several scholars have pointed out, in fact, the degree of directness comes with trade-offs. More indirect methods have permitted US officials to distance themselves strategically, morally and politically from the act of killing.[20] They have also provided higher levels of deniability. But less direct methods and the pressure to maintain deniability have – at times – left the US government with a reduced level of control.[21] Here, it should be noted that while mindful not to deprive local actors of agency,[22] the analysis recentres the role of the United States and – in several cases – presents new documentary evidence that establishes more explicitly US control of (and responsibility for) the operations.[23]

As the Soleimani case demonstrates, though, decisions surrounding assassination have involved the highest levels of the US

Introduction

government, including presidents and CIA directors. And, as the aftermath of the strike shows, assassination is also a practice that the US government has always tried to hide and deny. For this reason, the second thread running through the book follows the politics of assassination. It explores decision-making processes surrounding assassination and – with all the caveats surrounding the partial nature of the historical record – it assesses the degree of presidential control over the plots. Each president developed a different approach to covert action, both in terms of personal idiosyncrasies and in terms of the structures put in place to manage it. Each president also developed a different approach to laws and norms and a different understanding of what was acceptable. As James Baker put it, each president defines their political and normative expectations, and receives 'the process he tolerates, accepts, or demands'.[24]

Dominant as the president and the CIA are in the conduct of covert operations, though, the operations' breadth and character also depend on other political factors. If assassination plots depended on the international context and on the fortunes of international allies, they were also shaped by the domestic political environment. Public and Congressional attitudes – the 'mood', as CIA Director William Webster once called it[25] – towards assassination (and covert operations more broadly), as much as the nature and intensity of Congressional oversight, shape the environment in which US policymakers operate.[26] This is strongly connected to the third thread running through the book: language.

Through its final thread, the book explores how decision-makers viewed assassination, how they decided on it, and how they spoke about it. The analysis highlights how US officials defined (and redefined) assassination, separating it from other – less controversial – foreign policy practices. In the early Cold War, while euphemisms and innuendos prevailed, assassination was not completely absent from the language of decision-making. Efforts were still made to sanitise the historical record, but several officials understood assassination as a permissible weapon in the (covert) foreign policy arsenal. Looking at more recent times, the main turning point of the book is the establishment of the ban on assassination in 1975.

Here, the book builds and expands on existing International Relations (IR) scholarship, understanding the prohibition on assassination as a norm.[27] This norm (re)shaped and – to a certain extent – constrained the US government's behaviour. Contrary to existing scholarship,[28] this book shows that the norm did not put an end to the US government's involvement in assassination. Instead, it altered *how* the government conducted assassination and *how* it spoke about it. Starting in the 1980s, the ban entered a process of contestation.[29] Contestation targeted the meaning of the ban – in particular, definitional debates as to what activity amounted to assassination. It also targeted the remit of the ban (so-called applicatory contestation): that is, what areas of US foreign policy should be covered by the ban's provisions. More rarely – and in a sign of the weakened status of the norm – contestation also targeted the ban's appropriateness (validity contestation). Actors questioned whether the ban was detrimental to the successful conduct of US foreign policy, to US national security, and, finally, whether it was immoral.[30] At times, this contestation happened only among actors within the executive. At other times, contestation emerged in closed meetings between members of the executive and legislators, particularly from Intelligence Committees. More rarely, contestation played out in the open, involving the US media, Congress and the broader public.

This contestation often entailed the use of internal legal reviews.[31] Conducted by the Office of Legal Counsel and other (legal) branches of the executive, these reviews aimed at reinterpreting and redefining the ban, expanding the available policy options. In this sense, this 'secret law' – secretive legal reviews and legal opinions – amounted to 'legal work', that is, the development of new legal interpretation to suit the 'extra-juristic' preferences of decision-makers.[32] While most of these reviews remained secret, at times US officials engaged in selective disclosures. This 'quasi-secrecy' aimed at legitimating US government decisions without fully disclosing information and without fully revealing the extent of the legal (and political) reasoning behind them.[33] Covert (and overt) operations involving assassination were made possible by the internal and – at times – public discourses that surrounded them. These discourses provided legitimate 'reasons for action',

Introduction

and made assassination attempts against foreign officials possible.[34]

At the same time, the US government always publicly denied that what it was doing was assassination. In line with Stanley Cohen's 'interpretive denial', at times US officials did not deny the 'raw facts'; they did not deny the US government's involvement in an operation, nor the President's awareness of it. Instead, they introduced a new form of (im)plausible deniability. They gave a different meaning to what seemed like assassination to others. As Cohen wrote, 'officials do not claim that "nothing happened", but that what happened is not what you think it is, not what it looks like, not what you call it'.[35] Organisations, including the CIA and Congress, adapted to and adopted these new interpretations, in turn influencing the views and policies of their successors all the way to the contemporary, sprawling 'assassination complex'[36] and to the Soleimani strike.[37]

* * *

While these three threads run through the book, the analysis is divided into two main parts, separated by the emergence of the ban in the mid-1970s. The first part of the book shows that, until the mid-1970s, when covert operations occurred – largely – in secret beyond the reach of public scrutiny and Congressional oversight, the US government experimented with assassination, worked to establish an institutional capability for assassination, and used direct and indirect methods, often combining them against the same target. Several plots were carried out in the early Cold War era (Chapter 1), the main targets being Patrice Lumumba (Chapter 2), Fidel Castro (Chapter 3), the Dominican Republic's Rafael Trujillo (Chapter 4), South Vietnam's Ngo Dinh Diem (Chapter 5) and General René Schneider of Chile (Chapter 6).

As this list suggests, the CIA tended to use its 'dirtier' tricks against relatively weaker, Third World nations.[38] This approach had multiple rationales. First, at least in part, the US government had not completely abandoned the imperial prejudices and racism of its European allies.[39] Racism influenced not only intelligence collection and analysis but also the assessment of the leaders of newly independent states and of their capabilities. It also shaped assessments of rationality and of good (personal and international) behaviour.[40] Second, the 'Third World', or nations of the non-aligned movement – and the alternative socio-political models they proposed – were considered a threat and, hence, an area for forceful (covert) intervention.[41] And if harsh measures like assassination were needed, so be it. In this, the US government was no different from other Western powers who worked, including through assassination, to destroy national liberation movements.[42] Finally, in the zero-sum world of the Cold War, everything that was not pro-US and pro-capitalist was seen as a direct or potential loss to the Soviet Union. At times, some US officials argued – often unconvincingly – that leaders of the non-aligned movement were communists or puppets of the Soviet Union. At other times, US officials thought that – even if these leaders were not communists themselves – their inability to govern would have created chaos, a chaos that communists would have been ready to exploit.[43] Cold War dynamics also meant that – in this phase – assassination was also an explicit policy option against former allies. Here, the choice was often a strategic one. These allies had become a hindrance to the pursuit of US foreign policy objectives.

With its attention to language and discourse, this section of the book shows that assassination was often debated – at times explicitly, more often through circumlocutory language – among US officials. There was no public effort to justify the US government's conduct. To the contrary, the US government's involvement in assassination – as in other covert operations – had to be plausibly deniable. The same applied to the President's awareness and approval of the operations.[44] In the case of assassination, this plausible denial was not solely outward looking. Internally, those without a need to know often received what historian Thomas Powers has called the 'spiel': 'it's too tough, won't work, can't predict the consequences, might blow up in our faces etc.'. The spiel was a boilerplate argument restating the US government's and the CIA's moral and strategic opposition to assassination.[45] When this wasn't enough, the massaging or destruction of historical records also intervened. Legal and normative obstacles were largely non-existent. Moral qualms were exceedingly rare and often they concerned more the method of assassination than the act itself.[46]

The second part of the book shows how the situation changed radically in the mid-1970s. First, covert operations had to be reported to Congress. The 1974 Hughes-Ryan amendment aimed at undermining a president's plausible deniability. Before a covert operation could proceed, the President had to 'find' that the operation was important for US national security. The amendment translated into the practice of 'presidential findings' – that is, documents, signed by the President, notifying Congress of a covert action.[47] As John Rizzo – author of many of these findings – has argued, a new 'legal art-form' emerged in the drafting of the presidential findings.[48] The Agency created a new 'glossary', a vernacular for particularly controversial covert operations.[49] As Rizzo acknowledged, 'No president would affix his signature to a piece of paper that contained the word lie or kill, so the former sort of activity was dubbed "all forms of propaganda," while the latter was described as "lethal action."'[50]

Second, Congressional investigations of the US government's intelligence activities made the conduct of the CIA (and of other intelligence agencies) an object of public and Congressional scrutiny. The Senate Select Committee to Study Governmental Operations with Respect to Intelligence Activities – better known as the Church Committee – investigated (and published a report on) the US government's involvement in the assassination of foreign officials during the early Cold War. The report called for the establishment of a law prohibiting assassination. This law contained key criteria as to the activities that amounted to assassination and a set of conditions in which the prohibition applied. These legislative efforts were stymied by the Ford Administration's decision to publish an Executive Order reforming the intelligence community. While the order did contain a prohibition on assassination, compared to the Church Committee's recommendations, the ban was vague. Contained in an Executive Order, the ban was also subject to presidential amendment, suspension and/or reinterpretation. Third, the 'season of inquiry' led to an increased internal 'legalisation' of the conduct of covert operations. The CIA's Legal Counsel and the Department of Justice's Office of Legal Counsel became more involved in the evaluation of covert operations. This expanded the internal (and eventually public) need to better 'legalise' and justify covert operations.[51] These processes, detailed in Chapter 7, shaped the US government's conduct in the realm of assassination.

Starting in the 1980s, the US government again became involved in direct and indirect assassination attempts against foreign officials. These were often leaders understood as 'rogue', 'mad dogs', and irrational. They included Libyan leader Muhammar Qaddafi (Chapter 8), Panamanian leader Manuel Noriega (Chapter 9), Iraq's Saddam Hussein (Chapter 10), and Osama Bin Laden (Chapter 11). The methods used were primarily aerial bombing and the support of local actors in their coup efforts. Assassination attempts became a policy option only through the contestation of the ban and only to the extent that the policy could be justified as a 'non-violation' of the ban.[52]

* * *

Here – with two caveats: first, that definitional jousting[53] has long characterised and legitimated US assassination policy, and, second, that the US government has often pushed to blur the boundaries between peace and war to justify its own behaviour[54] – the analysis accepts the existing line of demarcation between assassination in wartime and in peacetime. In peacetime, assassination refers to the killing of an individual (at times, a foreign official) for political purposes. In wartime, not every killing is an assassination. Assassination requires an element of treachery and/or perfidy.[55] This book is concerned with the US government's involvement in the assassination of foreign officials during peacetime.

Given the scope of this inquiry, it is also important to be explicit as to what the book is not. It is not a general history of assassination.[56] The book distinguishes between state-sponsored assassination – the object of inquiry – and more general 'political murder'.[57] To set a manageable scope, it also separates the assassination of foreign officials from that of other prominent individuals.[58] Both internationally and within the United States, the targeting of foreign leaders and officials introduces a discrete set of strategic, normative and legal constraints.[59] Here, the book does

Introduction

make one exception: Osama Bin Laden.[60] While some have argued that he could be understood as the political equivalent of a state official,[61] his presence in this book depends on the importance of the pre-9/11 hunt for Bin Laden and the legal arguments that accompanied it in setting post-9/11 US policy, including the strike on Soleimani. The book also distinguishes between assassination plots and the broader (more indiscriminate) use of assassination as part of counterinsurgency and/or counterterrorism.[62] Finally, the analysis focuses on the developments of plots, the decision-making surrounding them, and the ways in which assassination is discussed and – at times – justified. It doesn't assess the utility of assassination for the pursuit of foreign policy.[63]

Importantly, the history and practice of assassination remain understudied, more the province of journalistic investigations than of academic research. When it features, assassination is a partial – often marginal – element in broader histories of the CIA[64] and in histories of US covert operations.[65] Here, assassination is the main object of inquiry. The aim is not to give undue weight to assassination, but to show its resilience in the history of US (covert) foreign policy. Like other practices in covert action, assassination has waxed and waned over the years but never completely disappeared.[66] A longer-term focus moves the scope of the book beyond the single case study approach.[67] It reveals continuities in practices, personnel and policies across decades and across multiple cases. It also separates this book from the many works that – to historicise and contextualise the development of the US drone programme and of its so-called 'targeted killing' policy after 9/11 – have made quick references to assassination and assassination debates.[68]

This book is not trying to devalue the importance of 9/11 in influencing US policy and rhetoric; 9/11 clearly changed the perception of the threat posed by terrorism. In its immediate aftermath, the US government engaged in an explicit repudiation of standards of international law, reshaping its domestic and foreign policies. The intelligence, institutional and technological developments that characterised the 'war on terror' have forever reshaped the US government.[69] But not everything changed on 9/11.[70] As Mathias Großklaus wrote, it is a fallacy to assume 'that a present moral status of a normative institution can explain its origins without factoring in past institutional dynamics that might have shaped the present structural constellation'. As he adds, 'separating historical state-sponsored assassination and present day targeted killing would be such a fallacy'.[71] This book showcases the continuities surrounding assassination between current practices and the US government's conduct throughout its recent history, starting with the Cold War.[72] As Branwen Gruffydd Jones has written, the present embodies 'in a stronger, more concentrated, developed or intensified form, features identifiable in the past'.[73]

A Note on Sources

Assassination is a very elusive subject. Rarely appearing in the historical records and often discussed through euphemisms and circumlocutory language. Assassination requires the piecing together of different sources. For such a long history, the types, quantity and quality of sources have varied markedly, with the two extremes in the Castro case on one side, and the Noriega one on the other.

Where possible, *The President's Kill List* has relied on archival records and primary sources. These sources have clear benefits. They provide a database that is 'reflective of what goes on behind the scenes'.[74] They capture how policymakers viewed the world at the time, the information they received, and how they interpreted it, without the benefit of hindsight bias and – in most cases – without concerns for public scrutiny.[75] Archival material also permits researchers to position themselves closer to the 'operational code' – that is, elite behaviour – as opposed to accepting the more public 'myth system' elites supposedly live by.[76] And yet, especially on a controversial topic like assassination, surviving and declassified records are bound to offer only a partial, biased and selective window on the operations of government.[77]

The analysis has deployed several strategies to strengthen rigour and limit biases.[78] First, it has combined multiple archives and primary sources.[79] Second, the analysis has triangulated archival material with several additional sources.[80] Newspapers and the work of (investigative) journalists have helped in both plugging gaps in the relevant chronologies and in giving a better

Introduction

picture of the environment in which decisions took place and of the partisan politics at play.[81] Memoirs are often self-serving and clearly targeted at a public audience, but they shouldn't be discounted out of hand. Particularly when the aim is to assess decision-makers' perspectives and efforts to justify their own choices, memoirs act as a 'suitable proxy, providing first-hand accounts, in their own words, of those who developed these policies'.[82] Secondary sources have informed and shaped the analysis of several cases. For the first part of the book, single cases and institutional histories abounded. In its second part, the book relied on more limited scholarship regarding covert operations in the late 1980s and 1990s, generally understood as a low point for the Agency. For more recent times, the book also took advantage of scholarship that has traced the origins of the US government's drone programme.[83] The analysis has worked to carefully select 'fingerprints' and identifying patterns, while at the same time being explicit about the strength of the claims[84] and the existence of alternative interpretations.[85]

Finally, where possible, the book has relied on unstructured and semi-structured qualitative interviews. One of the main targets for interviews was policymakers. Here, the research encountered several problems and sources of frustration. For older cases, not many policymakers survive and even fewer are willing to talk. For more contemporary cases, policymakers, especially those involved in controversial policies like assassination, are unwilling to talk about or even to acknowledge what is already available in the public record. Furthermore, interviewees often present a self-serving image of their conduct. This being said, many interviewees have been gracious with their time, often discussing their experiences at length. In all cases, caution has been necessary in both approaching a topic and in assessing the claims made.[86] The book has relied on purposive sampling, searching for policymakers with relevant experience, as well on a snowballing technique, asking each interviewee if they could recommend others.[87] Beyond policymakers, interviews with journalists and experts have helped with the chronology and with details of specific operations.[88] It is to the early Cold War and early assassination plots that the book now turns.

Notes

1. Jack Murphy and Zac Dorfman, '"Conspiracy is hard": Inside the Trump Administration's Secret Plan to Kill Qassem Soleimani', *Yahoo News*, 8 May 2021, available at https://news.yahoo.com/conspiracy-is-hard-inside-the-trump-administrations-secret-plan-to-kill-qassem-soleimani-090058817.html (accessed 17 October 2023).
2. Reuters, 'Trump Gives Dramatic Account of Soleimani's Last Minutes before Death', *Reuters*, 18 January 2020, available at https://www.reuters.com/article/us-usa-trump-iran-idUSKBN1ZH0G3 (accessed 17 October 2023).
3. Murphy and Dorfman, 'Conspiracy'.
4. US Department of Defense, 'Statement by the Department of Defense', 2 January 2020, available at https://www.defense.gov/News/Releases/Release/Article/2049534/statement-by-the-department-of-defense/ (accessed 17 October 2023).
5. Edward Wong and Lara Jakes, 'Pompeo Upended Middle East by Pushing Trump to Kill Iranian General', *New York Times*, 7 January 2020, available at https://www.nytimes.com/2020/01/07/world/middleeast/pompeo-trump.html.
6. Robin Wright, 'The Killing of Qassem Soleimani Is Tantamount to an Act of War', *The New Yorker*, 3 January 2020, available at https://www.newyorker.com/news/our-columnists/the-us-assassinated-suleimani-the-chief-exporter-of-irans-revolution-but-at-what-price?source=EDT_NYR_EDIT_NEWSLETTER_0_imagenewsletter_Daily_ZZ&utm_campaign=aud-dev&utm_source=nl&utm_brand=tny&utm_mailing=TNY_Daily_010320&utm_medium=email&bxid=5be9f6883f92a4046931394a&cndid=45877311&esrc=&mbid=&utm_term=TNY_Daily (accessed 17 October 2023).
7. Donald Trump, 'Iran Statement Speech Transcript', *Rev*, 3 January 2020, available at https://www.rev.com/blog/transcripts/donald-trump-iran-statement-speech-transcript-trump-orders-strike-on-qasem-soleimani (accessed 17 October 2023); Kate Riga, '"Imminent Threat"? Admin Shifts Goalposts around Rationale for Soleimani Strike', *Talking Points Memo*, 6 January 2020, available at https://talkingpointsmemo.com/news/imminent-threat-pompeo-soleimani-strike (accessed 17 October 2023); Samuel Osborne, 'Trump Approved Soleimani Assassination 7 Months Ago, Report Says', *The Independent*, 13 January 2020, available at https://www.the-independent.com/news/world/americas/us-politics/trump-soleimani-death-assassination-airstrike-drone-approved-presidential-directive-iran-iraq-a9281801.html (accessed 17 October 2023).

8. Patricia Zengerle and Lisa Lambert, 'Trump: Timing of threat from Soleimani "doesn't really matter"', *Reuters*, 13 January 2020, available at https://jp.reuters.com/article/us-iraq-security-trump-idUSKBN1ZC1QA (accessed 17 October 2023).
9. Helene Cooper, Eric Schmitt, Maggie Haberman and Rukmini Callimachi, 'As Tensions With Iran Escalated, Trump Opted for Most Extreme Measure', *New York Times*, 4 January 2020, available at https://www.nytimes.com/2020/01/04/us/politics/trump-suleimani.html (accessed 17 October 2023).
10. Marko Milanovic, 'The Soleimani Strike and Self-Defence Against an Imminent Armed Attack', *EJIL: Talk*, 7 January 2020 [blog], available at https://www.ejiltalk.org/the-soleimani-strike-and-self-defence-against-an-imminent-armed-attack/ (accessed 17 October 2023).
11. Scott Anderson, 'Did the President Have the Domestic Legal Authority to Kill Qassem Soleimani?' *Lawfare*, 3 January 2020, available at https://www.lawfareblog.com/did-president-have-domestic-legal-authority-kill-qassem-soleimani (accessed 17 October 2023).
12. Kathy Gilsinan, 'It Wasn't the Law That Stopped Other Presidents from Killing Soleimani', *The Atlantic*, 4 January 2020, available at https://www.theatlantic.com/politics/archive/2020/01/why-kill-soleimani-now/604441/ (accessed 17 October 2023).
13. Bob Woodward, *Veil: The Secret Wars of the CIA 1981–1987* (New York: Pocket Books, 1988), 446.
14. Investigative journalist Annie Jacobsen also told the history of the US government's involvement in assassination. Her book focused primarily on operators in the field; it did not distinguish between assassination of foreign officials and other foreign policy practices (e.g. assassination in counterinsurgency), and did not trace the evolution of the US government's language and legal position. Annie Jacobsen, *Surprise, Kill, Vanish* (New York: Little, Brown, 2019).
15. Lindsey O'Rourke, *Covert Regime Change* (Ithaca, NY: Cornell University Press, 2018), 63.
16. Fitzhugh Brundage, *Civilizing Torture* (Cambridge, MA: Harvard University Press, 2018), 6.
17. Victor Marchetti and John Marks, *The CIA and the Cult of Intelligence* (London: Jonathan Cape, 1974), 37.
18. Ruth Blakeley, *State Terrorism and Neoliberalism: The North in the South* (Abingdon: Routledge, 2009), 47.
19. Patrice McSherry, *Predatory States* (New York: Rowman & Littlefield, 2005), 249–52.

20. Ruth Jamieson and Kieran McEvoy, 'State Crime by Proxy and Juridical Othering', *British Journal of Criminology*, 45 (2005), 504–27.
21. Rory Cormac, *How to Stage a Coup* (London: Atlantic Books, 2022), 5.
22. James Lockhart, *Chile, the CIA, and the Cold War* (Edinburgh: Edinburgh University Press, 2019).
23. Daniel Bessner and Fredrik Logevall, 'Recentering the United States in the Historiography of American Foreign Relations', *Texas National Security Review*, 3.2 (2020), 39–55.
24. James Baker, 'Covert Action: United States Law in Substance, Process, and Practice', in Loch Johnson (ed.), *The Oxford Handbook of National Security Intelligence* (Oxford: Oxford University Press, 2010), 592.
25. Stephen Engelberg, 'C.I.A. Seeks Looser Rules on Killings during Coups', *New York Times*, 17 October 1989.
26. Loch Johnson, *Spy Watching* (Oxford: Oxford University Press, 2018), 4.
27. Simon Frankel Pratt, 'Norm Transformation and the Institutionalization of Targeted Killing in the US', *European Journal of International Relations*, 25.3 (2018), 1–25, doi: 10.1177/1354066118812178; Andris Banka and Adam Quinn, 'Killing Norms Softly: US Targeted Killing, Quasi-secrecy and the Assassination Ban', *Security Studies*, 27.4 (2018), 665–703.
28. For an exception, see Jonathan Ulrich, 'The Gloves Were Never On: Defining the President's Authority to Order Targeted Killing in the War Against Terrorism', *Virginia Journal of International Law*, 45 (2005), 1029–46; Luca Trenta, 'Death by Reinterpretation: Dynamics of Norm Contestation and the US Ban on Assassination in the Reagan Years', *Journal of Global Security Studies*, 6.4 (2021), doi: 10.1093/jogss/ogab012.
29. Antje Wiener, 'Enacting Meaning-in-use: Qualitative Research on norms and International Relations', *Review of International Studies*, 35.1 (2009), 175–93.
30. For a more extensive discussion of norm contestation, see Trenta, 'Death'.
31. Lisa Stampnitzky, 'The Lawyers' War: States and Human Rights in a Transnational Field', *The Sociological Review Monographs*, 64.2 (2016), 170–93; Craig Jones, *The War Lawyers* (Oxford: Oxford University Press, 2020).
32. Duncan Kennedy, 'A Left Phenomenological Alternative to the Hart/Kelsen Theory of Legal Interpretation', in Duncan Kennedy,

Introduction

Legal Reasoning, Collected Essays (Aurora, CO: The Davies Group Publishers, 2008); Noura Erakat, *Justice for Some: Law and the Question of Palestine* (Stanford: Stanford University Press, 2019).
33. Banka and Quinn, 'Killing Norms'; Brian Rappert and Chandré Gould, *The Dis-Eases of Secrecy* (Johannesburg: Jacana, 2017), 13.
34. Martha Finnemore, *The Purpose of Intervention: Changing Beliefs about the Use of Force* (New Delhi: Manas Publications, 2004), 14.
35. Stanley Cohen, *States of Denial: Knowing about Atrocities and Suffering* (Cambridge: Polity, 2001), 7–8.
36. Jeremy Scahill, *The Assassination Complex* (New York: Simon & Schuster, 2017).
37. Trenta, 'Death'.
38. Rhodri Jeffreys-Jones, *A Question of Standing* (Oxford: Oxford University Press, 2022), 43.
39. Thomas Borstelmann, *The Cold War and the Color Line* (Cambridge, MA: Harvard University Press, 2001), 130.
40. Oliver Kearns, *The Covert Colour Line* (London: Pluto Press, 2023), 29.
41. Vincent Bevins, *The Jakarta Method* (New York: Public Affairs, 2021).
42. Victoria Brittain, 'They Had to Die: Assassination against Liberation', *Race and Class*, 48.1 (2006), 60–74.
43. Christian Appy, 'Eisenhower's Guatemalan Doodle, or: How to Draw, Deny, and Take Credit for a Third World Coup', in Christian Appy (ed.), *Cold War Constructions* (Amherst: University of Massachusetts Press, 2000), 198–200.
44. Michael Poznansky, 'Revisiting Plausible Deniability', *Strategic Studies*, 45.4 (2022), 511–33.
45. Thomas Powers, *The man Who Kept the Secrets: Richard Helms and the CIA* (New York: Pocket Books 1979), 160.
46. Arturo Jimenez-Bacardi, 'From Lawless to Secret Law: The United States, the CIA and Extra-judicial Killing', in Alison Brysk and Michael Stohl (eds), *Contracting Human Rights* (Cheltenham: Edward Elgar, 2018).
47. Loch Johnson, *The Third Option* (Oxford: Oxford University Press, 2022), 182.
48. John Rizzo, *Company Man: Thirty Years of Controversy and Crisis in the CIA* (New York: Scribe, 2014), 72.
49. Rizzo, *Company Man*, 72.
50. Ibid., 73.
51. Jimenez-Bacardi, 'From Lawless', 127.

52. Here, the book agrees with Sanders's insights about 'plausible legality', but it suggests that the effort to provide plausible legality for seemingly prohibited foreign policy conduct started long before 9/11. Rebecca Sanders, *Plausible Legality* (Oxford: Oxford University Press, 2018).
53. Myriad definitions of assassination exist. In 2005, a review of the literature identified at least ten definitions. These often include the type of individual targeted, the means used to target them, the covert or overt nature of the operation, as well as the degree of intention and premeditation; see Asa Kasher and Amos Yadlin, 'Assassination and Preventive Killing', *SAIS Review of International Affairs*, 25.1 (2005), 41–57. Much of the definitional work – in the US context – has been carried out by legal scholars. This scholarship has emerged in three main waves, tracking the evolution of US government's policy. The first wave, from the late 1980s to the late 1990s, reacted to the Reagan Administration's 1986 attack on Libya, to the so-called CIA 'assassination manual' for the Nicaraguan Contras and to the early air strikes against Saddam Hussein during Desert Storm: see Michael Schmitt, 'State-Sponsored Assassination in International and Domestic Law', *Yale Journal of International Law*, 17.2 (1992), 609–85; Michael Reisman, 'Some Reflections on International Law and Assassination under the Schmitt Formula', *Yale Journal of International Law*, 17.2 (1992), 687–92. A second wave, between the early 1990s and 2000, started to debate the permissibility of strikes against both terrorists and – under certain circumstances – state officials; see Jonathan Fredman, 'Covert Action, Loss of Life, and the Prohibition on Assassination', *Policy and Law*, (1997), 15–25, Mark Vlasic, 'Cloak and Dagger Diplomacy: The Use of Assassination', *Georgetown Journal of International Affairs*, 1.2 (2000), 95–104. Finally, a third wave developed after 9/11 and coincided with the transition from the language of assassination to that of targeted killings and with the institutionalisation of the US government's 'drone wars'; see Jeffrey Addicott, 'Proposal for a New Executive Order on Assassination', *University of Richmond Law Review*, 37 (2002–3), 751–85; Robert Turner, 'It's Not Really Assassination: Legal and Moral Implications of Intentionally Targeting Terrorists and Aggressor-State Regime Elites', *University of Richmond Law Review*, 37.3 (2003), 787–810. It should be noted that this scholarship – often written by former government officials – and its work on redefinitions of assassination have, at times, served to legitimate the US government's preferred policy options.

54. Rebecca Ingber, 'Legally Sliding into War', *Just Security*, 15 March 2021, available at https://www.justsecurity.org/75306/legally-sliding-into-war/ (accessed 18 October 2023).
55. Schmitt, 'State-Sponsored'; William C. Banks and Peter Raven-Hansen, 'Targeted Killing and Assassination: The US Legal Framework', *University of Richmond Law Review*, 37 (2002–3), 667–749.
56. Franklin Ford, *Political Murder* (Cambridge, MA: Harvard University Press, 1987); John Withington, *Assassins' Deeds* (London: Reaktion Books, 2020); Michael Burleigh, *Day of the Assassins* (London: Picador, 2021); Kris Hollington, *How to Kill* (London: Arrow Books, 2008).
57. Understood here as the killing of (politically) prominent individuals conducted by single individuals or non-state groups. Several academic and popular works on assassination tend to conflate the two; see Murray Clark Havens, Carl Leiden and Karl M. Schmitt, *The Politics of Assassination* (Englewood Cliffs, NJ: Prentice Hall, 1970); Ford, *Political Murder*; Burleigh, *Day*.
58. The book does not deal with the US government's involvement in the assassination of foreign citizens who were not foreign officials (for example, Pablo Escobar), nor with US government agencies' involvement in the assassination of US citizens (for example, Fred Hampton, leader of the Black Panther Party). On Escobar, see Mark Bowden, *Killing Pablo* (New York: Atlantic Monthly Press, 2015); on Hampton, see Jeffrey Haas, *The Assassination of Fred Hampton* (Chicago: Lawrence Hill Books, 2019).
59. Ward Thomas, 'Norms and Security: The Case of International Assassination', *International Security*, 25.1 (2000), 107.
60. A second borderline case is left out of the book: Che Guevara. Guevara was not a state official at the time of his killing and the operation to capture and kill him was part of a broader counterinsurgency campaign. On this episode, see Henry Butterfield Ryan, *The Fall of Che Guevara* (Oxford: Oxford University Press, 1998); Michael Ratner and Michael Steven Smith, *Who Killed Che? How the CIA Got Away with Murder* (New York: OR Books, 2011).
61. Banks and Raven-Hansen, 'Targeted Killing', 723.
62. For example, in the Phoenix Program during the Vietnam War; see Mark Moyar, *Phoenix and the Birds of Prey* (Winnipeg: Bison Books, 2008); Douglas Valentine, *The Phoenix Program* (Bloomington: iUniverse, 2000). Several sources have debated the role of assassination and targeted killing in US counterterrorism. See, for example, Chris Woods, *Sudden Justice* (London: Hurst, 2015). Here, literature

on decapitation of non-state groups is also germane; see Jenna Jordan's seminal 'When Heads Roll: Assessing the Effectiveness of Leadership Decapitation', *Security Studies*, 18 (2009), 719–55.
63. Warner Schilling and Jonathan Schilling, 'Decision Making in Using Assassinations in International Relations', *Political Studies Quarterly*, 131.3 (2016), 503–39.
64. John Prados, *The Ghosts of Langley* (Stroud: Amberley Publishing, 2017); Jeffreys-Jones, *A Question*.
65. Loch Johnson, *The Third Option* (Oxford: Oxford University Press, 2022).
66. As the analysis will show, the possible exception here is the Carter years.
67. Dan Bohning, *The Castro Obsession* (Washington: Potomac Books, 2005); Susan Williams, *White Malice* (London: Hurst, 2021).
68. Christopher Fuller, *See It, Shoot It* (New Haven, CT: Yale University Press, 2017); Woods, *Sudden Justice*.
69. Michael Stohl, 'The War on Terror and the Law of War', in Lothar Brock and Hendrik Simon (eds), *The Justification of War and International Order* (Oxford: Oxford University Press, 2021).
70. Pratt, 'Norm Transformation'; Clifford Bob, 'Rival Networks and the Conflict over Assassination/Targeted Killing', in Alan Bloomfield and Shirley Scott (eds), *Norm Antipreneurs and the Politics of Resistance to Global Normative Change* (London: Routledge, 2017); Banka and Quinn, 'Killing Norms'; Jothie Rajah, *Discounting Life: Necropolitical Law, Culture, and the Long War on Terror* (Cambridge: Cambridge University Press, 2022).
71. Mathias Großklaus, 'Friction, Not Erosion: Assassination Norms and the Fault Line between Sovereignty and Liberal Values', *Contemporary Security Policy*, 38.2 (2017), 265–6.
72. For a similar point, see Jamieson and McEvoy, 'State Crime', 505.
73. Branwen Gruffydd Jones, 'Slavery, Finance and International Political Economy: Postcolonial Reflections', in Sanjay Seth (ed.), *Postcolonialism and International Relations: A Critical Introduction* (London: Routledge, 2013).
74. John Lewis Gaddis, 'Expanding the Data Base: Historians, Political Scientists, and the Enrichment of Security Studies', *International Security*, 12.1 (1987), 12.
75. Deborah Welch Larson, 'Archival Research in Foreign Policy', *World Politics*, 22 August 2017, available at https://oxfordre.com/politics/view/10.1093/acrefore/9780190228637.001.0001/acrefore-9780190228637-e-389?rskey=JKTQLC&result=1 (accessed 18 October 2023).

76. Michael Reisman and James Baker, *Regulating Covert Action* (New Haven, CT: Yale University Press, 1992), 23–4.
77. Richard Aldrich, "Grow Your Own': Cold War Intelligence and History Supermarkets', *Intelligence and National Security*, 17.1 (2002), 148; Christopher Darnton, 'Archives and Inference: Documentary Evidence in Case Study Research and the Debate over US Entry into World War II', *International Security*, 42.3 (2017), 92.
78. Scott A. Frisch et al., 'Taking the Road Less Travelled', in Scott A. Frisch, Douglas B. Harris, Sean Q Kelly and David C. W. Parker (eds), *Doing Archival Research in Political Science* (Amherst, MA: Cambria Press, 2012), 24.
79. See end of the volume for a list.
80. David Welch, *Justice and the Genesis of War* (Cambridge: Cambridge University Press, 1993).
81. Welch Larson, 'Archival Research'.
82. Stampnitzky, 'The Lawyers' War', 173.
83. Fuller, *See It*.
84. Ian S. Lustick, 'History, Historiography and Political Science', *American Political Science Review*, 90.3 (1996), 605–18.
85. McSherry, *Predatory*, xxvi, xxix.
86. Damien Van Puyvelde, 'Qualitative Research Interviews and the Study of National Security Intelligence', *International Studies Perspectives*, 19.4 (2018), 379.
87. Oisin Tansey, 'Process Tracing and Elite Interviewing: A Case for Non-Probability Sampling', *PS: Political Science and Politics*, 40.4 (2007), 770–1.
88. See the full list of interviewees at the end of the volume.

1 Experimenting with Assassination: Brainwashing, Poison and Early Cold War Plots

On 21 February 1952, the CIA's Morse Allen visited the home of a 'professional hypnotist of exceptionally good reputation'. Allen quickly introduced the real purpose of the meeting: to find out more about the potential uses of hypnosis in intelligence and national security. After a more general discussion, Allen tabled the main proposal: would the hypnotist be willing to act as a consultant for the Agency?

'Yes,' the hypnotist replied, 'I feel that we are at war, and if I can be of any help whatsoever, I shall be glad to give my time.'

Allen continued: 'Can individuals be made to do things under hypnosis that they would not do otherwise?'

Here the hypnotist's answer was circumspect. It was unlikely that an individual could be induced into doing something against their moral code. Through proper psychological conditioning and techniques, 'individuals could be taught to do anything including murder, suicide, etc.'. The obstacle of individual morality could be circumvented by using an immoral person to commit immoral acts.[1]

Assassination through hypnosis promised to be the perfect weapon for the CIA. If caught, the assassin would have no idea why he had committed the crime, he would not know who had ordered it, and under what circumstances; he would be completely disoriented. As historian Dominic Streatfeild put it: 'An amnesiac assassin was a perfect assassin.'[2]

In the early years of the CIA, assassination was pervasive both as a foreign policy practice and as a topic of research. As to the research, the CIA conducted several experiments with drugs and hypnosis in the search of a 'Manchurian candidate'. The term refers to the novel by Richard Condon – later adapted in a John Frankenheimer blockbuster movie – in which a US prisoner of war is brainwashed by communist officials into becoming an assassin.[3] The Agency also explored and developed poisons in collaboration with the US military. Beyond this ethically questionable – and at times deadly[4] – research, the Agency explored the use of assassination and engaged in several plots from the late 1940s to the mid-1950s. The evidentiary record for these plots is limited and many did not move beyond the drawing board. An overview of the plots, though, gives a sense of what Thomas Powers has called the US government's 'murderous mood' in the early Cold War.[5]

From the 'Manchurian Candidate' to the 'Poisoner in Chief:' The CIA's Experiments in Assassination

During the Second World War, assassination had featured in the Office of Strategic Services' (OSS) arsenal. Plans had been concocted – but eventually abandoned – to assassinate Hitler, other Nazi officials, and the Italian leader Benito Mussolini. German nuclear scientist Werner Heisenberg had also been a target.[6] During the war, several groups within the OSS – under the project 'Natural Causes' – had started experimenting with drugs and poisons. While some focused on the use of chemical and biological weapons in war, others explored their development as targeted weapons that could be used against selected individuals to incapacitate, disorient or kill them.[7] The aim was an assassination that could not be revealed through an autopsy.[8] At the centre of many of these activities was Stanley Lovell, head of the OSS Research and Development branch. Lovell also believed that a good way to kill Hitler would have been using a hypnotised German prisoner.[9] The CIA inherited much of the culture, elitism and personnel of the OSS.[10] It also inherited its interest in exotic methods of assassination and in drug experiments.

Many at the time reflected on the unsavoury nature of these practices, and on the perils for a democratic society in adopting the methods of totalitarian regimes. But these methods seemed to be made more cogent by the early Cold War paranoia and by the onset of the Korean War. As to the war, confessions of guilt and anti-war broadcasts made by American prisoners of war led US officials to conclude that the Soviets had developed capabilities to control the minds of individuals, to brainwash them.[11] As to the Cold War paranoia, while an element of ex-post rationalisation did exist, several US officials involved in assassination would later recall the early Cold War terror of being left behind in the superpower rivalry. A combination of fear of Soviet capabilities, ignorance about these capabilities, and US power and resources pushed the government and the CIA forward.[12] The famous Doolittle report on covert operations commissioned by President Dwight Eisenhower confirmed the necessity of unsavoury measures: 'We . . . must learn to subvert, sabotage, and destroy our enemies by more clever, more sophisticated and more effective methods than those used against us.' The American people needed to become acquainted with and support this 'repugnant philosophy'.[13]

Furthermore, as the Eisenhower Administration's doctrine of 'massive retaliation' took shape, many covert operators saw themselves as the first line of defence against communism. If nuclear weapons guaranteed a strategic stalemate, the 'real' war, the hot one, occurred at a lower level. As the CIA's Joseph Smith put it: 'The CIA had the only manpower that the US government had available to throw into the breach between the language of our policy . . . and the reality of our effective power.'[14] Most Cold Warriors interpreted the confrontation with the Soviet Union as a new global conflict, a continuation of the Second World War. Stalin, in this view, had simply replaced Hitler as the main enemy. This interpretation was made even more cogent by the continuities in personnel and culture between the OSS and CIA, and by the defining life experiences of early US covert warriors. Most of them had witnessed and participated in the Second World War, in either the military or the OSS. The few who had not taken part in the war felt the need to prove themselves to those who had.[15]

This war and 'derring-do' mentality shaped the early CIA and its initiatives. As a retired CIA official put it: 'It was the old OSS mentality: "Go out and do it." Doesn't matter if it's a good or bad idea, go do it. We're at war, so anything is justified . . . we know what the real threats are. No one else does.'[16] If the CIA was the first line of defence, it might as well use any weapon at its disposal.

* * *

Within the Agency, the umbrella project's name for the conduct of mind control operations and experiments changed over time – BLUEBIRD,[17] ARTICHOKE and eventually MKULTRA. Hypnosis experiments had initially been conducted under Project BLUEBIRD.[18] BLUEBIRD had been successful in obtaining information from willing and unwilling subjects but had obtained disappointing results in other areas such as control over the future activities of individuals. The agenda for future experiments read in part: Could an unwilling subject be conditioned in a matter of hours to 'perform an act for our benefit'? Could the subject be controlled against their basic moral principles? Could a subject be conditioned in a matter of hours and controlled to 'crash an airplane, wreck a train etc?'.[19]

ARTICHOKE was approved in August 1951. The project relied on a network of interrogation facilities and safe houses in the United States and abroad. Eventually, the project also used scientists from foreign countries to enable experiments prohibited under US law, such as those with anthrax.[20] Initially led by the Office of Scientific Intelligence, ARTICHOKE passed in 1953 to the Office of Security, under Sheffield Edwards.[21] Edwards reconfirmed the tasks and organisation of ARTICHOKE. Beyond more menial tasks like coordination with other agencies, one stands out: 'c. In coordination with TSS [Technical Services Staff] and the Medical Staff arrange for research and experimentation . . . for the development of means for the control of the activities and mental capacities of individuals whether willing or not.'[22]

Allen – whose interview with the hypnotist had covered similar ground – took charge of official and unofficial experiments in this area for the CIA. As to unofficial experiments, he relied on secretaries and other employees of the Agency. First, he hypnotised two secretaries, convincing one to steal 'secret documents' from a safe and to carry them to a safe place. Second, he convinced another secretary that an 'electrical timing device' was a bomb. The secretary was instructed to carry the device in a briefcase, set the bomb timer to 82 seconds, return to the operations room, and fall in a deep sleep on the sofa. In both cases the experiments were successful, and the secretaries had no recollection of what had happened.[23]

Eventually, the big question was posed in the form of a seemingly 'hypothetical problem' to an ARTICHOKE team: 'Can an individual of ***** descent be made to perform an act of attempted assassination involuntarily under the influence of ARTICHOKE?' The assassination target would be a prominent politician of 'Government ***' or an American official.[24] As reported to the team, the assassination was supposed to be the 'trigger mechanism' for a bigger project. Even if the problem was 'hypothetical', the team had a specific subject in mind, but he was likely to be unwilling to cooperate and access would have been limited. Since the subject was a 'heavy drinker', the always hypothetical project considered drugging his drinks and applying ARTICHOKE techniques in 'one involuntary uncontrolled social meeting'. After the act, the subject would be taken into custody by the '*** government' and 'disposed of'. Based on these conditions, the answer to the hypothetical problem was 'probably "no"'. The ARTICHOKE team stated that they would undertake the project if they had 'appropriate authority from headquarters', but they weren't sure about its chances of success, and it might jeopardise future applications of ARTICHOKE.[25]

Allen carried out another experiment in February 1954. He hypnotised one secretary and put her in deep trance. He hypnotised a second and told her that if she was unable to wake the first one up, her rage would be so great that she would kill her. He then left an unloaded pistol nearby. Having failed to awaken the first secretary, the second one pulled the trigger. Once awakened, she had no recollection of what had happened.[26] A 'Manchurian candidate' seemed possible. As historian John Marks has concluded, though, the difference between Allen's experiments and the ARTICHOKE team's experience was in the level of control over the setting and subjects.[27] While experiments with drugs and other substances continued under MKULTRA, ARTICHOKE

Experimenting with Assassination: Early Cold War Plots

experiments were seemingly shut down. The main problem was not their immorality, but their unreliability in the field.[28]

By the time of Allen's latter experiments, another star had risen within the CIA's Technical Service, one that preferred the certainty of poison to the unpredictability of hypnosis: Sidney Gottlieb. The son of Jewish Hungarian immigrants, Gottlieb was a stutterer since childhood and was born with a club foot which got him rejected from military service. Having received a PhD in biochemistry, the secretive and eccentric scientist moved with his family to a remote cabin in Virginia. He was living there when he was recruited by the CIA in 1948. In a few years, he rose to become a key figure in MKULTRA as well as the CIA's 'poisoner in chief'.[29]

* * *

The CIA's exploration of poison had started in the early 1950s, in collaboration with the Army's Special Operations Division (SOD). This collaboration – under the code name MKNAOMI – was formalised in an agreement signed in May 1952. It permitted the CIA to rely on Army facilities and expertise.[30] SOD developed 'darts coated with biological agents and pills containing several different biological agents which could remain potent for weeks or months'.[31] CIA and SOD also worked on biological weapons that could work on humans, animals and crops. The Agency developed (and stored) various toxins and other biological substances.[32] The methods of delivery included a gun able to fire a dart silently and below the threshold of pain so that it would not be perceived by the target and, in the case of certain substances, would not appear in an autopsy.[33] Poison featured prominently in the CIA's first assassination plots.

The CIA's Early Assassination Plots: Friends and Enemies

One of the first plots was developed within the Agency's Program Branch 7, or P/B7, then acting under the Office of Policy Coordination (OPC).[34] The head of the branch was Colonel Boris Pash.

Pash had been a security officer for the Manhattan Project. He had later overseen the US Army ALSOS teams. The teams had travelled to Italy after the Allied invasion and started collecting information on German advances in biological warfare.[35] ALSOS teams also worked to arrange the tracking and exfiltration of German nuclear scientists.[36]

Artie Lazarus, who worked under Pash at the CIA, recalled that the 'special operations' unit PB/7 had a charter[37] which included 'assassinations, kidnapping, and such other functions as from time to time may be given it . . . by higher authority'.[38] The Director of Operations Planning for OPC testified that everyone within OPC knew that assassinations and kidnappings were within the 'purview' of Pash's unit.[39] While admitting that he did oversee a unit called PB/7, Pash could not recall the precise wording of the charter, but he did not dispute Lazarus's testimony. His unit, Pash testified, never received any request to initiate an assassination plan. Yes, perhaps the possibility of assassination might have been raised, but so many crazy ideas were floating around at the time. This Pash attributed to the presence within the CIA of several OSS men. While many were dedicated, some had 'wild ideas and wild approaches'.[40] And yet, Pash did admit that – if assassination had been considered at the time – a request would have likely gone to P/B7 to start planning for such an eventuality.[41]

*　*　*

In the summer of 1949, with Pash out of the country, Lazarus met with the Chief of the CIA's Political Warfare Program Branch. The latter told him that during a planning meeting it had been decided that Chiang Kai Shek[42] – leader of the Chinese nationalist forces – 'must be sent to meet his ancestors'. An official acting as liaison between the CIA and the State Department told Lazarus that 'higher authority' – often a euphemism for the president – had approved the request. Lazarus reported the request to Frank Wisner, head of the OPC. A few days later, Wisner's assistant told Lazarus that the request had gone 'all the way to the top' and it had been denied. All documents and records of the exchange were to be destroyed.[43] While the plan was initially shelved, it resurfaced

Experimenting with Assassination: Early Cold War Plots

in May 1950, this time in a more indirect manner. Paul Nitze, then at the State Department, raised the possibility of removing Chiang. The United States had found in General Sun Liren the perfect, US-trained, candidate to replace Chiang. The general promised that upon taking power he would remove 'all prominent members of the Kuomintang'. The plan was never implemented due to the opposition of US officials and the start of the Korean War.[44]

Two years later, the CIA allegedly concocted a plot against Stalin timed to coincide with the Soviet Leader's planned trip to Paris. The plot relied on the extensive connections between the Agency and the French labour unions, particularly the vehicle maintenance workers. The CIA worked to have access to Stalin's limousine. The Technical Services were asked for the best options: sabotage, contamination of the circulation system, or just destruction of the car and its passengers. As historian Peter Grose reports, the plan was considered at several levels of authority, including then Deputy Director for Plans (DDP) Wisner, CIA Deputy Director Allen Dulles, and CIA Director Walter Bedell Smith. At no point was the plot rejected. Instead, it was shut down by the cancellation of the Paris summit and, eventually, by Smith's refusal to pursue any further plans.[45]

If these early plots did not move much past the drawing board, the Agency did make assassination a core component of larger covert operations. During Operation PBSUCCESS, the Eisenhower Administration's overthrow of the government of Jacobo Arbenz in Guatemala, the Agency developed lists of targets and – seemingly – worked with regional allies including Dominican dictator Rafael Trujillo to carry out assassinations.[46] The Agency prepared kill lists of communists, communist sympathisers, and individuals who had supported the Arbenz government.[47] Sessions on 'theory and techniques' of assassination featured prominently in the training schedules of the men working under Castillo Armas, the leader handpicked by the Agency to replace Arbenz. The Agency also recommended the creation and training of 'assassination specialist' teams.[48] The targeting of high-value targets was considered, potentially including Arbenz. The Agency, in fact, collected extensive intelligence on Arbenz's residences and on his patterns of behaviour.[49] Seemingly no assassination was carried out.

At the time of the coup, though, the Agency did produce a manual on assassination. 'A Study in Assassination' defined assassination as an 'extreme measure', one that will never be 'ordered or authorized by any US Headquarters', a reticence due, at least in part, to the need of committing orders to paper. 'No assassination instruction should ever be written or recorded', the manual advised. 'Decision and instructions should be confined to an absolute minimum of persons. Ideally, only one person will be involved.' The manual continued with a discussion of various techniques including drugs, edge weapons, blunt weapons, firearms (from precision rifles to submachine guns), explosives and contrived accidents. 'The most efficient accident, in simple assassination', the manual explained matter-of-factly, 'is a fall of 75 feet or more onto a hard surface. Elevator shafts, stair wells, unscreened windows and bridges will serve.' As to its justification, the manual identified several occasions in which assassination – while not morally justifiable – could be permissible. Self-defence, assassination as punishment against a person responsible for atrocities, as well as 'killing a political leader whose burgeoning career is a clear and present danger to the cause of freedom'[50] – these 'political leaders' were a favourite target of CIA assassination attempts, especially if they seemed to promise a socio-political alternative to the superpower confrontation.

The CIA and the Non-aligned Movement

The year after the Guatemala operation, the Agency targeted the premier of the People's Republic of China, Zhou Enlai. In 1975, then CIA Director William Colby admitted the Agency's awareness of two plots against Zhou. In April 1955, an Air India aircraft – the *Kashmir Princess* – had crashed after taking off from Hong Kong. The British Colonial Office had told the CIA that there was evidence that the Chinese Nationalists had bribed an airport employee as they thought Zhou would have been on board. After this failed plot, in late 1956, Chinese Nationalists notified the CIA that they had planned to kill the Chinese leader during a trip to Cambodia, but the plan had been thwarted by the arrest of their man in the

Experimenting with Assassination: Early Cold War Plots

country. Having reviewed these two plots, Colby acknowledged the long-standing intelligence and security relationship between the CIA and the Chinese Nationalist intelligence services but suggested that – in these cases – the Chinese Nationalists had acted independently.[51] Colby's account is incomplete.

Lazarus testified that, during his tenure at a CIA station in Asia (after his time at P/B7), an officer at the station recommended the assassination of Zhou to disrupt the upcoming 1955 Bandung Conference. Headquarters (HQ) disapproved of the operation and 'strongly censured' the station, also requesting that the station immediately burn all the relevant documents.[52]

As to the *Kashmir Princess* accident, Steve Tsang exonerated the CIA, concluding that the Chinese Nationalists were responsible for the assassination attempt. They hired an airport official to install an explosive device on the airplane while it was stationed at Hong Kong airport. The Chinese government and Zhou knew of the plot and – for this reason – changed the travel plans at the last minute but did not notify other members of the delegation and journalists who died in the crash. Tsang writes that the timer of the bomb was made in the United States, but it was also widely available at the time, thus exonerating the US and the CIA.[53]

But there is more to the story. In 1967, an alleged American defector (John Discoe Smith) confessed 'that he had delivered the explosive mechanism on behalf of the CIA to a Chinese Nationalist in Hong Kong'.[54] Tsang also writes that, with the Hong Kong police closing in, Zhou Zhu, the airplane saboteur, 'was assisted by a colleague, Yu Pui, to stow away in a little-used luggage compartment aboard a Civil Air Transport aircraft'.[55] According to Tsang, his escape could not have been arranged by Chinese Nationalist authorities as he was arrested soon after landing in Taipei as an illegal immigrant. Made aware of who he was, the Taiwanese government refused British requests to extradite him. The CIA's involvement, then, seems likely. At the time of the accident and extraction, the Civil Air Transport (CAT) operated under the CIA's control. It afforded 'air support for Agency and other U.S. national objectives, and the provision of cover for Agency personnel under which they could carry on other Agency activities'.[56] Furthermore, during the summer of 1952, 'the possibility

33

of developing a capability for successfully exfiltrating an agent or agents by an aerial pickup or "snatch" operation at night' had been discussed and later tested.[57]

After the air crash, assassination plots continued. Gottlieb was asked to develop a poison to be placed in a bowl of rice that Zhou Enlai would eat at the Bandung Conference's final banquet. The poison was supposed to take forty-eight hours to work, thus blurring the connection with the conference.[58] Rumours of the plot reportedly made their way to Lucien Truscott, selected by Eisenhower as the CIA's Deputy Director for Community Affairs. Truscott's role seemingly included keeping an eye on Dulles to make sure that the Agency stayed away from scandal. Having conducted his own investigation, Truscott informed Dulles that he knew about the plan and considered it unwise. Dulles shut it down.[59]

* * *

Gottlieb's poisons were required again for another leader prominent in the non-aligned movement: Indonesia's Sukarno. In the autumn of 1956, Frank Wisner, then Deputy Director for Plans, famously told Far East Division Chief Al Ulmer: 'I think it's time we held Sukarno's feet to the fire.'[60] After the statement, CIA officials in the field started developing contacts with local military personnel and other anti-Sukarno elements.[61]

Among the earliest contacts of the CIA was Lt. Col. Ahmad Hussein who, from the Central Sumatra region, had started defying the government. Links between the CIA and disgruntled military officials soon expanded beyond the collection of intelligence. Even before approval from Washington, the CIA provided extensive financial support under the pretence of repaying military officials for the intelligence they provided, and feigning ignorance when the money, instead, was used to purchase weapons.[62] Starting in the summer of 1957, the US government was aware of the activities and intent of Colonel Zulkifli Lubis, former Army intelligence chief and former deputy chief of staff. On 13 July, the CIA assessed that Lubis was 'planning new action which would involve the assassination of President Sukarno and the arrest of the army chief of staff, General Nasution'. Assassination remained a

Experimenting with Assassination: Early Cold War Plots

last resort. Lubis, the report added, was in constant contact with Hussein and Lt. Col. Sumual,[63] early and regular contacts of CIA officials in the field.[64]

Towards the end of November, Lubis took matters into his own hands. On the 30th, he masterminded an assassination attempt against Sukarno, the so-called Cikini incident. As Sukarno was exiting a school, hand grenades were thrown at him, but he miraculously escaped. One week after the attempt, the State Department settled on a policy of regime change; 'the point of no return' had been reached with Sukarno. The best option was to support right-wing elements who could form a new government. This new government would then receive economic and military support.[65] In the same months, the CIA ramped up its campaign to discredit Sukarno. Robert Maheu, then working for the CIA, was famously asked to produce a porn movie – Project 'Happy Days' – with a Sukarno lookalike.[66]

In later years, Richard Bissell revealed that a more direct assassination plot had also been considered. This – like the fake porn movie – was based on an understanding of Sukarno as primarily driven by his sexual appetites. As Bissell recalled, members of the CIA's Far Eastern division identified an asset for the job but, in Bissell's view, the plan never reached a stage at which it seemed feasible, and it was eventually dropped. For this reason, it was never discussed outside the agency.[67] The aim was to 'biologically immobilise' Sukarno by relying on a female associate of his. The order to produce the immobilising concoction once again went to Gottlieb.[68] The plot, though, went further than Bissell admitted. Codenamed HARPSTAR, the plan received the approval of the Director of Central Intelligence (DCI). The search for a suitable woman who could 'cultivate' Sukarno again involved Maheu.[69] The Agency eventually recruited a 'well-to-do widow approximately 35 years of age'. The woman reported that she understood her mission perfectly well and was told that she would travel with a female companion posing as her secretary. The companion, using the pseudonym 'Hogarth', was a member of the Agency's Far East division. The asset went as far as meeting Sukarno, but due to the Indonesian leader's frequent travels she was unable to cultivate him.[70]

A Choice of Enemies? The CIA in the Middle East

In 1957, with language similar to that employed in the case of Guatemala, the US government, this time in collaboration with Britain's Secret Intelligence Service, considered the use of assassination as part of a regime change operation in Syria. The Anglo-American Working Group on Syria developed a 'Preferred Plan' to deal with the Syrian crisis. The 'Preferred Plan' aimed at creating a moderate level of violence in Damascus, one that would not cause leading figures to increase their security details and protection.[71] This was important since the plan recommended that 'a special effort should be made to eliminate certain key individuals', in order to keep losses and destruction to a minimum, while achieving the operation's objectives.[72] As historian Matthew Jones showed, while it did not go very far, the plan – recommendations of assassination included – had received the support of the most senior political leaders in the United States and the United Kingdom.[73]

One of the allies the US and Britain had enlisted for their operation against Syria was Iraq, but revolution made its leader the CIA's next target. After overthrowing the Hashemite monarchy in 1958, General Abdul Karim Qassem had moved closer to the Soviet Union, thus threatening Western access to Middle Eastern oil and – in the minds of Eisenhower Administration officials – increasing the risk of falling dominoes in the Persian Gulf. Qassem's predicament had been discussed in a Congressional hearing where Senator Hubert Humphrey had recommended to Allen Dulles that – if Qassem feared assassination – maybe the US should also step up its game. 'Where are our liquidators?' he asked. He continued recommending that the US should threaten the life of Iraqi communists.[74]

Unwilling to conduct an open military intervention, the Administration established an Iraqi Committee to discuss covert options and developed an aggressive campaign to 'eliminate' the enemy. In October 1959, the Administration seemingly cooperated with Gamal Abdel Nasser of Egypt in an assassination plot against Qassem. The ambush, which included a young Saddam Hussein among the plotters, ended in failure.[75] After the failure, a CIA intelligence estimate concluded that only assassination could remove

Experimenting with Assassination: Early Cold War Plots

Qassem. Bissell concurred, suggesting that if assassination failed to remove Qassem, communist influence would grow.[76]

In February 1960, Gottlieb was asked to develop poison to 'immobilise' an Iraqi leader. Working as part of the euphemistically named 'Health Alteration Committee' (HAC), Gottlieb received a request from the CIA's Near East Division to target an Iraqi colonel who had been undermining US interests. There is some discrepancy among accounts as to who the target was: whether Qassem himself,[77] or more likely Colonel Fahdil Abbas al-Mahdawi who was in charge of firing squads and acting as Qassem's liaison with communist groups.

There is also discrepancy as to the purpose and outcomes of the operation. The Near East Division reported to Headquarters on 25 February 1960 that they were looking for a technique 'which while not likely to result in total disablement would be certain to prevent the target from pursuing his usual activities for a minimum of three months'. The telegram also added: 'We do not consciously seek subject's permanent removal from the scene; we also do not object should this complication develop.' In April, the HAC approved the request for a disabling operation.[78] The Agency green-lighted the plan aimed at delivering a 'monogrammed handkerchief' containing an incapacitating agent.[79]

CIA officials denied that the operation moved past the planning stage. Mahdawi, in their view, was simply killed by a firing squad of domestic opponents. Gottlieb, though, recalled mailing the handkerchief. According to Terry Lezner, Gottlieb's lawyer at the time of the 1970s Congressional investigations, Gottlieb was shocked when the Church Committee showed him a memorandum which mentioned the Mahdawi episode. 'That's the one,' he told Lezner, 'the one that worked.' Gottlieb confided to Lezner that the handkerchief had been infected with tuberculosis and the target had died weeks later.[80]

Conclusion

In the early Cold War, the Agency recognised the importance of maintaining assassination capabilities. ARTICHOKE, P/B7 and the 'Health Alteration Committee' clearly position assassination within the covert foreign policy arsenal. 'Assassination,' CIA Cold Warrior Joseph Smith confirmed, 'was always a contingency action to be included in the plans.'[81]

In terms of methods, the plots showcase features that characterised the US government's approach to assassination throughout the Cold War. The US government deployed direct methods such as the delivery of poison, as well as more indirect ones such as collaboration with local partners and international allies. Except for Gottlieb's handkerchief, the level of access to a target seemed to influence decisions as to the methods of assassination. When relying on local allies, the United States had various degrees of control. In certain episodes (Guatemala, for example), the collaboration was tight, and the US government shared clear expectations and goals with its local allies. In others, the US provided more indirect support to local actors, from intelligence sharing to the supply of weapons (for example in Indonesia). Contingency (as in the case of the cancelled Paris summit) as well as the risk of exposure (as in the case of Zhou Enlai) were often behind the cancellation of plans.

Beyond some references to 'higher authority' – often a pseudonym used to protect the president – the scant historical record of these early plots does not permit us to reach firm conclusions regarding the level of political control. At times, plots seemingly emerged organically from officials in the field. At other times, they were concocted at CIA Headquarters, where they received various levels of approval. The level of presidential involvement remains unclear. And yet, regardless of the limited window into these episodes, their sheer frequency demonstrates the pervasiveness of assassination and assassination plots in the early Cold War.

In these early plots, the language of US officials' deliberations highlights the use of – not too subtle – euphemisms. Furthermore, the US government established early the need to compartmentalise knowledge of assassination plots and to avoid putting anything on paper, as the assassination manual made clear. Assassination emerged as a suitable option to deal with troublesome leaders in the pursuit of broader US foreign policy goals. These goals included preventive measures in the superpower rivalry, regime change,

Experimenting with Assassination: Early Cold War Plots

and – in the case of the non-aligned movement – the discrediting of alternative socio-political projects.[82] The same rationale and methods shaped US policy in the assassination of Patrice Lumumba.

Notes

1. Morse Allen, 'Interview with [classified]', 25 February 1952, The Black Vault, available at https://documents2.theblackvault.com/documents/cia/mkultra/19-C00140394.pdf (accessed 18 October 2023).
2. Dominic Streatfeild, *Brainwash: The Secret History of Mind Control* (London: Hodder, 2007), 168.
3. Louis Menand, 'Brainwashed: Where the Manchurian Candidate Came From', *The New Yorker*, 8 September 2003, available at https://www.newyorker.com/magazine/2003/09/15/brainwashed (accessed 18 October 2023).
4. Stephen Kinzer, *Poisoner in Chief: Sidney Gottlieb and the CIA's Search for Mind Control* (New York: Holt and Co., 2019), chapter 7.
5. Thomas Powers, *The Man Who Kept the Secrets: Richard Helms and the CIA* (New York: Pocket Books, 1979), 184.
6. Douglas Waller, *Wild Bill Donovan* (New York: Simon & Schuster, 2011), 316.
7. Waller, *Wild Bill*, 5.
8. John Marks, *The Search for the Manchurian Candidate* (New York: Norton, 1991), 16–20; John Lisle, *The Dirty Tricks Department* (Cheltenham: The History Press, 2023), ebook, chapter 9.
9. There is also debate as to whether the killing of Admiral Isoroku Yamamoto amounted to assassination; Patricia Zengel, 'Assassination and the Law of Armed Conflict', *Mercer Law Review*, 43 (1992), 615–44.
10. Rhodri Jeffreys-Jones, *A Question of Standing* (Oxford: Oxford University Press, 2022), chapter 2.
11. CIA analysts also made frequent references to the Moscow show trials of the 1930s and to the seemingly incredible confession of Cardinal Mindszenty. But by the mid-1950s, the CIA had concluded that the Soviets relied on more traditional methods of torture and not brainwashing, and yet CIA experiments continued; John Ranelagh, *The Agency: The Rise and Decline of the CIA* (Cambridge: Sceptre, 1987), 202; Lisle, *Dirty Tricks*, chapter 16.
12. Kinzer, *Poisoner*, 238.

13. James Doolittle et al., 'Report on the Covert Activities of the Central Intelligence Agency', 26/7/1954, 2–3, available at https://www.cia.gov/readingroom/docs/CIA-RDP86B00269R000100040001-5.pdf (accessed 18 October 2023).
14. Joseph B. Smith, *Portrait of a Cold Warrior* (New York: Ballantine Books, 1976), 169.
15. For example, Sidney Gottlieb himself; Kinzer, *Poisoner*.
16. Kinzer, *Poisoner*, 80.
17. In 1947, the Navy had also carried out experiments with 'truth drugs' under Project CHATTER. Joint Hearing, Select Committee in Intelligence, Subcommittee on Health and Scientific Research, 'Project MKULTRA, the CIA's Program of Research in Behavioral Modification', 3 August 1977, 67, available at https://www.intelligence.senate.gov/sites/default/files/hearings/95mkultra.pdf (accessed 18 October 2023).
18. CIA, 'Memorandum for the Record: Project ARTICHOKE', National Security Archives (NSAr) 31/1/1975, available at https://nsarchive2.gwu.edu/NSAEBB/NSAEBB54/st02.pdf (accessed 18 October 2023).
19. Memorandum, 'Subject: Special Research, Bluebird', undated, CIA MKULTRA/Mind Control collection, Cryptocomb, available at https://documents2.theblackvault.com/documents/cia/mkultra/26-C00140401.pdf (accessed 18 October 2023).
20. 'Project MKULTRA', 101.
21. Ibid., 68.
22. Director of Security (Edwards), Draft memorandum to ARTICHOKE representatives, Subject: Artichoke, restatement of program, undated, CIA CREST, CIA-RDP83-01042R000800010010-3.
23. Streatfeild, *Brainwash*, 166–7.
24. A * appears after 'American Official' and a note at the end of the document reads '* simulated only'.
25. Memorandum to [redacted] from Security Representative [redacted], Subject: Security, ARTICHOKE Report, 22/1/1954, CIA Reading Room, available at https://www.cia.gov/readingroom/docs/DOC_0000140399.pdf (accessed 18 October 2023).
26. Marks, *The Search*, 194–5.
27. Ibid., 203.
28. According to the CIA, the project ended in 1956. A Congressional investigation concluded that the use of 'special interrogation' techniques continued long thereafter. 'Project MKULTRA', 68.
29. Kinzer, *Poisoner*; CIA, 'Memorandum for the Record: Project ARTICHOKE', 5.

30. US Senate, 'Unauthorized Storage of Toxic Agents', Hearing, Select Committee to Study Governmental Operations with Respect to Intelligence Activities, 16, 17, 18/9/1975, 6, available at https://www.intelligence.senate.gov/sites/default/files/94intelligence_activities_I.pdf (accessed 18 October 2023).
31. 'Project MKULTRA', 69.
32. US Senate, 'Unauthorized Storage', 16, 39.
33. Ibid., 17. US Patent Office, 'Javelin Stabilized Quiet Round', 3/10/1967, available at https://archive.org/details/Javelin_Stabilized_Quiet_Round_-_US_Patent_3344711/page/n3/mode/2up
34. Peter Grose, *Gentleman Spy: The Life of Allen Dulles* (London: André Deutsch, 1994), 320; Sarah-Jane Corke, *US Covert Operations and Cold War Strategy* (London: Routledge 2008), 44.
35. Dan Kaszeta, *Toxic* (London: Hurst, 2022), 65.
36. Boris Pash, Atomic Heritage Foundation, available at https://www.atomicheritage.org/profile/boris-pash (accessed 18 October 2023).
37. Testimony, Boris Pash, 7/1/1975, Senate Select Committee to Study Governmental Operations with Respect to Intelligence Activities (SSCIA) Committee, Digital National Security Archives (DNSA) Covert Operations II, 16.
38. SSCIA, 'Addenda to the Interim Report on Alleged Assassination Plots', *Supplementary Detailed Intelligence Staff Reports on Foreign and Military Intelligence*, book 4, 1976, 128.
39. SSCIA, 'Addenda', 129.
40. Ibid., 130.
41. Testimony, Pash, 12, 30. Pash was also allegedly contacted by Howard Hunt with a proposal to assassinate a suspected Albanian double agent during BGFIEND. See Pash, Testimony; Howard Hunt, Testimony to the Church Committee, 10/1/1976, DNSA CovOps II.
42. Also a target of the OSS during the Second World War; Lisle, *Dirty Tricks*, chapter 7.
43. SSCIA, 'Addenda', 132.
44. Hsiao-ting Lin, 'Taiwan's Secret Ally', *Hoover Digest*, 6 April 22, available at https://www.hoover.org/research/taiwans-secret-ally (accessed 18 October 2023).
45. Grose, *Gentleman Spy*, 328–9.
46. Memorandum for the Record, 'Weekly PBSUCCESS Meeting, 9/3/1954', FRUS, Guatemala 1952–1954, doc. 113, and Memorandum for All Staff Officers, 'Selection of Individuals for Disposal by

Junta Group', 31 March 1954, NSAr, The CIA and Assassination: The Guatemalan Documents, available at https://nsarchive2.gwu.edu/NSAEBB/NSAEBB4/docs/doc03.pdf accessed 18 October 2023).
47. Gerald K. Haynes, 'CIA and Guatemala Assassination Proposals, 1952–1954', CIA History Staff Analysis, June 1955, 9, available at https://nsarchive2.gwu.edu/NSAEBB/NSAEBB4/docs/doc01.pdf
48. Memorandum for C/P, Basic [redacted] document 1, 10/2/1954, CIA Record, Guatemala, Folder, Documents on Assassinations Proposal 2 and Memorandum to [redacted], Letter of instruction, 23/12/1953, CIA Records Guatemala Box 4, Folder Stage One Report – Annex C – Eyes only – 15/12/1953, National Archives and Records Administration [hereafter NARA], College Park, MD.
49. Memorandum Guatemala City to Lincoln, 'Operation KEIs', 17/3/1954, Folder Weekly PBSUCCESS Meeting with DD/P – 16 March 1954, CIA Records Guatemala – Container 7, NARA.
50. 'A Study of Assassination', undated, NSAr, available at https://nsarchive2.gwu.edu/NSAEBB/NSAEBB4/ciaguat2.html (accessed 18 October 2023).
51. William Colby, Testimony to the SSCIA, 23/51975, John F. Kennedy Assassination Records (JFKAR), 178-10004-10112, 15.
52. SSCIA, 'Addenda', 133.
53. Steve Tsang, 'Target Zhou Enlai: The "Kashmir Princess" Incident of 1955', *The China Quarterly*, 139 (1994), 780.
54. Arthur Schlesinger, *Robert Kennedy and His Time* (Boston, MA: Houghton Mifflin, 1978), 481.
55. Tsang, 'Target Zhou', 770.
56. Clandestine Services Industry, *Civil Air Transport – A Proprietary Airline 1946–1955*, vol. 1, 1, The University of Texas at Dallas, Eugene McDermott Library, available at https://utd-ir.tdl.org/handle/10735.1/1791 (accessed 18 October 2023).
57. The downing of a CAT plane led to the capture of CIA officers John Downey and Richard Fecteau. Clandestine Services Industry, *Civil Air Transport – A Proprietary Airline 1946–1955*, vol. 3, TAB J, 2, available at https://utd-ir.tdl.org/handle/10735.1/1792 (accessed 18 October 2023); Nicholas Dujmovic, 'Two CIA Prisoners in China, 1952–73', *Studies in Intelligence*, 50.4 (2006).
58. Kinzer, *Poisoner*, 133.
59. William Corson, *The Armies of Ignorance: The Rise of the American Intelligence Empire* (New York: Dial, 1971), 361–5.
60. Smith, *Portrait*, 197.
61. Ibid., 221.
62. Ibid., 225.

63. CIA, Current Intelligence Bulletin, 13/7/1957, CIA Crest Archive, 15757402, 5.
64. Audrey Kahin and George McT. Kahin, *Subversion as Foreign Policy: The Secret Eisenhower and Dulles Debacle in Indonesia* (Seattle: University of Washington Press, 1995), 105.
65. Message Robertson to Allison, 7/12/1957, FRUS South-East Asia, 1955–1957, vol. XXII, doc. 314.
66. James O'Connell, Testimony to the SSCIA, 30/5/1975, 162, JFKAR, 157-10002-10148. CIA Report, Subject: Robert Maheu, undated, JFKAR, 104-10122-10141, 2; James Risen, *The Last Honest Man* (New York: Little, Brown, 2023), 205–6.
67. Richard Bissell, 'Testimony, President's Commission on CIA's Activities, 21/4/1975, DNSA Covert Operations II, 2299.
68. Evan Thomas, *The Very Best Men* (New York: Simon & Schuster 1996), 212–14.
69. Memorandum Michael Madigan to Committee, 'Robert Maheu Appearance before the Committee', 10/6/1975, JFKAR 157-10002-10379.
70. CIA Report, Subject: Robert Maheu, 3–4 and SSCIA, Interim Report, 'Alleged Assassination Plots Involving Foreign Leaders' (Washington, DC: US Government Printing Office, 1975), 4. In the late 1990s, leading experts on Indonesia revealed that they had initially been contacted by the Church Committee to investigate the CIA's links to the Lubis plot. The invitation was rescinded, and the Committee had refused to conduct a serious investigation on the Sukarno case. Kahin and Kahin, *Subversion*, 115.
71. Matthew Jones, 'The "Preferred Plan": The Anglo-American Working Group Report on Covert Action in Syria, 1957', *Journal of Intelligence and National Security*, 19.3 (2004), 407.
72. Jones, 'Preferred Plan', 408.
73. Ibid., 409. Nasser was also a target for assassination, but this seems primarily a UK operation. Hugh Wilford, *America's Great Game* (New York: Basic Books, 2013), 225; Hugh Wilford, Zoom interview with the author, March 2022.
74. David M. Barrett, *The CIA and Congress* (Lawrence: University Press of Kansas, 2005), 35.
75. Kenneth Osgood, 'Eisenhower and Regime Change in Iraq', in David Ryan and Patrick Kiely (eds), *America and Iraq* (London: Routledge, 2009), 19–21.
76. Osgood, 'Eisenhower', 23.
77. Powers, *The Man*, 161; Seymour Hersh, *The Dark Side of Camelot* (London: HarperCollins, 1997), 194; Osgood, 'Eisenhower', 24.

78. SSCIA, Interim Report, 181.
79. Thomas, *The Very Best*, 215.
80. See Kinzer, *Poisoner*, 227; Terry Lezner, *The Investigator* (New York: Blue Rider Press, 2013), 199.
81. Smith, *Portrait*, 71.
82. Vincent Bevins, *The Jakarta Method* (New York: Public Affairs, 2020).

2 Patrice Lumumba: Eisenhower's Order to Kill

On 30 June 1960, delegations from all over the globe gathered to mark Congo's independence. The ceremony started with a patronising speech by Belgian King Baudoin who celebrated independence as the 'crowning of the work conceived by the genius of King Leopold II'. After a perfunctory speech by newly elected President Joseph Kasavubu, the tone of the ceremony changed with a speech by the new prime minister, Patrice Lumumba:

> We have known laws which differed according to whether it dealt with a black man or a white.
> We have known the atrocious sufferings of those who were imprisoned for their political opinions or religious beliefs and of those exiled in their own country.

The speech was so incendiary that at one point the Belgian monarch threatened to leave.[1] Royal shock notwithstanding, Lumumba's speech represented the views of a country that had long suffered under Belgium's colonial brutality.[2] Lumumba's message was also one of hope: 'We shall show the world what the black man can do when working in liberty, and we shall make the Congo the pride of Africa.'[3]

* * *

Born in 1925, Patrice Lumumba attended both Catholic and Protestant schools, as well as a training school for the Belgian Congo government postal service. His career as a postal clerk – something open to the so-called *évolués* in the Belgian Congo – ended when he was arrested for embezzlement. He later became a sales representative for Polar, one of Congo's beers, a role that helped refine his rhetorical skills. At the same time, he developed an interest in journalism and politics. He abandoned an early position of accommodation with the Belgian colonial government and started exploring themes of nationalism and anti-imperialism. While initially a member of the Liberal Party, he later helped found the Mouvement National Congolais (MNC) and became one of the leading voices in the organisation.[4] His participation at the All-African People's Conference in 1958, in Accra, Ghana, made of him a convinced pan-Africanist. Ghana's Kwame Nkrumah, prime minister and later president of Ghana, became Lumumba's mentor and supporter in a common anti-colonial struggle.[5]

* * *

In January 1959, uprisings in the Congolese capital Leopoldville convinced Belgian authorities to expedite the process of independence. A hastily organised roundtable in Brussels agreed on a new constitution and on a date for elections. During the electoral campaign, the CIA adopted an ambivalent policy. Its views informed by Brussels, the Agency feared Lumumba's (alleged) communist sympathies, but it also recognised him as the only leader with national appeal. A proposal to flood the elections with CIA money was abandoned in favour of smaller donations to sympathetic politicians (likely including Lumumba).[6]

In the elections, held on 22 May, Lumumba led the MNC – L (Lumumba)[7] to a plurality of votes (23%), receiving votes throughout the nation, not based on regional ethnicity. Before Lumumba's government could receive approval from the Congolese parliament, the Belgian parliament modified the provisional constitution to permit the election of provincial governments without a two thirds majority. This allowed the Conakat party of the pro-Belgian Moise Tshombe to take power in the region of Katanga, a rich mining region in the south of the country.[8] Beyond these machinations, Belgium's efforts to prevent Lumumba from becoming prime minister failed.[9] On 23 June, Lumumba's coalition government was approved by the Congolese parliament.

The assassination of Lumumba is as close as we come to a Presidential order to assassinate. The order was executed at all levels of the Agency's hierarchy, from Director Allen Dulles to Larry Devlin, the CIA Chief of Station in Congo. Few US officials showed moral qualms about the assassination, and they soon put them to rest. Two main tracks emerged and developed in parallel. One was a more direct approach aimed at killing Lumumba by poisoning him or shooting him from a distance; the other a less direct approach aimed at delivering Lumumba to his domestic enemies, with full awareness that this meant the death of the first Congolese prime minister.

'A Castro or worse'

After the independence celebrations, the situation in the country worsened. On 4 July, Congolese troops mutinied. While economic conditions mattered, the spark for the escalation was the intentionally provocative behaviour of Belgian general Émile Janssens, commander of the Force Publique, who famously wrote on a blackboard that 'before independence = after independence'.[10] European fears were increased by – largely inflated – claims of violence against white people, especially the rape of white women; a well-known racist trope. The following day, to placate the soldiers, Lumumba promoted all of them by one grade and dismissed Janssens. On the 9th, Lumumba replaced all Belgian officers with Congolese ones and renamed the Force Publique as the Congolese National Army. He picked Joseph Mobutu, who had just been promoted to colonel, to be chief of staff.[11] The mutiny and the chaos persisted.

With the justification of protecting Belgian citizens, Belgium started reinforcing its military position in bases it had maintained in the country. Before independence, an agreement had been reached for Belgium to station troops in selected military bases. On 10 July, Lumumba and Kasavubu met with US Ambassador to Congo Clare Timberlake to ask for support and technical assistance to restore order in the country. Timberlake replied that any such help would have to come from the United Nations (UN).[12] The two

Congolese leaders immediately contacted Ralph Bunche, the personal representative of UN Secretary Dag Hammarskjöld in Congo. The option of a military technical mission started to take shape.[13]

At this stage, as the pre-independence agreement shows, Lumumba was not opposed to the Belgian presence. Two events changed the picture. First, on the 11th, Belgian forces landed at the port of Matadi – an area where no Europeans were in danger – and the landing turned into a massacre which included an aerial bombing of Congolese troops and civilians. Second, on the same evening, Tshombe – supported by the Belgian government and Western corporations, and with Washington turning a blind eye[14] – declared the independence of Katanga, asking for Belgian recognition and assistance. Lumumba and Kasavubu immediately tried to fly to the breakaway province but were prohibited from landing by Belgian troops.[15] Unbeknown to Lumumba, Albert Kalonji, one of his long-term opponents, had already met with Timberlake to ask for funds to overthrow Lumumba.[16] On the 12th and 13th, Lumumba and Kasavubu appealed again to the UN, this time to stop Belgian aggression and compel Belgian troops to withdraw. The US took a more prominent role in the country.

* * *

Until the crisis in Congo erupted, the US government had paid little attention to the country and to the African continent as a whole. It was only in 1958 that the US State Department created a Bureau of African Affairs, and only in November 1959 that the CIA established an Africa Division. US policy on the continent – and on Congo – was informed by the perspectives of its European allies. US policy showcased a conservative Eurocentrism that ignored the Third World and put a premium on NATO (North Atlantic Treaty Organization) cohesion.[17] European influences were also visible in the racist attitudes towards African people and the new African leaders.[18] A refrain that emerges from early US assessments of Lumumba was his inherent untrustworthiness, an ability to tell an audience what it wanted to hear.[19] The capabilities and intentions of Lumumba as well as of other African leaders were questioned since they had only recently 'come down from the trees'.[20] The racist tones only increased with the worsening of the crisis.[21] Several US officials also had investments in Belgian companies in Congo or family connections to such investments.[22] Finally, the United States was quick to superimpose its rigid Cold War lens on developments in Africa and in Congo. Lumumba, most US officials assumed, was probably a communist, and even if he wasn't one, his (alleged) inability to govern the country created a vacuum that the Soviets could exploit.[23]

* * *

After fighting in the Second World War, Larry Devlin was recruited by the CIA in the manner typical of the time, a touch on the shoulder and a quick meeting with a professor – and later with McGeorge Bundy – during his Master's degree at Harvard University. Devlin was initially stationed in Brussels where he established contacts with Congolese politicians, and possibly with Mobutu. At the time, Mobutu was working in Brussels as a journalist and was already collaborating with Belgium's information agency INFORCONGO[24] and Belgian intelligence.[25] Devlin arrived at the US Embassy in Leopoldville, to take up his new post of Chief of Station in the early days of July 1960. All around the Embassy's building, violence was flaring.[26]

In July, as the US government's posture towards Lumumba hardened,[27] the UN Security Council approved Resolution 143, calling on Belgian troops to withdraw and authorising the Secretary General to assemble a multinational force and dispatch it to Congo. On the same day, the crisis escalated. Due to Belgium's refusal to withdraw troops, Lumumba and Kasavubu agreed to break diplomatic relations with Belgium. Belgium replied by installing a 'technical mission' in Katanga, a 'shadow government' directed from Brussels.[28] Afraid that the situation might worsen before UN troops could be deployed, Lumumba and Kasavubu wrote to Soviet premier Nikita Khrushchev asking him to follow the situation closely and hinting that the Congolese government might request future Soviet assistance if Western powers failed to put an end to Belgian aggression.[29] The Soviet Union made this request public, seemingly confirming the United States' fears.

In a National Security Council (NSC) meeting on the 15th, Lumumba was described as 'especially anti-Western'.[30] Several US officials came to agree with their Belgian counterparts that Lumumba was acting under Soviet influence.[31] In the first few days of the UN mission, the multinational force had moved slowly and – contrary to the Congolese government's expectations – had not acted to remove Belgian troops. Disappointed by the slow pace of UN activities, Lumumba and Kasavubu issued an ultimatum to the UN to expel all Belgian troops within seventy-two hours and threatened to call in Soviet troops if the request was not carried out.[32] The request was later withdrawn, when the UN passed a new Security Council resolution on Belgian withdrawal.

On the 17th, US Ambassador Timberlake sent an urgent 'night action' telegram to Washington and Brussels warning that Congo as a nation seemed in 'its death throes'. It was time to make a major policy decision, Timberlake wrote.[33] From the UN, Hammarskjöld made clear that the multinational force was a temporary measure. The force would not become part of 'internal conflicts' and would not be used to 'impose a political solution' to pending conflicts.[34] This interpretation conformed with Belgian and Western interests, but it was disingenuous. The secession of Katanga was not solely an internal matter; it was propped up politically and militarily by Belgium.

At this stage, US Ambassador in Belgium William Burden made the first explicit call for the overthrow of Lumumba: 'A principal objective of our political and diplomatic action,' he told the Department of State, 'must . . . be to destroy Lumumba government as now constituted, but at same time we must find or develop another horse to back.' The US government needed to launch a political campaign to overthrow Lumumba and a propaganda campaign to paint him as a 'witting or unwitting instrument of Soviet intervention'.[35]

In later years, Burden was more explicit. 'It was perfectly obvious,' he declared, 'that the way to get rid of him [Lumumba] was through political assassination.' For this reason, since the Belgians were 'toying' with the idea, he went beyond his instructions and told them that he thought it was a good idea. He discussed the option extensively with Belgian authorities without reporting it explicitly to Washington.[36] Burden also revealed that he enjoyed cutting bureaucratic red tape and having direct contacts with the President and the Secretary of State to discuss 'matters of key importance' related to Belgium and Congo.[37]

Two days after Burden's telegram, Dulles declared that in Lumumba the United States confronted a 'person who was a Castro or worse'. The Pentagon agreed, suggesting that the chaos in Congo was communist-inspired.[38] Devlin, recalled to Washington, also painted for Dulles a terrifying (if fanciful) picture of a Soviet plot that – via Congo – would eventually threaten the Mediterranean.[39] Only the State Department's Bureau of Intelligence and Research held out against this alarmism: Lumumba was more likely to be an 'African nationalist'.[40] This view was not shared by Secretary of State Christian Herter.

With US policy coming into focus, Lumumba visited the United States. In New York, meetings with Hammarskjöld did not go well.[41] As to Washington, President Eisenhower snubbed Lumumba, who was instead received by Secretary Herter and Undersecretary Douglas Dillon. Dillon later recalled that Lumumba 'would never look you in the eye . . . He looked up at the sky. And a tremendous flow of words came out . . . You had a feeling that he was a person that was gripped with this fervor that I can only characterise as Messianic.' He was 'impossible to deal with'.[42] Bissell, on the contrary, recalled that Lumumba's meeting with Herter had been somewhat successful.[43] Certainly, Lumumba confounded the expectations of US officials, no doubt influenced by racial stereotypes.[44] Racist assumptions are also likely to have fed the shock at Lumumba's alleged request for a blonde companion for the night.[45] On the policy side, the United States had – in any case – no intention of listening to any of his requests or providing support.

Meanwhile, in Congo, the situation had deteriorated after the UN's refusal to impose the withdrawal of Belgian troops from Katanga. On 8 August, Albert Kalonji – who led the other wing of the MNC party – announced the secession of South Kasai, a province bordering on Katanga. Lumumba correctly concluded that further Belgian interference was behind the secession.[46] Having failed in another bid to get the UN to end Katanga's secession, and now facing a second seceding province, Lumumba declared a state of emergency and, later, martial law. Political figures suspected of threatening the government were arrested.[47]

For Devlin, these developments seemed to confirm his warnings about an increased communist influence in Congo.[48] CIA Headquarters had initially been more cautious, warning that the 'removal' of Lumumba 'might breed more problems than [it] would solve'. Headquarters had instructed the Embassy and the Station to refrain from advocating the 'illegal overthrow Lumumba'.[49] The situation changed with Devlin's momentous cable on 18 August.

Getting Rid of Lumumba

'Embassy and Station believe Congo experiencing classic Communist effort take over government,' Devlin wrote. 'Whether or not Lumumba actually Commie or just playing Commie game to assist his solidifying power . . . there may be little time left in which take action to avoid another Cuba or Guinea.' The Station – with the concurrence of Timberlake – recommended a sweeping plan of political action against Lumumba, including financial support to his opposition, and broad authorities to act independently.[50]

On the same day, Devlin's telegram was discussed at the NSC. Dillon expressed concern for the future of the UN mission in Congo. Dulles reminded participants that Lumumba was probably a Soviet stooge. The president agreed with Dillon. It was 'inconceivable' that the UN should leave; the United States needed to do anything in its power to prevent this.[51] Not reported in the minutes was Eisenhower's order to kill Lumumba. Robert Johnson, who attended the NSC meeting as a substitute, recalled: 'At some time during that discussion, President Eisenhower said something, I can no longer remember his words, that came across to me as an order for the assassination of Lumumba . . . There was no discussion, the meeting simply moved on.'[52]

The 5412 Special Group (often referred to simply as Special Group)[53] – tasked with developing covert operations – met to discuss the situation on the 25th. Having listened to the plans being devised by the Agency, Gordon Gray – Eisenhower's National Security Advisor – reported that 'his associates had expressed

Patrice Lumumba: Eisenhower's Order to Kill

extremely strong feelings on the necessity for very straightforward action in this situation, and he wondered whether the plans as outlined were sufficient to accomplish this'. In other words, Eisenhower – Gray's associate – wanted to get rid of Lumumba and did not think that the measures being taken would be sufficient. Having understood the implications of Gray's statement, Dulles replied that he 'had every intention of proceeding as vigorously as the situation permits or requires . . . within the bounds of necessity and capability'. The meeting concluded with an agreement that 'planning for the Congo would not necessarily rule out "consideration" of any particular kind of activity which might contribute to getting rid of Lumumba'.[54] No clearer statement of US policy was needed. Assassination was fair game. Belgium agreed. The Belgian Foreign Ministry told ambassadors from the US, UK and France that 'the essential thing' was to get rid of Lumumba.[55] Belgian policy quickly settled on assassination.[56]

Having received presidential instructions, Dulles wrote to Devlin that 'high quarters' – another euphemism for the president – had reached a 'clear cut conclusion'. If Lumumba stayed in office chaos would ensue, paving the way for a communist takeover. 'Consequently,' Dulles continued, 'his removal must be an urgent and prime objective . . . a high priority of our covert action.' For this mission, Devlin was granted all the authority he needed. He had already received broad authorities in previous cables and now he was being authorised to conduct 'even more aggressive action if it can remain covert'. Since 'targets of opportunity may present themselves', money was set aside for Devlin to conduct 'crash programs' without consulting with headquarters. Devlin was also given permission to act on his own authority and to consult the ambassador only if the latter wished to be consulted. The message also had the support of the Department of State.[57] The US government's bureaucracy was speaking with one voice.

As Devlin was receiving this unprecedented démarche, Lumumba had ordered Mobutu and the army to start the attack on Kasai. The attack was seen as the first step in a broader effort to retake Katanga.[58] The army confronted little resistance in Kasai but conducted extensive attacks against the civilian population; thousands were killed including many civilians from the local

53

ethnic Baluba population. The attack shocked the UN Secretary General, who considered it 'genocidal',[59] and convinced him that Lumumba was not only inept, but an evil villain, a new Hitler.[60] Such a view signalled the coming of a stronger confrontation between UN officials and Lumumba.

Throughout August, the Station and Ambassador Timberlake had been pushing for 'instructions that would allow them to pursue a course that would lead to change of government'.[61] On 1 September, the Special Group launched Project Wizard,[62] a political action programme aimed at strengthening and financing Congolese politicians opposed to Lumumba.[63] Having heard that Kasavubu was considering Lumumba's dismissal, Devlin and the CIA prepared a brief for the Congolese president on how to carry out such action. The US plan was for Kasavubu and the CIA to convince enough senators to take a vote of no confidence against Lumumba and dismiss him. Joseph Ileo – one of Lumumba's main rivals and the man the CIA had helped elect President of the Senate – was considered Lumumba's ideal replacement.[64]

On 5 September, though, before a parliamentary vote could take place, Kasavubu – following instead Belgium's advice – went on the radio to announce that he was dismissing Lumumba. The Prime Minister immediately responded with his own announcement, dismissing the President. The following day, Hammarskjöld's personal representative, Andrew Cordier – who was in regular contact with the United States – ordered UN troops to close the airport, thus preventing the airlift of troops loyal to Lumumba. He then proceeded to close the radio stations.[65] Cordier justified the move as an impartial effort to maintain law and order. This was disingenuous. Cordier knew full well that the closure of the radios prevented Lumumba from speaking to his supporters and to the Congolese people. Kasavubu, on the contrary, had access to radio facilities in the neighbouring Congo Brazzaville.[66]

On the 12th, Mobutu – on orders from Kasavubu – tried to have Lumumba arrested, but the Congolese leader was soon released. Mobutu also requested financial support from the UN to pacify – read buy the loyalty of – Congolese troops. Again, Cordier authorised the UN to release food and as much as US$1 million to be distributed among Congolese troops.[67] Another UN official, the Moroccan General Ben Hammou Kettani, worked on the transfer and soon became a personal adviser to (and close friend of) Mobutu.[68] Kettani also trained Mobutu's troops.[69] And yet, support for Lumumba remained strong. Lumumba took the stage in parliament and received confidence votes. Parliament also refused the dismissal of both Kasavubu and Lumumba.

Having had to abandon the more constitutional – if still illegal – plan centred on Kasavubu, Devlin intensified his meetings with Mobutu. The Congolese colonel discussed a possible plan to have Lumumba assassinated by a mob. The leader could be convinced to show up at a rally of his opponents and the army could be made to arrive too late. Devlin thought the plan unlikely to succeed since UN troops would be able to intervene.[70]

In Washington, assassination remained on the table. During a Special Group meeting, Gray reminded Dulles that the President and the CIA Station wanted 'vigorous action'. Dulles agreed: 'Lumumba was not yet disposed of and remained a grave danger as long as he was not disposed of.'[71] Following developments from Langley, Bronson Tweedy, the CIA Africa Division's chief, wrote to Devlin. He commended the work being done, especially considering the 'naïve human material' Devlin had at his disposal. He also recognised that Lumumba's talents and dynamism made sure that he was always able to re-establish his position even when all seemed lost[72] – another call to permanently dispose of him. Devlin agreed. Only Lumumba's physical elimination could solve the situation.[73] The same point was discussed in a meeting between US officials and the French Ambassador to the United States. Livingston Merchant, Undersecretary of State for Political Affairs, told attendees that 'everything appeared hopeless so long as Lumumba was on the scene'.[74]

Any veneer of constitutionality was abandoned. UN and US officials identified Mobutu as the only one able to remove Lumumba. Devlin started thinking in terms of a coup.[75] Mobutu – who over the course of the crisis became Devlin's friend and his main point of contact – told Devlin that the army was ready to overthrow Lumumba but only if the US government could support the government put in place to replace him. Devlin asked what would happen in these circumstances to Kasavubu and Lumumba and

Mobutu replied that they would have to be 'neutralized'. Without consulting Washington, Devlin offered US support for the coup and for the government of civilian technocrats that would replace Lumumba.[76] As Devlin recalled, Mobutu's coup 'was arranged and supported, and indeed managed, by the CIA'.[77]

With UN funds and US support, Mobutu sprang into action. On the 14th, with Parliament still backing Lumumba, and Kasavubu still refusing to recognise Parliament's decision, Mobutu went on the radio to announce that he was taking over the government and he was 'neutralizing' both Kasavubu and Lumumba. He expelled Soviet diplomats and nominated a Council of Commissioners. For a few days, confusion reigned about the outcome of Mobutu's coup. When the dust settled on the 16th, Lumumba was again almost arrested by Congolese troops, but the UN prevented this move, surrounding the Prime Minister's residence. Devlin notified the CIA that it was unclear whether Lumumba was out of the equation. The (former) Prime Minister was still an able politician and the option of a reconciliation with Kasavubu was in the air. The only solution was to 'remove him from scene soonest'.[78] Devlin started working as 'adviser' to the Congolese to 'eliminate' Lumumba.[79]

Sid from Paris: The Poison Plot

In the same weeks, Deputy Director for Plans Richard Bissell had asked Tweedy to explore capabilities and opportunities to assassinate Lumumba. Bissell made clear that 'higher authority' had cleared the action. Both Bissell and Tweedy held several meetings with Sidney Gottlieb and asked him to develop poison for use against an unspecified African leader. Gottlieb worked on a poison that could dissolve in food and drink, as well as on toxic biological material. With the materials ready, Gottlieb was told to travel to Congo and work with Devlin to eliminate Lumumba.[80]

On 19 September, Headquarters notified Devlin of the imminent arrival of 'Sid from Paris'. 'Sid from Paris' was none other than Gottlieb. As Tweedy recalled, Gottlieb was a 'technician', and the only purpose of his trip was to facilitate assassination.[81]

The Agency also established a new super-secret channel of communication. Any information surrounding the assassination of Lumumba would go through the PROP channel, with only five officials cleared: Dulles, Bissell, Tweedy, Glenn Fields (Tweedy's deputy) and Devlin himself. PROP was to have priority over other communications.[82]

Gottlieb travelled to Leopoldville and met Devlin at a local cafe. After a few pleasantries, he told Devlin that the poison he had brought with him could be used in food or toothpaste. He passed to Devlin rubber gloves, a mask and a syringe, as well as vials with poison. Gottlieb assured the station chief that such a dangerous and controversial mission had been approved by higher authority, by President Eisenhower himself. According to Devlin, Gottlieb told him:

> I wasn't there when he approved it, but Dick Bissell said Eisenhower wanted Lumumba removed... It's your responsibility... The details are up to you, but it's got to be clean – nothing that can be traced back to the US government... With the stuff that's in there, no one will ever be able to know that Lumumba was assassinated.[83]

After chatting with Gottlieb, Devlin cabled Headquarters to check whether the operation had been fully authorised. Having received confirmation, he was ready to act. 'They were serious about it,' he later recalled, 'it was clear that the policy decision to assassinate Lumumba had been made.'[84] In spite of his later denials and professed shock, Devlin wrote to Tweedy that he and Gottlieb were 'on same wave length'.[85]

With Lumumba now under protective UN custody and with Gottlieb in Congo, Devlin explored options for assassination with the Agency. He had contacts with various groups who intended to kill Lumumba. Some needed weapons. The option of providing training had been considered.[86] More directly, Devlin proposed asking an agent to 'take refuge with big brother'[87] to poison him. The agent could have access to Lumumba's kitchen. He 'would thus act as inside man to brush up details to razor edge. Also would provide info on food and agricultural problem' – a clear reference to the poison Gottlieb had prepared. A second possibility involved a different agent who had promised to take care of Lumumba but had initially failed. However, 'if price right might get show on road'. At the Agency, Tweedy agreed that the station should proceed with its options and reminded Devlin that for the assassination operation the main concern in Washington was to guarantee plausible deniability, unless 'an outstanding opportunity' materialised 'which made a calculated risk a first class bet'.[88]

In the following days, Devlin explored and put in motion the poisoning option. He asked headquarters for permission to continue discussions with the asset and eventually asked for an opinion as to whether he should cancel the operation or 'accept calculated risk of varying degrees'. This referred to the extent to which the operation could remain plausibly deniable. This, Devlin believed, would have improved if the asset had left the scene before the effects of the poisoning started to appear. Headquarters authorised these discussions. Devlin reported that the asset was willing to 'take any role necessary' but asked Headquarters whether due to the asset's personal circumstances,[89] it would have been better to send a third-country national.[90] As these options were considered, the Agency continued to express support for assassination.[91]

At this point, US policies and views coincided with those of other European allies. In a meeting with British Foreign Secretary Alec Douglas-Home, President Eisenhower reportedly 'expressed his wish that Lumumba would fall into a river full of crocodiles', to which Home regretfully replied that many of the 'old-fashioned techniques of diplomacy' had gone lost.[92] British officials were also explicitly debating the assassination of Lumumba.[93] As to Belgium, Colonel Louis Marlière – a former officer in the Belgian colonial army – had been assigned as Mobutu's personal adviser, albeit in an unofficial capacity. According to Belgian intelligence officer Andre LeHaye, Marlière, in his new role, was in regular contact with Devlin.[94] On 6 October, the Belgian government made a final decision that only Lumumba's 'definitive elimination' could guarantee the interests of Belgium and Katanga.[95]

The United States needed little convincing. On the 7th, Tweedy reassured Devlin that he did not anticipate the immediate success of the assassination plan.[96] He also accepted Devlin's request to send a third-country national. Devlin should assess the candidate on his arrival and – if deemed useful – he could play an 'active or cutout role on full time basis'.[97] The third-country national was Jose Marie Andre Mankel, better known through his CIA cryptonym QJWIN-1.[98] A former member of the French Resistance, with experience of illegally exporting nickel to countries of the Eastern bloc, he had been recruited by the CIA.[99] In the Agency's own assessment, Mankel was not a man of 'many scruples' and he could certainly carry out an assassination.[100]

As preparations regarding Mankel continued, Devlin and Tweedy continued to explore options for assassination. Looking at more direct options, Tweedy asked whether a commando-type operation against Lumumba – such as an assault on his house – could work. Devlin admitted that he had not been able to penetrate Lumumba's entourage and that a commando operation looked unlikely. He also lamented that he was overburdened and recommended the dispatch of a senior case officer.[101] 'If case officer sent,' Devlin added, 'recommend HQS pouch soonest high-powered foreign make rifle with telescopic scope and silencer. Hunting good here when lights right.' Devlin would keep the rifle at the station until 'hunting season'.[102]

Responding to Devlin's request for a senior officer, Bissell asked Justin O'Donnell to go to Congo and kill Lumumba. O'Donnell balked at Bissell's request – conspiracy to murder was a federal crime in Washington, DC – but the DDP still asked him to meet with Gottlieb, who had by then returned to Washington. Gottlieb assured O'Donnell that several methods for assassinating Lumumba were still available in Congo; these included a virus and poison. O'Donnell insisted that he found the idea of poisoning Lumumba immoral but agreed to travel to Congo. He told Bissell that he had 'no compunction' about running an operation to draw Lumumba out of protective custody. O'Donnell also understood that such an operation would have a 'very, very high probability' of resulting in Lumumba's assassination, but he was still able to make a distinction. Directly assassinating Lumumba would have been immoral. An effort to deliver him to his enemies was a different matter, however; 'it would have been a Congolese, being judged by Congolese, for Congolese crimes'. Bissell, unwilling to relent, told O'Donnell not to completely discount the possibility of assassinating Lumumba more directly.[103]

Having accepted Bissell's request, O'Donnell met personally with QJWIN in Frankfurt and asked him to travel to Leopoldville for a mission that included a high degree of personal risk. The idea was for QJWIN to penetrate the two protective rings around Lumumba and trick the (former) Congolese prime minister out of his residence.[104] O'Donnell arrived in Leopoldville before his asset and met with Devlin. The Chief of Station told O'Donnell that some of Gottlieb's viruses were still in the Station safe, but the latter shifted the discussion to his own (kidnap) plan.[105]

Devlin had also increased his contacts with Mobutu. The latter often visited Devlin's house to unwind and plot his next moves. At one point, Mobutu suggested that he was considering a second coup, this time taking over the government. Devlin convinced him to desist. The Chief of Station feared that the plot might fail and result in Lumumba's return. It was much better, Devlin thought, for Mobutu to remain behind the scenes as the strong man pulling the strings. After all, Kasavubu had shown his support for the Council of Commissioners installed by Mobutu, many of the Commissioners were on the CIA's pay roll, and Devlin was in constant contact with Congolese politicians through the informal Binza Group.[106] The Agency also made sure to further buy Mobutu's loyalty. The Special Group set aside $250,000 to convince Congolese politicians to back Mobutu's government in Parliament. When Parliament refused – showing once against its loyalty to Lumumba and the constitution – the funds were transferred to Mobutu personally.[107]

On 15 November, Devlin expressed his frustration about the protection surrounding Lumumba and the lack of access. 'Concentric rings of defense make establishment of observation post impossible.' Under these conditions a renewed attempt to poison Lumumba and attempts to shoot him were unlikely to succeed. A more plausible option remained an effort to kidnap him in case Lumumba escaped. The Station, Devlin assured, had 'several possible assets' to use in such a contingency and several 'plans of action' were under study.[108]

Lumumba's Escape and Death: Too Many Coincidences?

As the crisis evolved, Hammarskjöld, his new personal representative Rajeshwar Dayal and the UN had come to adopt a policy less aligned with US and Belgian interests. Influenced by the African nations contributing to the UN force, they had started to work towards a constitutional solution, one that would include Lumumba. On 5 November, the UN established a (re)conciliation commission to broker a deal between Lumumba and Kasavubu.[109] Things were looking up for Lumumba and there was hope that the recently elected John Kennedy might eventually adopt a different policy towards Congo.[110]

In New York, the UN Credentials Committee also met to assess which delegation should be admitted as the representative of Congo: one led by Lumumba's government and supporters, or one led by Kasavubu. US threats and arm-twisting, as well as the bribing of several delegations – delivered through the bland-sounding Overseas Regional Survey Associates, a CIA front acting as a consultancy firm in New York – ensured the admission of Kasavubu's delegation.[111] This decision seemingly convinced Lumumba that there was no political path for a return to power. He decided to flee his house arrest and join his supporters in Stanleyville.[112] On 27 November, Lumumba escaped in mysterious circumstances, possibly hidden under the feet of a passenger in a car driven by some of his servants.[113]

A Lumumba escape from UN custody coincided with US objectives, with O'Donnell's mission, and with the brief he had allegedly given QJWIN on their first meeting. The telegram Devlin sent after the escape raises questions as to whether the escape was more than a coincidence:

> QJWIN arrived Leop. November 21. View delicate nature of op. station did not surface him to [name withdrawn]. Unilaterally and on own initiative he made contact with Iden who agreed 26 November in following plan against target: Iden to supply for UNO vehicles and six Congolese Soldiers with UNO brassards and berets. QJWIN posing as [withdrawn] officer to enter target's home and provide escort out of residence. Iden said could easily provide vehicles and man (UNO announced fifty-five of its vehicles have been stolen and station knows where [withdrawn] uniforms available). Iden A organization needed to pierce both Congolese and UNO guards.[114]

The telegram is cryptic, and two mysteries remain. First, a handwritten note added 'Mobutu' to the first name withdrawn. It seems that 'Iden A' referred to a contact developed by QJWIN, Major Djurorie Dujare Djurovic, a pilot of the Yugoslav Air Force who was delivering supplies for the UN in Congo. Iden and Iden A, however, are two different individuals. Who is Iden?

Some scholars have suggested that QJWIN simply approached Mobutu to provide UN vehicles and other resources.[115] This interpretation seems unconvincing since Mobutu's name was completely withdrawn in the telegram and added in a handwritten note. Others conclude that Iden must have been someone with good access to the UN mission, if not a member of the mission.[116] In a later chronology, the US State Department hinted that Lumumba's escape had happened with the 'connivance of Moroccans on the UN force'. Is this the nationality withdrawn in the telegram? Dayal confirmed that 'the first report was from the Moroccan guard posted at the Prime Minister's residence'.[117] And if that is the case, could General Kettani be Iden? He was, after all, in the Moroccan UN contingent. He had become Mobutu's close friend and adviser.[118] We know that Kettani was in close contact with the CIA Station and had helped in transferring $1 million to Mobutu for the Congolese troops.[119] Reportedly, Kettani later became a CIA informant.[120]

Second, it is quite a coincidence that Lumumba's escape developed precisely along the lines set out by QJWIN. On the 29th, Devlin told Tweedy that QJWIN had begun the implementation of a plan to 'pierce both Congolese and UN guards' and 'provide escort out of residence'. O'Donnell also confirmed that QJWIN had become acquainted with members of the UN force the agent would have needed to snatch Lumumba.[121] In later years, Devlin and O'Donnell denied that the CIA played any part in Lumumba's escape. Lumumba's supporters also argue that the escape was Lumumba's idea for both political and personal reasons.[122] Some, however, are less convinced. The episode, the UN's Dayal argued, was hard to explain, 'unless his escape was actually encouraged to get rid of an inconvenient element'.[123]

What is certain is that the timing of communication is interesting here. Devlin only told Washington of Lumumba's escape two days after it had happened. By the time of Devlin's cable to the Agency, Lumumba was already on the run and a hunting party had formed. Devlin further reported that 'QJWIN had displayed great initiative, imagination, and courage since arrival'. The Station knew that Lumumba was heading to Stanleyville to reunite with his supporters. 'QJWIN anxious go Stanleyville and expressed desire execute plan by himself without using any apparat.'[124] The Agency approved the use of 'direct action' by QJWIN in Stanleyville but only after an assessment by Devlin of the security of the operation and of the risk of US exposure.[125]

Devlin, Belgian officials, Mobutu's men and Victor Nendaka's Sûreté Nationale worked to track Lumumba. The Belgians made available a low-flying surveillance plane. Devlin and Marlière worked with Mobutu to set up roadblocks. MI6's Daphne Park (who had collaborated with the other Western powers against Lumumba) and her contacts were also involved in the chase.[126] UN forces came to play a prominent role. After Lumumba's escape the UN adopted a policy of 'neutrality' towards Lumumba's safety. When Mobutu's men first reached Lumumba's group, Ghanaian troops working for the UN mission disobeyed the orders of their British officers and helped Lumumba forward. On 1 December, though, as Lumumba reached the Sankuru River, he was caught. Lumumba and one of his emissaries shouted and asked the nearby UN troops for help, but British officers in charge of the Ghanaian troops ignored their pleas. Lumumba was captured.[127]

Mobutu's troops mistreated Lumumba in front of cameras as they flew him to Leopoldville. Two days later, he was imprisoned with one member of his government – Maurice Mpolo, Minister of Youth and Sports – and with Joseph Okito, Second Vice-President of the Senate at Camp Hardy in Thysville.

Alongside these developments, the CIA had also strengthened its presence on the ground, by sending another third-country national, David Tzitzichvili, under the cryptonym WIROGUE-1.[128] Tzitzichvili, born in Georgia, fought with the Foreign Legion. During the Second World War, he was involved with the French Resistance and in the counterfeiting of documents. Arrested and sentenced to death by the Germans, he was liberated by the US Army in 1945. After the war, he moved to France where he was arrested after a bank robbery. He was released for good behaviour and recruited by the CIA. Initially, he was trained for Project AESENTINEL, infiltration and exfiltration operations in the Soviet Union. When the project collapsed, he was reassigned to the Technical Service Division.[129]

In the Agency's own assessment, WIROGUE-1 was a stateless soldier of fortune, a man with a 'peculiar turn of mind which leads itself remarkably to nefarious and illegal activities', able to distinguish right and wrong but also to rationalise and carry out any activity he is ordered to 'without pangs of conscience'. Before his travel to Congo the CIA had provided him with plastic surgery and a toupee to disguise his appearance. The Africa Division also reported that – since October 1960 – every effort had been made to train and prepare psychologically WIROGUE for his assignment in Africa.[130] In Congo, he was to be used as a 'utility agent' for '(1) organizing and conducting surveillance team (2) interception of pouches (3) blowing up bridges and/or (4) executing other assignments requiring positive action',[131] another reference to assassination. His training and expertise also made him suitable for 'paramilitary activities'.[132]

With Lumumba under arrest, Devlin told WIROGUE to lie low and start developing contacts. But Devlin was having trouble controlling his agent. On 14 December, for example, dropping his cover and without realising that he was dealing with another US asset, WIROGUE approached QJWIN and asked him whether he wanted to be part of an 'execution squad', offering $300 per month in compensation.[133] In making this offer, as well as in showing off his embassy contacts to QJWIN, WIROGUE clearly breached protocol. Devlin allegedly raised concerns about his behaviour.[134]

By early January, Lumumba was neutralised, out of politics and in prison, but his prospects seemed to improve. Antoine Gizenga, who had been leading the pro-Lumumba forces, declared himself prime minister of a provisional government in Stanleyville. Having achieved quick military victories against Mobutu's army, he seemed ready to attack Katanga. Politics in the Congo also became intertwined with the impending change in administration in the United States. Devlin feared that the incoming Kennedy Administration might decide to turn the page on Congo and work with Lumumba.[135] Furthermore, confirming Devlin's and the CIA's fears that – until assassinated – Lumumba might always make a comeback, on 13 January the troops at Camp Hardy in Thysville, where Lumumba was being held prisoner, mutinied. Disregarding Devlin's advice, Congolese officials including Mobutu travelled to Camp Hardy to try and calm the troops.[136] The Chief of Station, though, had also decided to keep a close eye on developments in Thysville by sending along WIROGUE.[137]

At this stage, regardless of what the Kennedy Administration's policy towards Lumumba might have been (and one should look with great scepticism at claims that it would have been radically different),[138] Devlin played a crucial role in sealing Lumumba's fate. After Lumumba's mistreatment at the airport, calls for humane treatment had emerged. The State Department had refused Devlin's request to provide funds to calm – that is, buy the loyalty of – the police and the military. With the impending change of administration, the State Department considered this too big a policy decision. Confronted with this situation, and aware since 14 January that Lumumba would be transferred to Bakwanga, Devlin did not report news of the transfer to Washington.[139] In a pattern like the one seen in the cable detailing QJWIN's effort to enter Lumumba's residence, Devlin communicated the transfer only on the 17th, three days later. Devlin knew that in Bakwanga, Lumumba would be killed. He wanted to make sure that the US government did not interfere.[140] He also did nothing to restrain Mobutu and the other henchmen, when requests for humane treatment arrived from the State Department.[141] In this sense, even if the more direct assassination plot (poisoning or shooting Lumumba) had been dropped, the CIA's role was essential for the success of the more indirect one.

Eventually, Lumumba's destination became Elizabethville, in Katanga. Like Bakwanga, Elizabethville meant death. Lumumba arrived in Katanga on the 17th having been brutally beaten and tortured on the flight.[142] On the 18th, David Doyle, the CIA man in Elizabethville, wrote to the Agency and Devlin: 'Thanks for Patrice. If we had known he was coming we would have baked a snake.' While some controversy surrounds the meaning of the sentence, the celebratory tone is clear. Doyle,[143] like Devlin, understood that Lumumba would no longer threaten a political return; he would not leave Katanga alive.[144] Although Doyle later used the telegram as a demonstration of his innocence,[145] at the time he ignored Lumumba's terrible state, and he delayed communication of Lumumba's arrival to avoid any last-minute surprises.

By the time of Doyle's celebratory telegram, Lumumba was already dead. Belgian officials had gathered in Katanga and took charge of the final execution. After being the subject of additional mistreatment and torture, Lumumba, Mpolo and Okito were shot on 17 January by a firing squad of Congolese (Katangans) commanded by Belgian officials.[146]

Conclusion

Assassination plots against Lumumba developed along two main tracks. Direct options relied on individual assets to poison or shoot Lumumba, whereas more indirect approaches relied on creating favourable political conditions to remove Lumumba from power and 'deliver' him to his internal enemies and executioners. It is possible, though by no means confirmed, that Devlin, O'Donnell and CIA agent QJWIN played a part in Lumumba's escape. O'Donnell's moral qualms are important here. They showcase the distinction between more direct approaches that some – but not all – considered unsavoury, and more palatable indirect ones.

Several Western powers were involved in Lumumba's demise. As to the US government, all levels of the CIA – from Director Dulles to Tweedy, from Bissell and Gottlieb to O'Donnell, Devlin and Doyle in the field – were involved in the assassination. All agreed that Lumumba's political neutralisation was not enough; he had to be completely disposed of, to prevent any risk of a political return. But was the CIA acting independently or was it following presidential orders? The Church Committee's investigation surrounding the assassination of Lumumba concluded that the evidence was 'strong enough' to permit a 'reasonable inference that the plot to assassinate Lumumba was authorized by President Eisenhower'. It also added that countervailing evidence and circumlocutory language could be used to question whether the President wanted Lumumba assassinated.[147] This conclusion seems to miss the mark.

Patrice Lumumba: Eisenhower's Order to Kill

At the NSC meeting on 18 August, Robert Johnson heard a presidential order for assassination. One week later, in a Special Group meeting, Gordon Gray reported the President's request for 'very straightforward action'. The Church Committee's senators deposing Gray accepted his statement that he did not consider 'very straightforward action' to include assassination.[148] This is surprising. A few days before his testimony Gray had been interrogated by Church Committee's staffer Frederick Baron and had given a different interpretation. 'When I said very straightforward action,' Gray told Baron, 'Certainly, assassination would be a possibility.'[149] The same Special Group meeting concluded with the understanding that no option should have been excluded in the pursuit of Lumumba's removal.

As Richard Bissell put it, this type of language is the point where assassination and plausible deniability meet:

> When you use the language that no particular means were ruled out, that is obviously what it meant, and it meant that to everybody in the room ... if it had to be assassination, that was a permissible means. You don't use language of that kind except to mean in effect, the Director is being told to get rid of the guy and, if you have to use extreme means up to and including assassination, go ahead.[150]

The evidence of a presidential order and of the US government's responsibility in the case of the assassination of Patrice Lumumba is convincing. The US government and the CIA made extraordinary preparations to have Lumumba killed, and they were at the centre of Lumumba's enemies' plots. By the time of the Congolese leader's death, the Agency was already embroiled in a long campaign against one of its archenemies, Fidel Castro.

Notes

1. The Guardian, 'Marred: M. Lumumba's Offensive Speech in King's Presence', *The Guardian*, 1 July 1960, available at https://www.theguardian.com/world/1960/jul/01/congo (accessed 19 October 2023).

2. Emmanuel Gerard and Bruce Kuklick, *Death in the Congo: Murdering Patrice Lumumba* (Cambridge, MA: Harvard University Press, 2015), 25.
3. Patrice Lumumba, 'Independence Day Speech', 30 June 1960, available at https://africanlegends.files.wordpress.com/2011/06/patrice-lumumba-speech.pdf (accessed 19 October 2023).
4. Georges Nzongola-Ntalaja, *Patrice Lumumba* (Athens: Ohio University Press, 2014).
5. Susan Williams, *White Malice: The CIA and the Neocolonisation of Africa* (London: Hurst, 2021).
6. Stuart Reid, *The Lumumba Plot* (New York: Knopf, 2023), chapter 6.
7. A splinter group, MNC – K, was led by Albert Kalonji.
8. Lise Namikas, 'Chronology US Soviet Competition in West/Central Africa and the Congo Crisis 1945–1965', Wilson Center, 3, available at https://www.wilsoncenter.org/sites/default/files/media/documents/publication/Congo1960-61_1.pdf (accessed 19 October 2023).
9. In March 1960, Belgian authorities had already started developing plans to eliminate Lumumba or – at a minimum – prevent him from taking power; Williams, *White Malice*, 138.
10. Nzongola-Ntalaja, *Patrice Lumumba*, 91–2.
11. Gerard and Kuklick, *Death in the Congo*, 29.
12. Memorandum of conversation, Subject: 'American Ambassador Advises Congolese Chief of State and Prime Minister to Call upon United Nations for Assistance', 10 /7/1960, Folder Political Activities, General Records Dep of State 755a (Congo), Box 1831, NARA.
13. US State Department, Analytical Chronology, File Congo: Analytical chronology, 25/1/1961, President's Office File, JFK Library, 10, available at https://www.jfklibrary.org/asset-viewer/archives/JFKPOF/114/JFKPOF-114-015 (accessed 19 October 2023).
14. Christopher Othen, *Katanga 1960–1963* (Brimscombe Port: The History Press, 2018), 54.
15. Stephen Weissman, *American Foreign Policy in the Congo 1960–1964* (Ithaca, NY: Cornell University Press, 1974), 58–9.
16. State Department, Analytical Chronology, 11.
17. Ibid., 2.
18. Thomas Borstelmann, *The Cold War and the Color Line* (Cambridge, MA: Harvard University Press, 2001), 130.
19. William Burden, 'Memorandum of Conversation between the Ambassador in Belgium and Patrice Lumumba', 25/2/1960, doc. 97 and Telegram Embassy Congo to State, 'Ambassador Murphy's Meeting with Lumumba, 4/7/1960, doc. 107 in Foreign Relations of the United States [FRUS], 1958–1960, Africa, vol. XIV.

20. Gerard and Kuklick, *Death in the Congo*, 56.
21. Borstelmann, *The Cold War*, 130.
22. Williams, *White Malice*, 123.
23. Memorandum Cumming to Herter, 25/7/1960. Subject: Communist Influence in Congo. FRUS vol. XIV, doc. 149.
24. Memorandum, Secret, 'Joseph Mobutu', 14/9/1960, Folder Political Activities, General Records State Department – Office of African Affairs – Records on Congo, box 4, NARA.
25. Williams, *White Malice*, 86. Devlin repeatedly denied the accusations that he recruited Mobutu then or later. See Wilson Center, 'The Congo Crisis, 1960–1961: A Critical Oral History Conference', 23–24 September 2004, 39, available at https://www.wilsoncenter.org/sites/default/files/media/uploads/documents/The%20Congo%20Crisis%2C%201960-1961.pdf (accessed 19 October 2023).
26. Wilson Center, 'The Congo Crisis', 61–6.
27. Telephone conversation Eisenhower – Herter, 13/7196 and Telegram Department of State to US Mission UN, 13/7/1960 in FRUS vol. XIV, docs. 120 and122.
28. Georges Nzongola-Ntalaja, 'Patrice Lumumba and the Unfinished Business of Liberation', *Review of African Political Economy*, 15 January 2021, available at https://roape.net/patrice-lumumba-and-the-unfinished-business-of-liberation/ (accessed 19 October 2023).
29. Stephen Kinzer, *The Brothers* (New York: Times Books, 2013), 263.
30. Memorandum of discussion at 451st NSC Meeting, 15/7/1960, FRUS vo;. XIV, doc. 126.
31. Memorandum of a conversation, 15/7/1960, FRUS vol. XIV, doc. 128.
32. Williams, *White Malice*, 202.
33. Telegram US Embassy Congo to State. 17/7/1960, FRUS vol. XIV, doc. 130.
34. United Nations Security Council, 'First Report of the Secretary general on the Implementation of Security Council Resolution S/4387 CF 14 July 1960', 18/7/1960, available at https://documents-dds-ny.un.org/doc/UNDOC/GEN/N60/171/85/PDF/N6017185.pdf?OpenElement
35. Telegram US Embassy Belgium to State, 19/7/1960, FRUS vol. XIV, doc. 136.
36. John Luter, 'William Burden, Interview', Eisenhower Administration, Oral History Research Office, Columbia University, 1971, 41–2, available at https://dlc.library.columbia.edu/catalog/cul:qfttdz0bjp (accessed 19 October 2023).
37. Luter, 'Burden, Interview', 18, 23, 25.

38. Memorandum of Discussion, 452nd NSC Meeting, 21/7/1960, doc. 140, FRUS vol. XIV.
39. Larry Devlin, *Chief of Station, Congo: Fighting the Cold War in a Hot Zone* (New York: Public Affairs, 2007), 46–7.
40. Memorandum Cumming to Herter, 25/7/1960, FRUS vol. XIV, doc. 149.
41. Reid, *The Lumumba Plot*, chapter 19.
42. Evan Thomas, *The Very Best Men* (New York: Simon & Schuster 1996), 221.
43. Richard Bissell, *Reflections of a Cold Warrior* (New Haven, CT: Yale University Press, 1996), 143.
44. Oliver Kearns, *The Covert Colour Line* (London: Pluto Press, 2023).
45. Ironically, Allen Dulles's obsessive philandering was not a problem; Borstelmann, *The Cold War*, 131.
46. Williams, *White Malice*, 138.
47. Gerard and Kuklick, *Death in the Congo*, 86.
48. Telegram Station Leopoldville to CIA, 11/8/1960, FRUS 1964–1968 vol. XXIII: Congo, 1960–1968 (FRUS vol. XXIII), doc. 8.
49. Telegram CIA to Station Leopoldville, 12/8/1960, FRUS vol. XXIII, doc. 9.
50. Telegram Station Leopoldville to CIA, 18/8/1960, FRUS vol. XXIII, doc. 10.
51. NSC meeting, 18/8/1960, Editorial Note, FRUS vol. XXIII, doc. 10.
52. Testimony of Robert Johnson to Senate Select Committee to Study Governmental Operations with Respect to Intelligence Activities (SSCIA), 13/9/1975, Digital National Security Archives (DNSA), Covert Operation II, 10.
53. Note on US Covert Action, FRUS vol. XII, 1964–1968, Western Europe.
54. Memorandum for the Record, Minutes of Special Group Meeting, 25/8/1960, FRUS vol. XIII, doc. 12.
55. State Department, Analytical Chronology, 18.
56. Ludo De Witte, *The Assassination of Lumumba* (London: Verso, 2002).
57. Telegram CIA to Congo Station, 27/8/1960, FRUS vol. XXIII, doc. 14.
58. Nothing came of this broader operation as Lumumba and Mobutu fell out over the matter; Reid, *The Lumumba Plot*, chapter 30.
59. Nzongola-Ntalaja, *Patrice Lumumba*, 97.
60. Gerard and Kuklick, *Death in the Congo*, 90.
61. Victor Hedgman (Larry Devlin), 'Interview and Meeting Summary', 22/8/1975, Miscellaneous Records of the Church Committee, JFKAR 157-10014-10185, 6.

62. Stephen Weissman, 'The Lumumba Assassination and CIA Accountability', Wilson Center, 9/4/2012, available at https://www.wilsoncenter.org/event/the-lumumba-assassination-and-cia-accountability (accessed 19 October 2023).
63. Nzongola-Ntalaja, 'Unfinished Business'.
64. Devlin, *Chief of Station*, 67.
65. David Gibbs, 'Secrecy and International Relations', *Journal of Peace Research*, 32.2 (1995), 221.
66. Gerard and Kuklick, *Death in the Congo*, 97.
67. Carole J. T. Collins, 'The Cold War Comes to Africa: Cordier and the 1960 Congo Crisis', *Journal of International Affairs*, 47.1 (1993), 262.
68. Weissman, *American Foreign Policy*, 96.
69. Rajeshwar Dayal, *Mission for Hammarskjold* (Delhi: Oxford University Press, 1976), 65.
70. Reid, *The Lumumba Plot*, chapter 33.
71. Gerard and Kuklick, *Death in the Congo*, 146–7.
72. Telegram CIA to Congo Station, 13/9/1960, FRUS vol. XXIII, doc. 20.
73. SSCIA, Interim Report, 'Alleged Assassination Plots Involving Foreign Leaders', (Washington, DC: US Government Printing Office, 1975), 17.
74. Memorandum of conversation, 13/9/1960, FRUS, 1958–1960, Africa, vol. XIV, doc. 211.
75. Devlin, 'Interview and Meeting', 6.
76. Devlin, *Chief of Station*, 78–9.
77. Devlin, 'Interview and Meeting', 6.
78. Telegram Station to CIA, 16/9/1960, FRUS vol. XXIII, doc. 22.
79. SSCIA, Draft Assassination Report, 16/10/1975, JFKAR 157-10014-10136, 259.
80. SSCIA, Interim Report, 19–21.
81. Bronson Tweedy, SSCIA Testimony, 9/10/1975, JFKAR 157-10014-10068, 10.
82. Richard Bissell, SSCIA Testimony, 10/9/1975, JFKAR, 157-10014-10093 (December 2022), 10; Devlin, *Chief of Station*, 94; SSCIA, Interim Report, 31.
83. Devlin, *Chief of Station*, 95.
84. Frederick Baron, Interview with Congo Chief of Station: Lumumba Assassination Plan and Related Events in the Congo, 20/8/1975, SSCIA, Miscellaneous documents, JFKAR 157-10014-10178, 5.
85. Editorial Note, FRUS vol. XXIII, doc. 28.
86. SSCIA, Draft Report, 263.
87. Lumumba.

88. Editorial Note, FRUS vol. XXIII, doc. 28.
89. The asset had seemingly spent time in the United States, thus undermining plausible deniability. Reid, *The Lumumba Plot*, chapter 38.
90. SSCIA, Draft Report, 276.
91. Allen Dulles, 'Telegram', 24/9/1960, CIA Reading Room Archive, DOC_0000095210.
92. Gordon Corera, *MI6* (London: Weidenfeld & Nicholson, 2011), 124.
93. Rory Cormac, *Disrupt and Deny* (Oxford: Oxford University Press, 2018), 152.
94. Lise Namikas, *Battleground Africa: Cold War in the Congo 1960–1965* (Stanford: Stanford University Press, 2013), 116.
95. De Witte, *The Assassination*, 47.
96. The historical record shows some discrepancy as to what happened to Gottlieb's poisons. SSCIA, Interim Report, 30.
97. Editorial Note, FRUS vol. XXIII, doc. 30.
98. QJWIN was a programme headed by CIA Chief of Station in Luxembourg Arnold Silver to spot and recruit agents for sabotage and covert intelligence activities. The two-letter digraph QJ refers to Luxembourg. Williams, *White Malice*, 309.
99. Reid, *The Lumumba Plot*, chapter 40.
100. SSCIA, Interim Report, 43.
101. Wilson Center, 'The Congo Crisis', 133.
102. SSCIA, Interim Report, 32.
103. Ibid., 39.
104. Richard D. Mahoney, *JFK's Ordeal in Africa* (Oxford: Oxford University Press, 1983), 52.
105. SSCIA, 'Summary Chronology of ZRRIFLE/QJWIN activities', JFKAR 157-10004-10068.
106. Stephen Weissman, 'What Really Happened in Congo: The CIA, the Murder of Lumumba, and the Rise of Mobutu', *Foreign Affairs*, 93.4 (July/August 2014), 17–18.
107. Namikas, 'Chronology', 10.
108. Telegram Station to CIA, 15/11/1960, FRUS vol. XXIII, doc. 43.
109. Namikas, 'Chronology', 11.
110. Reid, *The Lumumba Plot*, chapter 39.
111. Mahoney, *JFK's Ordeal*, 53.
112. Nzongola-Ntalaja, *Patrice Lumumba*, 124.
113. De Witte, *The Assassination*, 52.
114. Telegram Leopoldville to Director, 29/11/1960, CIA Reading Room, DOC_0001366113.

115. Namikas, *Battleground*, 118.
116. Williams, *White Malice*, 337.
117. Dayal, *Mission*, 142.
118. Weissman, *American Foreign Policy*, p. 96.
119. Farid Boussaid, 'Brothers in Arms: Morocco's Military Intervention in Support of Mobutu of Zaire during the 1977 and 1978 Shaba Crises', *International History Review*, 43 (2021), available at https://www.tandfonline.com/doi/full/10.1080/07075332.2020.1739113 (accessed 19 October 2023).
120. Rif Time, 'Kettani Ben Hammou, from Collaborator to CIA Informant', 29 November 2020, available at https://riftime.com/kettani-ben-hammou-from-collaborator-to-cia-informant/ (accessed 19 October 2023).
121. SSCIA, Draft Report, 319.
122. Williams, *White Malice*, 338–9.
123. Ibid., 344.
124. Telegram from Leopoldville to Director, 29/11/1960, FRUS vol. XXIII.
125. Footnote in Telegram Station to CIA, 29/11/1960, FRUS vol. XXIII.
126. Paddy Hayes, *Queen of Spies: Daphne Park, Britain's Cold War Spymaster* (London: Duckworth Overlook, 2015), 174.
127. Gerard and Kuklick, *Death in the Congo*, 179.
128. The WIROGUE project used foreign agents to recruit assets for sabotage, intelligence gathering and proposed assassinations. See Mary Ferrell Foundation [MFF] Archive, 'Cryptonym: WIROGUE', available at https://www.maryferrell.org/php/cryptdb.php?id=WIROGUE&search=WIROGUE (accessed 19 October 2023).
129. CIA File on WIROGUE, JFKAR 104-10182-10069; CIA, WIROGUE, vol. III, 104-10182-10057 at MFF Archive.
130. Chief Africa Division to Chief of Station Leopoldville, 14/11/1960, JFKAR 104-10182-10057.
131. Editorial Note, FRUS vol. XXIII, doc. 50
132. Meeting with Mr Burt Wides, 20/6/1975, JFKAR 104-10059-10236.
133. SSCIA, Interim report, 46.
134. WIROGUE's services in Congo were allegedly terminated for 'poor performance and lack of operational security'. The same file, however, recognised that he had been able to establish himself in a position of 'potential value' and 'therein implement the objective of the project'. Termination, Project WIROGUE, undated. JFKAR 104-10182-10057, 81.
135. Gerard and Kuklick, *Death in the Congo*, 191.
136. Ibid., 195.

137. Williams, *White Malice*, 387.
138. Gerard and Kuklick, *Death in the Congo*, 190; Mahoney, *JFK's Ordeal*, 64–6.
139. Weissman, 'The Lumumba Assassination'; Weissman, 'What Really Happened', 17.
140. Namikas, *Battleground*, 125.
141. Weissman, 'The Lumumba Assassination'.
142. Gerard and Kuklick, *Death in the Congo*, 190.
143. David Doyle, *True Men and Traitors* (New York: John Wiley & Sons, 2001), 148.
144. Telegram Elizabethville to Director, 18/1/1961, CIA Reading Room, DOC_0001366116; Gerard and Kucklik, *Death in the Congo*, 191.
145. Doyle, *True Men*, 147–8.
146. According to CIA renegade official John Stockwell, men very close to the CIA were part of the firing squad and worked to dispose of Lumumba's body; Williams, *White Malice*, 383.
147. SSCIA, Interim Report, 263.
148. Gordon Gray, SSCIA Testimony, 9/7/1975, DNSA Covert Operations II, 32.
149. Frederick Baron, 'Summary of interview with Gordon Gray', Memorandum to file, 5/7/1975, JFKAR 157-10014-10100.
150. SSCIA, Interim Report, 61.

3 Fidel Castro: The US Government's Assassination Campaign against Cuba

On 13 March 1961, Miami was buzzing for the third heavyweight championship fight between Floyd Patterson and Ingemar Johansson. An ecstatic crowd of 15,000 was packed inside the Miami Convention Center. In the crowd two shady characters witnessed the fight: Robert Maheu and Joseph Shimon.

Maheu had started his career in the FBI (Federal Bureau of Investigation). In 1947 he had left the Bureau and opened Robert Maheu & Associates, a private detective firm in Washington, DC which had initially received financial support from the CIA. In 1955 he had started working for the magnate Howard Hughes. This, however, was not the reason why he was in Miami. Shimon was Inspector General in the Detective Bureau of the Metropolitan Police Department in Washington, DC, but he had extensive contacts with the underworld. He knew Maheu socially and would sometimes help him out as a friend.[1]

At the time, Maheu needed all the help he could get. Working as a 'cut-out' for the CIA, he had just brokered a dangerous deal between the Agency, the Mafia and Cuban exiles: an assassination plot. As Patterson knocked out Johansson in the sixth round, another knockout was on Maheu's mind: that of Fidel Castro, the charismatic leader of Cuba.

* * *

Castro, his influence, and his foreign and domestic policies, were seen as a major threat to US economic and strategic interests in the hemisphere. Between 1960 and 1965 the US government conducted a long and multifaceted assassination campaign against Castro, a campaign that covered two CIA directors and three presidencies.

The President's Kill List

At various points, this campaign relied on elements of the underworld, as well as on various groups of Cuban exiles. Assassination plots – which peaked between 1960 and 1963 – covered most of the continuum identified in the Introduction, from more to less direct. They all failed.

The Eisenhower Years

On 1 January 1959, Fidel Castro triumphally entered Havana. Early US efforts by the State Department and the US Ambassador to Cuba to bribe Castro into political retirement had failed.[2] Last-minute attempts to establish a 'third force' that could replace the dictatorial regime of Fulgencio Batista while preventing Castro's rise had also floundered,[3] mostly due to the overwhelming support Castro enjoyed.[4]

By March 1959, CIA Director Allen Dulles had concluded that the Castro regime was moving towards dictatorship. In April, Eisenhower refused to meet Castro during the Cuban leader's visit to the United States, sending Vice-President Richard Nixon instead. With the mood in Washington rapidly turning against Castro, CIA Deputy Director Charles Cabell reasoned that the Agency would soon be asked to conduct paramilitary operations in Cuba and that early preparations were needed.[5]

The US government's response to Cuba's first reforms and expropriations was to support an early attempt – financed by Dominican Republic Dictator Rafael Trujillo – to retake the island. Chief of the CIA's Western Hemisphere Division J. C. King told the Havana Station to follow the development closely.[6] William Pawley – former diplomat, close friend of Eisenhower, and fixer for his administration – was also involved in the operation. Pawley – who had agreed to bug his own US office – acted as liaison between Cuban exiles and Dominican officials. He confirmed that the plan envisaged the 'physical elimination' of Castro and the leading figures in his government.[7] The invasion ended in failure when it became apparent that the 'Cuban exiles' gathered by Trujillo were instead Cuban agents.[8]

On 5 November 1959, based on Secretary of State Christian Herter's recommendations, Eisenhower approved a more confrontational

Fidel Castro: The Assassination Campaign against Cuba

policy towards Cuba.[9] As the new policy took shape, assassination was on the cards. King recommended to Dulles that 'thorough consideration be given to the elimination of Fidel Castro' since none of those close to him had 'the same mesmeric appeal on the masses'. Richard Bissell, Deputy Director for Plans, agreed, as did Dulles.[10] One month later, the covert war and the overthrow of the Castro government received full support in a NSC meeting.[11] The CIA responded by setting up Western Hemisphere, Branch 4 (WHB4) in charge of operations against the island.[12]

On 17 February 1960, Dulles presented the President with a plan for the harassment of the Cuban regime, focused on the sabotage of sugar refineries.[13] The President wasn't impressed. He told Dulles: 'Well, Allen, this is fine, but if you're going to make any move against Castro, don't just fool around with sugar refineries. Let's get a program which will really do something about Castro.'[14] One month later, the Special Group approved a new, more aggressive programme of covert action.[15] This time, Eisenhower was effusive in his praise; however, worried about leaks, he warned them to keep communication to a minimum to hide the US government's hand.[16] It is in this context of high presidential involvement and attention to plausible deniability that CIA-sponsored assassination plots developed.

Early efforts against Castro aimed more at discrediting than killing him. One scheme suggested the contamination with LSD of the air in a studio where Castro broadcast his speeches. Jake Esterline, head of WHB4, also recalled having in his office a box of contaminated cigars. It is unclear whether the chemical used in the cigars aimed at disorienting Castro or at making his beard fall off. Still targeting his beard, the CIA's Technical Services Division developed a plan to dust Castro's boots with thallium salts, a depilatory substance. The plan progressed only as far as animal testing.[17] The shift from these early 'dirty tricks' to assassination plots was rapid.

The Agency's Early Plots

One of the earliest assassination plots had a limited connection to the Agency. It involved the shadowy character Frank Sturgis, also known as Frank Fiorini. Long before being caught up in the Watergate Hotel break-in, Sturgis had worked for Castro's rebels. In 1957 he had travelled to Cuba on an intelligence mission for former Cuban president Carlos Prio. Sturgis reached the Sierra Maestra and started smuggling weapons to Castro's rebels. After Castro's victory, Sturgis was rewarded with a role in the Cuban Air Force. By then, though, Sturgis had been working as a double agent. He provided intelligence to the US Embassy and to the military attaché to the Cuban Air Force, a 'Colonel Nichols', on the 26 July Movement and eventually on Castro's government. Sturgis allegedly proposed to Nichols that he was willing to kill Castro while he visited the Air Force base where he worked, but never got the green light.[18] With Castro's G-2 intelligence services closing in, Sturgis fled to Miami.[19] There, he started working with the CIA on anti-Castro operations in the secretive Operation 40, which gathered a group of (initially forty) Cuban exiles with both Mafia and CIA connections and served different intelligence and political warfare purposes.[20]

In Miami, Sturgis recruited Marita Lorenz, one of Castro's lovers, as a honeytrap.[21] 'She was pure gold,' Sturgis later said. 'And I cultivated her until she was ready to poison Castro.'[22] Sturgis introduced Lorenz to key figures in the Mafia including mobster Johnny Rosselli. In January 1960, Lorenz was ready to travel to Cuba. After a few trips to rekindle the love story with Castro, she met him at the Havana Libre Hotel. Before the trip, Lorenz had been provided with two botulism toxin pills for the Cuban dictator and had stored the pills in a small jar of face cream. By the time she landed in Havana, Lorenz had changed her mind. When she met Castro in the hotel room, she also discovered that the pills had dissolved in the face cream. In a perhaps romanticised version of events, Castro having quickly uncovered the purpose of their encounter, passed his own revolver to Lorenz, giving her the chance to kill him – a chance Lorenz did not take.[23]

According to Colonel Fletcher Prouty,[24] in the same months the CIA's Operations Division, then working to support Cuban exiles, also entered the assassination business, concocting a plan – approved at all levels of the Agency – to arm and fly Cuban exiles to the island for an assassination mission.[25] While nothing came

Fidel Castro: The Assassination Campaign against Cuba

of this operation, in Washington, assassination remained on the agenda. In a NSC meeting on 10 March 1960, chaired by the President, Admiral Arleigh Burke commented that 'any plan for the removal of Cuban leaders should be a package deal, since many of the Cuban leaders . . . were even worse than Castro'.[26] A Special Group meeting four days later, not attended by Eisenhower, went over the same ground, including a 'general discussion as to what would be the effect on the Cuban scene if Fidel and Raul Castro and Che Guevara should disappear simultaneously'.[27]

In the summer of 1960, assassination attempts went into overdrive. The Agency took on a more direct role, but the first confirmed plot was not against Fidel but against his brother, Raul. William Murray, a CIA officer in Havana, had been cultivating an asset, Jose Raul Martinez Nunez, a pilot for Cuba's airline. On 18 July, Martinez requested an emergency meeting with Murray. He had been selected to fly Raul Castro from Havana to Prague on the 21st. Murray discussed the opportunities this presented with CIA Headquarters. The station in Havana received a response: 'possible removal top three leaders is receiving serious consideration at HQS'. Headquarters wrote that if the asset's motivation was sufficient for him to arrange an accident during the return trip, HQ was happy to pay the asset $10,000 or more (within reasonable bounds) and to arrange for a rescue operation if required. No advance payment could be made to avoid risks that the asset might be a 'provocator [sic]'. The station was authorised to go ahead with the plan and finalise details with the asset.[28]

Murray arranged another meeting with Martinez, who stated that he was willing to take the risk. The options included either an engine burnout on take-off or (potentially) 'water ditching' three hours out of Cuba.[29] Martinez warned that it was unlikely that the operation could pass as an accident and asked for US support for the college education of his children. This was granted. With Martinez already departed, a second cable reached the station: 'Do not pursue. Would like to drop matter.' The cable had deliberately been sent too late, to cover the US government's tracks in case the operation succeeded. Martinez returned having been unable to cause an accident.[30]

The Mafia Connection under Eisenhower

While it remains unclear where the idea originated, sometime in the summer of 1960 Deputy Director for Plans Bissell asked Colonel Sheffield Edwards whether he had any contacts within the gambling syndicate (the Mafia) that was active in Cuba.[31] As Edwards later testified, while Bissell studiously avoided the term 'assassination', the purpose of the mission was clear.[32]

Edwards – then Director of Security – relayed the request to James O'Connell, Chief of the Operation Support Division in the Office of Security, and recommended that he get in touch with Robert Maheu.[33] Maheu had helped the Agency in various covert activities including the campaign to discredit Sukarno.[34] In their first meeting, Maheu was allegedly unconvinced. He was working for the secretive billionaire Howard Hughes and this role was taking most of his time. Working as a 'cut-out' between the CIA and the Mafia in an assassination plot was hardly a decision to be taken lightly. Having slept on it, Maheu agreed to put O'Connell in touch with Rosselli.[35]

On 14 September 1960, Maheu met Rosselli, who wanted government assurances before embarking on such a dangerous task and requested a meeting directly with the CIA. Meeting Rosselli and Maheu at the Hilton Savoy Plaza, the CIA's O'Connell maintained the fiction that he was just 'Jim Olds' representing the interests of concerned businessmen, but Rosselli already knew that O'Connell was CIA.[36] Rosselli agreed to introduce Maheu and O'Connell to a 'Sam Gold' (the Chicago Mafia boss Sam Giancana), who had contacts in Cuba, to carry out the mission.

With a plan taking shape, it was time to brief Dulles. Edwards's language with the DCI was 'circumspect'. The plan was described as an 'intelligence operation'. Edwards described the connection 'as being from A to B to C . . . "A" was Maheu, "B" was Rosselli, and "C" was the principal in Cuba'. Dulles simply nodded in agreement and did not express opposition. The lack of formal approval provided Dulles with a veneer of plausible deniability,[37] but given the individuals involved and the subject of the meeting, there should be little doubt that any misunderstanding might have existed. As intelligence historian John Prados concluded, as Deputy Director for Operations, Bissell had no independent authority over an officer of the Support Directorate. 'For Bissell to have asked Edwards to do anything required sanction from Dulles.'[38]

In late September, Rosselli, Maheu and Giancana met at the Fontainebleau Hotel in Miami. At the meeting, Giancana introduced the two to 'Joe' who would act as a courier to Cuba. 'Joe' was another mobster, Santo Trafficante.[39] Despite describing himself as only a humble interpreter,[40] he was the ideal contact for the plot being concocted. Gambling was still permitted in Havana, and Trafficante maintained several associates in Cuba and interests in casinos, which gave him a reason to travel to the island.[41]

By the time of the meeting with Trafficante, Edwards had also started taking matters into his own hands, looking for more direct methods to kill Castro. In August, he had passed to Dr Edward Gunn (Chief, Operations Division, Office of Medical Service) a box of Castro's favourite cigars with the instruction to contaminate them with a suitable poison. It seems that the poisoned cigars were ready for use on 7 October 1960 and were delivered in February 1961 to a contact. It is unclear what happened to the poisoned cigars, but around the same time, the CIA had also considered another plot involving cigars. This time, they were to be delivered to Castro's room at the Waldorf Astoria, during his visit to the UN in September. The CIA asked New York City's chief inspector, Michael J. Murphy, to put the cigars in Castro's room. These cigars were explosive, not poisoned. In any case, Murphy refused to deliver them.[42]

For the Mafia plots, Giancana rejected the CIA's early proposal for a gangster-style shooting. It would have been a suicide mission. Instead, he recommended poison. Bissell consulted the Chief of Technical Services, Cornelius Roosevelt. According to Roosevelt, various delivery methods were considered before settling on pills,[43] and Dr Raymond Treichler was assigned to develop them.[44] In the following weeks, Maheu and the mobsters worked out the details of the plan. The pills would be passed to Rosselli, who would give them to Rafael 'Macho' Gener, a contact of a leading Cuban exile, Tony Varona. After reaching Cuba, Gener would pass the pills to Juan Orta, then Office Chief and Director General of the Office of the Prime Minister. Orta, who had received Mafia kickbacks from gambling interests under Batista, had quickly become disaffected with the Castro regime.[45]

At this juncture, Giancana's gossiping and sex life threatened to derail the plans. In October, FBI Director J. Edgar Hoover contacted Bissell to let him know that surveillance on Giancana had revealed that the mobster had been talking to associates about a plan to kill Castro involving a girl who would drop 'pills' into Castro's food.[46] It was a second wiretap, however, that would have much stronger reverberations: the so-called Balletti case. On 31 October, the Las Vegas police arrested Arthur Balletti.[47] Maheu had hired Balletti to install a wiretap in the hotel room of comedian Dan Rowan. At the time, Rowan was in a relationship with singer Phyllis McGuire, one of Giancana's mistresses. The Agency had provided financial support for the operation but it had refused to provide technical assistance. The wiretap operation collapsed when a bug was found in Rowan's phone by the hotel maid. The reason for the wiretap remains unclear – maybe Giancana's jealousy or maybe a CIA effort to keep tabs on Giancana's gossiping.[48] Whatever the rationale, wiretapping was a federal offence, and the FBI started an official investigation.

* * *

Meanwhile, in Washington, talk of assassination re-emerged. In a Special Group meeting on 3 November 1960, Undersecretary of State for Political Affairs Livingston Merchant asked whether 'any real planning' had been done for 'taking direct positive action against Fidel Castro, Raul, and Che Guevara'. The CIA's Cabell replied that the Agency did not do such things.[49] The reality was different. Eisenhower's National Security Advisor, Gordon Gray, knew that direct positive action 'could have included assassination',[50] something CIA in-house historian Jack Pfeiffer later confirmed.[51] Cabell's response was just another case of what Thomas Powers called the 'spiel', a boilerplate response for the benefit of the historical record.[52]

On 25 November, Dulles held a secret meeting with President Eisenhower. Both Gray and Thomas Parrott – minute taker for the Special Group (also known as 5412 Group under Eisenhower) – while initially incredulous that Dulles could have done something without their being aware, had to admit that Dulles had a direct channel of communication with the President that excluded them.[53] In this sense, whether Dulles briefed Eisenhower on the assassination plots at this meeting or at any other time is immaterial. It is unlikely that Dulles would have pursued such a policy without proper authorisation.[54]

At the CIA, technical difficulties pushed the poison pills plot beyond Eisenhower's term in office. The Technical Services Division (TSD) took a long time to develop the pills. A first batch would not dissolve in water. A second batch of botulinum pills was initially tested on guinea pigs, but nothing happened. It turned out that guinea pigs have a strong resistance to botulinum. A later test on monkeys worked. The pills were ready only sometime after 10 February 1961 and were eventually passed to Rosselli and then to Orta in Cuba, but the latter was no longer in a position to use them, having lost his post in the prime minister's office.[55]

The Kennedy Years: Executive Action and the Mafia Redux

The Kennedy Administration started, or so it seems, with a (planned) bang. In January 1961, Bissell reportedly received two separate requests from the White House to set up an 'executive action' capability.[56] According to the CIA's Sam Halpern, the request had come directly from the President.[57] White House officials vehemently denied that such a request was made – and, especially, that it came from the President.[58]

In any case, William Harvey, a legendary and controversial figure in the Agency, was the man tasked by Bissell to develop 'executive action'.[59] Harvey understood the request to be an order to start exploring capabilities, assets, and pros and cons for the use of assassination as a tool of foreign policy.[60] To Harvey, 'executive action' meant:

> Any direct action taken against any target . . . to eliminate or destroy the effectiveness of that target. And this is generally considered to cover a rather wide gamut of possible techniques . . . but . . . it is generally considered a synonym for assassination.[61]

Harvey was then in charge of the CIA's Foreign Intelligence (Staff D). Staff D carried out operations which involved the breaking and stealing of codes, as well as communication interceptions in collaboration with the National Security Agency.[62] Harvey folded 'executive action' within a Staff D project codenamed ZRRIFLE. This provided cover for both operations and expenditures.

Harvey understood the project as 'the magic button', a 'last resort beyond last resort', but also that – as part of the project – the word 'assassination' should never be mentioned. The project aimed at finding and recruiting assassins under the 'Pretext: KUTUBE/D[63] search'. The sensitive nature of the project meant that no American citizens or individuals with US connections should be recruited – something that might have stopped Devlin's asset against Lumumba – preferring instead members of the underground. It would have been even better to recruit personnel from the Soviet bloc. Personnel files could be 'forged and backdated'. ZRRIFLE used QJWIN as principal agent in charge of recruiting additional individuals.[64] QJWIN had first been recruited in November 1959 'to undertake a one-shot mission to the Belgian Congo' in pursuit of Lumumba.[65] Getting to work in early 1961, Harvey discussed options and assassination techniques with the Agency's scientists.[66]

As these discussions proceeded, the CIA and other US government agencies also engaged in more indirect assassination plots. They gave technical and logistical support to initiatives of Cuban exiles. The National Photographic Interpretation Center (NPIC), the secretive agency producing satellite and other advanced images, was seemingly involved in two plots. For one of the plots, NPIC provided 'annotated photographs and line drawings' of the Dupont Varadero Beach estate where Castro vacationed. Carl Jenkins, a Marine and CIA (para)military trainer at the time, confirmed the plot.[67] Another plot, codenamed PATHFINDER, entailed the assassination of Castro in the Bay of Pigs resort area where he maintained a yacht.[68] While evidence is scarce and a later investigation concluded that none of the NPIC-related plans were executed, some authors have connected PATHFINDER with Cuban exile Felix Rodriguez's mission to kill Castro by shooting him at his Varadero residence.[69] Here, the NPIC's provision of pictures seems to suggest approval beyond Miami and the exile community.[70] After three failed attempts, Rodriguez's plot was abandoned.

The CIA might have considered that – by early 1961 – better options were available. The Mafia plots had not stopped with Orta's failure. Trafficante had proposed an alternative strategy to O'Connell. Trafficante and Varona had become acquainted in 1960 and a quid pro quo emerged around the plot to kill Castro. Varona would use members of his organisation in Cuba to kill Castro. In return, Trafficante would provide $1 million and an agreement to share the profits of his gambling business once the Castro government had been dislodged from the island.[71] Varona confirmed having a suitable contact in Cuba and obtained money and communication equipment from the Agency.[72] Bissell testified that it was his 'pure personal opinion' that, at this juncture, Dulles briefed President Kennedy about the Mafia plots, something that White House officials denied.[73]

The transfer of money and a new batch of poison pills occurred in Miami at the time of the Patterson–Johansson fight. Varona had a contact in a restaurant frequented by Castro and the pills would be put into Castro's food. According to Maheu, the pills were in place, and everything was ready, but the order never came.[74] The contact in Cuba was told to wait for Varona's phone call confirming a green light. The assassination plan, though, coincided with the Bay of Pigs invasion. Varona was supposed to be one of the members of the Cuban Revolutionary Council taking over the island after the successful invasion. With the invasion ready to launch, Varona was sequestered by the CIA in a safe house. When O'Connell phoned Maheu to give the order, Varona could not be reached.[75] As the assassination plot failed, so did the Bay of Pigs invasion.

* * *

In the aftermath of the Bay of Pigs, President Kennedy asked General Maxwell Taylor to form a commission to investigate the fiasco. Taylor's work coincided with potentially explosive developments in the FBI's own investigation of the Balletti wiretap. Under questioning from the FBI, Maheu had told the Bureau to contact Edwards for confirmation that the wiretap was part of a CIA operation. To the FBI, Edwards denied any knowledge of the rationale for the wiretap but admitted that he had contacted Maheu as a 'cut-out' in an operation that involved Giancana. Later, Edwards also recalled that – as part of the Taylor commission's investigation – Bissell had briefed Taylor and Attorney General Kennedy regarding 'the use of Giancana and the underworld against Castro'.[76] On 22 May, Hoover reported to Attorney General Kennedy Edwards's admission that Maheu and Giancana had been used for 'dirty business' against Castro. Hoover also told Kennedy that – since the purpose of Balletti's wiretap had not been established – the FBI investigation would continue.[77]

The War before the 'Secret War': Assassination Plots between the Bay of Pigs and Mongoose

The US government's contacts with the Mafia continued in the immediate aftermath of the Bay of Pigs, as did the plotting with Cuban exiles[78] In Cuba, the Bay of Pigs disaster had been accompanied by arrests and disarray among counter-revolutionary forces. In an effort to pick up the pieces and re-establish a functioning network, these groups sent Alfredo Izaguirre de la Riva to contact US officials. Izaguirre was interviewed by the Taylor Commission. The meeting gave Izaguirre the impression that there was very little chance of a new US invasion unless a pretext could be found.[79]

With Izaguirre's return to Cuba, Operation Patty started to take shape. It envisaged sabotage activities in Cuba's largest cities, assassination attempts against the Castro brothers, and incidents around the Guantanamo base to create the pretext for a US invasion.[80] At the base, Cuban exiles and the CIA were working hand in hand with the Office of Naval Intelligence (ONI).[81] Naval Intelligence Officer John Gordon recalled that he was transferred to the Guantanamo base in June 1961. There, he witnessed how Cuban counter-revolutionaries – with US complicity – used the base as a launching pad to conduct raids on the island. The liaison officer between the ONI and the CIA told Gordon of an individual – Alonzo Gonzales— who had offered to kill Castro. In July (the time of Operation Patty), Gordon discovered that dynamite had been brought onto the base surreptitiously. Gordon reported this to his superiors as he suspected that Gonzales was responsible. One hour after the phone call, instead of stopping Gonzales, the Shore Patrol arrested Gordon and put him in a psychiatric ward. He was then sent to various naval hospitals and discharged only in late 1961, to resume the role of intelligence officer in New Orleans.[82]

Operation Patty was just one of the many plots concocted by Cuban exile groups and eventually foiled by the Cuban government. These plots tended to rely on sabotage operations in Cuba's major cities and on the assassination of Castro and other members of the Cuban leadership. In most cases, these were financially and logistically supported by the CIA with a full understanding that the aim was assassination. The amount and type of weapons delivered also indicated that assassination of Castro and the Cuban leadership was part of these plans.[83]

* * *

While these plots developed (and were foiled), back in Washington members of the Administration, including the Kennedy brothers, seemed to rekindle their interest in assassination. On 5 October, Robert Kennedy (RFK) made inquiries to the FBI regarding developments in the Balletti wiretap case. As historian Evan Thomas writes, it is certainly curious that RFK's inquiries regarding a case that risked exposing the CIA's assassination plots coincided with extensive contingency planning regarding the possible removal of Castro.[84] On the same day, in fact, National Security Advisor McGeorge Bundy asked State to review the possibilities that would open for the United States if Castro were removed from Cuba and to prepare contingency plans with the Pentagon for a US invasion in that event.[85] Thomas Parrott, a CIA officer who served in the White House as Taylor Assistant and as member of the NSC, believed that what was needed 'was a plan against the contingency that Castro would, in some way or the other, be removed from the Cuban scene'.[86] Parrott also specified that the President had expressed a keen interest in such a contingency. Immediately, he was reprimanded by Taylor and warned that the President's interest should be kept private.[87]

It seems clear that the Kennedy White House was ramping up its efforts against Castro. Perhaps, some diversion was in order. On 9 November, following a suggestion by his Special Assistant Richard Goodwin, President Kennedy met with journalist Tad Szulc. Szulc was connected to elements in the Cuban exile world and had also recently returned from a trip to Cuba in which he had interviewed Fidel Castro. After a general discussion of the situation in Cuba, the President asked: 'What would you think if I ordered Castro to be assassinated?' A shocked Szulc responded that for both strategic and moral reasons, the US government should not be involved in assassination. According to Szulc, the President replied that he was simply testing Szulc and he agreed but was under intense pressure from elements within the intelligence community.[88] Szulc and Goodwin later understood the President's question as evidence that he was not seriously considering assassination. If he was, why would he mention it to a journalist who was likely to publish the story if something happened?[89] The reverse is also true. A president then considering assassination might have raised the point with a friendly audience to give precisely the impression recorded by Szulc and Goodwin.[90]

Mongoose: The Kennedys' War against Castro

Around mid-October 1961, Bissell reported that he had been 'chewed out in the Cabinet room of the White House by both the President and the Attorney general for . . . sitting on his ass and not doing anything about getting rid of Castro'. He ordered Halpern and another CIA official to make it happen.[91] In mid-November, Bissell asked Harvey to expand Executive Action/ZRRIFLE to Castro. As part of this transfer, Harvey took over the Mafia connection from Edwards.[92] In the same month, John McCone, a lifelong Republican, replaced Dulles as Director of the CIA. McCone tapped Helms as the new man in charge of Cuban operations. With this setting, Harvey had 225 people on staff at CIA headquarters. The CIA station in Miami had 400 employees,

Fidel Castro: The Assassination Campaign against Cuba

approximately 2,000 Cuban agents and a budget of about $50 million a year.[93]

At the end of November, the US government's secret war against Castro was put on a stronger footing. Mistrustful of the CIA after the Bay of Pigs debacle, President Kennedy added his brother and General Taylor to the Special Group. The new Special Group Augmented (SGA) became the main forum for the discussion and approval of covert operations against Cuba. This combined with the establishment of Operation Mongoose, led by Colonel Edward Lansdale. Mongoose envisaged an aggressive sabotage and harassment campaign, which could undermine and eventually overthrow the Castro regime.[94] Mongoose soon turned into a sprawling campaign of 'state-sponsored terrorism',[95] which included, but was not limited to, assassination attempts.

The main driving forces behind Mongoose were clearly Robert Kennedy and Lansdale himself. Within this structure, RFK became the overseer of clandestine activities in Cuba[96] with a direct and constant channel of communication to Lansdale and, presumably, to his brother. The Attorney General set the tone of the operation, identifying Cuba as the 'top priority'. 'The agency heads understand that you are to have full backing on what you need,' he added. The president believed – RFK reported – that 'the final chapter on Cuba' had not been written.[97]

Lansdale told the SGA that – based on RFK's words – US government agencies needed to abandon a 'business as usual' attitude and consider themselves in a 'combat situation' where they had been given 'full command'.[98] Helms and the rest of the CIA understood the message – not unreasonably – as giving them free rein in the war against Castro, including assassination.[99] Helms named Harvey head of the CIA's new Task Force W, the Agency outfit working for Mongoose. Harvey, who had fully briefed Helms on ZRRIFLE, started to oversee both the overall covert war and the assassination plots.[100] Some of the most explicit high-level discussions of assassination emerged in the context of Mongoose and the SGA.

By 18 January, Lansdale had readied the tasks for the agencies working under Mongoose. He reported the tasks to RFK with a cryptic handwritten note: 'My review does not include the sensitive work I have reported to you; I felt you preferred informing the president privately.'[101] Lansdale later denied that he ever discussed assassination with RFK. The 'sensitive work' instead referred to a visit Lansdale had made under pseudonym to a group of Cuban exiles.[102]

Only eleven days after setting his tasks, Lansdale told RFK that he felt the United States could 'uncork the touchdown play independently of the institutional program the US had created'. Since the tasks covered most aspects of the operation, the 'touchdown play' yet to uncork was assassination, something Lansdale denied.[103] At the end of the month, Lansdale discussed with RFK Operation Bounty. The operation offered a series of financial rewards for the killing of Cuban leaders. The bounty on Castro's head was put at two centavos in order to denigrate him in the eyes of the Cuban people.[104] A very similar plan appeared in the record when Lansdale presented an updated plan for Mongoose, divided into six phases. The 'Resistance' phase included a 'Special Target' operation for the killing of Cuban intelligence officials and other 'key leaders'. Lansdale suggested that 'gangster elements' would have been ideal to conduct such an operation. He added that 'bloc technicians' should be included in the list of targets and that 'CW [Chemical Weapons] agents should be fully considered'.[105] The Joint Chiefs of Staff also recommended to 'assassinate Castro and his handful of top men',[106] as an option to improve Mongoose's prospects.

On 16 March, members of the SGA gathered at the White House with the President. RFK mentioned Mary Hemingway – wife of Ernest Hemingway – and commented on reports that Castro was drinking heavily, and that the US government could take advantage of the 'opportunities offered by the "shrine" to Hemingway'. As the CIA's William Elder[107] explained, RFK's cryptic remark referred to the possibility of 'luring Castro into an ambush at Hemingway's farm outside Havana'. Mary Hemingway had reported that – soon after the writer's suicide – Castro had visited Hemingway's farm in Cuba with minimal security and had remained impressed.[108] Lansdale responded that rumours coming from Hemingway's reports were worth 'assessing firmly and pursuing vigorously' since the CIA was receiving similar information from other sources. Lansdale added that – if there were grounds

Fidel Castro: The Assassination Campaign against Cuba

for action – the CIA had assets committed to such an effort. Lansdale also assured McCone that he had discussed with the CIA the options and that they agreed that 'the matter was so delicate and sensitive that it shouldn't be surfaced to the Special Group' until the assets were ready to go and, even then, not in detail. It was, after all, a matter of 'fractioning the regime'.[109] Ted Shackley, the CIA's Chief of Station in Miami, later remarked that the discussion certainly had 'the earmarks of an assassination plot'. Another official acknowledged that Lansdale's memo was as close as we are likely to come to have proof of the Kennedys' knowledge of assassination plots.[110] FBI Director Hoover was also on the case.

* * *

According to the CIA, on 7 February 1962 Edwards briefed RFK on the 'circumstances involving Maheu's involvement in the wiretap'.[111] On the 26th, the FBI re-entered the picture. The combined surveillance of Frank Sinatra – long associated with the mob and with the Kennedys – and Giancana had permitted the FBI to piece together the love life of Judith Campbell. Since 1960, Campbell had been the mistress of both Giancana and President Kennedy. She also had extensive contacts with another mobster involved in the assassination plots, Rosselli, and had often called the White House. A review of the FBI files would have permitted Hoover to conclude that Giancana was involved in assassination attempts (the October 1960 tap), that he was involved in CIA operations against Castro (the Balletti wiretap), and that he and the President shared a mistress. Likely armed with this information, Hoover held a lunch with the President on 22 March. No record exists of what the President and the FBI Director discussed. It is difficult to imagine that assassination was not discussed. Certainly the President cut his ties with Sinatra and – seemingly – with Campbell.[112]

In the first week of May, RFK also received a second briefing by the CIA on the Agency's operations and involvement with Giancana. Lawrence Houston, the CIA's general counsel, and Sheffield Edwards briefed the Attorney General. The briefing discussed the use of Rosselli and Giancana in assassination attempts, Maheu's role as a 'cut-out', and the alleged transfer of money to Mafia dons to seal the deal. Kennedy was allegedly irate,[113] but it remains unclear whether RFK's unhappiness was directed at the use of assassination, at the relations with the underworld,[114] or at the fact that he had been – allegedly – left out of the loop. He simply told Edwards and Houston that he wanted to be informed if the CIA ever recontacted the Mafia.[115] During the meeting, RFK was told that the plots, as well as the collaboration with the Mafia, had stopped – but it was a lie and Edwards knew it.

In early April 1962, Edwards had briefed Harvey on the Mafia plots and had introduced him to Rosselli. With ZRRIFLE, Harvey had taken over the assassination plots and the Mafia connection and decided to increase the security of the operation by dropping Giancana and Maheu and dealing directly with Rosselli.[116] On the 21st, Rosselli re-established contacts with Varona who claimed to have another asset in a Cuban restaurant who could poison Castro. This time, Varona asked for the delivery of weapons. Harvey – with the help of Shackley, chief of the Agency's Station in Miami (JMWAVE) – obliged and delivered the weapons by leaving a U-Haul truck unattended in a parking lot.[117] By the end of April, the weapons and the poison pills – this time developed by Gottlieb – were in Cuba. The pills were divided among members of Rescate (Varona's organisation in Cuba) who were then working in various hotels and restaurants frequented by Castro. Fidel did not show up at any of the hotels.[118]

* * *

In the summer of 1962, with the first signs of a Soviet military build-up in Cuba, the scolding from RFK increased. At one point he asked Harvey, who had allegedly been presented to JFK as the American James Bond, 'Why can't you get things cooking like 007?'[119] CIA officials recalled how this pressure expanded 'the extent of the means that one thought available'.[120] The option of assassination was explicitly raised on 10 August 1962, during a SGA meeting attended by all SGA members with the addition of Secretary of Defense Robert McNamara, Secretary of State Dean Rusk, and United States Information Agency Director Edward Murrow.[121] During the meeting Secretary McNamara raised the question of assassination of the Cuban leaders.[122] As Goodwin reported, the Secretary grabbed his shoulder and stated: 'The only thing to do is eliminate Castro.' The CIA representative (presumably Harvey or McCone) replied: 'You mean Executive Action.' McNamara nodded and then told Goodwin: 'I mean it, Dick, it's the only way.'[123]

Participants recalled that the proposal was received with a mixture of shock and incredulity, and it was quickly shut down. McCone admitted that while he strongly objected to the proposal, there was no decision at the meeting 'not to include assassination in the program'. Harvey agreed, saying that the reaction suggested an effort to swipe the whole thing under the rug.[124]

The day after the meeting, Lansdale assigned Harvey a series of intelligence and political tasks 'including the elimination of leaders'. When he read the memorandum, Harvey went berserk. He wrote to Helms expressing his concerns. There was a consensus in the meeting, he told Helms, that 'this is not a subject which *has been made* a matter of official record' (emphasis added).[125] Having failed to reach Lansdale, Harvey berated Lansdale's assistant, Frank Hand, lamenting the stupidity of putting such an instruction on record. He told Hand that he 'would write no document pertaining to this and would participate in no open meeting to discuss it'.[126] Having excised the three letters from the memorandum, Harvey also complained to McCone. Harvey's main problem was not assassination, but the explicit discussion of assassination in a memorandum.[127] The memorandum was withdrawn. The episode shows how the SGA clearly discussed the option of assassinating the Cuban leaders and, while the suggestion was dropped, no explicit prohibition emerged. Events took over with the emergence of the Cuban missile crisis which temporarily halted assassination plots.[128]

By the end of 1962, the CIA–Mafia relation was breaking apart. Harvey had already become disillusioned with the Mafia assassination plots. His relationship with RFK had also broken down.[129] On his part, Helms testified that he always thought the Mafia plots were a 'cock and bull' story, with the Mafia and the Cubans involved scamming the Agency.[130] In March 1963, Castro visited one of the hotels used in Varona's poison pills plot. The

Cuban leader asked for his favourite drink: a chocolate milkshake. One the men involved in the plot, still working at the hotel, prepared the drink. He reached for the poison capsules he had stored in the hotel freezer, but they broke as he tried to dislodge them from the freezer's wall.[131]

New Exotic Plots and the AMLASH Operation

In early 1963, Desmond Fitzgerald had replaced Harvey as head of Task Force W, renamed Directorate of Operations Special Affairs Staff. With Mongoose out of the picture, Fitzgerald became the point man on Cuban matters. Fitzgerald established a strong working relationship with the Attorney General. According to CIA officials, he was 'encouraged by Kennedy's boldness, his willingness to cut through the bureaucracy', but the pressure from RFK also spurred Fitzgerald's worst instincts.[132] Officials within the Administration seemingly understood that assassination plots had restarted. Gordon Chase – Bundy's assistant – asked Bundy whether the United States should consider learning to live with Castro, since he was aware that the President was ready to consider 'more violent solutions'.[133]

While operations run by Cuban exiles with the Agency's financial and logistical support continued, often with farcical elements,[134] the CIA re-entered the assassination business more directly.[135] In the early month of his tenure, Fitzgerald made inquiries to TSD regarding possible 'exotic' means to assassinate Castro, exploiting his passions. In one case, aware of Castro's passion for scuba diving, he asked TSD to explore whether an explosive seashell could be developed. Fitzgerald even bought a book on Caribbean mollusca. At the CIA, Halpern had questioned the legality of the plan and discussed it with Houston. CIA lawyers concluded that if the plan had been authorised by the President and Attorney General, it was legal.[136] But the plan was impractical. There was no guarantee that the seashell would be spectacular enough and no guarantee that Castro would be the first to pick it up. Furthermore, no shell in the area was large enough to contain enough explosive and the mini submarine tasked with deploying it did not have enough range.

A second scheme involved the use of a poisoned scuba diving suit. James Donovan (then leading the negotiations with Castro for the release of the Bay of Pigs prisoners) was asked to give the poisoned suit to Castro as a gift.[137] According to Gottlieb, the plan went as far as developing the poisoned suit with Madura foot (fungal infection) and contaminating the breathing apparatus with tuberculosis. The plan was abandoned after Donovan revealed that he had just given a scuba diving suit to Castro as a gift on his own initiative.[138]

As intelligence historian James Callanan wrote, while the CIA had been very proficient at developing methods to kill Castro, it had always lacked an adequate and secure 'delivery system'.[139] Fitzgerald's most ambitious attempt in this context involved a contact established in 1961 who seemed poised to solve the Agency's problems. The contact was Rolando Cubela, the operation was codenamed AMLASH.[140]

* * *

In March 1961, Carlos Tepedino (AMWHIP, a long-time agency collaborator) had arranged a meeting between a CIA case officer[141] and Cubela in Mexico City. Cubela – 'a high-strung, loose-lipped, violent man'[142] – had been the leader of the Directorio Revolucionario, a group of student activists that had participated in anti-Batista activities. Cubela himself had taken part in the assassination of Lt. Col. Antonio Blanco, Batista's chief of military intelligence. Cubela's group had reluctantly conceded the leadership of the Revolution to Castro. From the early months of Castro's government, Cubela had privately expressed dissatisfaction with the political direction of the country as well as a willingness to kill the Cuban leader.[143] Publicly, he had remained close to Castro and was free to travel abroad in his role as military attaché in Spain.[144]

The CIA held a series of meetings with Cubela in various European cities. Cubela's commitment to his mission waxed and waned, but he repeatedly told the CIA that any hope of arranging a coup in Cuba depended on the elimination of Castro. As William Weatherby, Cubela's case officer, wrote, Cubela strongly objected to assassination. His objection, though, had to do with the word itself, not with the act; he much preferred 'elimination'.[145]

In the summer of 1962, Cubela told his CIA handlers that he desired to execute 'Carlos Rodriguez [a top-ranking Castro subordinate] and the Soviet ambassador, and also to eliminate Fidel, by execution if necessary'. Weatherby later denied that these conversations amounted to much. They were simply an expression of Cubela's irascible character and frustration, and the CIA never provided any indication of support.[146] At the time, though, Weatherby had told Cubela that 'schemes like he envisioned certainly had their place' but required careful preparation.[147] The CIA did provide support to Cubela including training in secret writing and in demolitions. When the Agency requested Cubela to undergo a polygraph test, he indignantly refused. Officers dealing with Cubela and CIA headquarters initially agreed that no assassination mission should be entrusted to him.[148]

The collaboration with Cubela was stepped up in the autumn of 1963, as Nestor Sanchez took over as case officer. By that time, the CIA was aware that Cubela had contacted a series of disgruntled Cuban military officials. Cubela wanted assurances of the US government's support. During a meeting with Sanchez, in Paris, he asked the case officer to meet with a senior US official, preferably Robert Kennedy.[149] Sanchez wrote back that 'highest and profound consideration' should have been given to Cubela's request since he seemed determined to act against Castro with or without US support. The CIA refused Cubela's request, but Helms gave Fitzgerald permission to meet Cubela in person, pretending to be a personal representative of RFK. Fitzgerald and Helms also agreed not to brief RFK of this development since (or so Helms later argued) the plan was still at an early stage, and it was perfectly in line with US government policy against Castro.[150]

At the meeting with Cubela, Fitzgerald, under the pseudonym James Clark, told the Cuban that the United States would not support a quick insurrection that was likely to fail, but that it would render 'all necessary assistance' to a group which would succeed in 'neutralizing the present Cuban leadership' and exert enough control on the island to request the US government's official assistance. Fitzgerald also told Cubela that the US government could not get involved in assassination.[151] Disappointed at the alleged rebuff, Cubela started venting his frustration to his CIA contacts. It didn't take long for Fitzgerald to change his mind. On 19 November he wrote to Sanchez approving a message to Cubela. He would be given a cache of weapons dropped inside Cuba. If he so requested, the cache would also include a high-power rifle with scopes, the weapon Cubela had long requested for his assassination plan.[152]

Cubela confessed to Sanchez that – while eager to get rid of Castro – he was not suicidal and was sure the CIA could also come up with some alternative means of assassination. Back in the US, Sanchez and Halpern discussed options with Dr Gunn. The three settled on Black-Leaf 40, a commonly available insecticide. The means to administer the poison was a rigged Paper-Mate ballpoint pen fitted with a hypodermic needle. On 22 November, Sanchez arrived in Paris to meet with Cubela and gave him the pen. Famously, the pen – which according to some accounts Cubela refused – was passed at the same time as Kennedy's assassination.[153]

Assassination Plots after the Assassination

Kennedy's assassination did not stop Cubela's operation, nor the CIA's support for it, but it moved them further underground. In early 1964, Cubela received a cache of weapons in Cuba from the CIA's Miami Station. Cubela still insisted on the delivery of sniper rifles (Belgian FALs) with sights for poor lighting conditions and silencers. The CIA's TSD went to work on producing the silencers. By this time, the Agency had been able to put AMLASH (Cubela) in contact with Manuel Artime.

Since June 1963, Artime had been building a Cuban exiles brigade in the United States, with bases in Nicaragua. The US government financed the brigade and released assets like leading Cuban exile Felix Rodriguez who was at the time training with the US military. Rodriguez took this as a sign of US government involvement in (and support for) Artime's venture.[154]

Over time, Artime's brigade (Project AMWORLD) became part of a three-pronged approach that included contacts with dissident Cuban military officials (codenamed AMTRUNK) and the assassination component provided by Cubela (AMLASH).[155] As Shackley put it, Artime's operation aimed at assessing whether with 'x number of dollars, some equipment, some guidance', these groups could be given the opportunity to find a Cuban solution to a Cuban problem,[156] but the Agency was never far behind and it kept a tab on meetings between Artime and Cubela in European cities throughout 1964.[157] The CIA Paris Station clearly saw Artime as the perfect option to provide deniable support for what Cubela considered the first step in the overthrow of the Castro regime: the assassination of Fidel.[158]

At this stage, US policy towards Cuba seemed somewhat schizophrenic. McCone told President Johnson, on 7 April, that US policy towards Cuba needed to 'encourage dissident elements in the military and other power centers of the regime to bring about the eventual liquidation of the Castro/communist entourage'.[159] And yet, perhaps influenced by the history of failure surrounding this type of venture, the Johnson Administration also made efforts in 1964 to undermine plots to assassinate Castro that had developed among underworld and business figures and of which the CIA and Helms had become aware.[160]

In early 1965, the Artime/Cubela plot, with an expected D-day of 13 March, was discussed in a memorandum to McGeorge Bundy.[161] Artime met again with Cubela and provided him with the required FAL rifles and the silencers. CIA cable traffic shows that the weapons came from the United States, procured by Carl Jenkins.[162] But, by mid-1965, suspicions surrounding Cubela had increased. Some CIA officials had always believed that Cubela was a 'dangle', a double agent of the Castro government.[163] Dangle or not, Cubela was arrested by the Castro government on 1 March 1966. Years of CIA assassination attempts had come to nothing.

Conclusion

No other case gets close to the extent and intensity of the assassination campaign against Fidel Castro. The campaign included a multiplicity of direct and indirect methods of assassination, from poison to various kinds of support for (and training of) Cuban exiles. It also involved multiple organisations. No legal opposition to assassination emerged and neither did moral qualms. The language of decision-making remained ambiguous and rich in euphemisms. An

Fidel Castro: The Assassination Campaign against Cuba

explicit effort was made to prevent (and remove) the appearance of 'assassination' in the historical record.

In the case of Castro, then, the more interesting question surrounds political control. As to the CIA, Dulles was briefed by Edwards and Bissell at the time of the first round of Mafia plots. He approved of the 'intelligence operation' with a full understanding of what it entailed. The picture is more complicated when it comes to DCI McCone. A consensus exists that McCone was not briefed about the assassination plots and the Mafia until August 1963. In that month, two media stories connected the CIA with the underworld. Deputy Director for Plans Helms then briefed McCone on the CIA–Mafia collaboration including the assassination plots using the memorandum prepared by Edwards after the Robert Kennedy briefing in May 1962.[164]

McCone repeated that he was opposed to assassination for moral and religious reasons and that such opposition was known within the Agency.[165] Helms, Bissell and Harvey found various *ex post* rationalisations as to why they had not briefed McCone sooner.[166] But was McCone unwitting until 1963? After all, he attended several meetings of the SGA where assassination was discussed, including the 'Hemingway shrine', and August 1962 meetings. McCone might not have been briefed because CIA officials knew of his (moral) opposition. In this understanding, plausible deniability extended to the DCI. As Elder put it, 'if you are given a charter to overthrow a government, any number of actions may be taken, not each and every one of which needs to be referred'.[167] At a CIA seminar in 1991, Elder went further. McCone had explicitly instructed Helms to keep him 'uninformed' of the assassination plots.[168]

If CIA directors knew, what about the presidents they served? In the case of Eisenhower, the evidence suggests that Dulles might have briefed him on the Mafia assassination plots. George Kistiakovski, White House Science Advisor, also recalled how Eisenhower insisted that all plans that entailed the use of force should be brought to him for decision.[169] According to Bissell, Dulles is likely to:

> Have indicated . . . the general objective of the operation that was contemplated to make that sufficiently clear so that the President . . . could have ordered the termination of the operation, but to give the President just as little information about it as possible beyond an understanding of its general purpose.[170]

No order for termination ever emerged. Bissell also held several one-to-one meetings with Eisenhower.[171] Eisenhower's background and his experience in the Second World War might also have made him more open to covert action, and even assassination, as a way of preventing escalation and mass slaughter.[172]

As to the Kennedys, a starting point is probably the fair assumption that no secrets existed between the two brothers and that – in many decision-making contexts – Robert Kennedy acted as a proxy (as well as a shield) for the President.[173] The requests to establish an 'executive action' capability' might have come from the White House. Before the Bay of Pigs, according to CIA officials, Dulles is likely to have briefed President Kennedy about the assassination plots, a point strongly contested by White House officials and Kennedy loyalists.[174] Some of them blamed the tendency of the CIA under Dulles to act in a semi-autonomous manner.[175]

In the aftermath of the failed invasion, it is likely that Bissell briefed RFK on the assassination plots during his deposition at the Taylor Commission. Bissell assumed that from his circumlocutory language, Kennedy had understood that the activities against Castro included assassination.[176] The Kennedys also had extensive meetings with Hoover, who is likely to have exploited any chance he might have had to embarrass the President, his brother and the CIA.[177] It was through the FBI investigation that Robert Kennedy was eventually officially briefed on the first wave of Mafia–CIA assassination plots; no explicit order to stop the assassination plots was given. According to Evan Thomas, this was 'the dog-that-didn't-bark in the mystery over presidential authorization'.[178] During Mongoose, discussions of assassination abounded, at times with the Kennedy brothers present.[179] As to AMLASH, especially in its early stage, the operation coincided with intense pressure from Attorney General Kennedy to do more about Cuba.[180] Only a partial conclusion can be reached. It seems that a suspension of disbelief is required to conclude that the Kennedys knew nothing of the underworld and that they did not know and – at a minimum – acquiesced to the CIA's sprawling campaign of assassination plots. If the campaign against Castro had shown a remarkable continuity in policy between the Eisenhower and the Kennedy administrations, the same applied to the US government's next target: Rafael Trujillo.

Fidel Castro: The Assassination Campaign against Cuba

Notes

1. Joseph Shimon, Testimony to the Senate Select Committee to Study Governmental Operations with Respect to Intelligence Activities (SSCIA), 12/9/1975, Digital National Security Archives (DNSA) Covert Operations II, 4.
2. Memorandum of conversation Smith-Guell, 'General Political Situation', 15/8/1958, FRUS vol. VI – Cuba (FRUS vol. VI), doc. 123.
3. Jack Colhoun, *Gangsterismo: The United States, Cuba and the Mafia, 1933 to 1966* (New York: OR Books, 2013), 38.
4. Telegram Embassy Cuba to State, 9/1/1959, FRUS vol. VI, doc. 220.
5. Deputies' Meeting, 20/4/1959, CIA FOIA, available at https://www.cia.gov/readingroom/docs/CIA-RDP80B01676R002400060129-0.pdf (accessed 20 October 2023).
6. Telegram Director to Havana, 1/8/1959, JFK Assassination Records (JFKAR), 104-10177-10036.
7. Anthony Carrozza, *William D. Pawley* (Washington, DC: Potomac Books, 2012), 231–2.
8. Fabian Escalante, *The Secret War: CIA Covert Operations against Cuba 1959–1962* (New York: Ocean Press, 1995), 24–7; Alex Von Tunzelmann, *Red Heat* (New York: Simon & Schuster 2011), 168–9; Michael Hall, *Sugar and Power in the Dominican Republic* (London: Greenwood Press, 2000), 91.
9. Memorandum Secretary of State to President, 5/11/1959, FRUS vol. VI, doc. 387.
10. Dulles's handwritten correction crossed out 'elimination' and replaced it with 'removal from Cuba'. JC King, Memorandum for DCI, 'Subject: Cuban Problems', 11/12/1959, Digital National Security Archives (DNSA) Collection, Cuban Missile Crisis Revisited.
11. Memorandum of Discussion 432nd NSC Meeting. 14/1/1960. FRUS vol. VI, doc. 423.
12. NSA, 'Bay of Pigs 40 Years After: A Chronology', available at https://nsarchive2.gwu.edu/bayofpigs/chron.html (accessed 20 October 2023).
13. Simon Hall, *Ten Days in Harlem* (London: Faber, 2020), 72.
14. Rebecca Friedman, 'Crisis Management at the Dead Center: The 1960–1961 Presidential Transition and the Bay of Pigs Fiasco', *Presidential Studies Quarterly*, 41.2 (2011), 311.
15. Paper prepared by the 5412 Committee, 'Subject: A Program of Covert Action against the Castro Regime', 16/3/1960, FRUS vol. VI, doc. 481.
16. Memorandum of Conference with President, 17/3/1960, FRUS vol. VI, doc. 486.

17. CIA Inspector General, 'Report on Plots to Assassinate Fidel Castro' (CIA IG Report) 23/5/1967, JFKAR, 104-10213-10101, 11–13.
18. Frank Sturgis, Testimony before House Select Committee on Assassination (HSCA), 11/5/1979, 44–45, 48, available at https://www.archives.gov/files/research/jfk/releases/docid-32252528.pdf (accessed 20 October 2023).
19. Colhoun, *Gangsterismo*, 57–60; Escalante, *Secret War*, 11–18.
20. Marita Lorenz, Testimony HSCA, 31/5/1978, JFKAR, 180-10118-10129, 24; Frank Sturgis, Testimony HSCA, 20/3/1978, JFKAR 180-10088-10087, 68. See also Warren Hinckle and William Turner, *The Fish Is Red* (New York: Harper & Row, 1981), 308.
21. Sturgis, Testimony, 41; Jonathan Marshall, 'The White House Death Squad', *Inquiry*, 5 (March 1979), 18.
22. Thomas Maier, *Mafia Spies: The Inside Story of the CIA, Gangsters, JFK, and Castro* (New York: Skyhorse Publishing 2021), 80–1.
23. Ann Louise Bardach, 'The Spy Who Loved Castro', *Vanity Fair*, November 1993.
24. Michael Carlson, 'L. Fletcher Prouty: US Officer Obsessed by the Conspiracy Theory of President Kennedy's Assassination', *The Guardian*, 22 June 2001, available at https://www.theguardian.com/news/2001/jun/22/guardianobituaries (accessed 20 October 2023).
25. Fletcher Prouty, Testimony SSCIA, 16/7/1975, DNSA Covert Operations II, 29–30.
26. SSCIA, Interim Report, 'Alleged Assassination Plots Involving Foreign Leaders' (Interim Report) (Washington, DC: US Government Printing Office, 1975), 114.
27. SSCIA, Interim Report, 115.
28. CIA Cable, Top Secret, 21/7/1960, available at https://nsarchive.gwu.edu/document/20838-2 (accessed 20 October 2023).
29. SSCIA, 'Draft Interim Report', JFKAR 157-10014-10136, 30.
30. William J. Murray, Memorandum for Inspector General, 'Subject: Questionable Activities', 17/1/1975, available at https://nsarchive.gwu.edu/document/20837-1 (accessed 20 October 2023).
31. Carrozza, *William Pawley*, 240.
32. CIA, IG Report, 14.
33. James O'Connell, Testimony to SSCIA, 30/5/1975, JFKAR 157-10002-10148, 7.
34. James Risen, *The Last Honest Man* (New York: Little, Brown, 2023), 205; CIA Memorandum, 'Robert Maheu', undated, JFKAR, 104-10122-10141.
35. Bryan Smith, 'How the CIA Enlisted the Chicago Mob to Put a Hit on Castro', *Chicago Magazine*, 23 October 2007, available at https://

www.chicagomag.com/chicago-magazine/november-2007/how-the-cia-enlisted-the-chicago-mob-to-put-a-hit-on-castro/ (accessed 20 October 2023).
36. Maier, *Mafia Spies*, 49.
37. Confirmation of Dulles's knowledge and approval of the Mafia plots can be found in CIA documents. Security Analysis Group, 'Rosselli/Maheu Matter', 23/5/1975, JFKAR, 104-10133-10041. See also David Belin, 'Transcript Interview with Sheffield Edwards', 30/4/1975, DNSA Family Jewels, 5; William Colby, Testimony to the SSCIA, 21/5/1975, DNSA Covert Operations II, 49.
38. John Prados, *Safe for Democracy* (Chicago: Ivan Dee, 2006), 230.
39. HSCA, 'The Evolution and Implications of the CIA-sponsored Assassination Conspiracies against Fidel Castro', March 1979, Report Appendix, vol. X, 166.
40. Santo Trafficante, Testimony before HSCA, 14/11/1977, JFKAR, 180-10118-10137, 15.
41. Maier, *Mafia Spies*, 73. The HSCA raised the possibility that Trafficante was a double agent. HSCA, 'The Evolution', 185, Mary Ferrell Foundation (MFF) Archive; Jose Aleman, Testimony to HSCA, Appendix Hearing, vol. 5, MFF Archive, 323.
42. Maier, *Mafia Spies*, 13; Escalante, *Secret War*, 55.
43. CIA, IG Report, 23–4.
44. Howard Osborn, Memorandum to DDCI, Subject: Robert A. Maheu, 24/6/1966, available at https://www.archives.gov/files/research/jfk/releases/docid-32403481.pdf (accessed 20 October 2023).
45. CIA, IG Report, 25.
46. SSCIA, Interim Report, 79.
47. HSCA, 'The Evolution', 152.
48. SSCIA, Interim Report, 78.
49. Jack Pfeiffer, *Official History of the Bay of Pigs Operation*, vol. III: *Evolution of the CIA's Anti-Castro Policies*, 281, available at https://www.archives.gov/files/research/jfk/releases/104-10301-10004.pdf (accessed 20 October 2023).
50. Frederick Baron, 'Summary of Interview with Gordon Gray', Memorandum to file, 5/7/1975, JFKAR 157-10014-10100, 68.
51. Pfeiffer, *Official History*, 282.
52. Thomas Powers, *The Man Who Kept the Secrets: Richard Helms and the CIA* (New York: Pocket Books 1979), 160.
53. Baron, 'Summary of Interview', 65; Thomas Parrott, Testimony to SSCIA, 10/7/1975, 15, DNSA Covert Operations II, 17.
54. Peter Grose, *Gentleman Spy* (London: André Deutch, 1994), 505; John Prados, *The Family Jewels* (Austin: University of Texas Press,

2014), 169; Stephen Ambrose, *Ike's Spies* (New York: Anchor Books, 1981), 306.
55. In some versions of events, Orta simply got cold feet as Castro's intelligence directorate (G-2) closed in on him. CIA, IG Report, 27 and SSCIA, Interim Report, 80.
56. Bissell identified either National Security Advisor McGeorge Bundy or his Deputy Walt Rostow as originators of the request. SSCIA, Interim Report, 185.
57. Halpern knew – or so he testified – because back in 1975, before being called in front of the Church Committee, he had reviewed all 'executive action' files. Ralph Weber, 'Secret Interview with Sam Halpern', 23-30/10/1987, JFKAR 104-10324-10002, 99.
58. William Rostow, Testimony to SSCIA, 9/7/1975, DNSA Covert Operations II, 12–13.
59. Undated Chronology, Interview, Meeting Summary with Harvey, available at https://www.archives.gov/files/research/jfk/releases/2018/157-10014-10102.pdf (accessed 20 October 2023).
60. William Harvey, Testimony to SSCIA, 11/7/1975, DNSA Covert Operations II, 16.
61. William Harvey, Testimony to SSCIA, 25 /6/1975, DNSA Covert Operations II, 10.
62. Colhoun, *Gangsterismo*, 99.
63. The cryptonym for Agency Staff D.
64. William Harvey, Handwritten notes, JFKAR 104-10103-10318, MFF Archive.
65. David Martin, *Wilderness of Mirrors* (New York: Skyhorse Publishing, 2018), 123.
66. Colhoun, *Gangsterismo*, 99; CIA, IG Report, 27.
67. Jefferson Morley, 'If You Need a Dirty Job Done', *Military.com*, 16 June 2022, available at https://www.military.com/daily-news/2022/06/16/if-you-need-dirty-job-done-straight-talk-marine-vet-about-cia-plot-assassinate-castro.html (accessed 20 October 2023).
68. Edward Cates, Memorandum for the record, 21/3/1975, HSCA, Security File on Frank Sturgis, NARA Record Number: 1993.08.05.14:42:12:750028, MFF Archive, 15–16.
69. Felix Rodriguez, *Shadow Warrior* (New York: Pocket Books, 1989), 70; Escalante, *Secret War*, 74–5.
70. Larry Hancock, *Shadow Warfare* (Berkeley, CA: Counterpoint, 2014), 204.
71. IG Report, 29–30.
72. IG Report, 32, SSCIA Interim Report, 81.
73. SSCIA, Interim Report, 117–20.

74. IG Report, 32; SSCIA Interim Report, 82.
75. Escalante, *Secret War*, 85; IG Report, 32.
76. Memorandum, Belmont to Parsons, 'Arthur James Balletti et al.', 4/5/1961, FBI Freedom of Information, Privacy Acts section, Subject: Fidel Castro, File Number: 139-1201, Part 1, FBI Vault, 195–6.
77. Memorandum, FBI Director to Attorney General, 22/5/1961, FBI Freedom of Information, Privacy Acts section, Subject: Fidel Castro, File Number: 139-1201, Part 1, FBI Vault, 198–201.
78. Colhoun, *Gangsterismo*, 127; HSCA Appendix Volumes, vol. X, MFF Archive, 183.
79. Operation Northwoods, 'Annex to Appendix to Enclosure A: Pretext to Justify US Military Intervention in Cuba', 9/3/1962, National Security Archives (NSAr), available at https://nsarchive2.gwu.edu/news/20010430/northwoods.pdf (accessed 23 October 2023).
80. Escalante, *Secret War*, 89–94.
81. Journalist Tad Szulc also became aware of an operation involving ONI in the immediate aftermath of the Bay of Pigs. Tad Szulc, 'Notes on TS Conversation with JFK, at White House – Nov. 9, 1961', NSAr, available at https://nsarchive.gwu.edu/document/19619-national-security-archive-doc-08-tad-szulc-notes (accessed 23 October 2023); Tad Szulc, 'Cuba on Our Mind', *Esquire*, February 1974, 90.
82. Gordon's testimony continues by saying that he did not hear about Gonzales until 1966 when he read that he had been arrested by Castro. In 1969, Gordon allegedly wrote to the new Secretary of the Navy and discussed the episode with him. After the meeting, he was again confined to the Psychiatric Ward of Bethesda Naval Hospital. When he was released, he retired from the Navy in 1969. Mason Cargill, Memorandum to File: John Gordon, 29/5/1975, JFKAR 178-10002-10320, MFF Archive.
83. Antonio Veciana, *Trained to Kill* (New York: Skyhorse Publishing, 2017), chapter 1, ebook; Aleksandr Fursenko and Timothy Naftali, *"One hell of a gamble": Khrushchev, Castro, and Kennedy 1958–1964* (New York: W. W. Norton, 1997), 136; Escalante, *Secret War*, 96–8; FBI Memo, 'Cuban Rebel Activities in Cuba', 7/12/1961, JFKAR 104-10217-10247, MFF Archive, 2.
84. Evan Thomas, *Robert Kennedy: His Life* (New York: Touchstone, 2000), 157–8.
85. National Security Action Memorandum 100, 'Contingency Planning for Cuba', 5 October 1961, available at https://www.jfklibrary.org/asset-viewer/archives/JFKNSF/332/JFKNSF-332-002 (accessed 23 October 2023).
86. SSCIA, Interim Report, 136.

87. Colhoun, *Gangsterismo*, 146. See Thomas Parrott, Memorandum for the record, 5/10/1961, FRUS vol. X, Cuba, January 1961–September 1962 (FRUS vol. X), doc. 266.
88. Tad Szulc, SSCIA Testimony, 10/6/75, DNSA Covert Operations II, 26–7.
89. Szulc, Testimony, 27.
90. Kennedy had had a somewhat similar conversation regarding the appropriateness of assassinating Castro with Senator George Smathers of Florida in March 1961, another high point of assassination plots. SSCIA, Interim Report, 123–4.
91. Sam Halpern, Testimony to SSCIA, 18/6/1975, JFKAR, 157-10002-10087, 8.
92. CIA, IG Report, 39.
93. James Johnston, *Murder Inc.* (Lincoln, NE: Potomac Books, 2019), 31.
94. Luca Trenta, *Risk and Presidential Decision-Making* (London: Routledge, 2016), 91–4.
95. Lars Schoultz, *That Infernal Little Cuban Republic* (Chapel Hill: University of North Carolina Press, 2009), 175.
96. Tim Weiner, Zoom interview with the author, 3 February 2022.
97. Memorandum Helms to DCI McCone, 19/1/1962, FRUS vol. X, doc. 292.
98. Philip Buchen, Report Castro, JFKAR 178-10003-10318, 10–11.
99. SSCIA, Interim Report, 141.
100. Bayard Stockton, *Flawed Patriot* (Lincoln, NE: Potomac Books 2006), 112.
101. SSCIA, Interim Report, 142.
102. Edward Lansdale, Testimony to SSCIA, 8/7/1975, 29.
103. Lansdale, Testimony, 46–7.
104. Ibid., 30.
105. SSCIA, Interim Report, 143; Buchen, Report Castro, 11a.
106. Buchen, Report Castro, 17.
107. Then McCone's executive assistant and later author of a secret history of the CIA under McCone.
108. William Elder, 'John McCone as Director of Central Intelligence 1961–1965', NSAr, available at https://nsarchive.gwu.edu/document/21523-document-09 (accessed 23 October 2023), 99.
109. Edward Lansdale, Memorandum for the record, 16 March 1962, JFKAR, 198-10004-10020, 24–5.
110. Elder, 'John McCone', 99
111. CIA Report, 'The Johnny Rosselli Matter', undated, JFKAR 104-10122-10141, 3.

112. Jeff Leen, 'AKA Frank Sinatra: The Singer and the Senator', *Washington Post*, 7 March 1999.
113. HSCA, 'The Evolution', 188.
114. This seems unlikely since RFK had his own contacts with the underworld through the shady figure of Charles Ford. Ford Was working for Task Force W and seemingly had frequent meetinsg with the Attorney General who had expressed an interest in a group of Cuban exiles who could cause an uprising in Santiago. While Ford often discussed assassination with the exiles, the topic seemingly did not surface with RFK. CIA Task Force to Review Staff, 28/8/1975, JFKAR, 104-10303-10001. Robert Gambino, Memorandum for Review Staff, 'Senate Select Committee Report: Charles Ford', 4/9/1975, JFKAR, 104-10309-10014; Charles Ford, Memorandum for the Record, Subject: Interview with the Senate Committee Investigators, 19/9/1975, JFKAR, 104-10303-10001.
115. SSCIA, Interim Report, 133.
116. Sheffield Edwards, Testimony to SSCIA, 30/5/1975, DNSA Covert Operations II, 4 and 16.
117. IG Report, 49–50.
118. Escalante, *Secret War*, 133.
119. Thomas, *Robert Kennedy*, 151.
120. Quote from Richard Helms in SSCIA, Interim Report, 149.
121. SSCIA, Interim Report, 163; John McCone, Testimony to SSCIA, 6/6/1975, DNSA Covert Operations II, 38.
122. SSCIA, Interim Report, 162.
123. Richard Goodwin, *Remembering America: A Voice from the Sixties* (Boston, MA: Little, Brown, 1988), 189.
124. SSCIA, Interim Report, 164.
125. Memorandum, Harvey to Helms, 14/8/1962, NSAr, CIA File, Robert Borosage Collection, Washington, DC.
126. SSCIA, Interim Report, 162.
127. McCone, Testimony, 38.
128. Trenta, *Risk*.
129. Johnston, *Murder Inc.*, 52; Trenta, *Risk*, 93.
130. Richard Helms, Testimony to SSCIA, 13/6/1975, DNSA Covert Operations II, 44.
131. Escalante, *Secret War*, 133–4; Anthony Broadle, 'Closest CIA Bid to Kill Castro Was Poisoned Drink', *Reuters*, 5 July 2007, available at https://www.reuters.com/article/us-cuba-cia-idUSN0427935120070705 (accessed 23 October 2023).
132. Evan Thomas, *The Very Best Men* (New York: Simon & Schuster, 2006), 297.

The President's Kill List

133. SSCIA, McGeorge Bundy: Trujillo Summary, JFKAR 151-10014-10095, 9 (of chronology) and 6 (of interview with Bundy).
134. Operation Red Cross, also known as Operation Tilt or the Pawley/Bayo raid. Telegram, Chief of Station JMWAVE to Chief Special Affairs Staff, 'Status Report: Operation Tilt', 26/2/1964, JFKAR 104-10057-10102, available at https://www.maryferrell.org/showDoc.html?docId=50552&relPageId=4 (accessed 23 October 2023); Carrozza, *William Pawley*, 260–4.
135. In the same months, the Administration was also considering options on how to remove Duvalier from Haiti. Greg Treverton to F.A.O. Schwartz, 'Trujillo Assassination: missing documents', 2/7/1975, JFKAR 157-10008-10238, 7.
136. Prados, *Safe*, 322; CIA, IG Report, 77.
137. Dan Bohning, *The Castro Obsession* (Washington, DC: Potomac Books, 2006), 182.
138. CIA, IG Report, 75.
139. James Callanan, *Covert Action in the Cold War* (London: I.B. Tauris, 2010), 181.
140. Bohning, *The Castro Obsession*, 178.
141. SSCIA, 'Chronology of Castro Assassination Plans', JFKAR 157-10004-10147, 6.
142. Tim Weiner, *Legacy of Ashes* (New York: Doubleday, 2007), 208.
143. CIA, IG Report, 78–9.
144. Powers, *The Man*, 190.
145. CIA, IG Report, 85.
146. William Weatherby, Testimony to SSCIA, 1/8/1975, JFKAR 157-10005-10258, 48.
147. CIA, IG Report, 84; Weatherby, Testimony, 48.
148. CIA, IG Report, 85.
149. Ibid., 87.
150. SSCIA, Interim Report, 88.
151. CIA, IG Report, 89.
152. Ibid., 91.
153. IG Report, 94.
154. CSPAN, Interview with Felix Rodriguez, 1989, available at https://www.youtube.com/watch?v=wjXUPbXczKQ
155. Hancock, *Shadow Warfare*, 204.
156. Testimony Mr Halley (Ted Shackley) to SSCIA, 19/8/1975, JFKAR 157-10002-10084, 84.
157. FRUS, 1964–1968, vol. XXXII: Dominican Republic; Cuba; Haiti; Guyana, Editorial Note, doc. 315.

158. CIA, IG Report, 100.
159. Memorandum, Cargill to Belin, 'Search for files for material relevant to assassination plans', 1/5/1975, HSCA (RG233), JFKAR 157-10005-10158, 4.
160. Loch Johnson, 'LBJ Library National Security papers touching on assass. And covert action in Cuba', Miscellaneous Records of the Church Committee, 21/7/1975, JFKAR 157-10014-10096.
161. Gordon Chase, Memorandum for Bundy: 'Artime's contact with dissident leader', 5/1/1965, in Loch Johnson, 'LBJ Library National Security papers'.
162. Morley, 'If You Need a Dirty Job Done'.
163. CIA, AMLASH Operation, undated, JFKAR104-10065-10094.
164. George Manfredi, 'Examination of a portion of the record of Richard Helms', 19/3/1975, JFKAR, 178-10003-10439.
165. McCone, Testimony, 15.
166. SSCIA, Interim report, 102–4.
167. William Elder, Testimony to SSCIA, 13/8/1975, DNSA Covert Operations II, 28–9.
168. David Corn and Gus Russo, 'The Old Man and the CIA', *The Nation*, 26 March 2001, available at https://www.thenation.com/article/archive/old-man-and-cia-kennedy-plot-kill-castro/ (accessed 23 October 2023).
169. Grose, *Gentleman Spy*, 505.
170. SSCIA, Interim Report, 118.
171. Stephen Kinzer, *The Brothers* (St. Martin's Griffin, 2013), 287.
172. Stephen Kinzer, Zoom interview with the author, 14 February 2021.
173. Thomas, *Robert Kennedy*; Arthur M. Schlesinger, *Robert Kennedy and His Times* (New York: Mariner Books, 2018).
174. Theodore Sorensen, Testimony to SSCIA, 21/7/1975, DNSA Covert Operations II, 7.
175. Rostow, Testimony, 29.
176. SSCIA, Interim Report, 121–3.
177. Anthony Summers, *The Secret Life of J. Edgar Hoover* (London: Ebury Press, 2011), 345–6.
178. Thomas, *The Very Best Men*, 398.
179. CIA, IG Report.
180. SSCIA, Interim Report, 175–8.

4 Rafael Trujillo: Assassination and the US Role in Covert Regime Change

> The members of our club are now prepared in their minds to have a picnic but do not have the ingredients for the salad ... They have asked us for a few sandwiches, hardly more, and we are not prepared to make them available. Last week we were asked to furnish three or four pineapples for a party ... but I could remember nothing in my instructions that would have allowed me to contribute this ingredient. Don't think I wasn't tempted.[1]

On 16 March 1961, Henry Dearborn – Consul in the Dominican Republic and main contact between the US government and Dominican dissidents – sent a not-so-subtle letter to the State Department. He complained about the US government's refusal to provide weapons and fragmentation grenades – 'sandwiches' and 'pineapples' – to a group of anti-Trujillo dissidents. This refusal notwithstanding, by March 1961 Dearborn and the dissidents had agreed on the need to assassinate Dominican Republic dictator Rafael Trujillo. The picnic was on.

* * *

Trujillo had risen within the ranks of the Dominican National guard, put in place by the United States government during its occupation of the country. He seized power in 1930, six years after the end of the occupation. For almost thirty years, Trujillo acted as a loyal US ally internationally and a brutal dictator domestically.[2] While the dictator's hawkish Cold War posture contributed to the US government's support, his grip on US politics also relied on diplomacy, on public relations campaigns,[3] and on corruption and on the blackmail of members of Congress, including through the use of a 'sex den'.[4] Things started to unravel in March 1956, when Trujillo's men – possibly helped by Robert Maheu's firm[5] – kidnapped on US soil Jesus de Galindez, a Spanish-Dominican academic at Columbia University. Badly beaten, Galindez was flown to the Dominican Republic by an unwitting US citizen, Gerry Murphy. Brought in front of Trujillo, Galindez was ordered to eat a copy of his dissertation which had criticised the regime. Still alive, his body was slowly lowered into boiling water and the corpse fed to sharks.[6] Aiming to leave no witnesses, the regime proceeded to kill Murphy and Octavio de la Maza, a pilot, member of a prominent Dominican family, who had befriended Murphy. Trujillo also left a forged final 'suicide' letter from de la Maza.[7]

Certainly, the killing of Murphy and the inquiries by US Congressmen from Oregon (Murphy's home state) caused headaches for the dictator and the Eisenhower Administration. Similarly, the emergence of democratic governments in the region – such as Venezuela under Romulo Betancourt – made US support more problematic. No other development was more consequential than the rise of Fidel Castro in Cuba. This posed two main challenges for the United States. First, US allies and the Organization of American States (OAS) refused to move against Castro until the US dropped its staunch support for Trujillo. Second, the United States feared that the Trujillo regime's elimination of even moderate opposition might lead to the rise of another pro-Castro government. The US support for Trujillo had moved from an image problem to a strategic liability.[8]

Both the Eisenhower and Kennedy administrations developed methods to remove Trujillo. Non-violent methods were considered, such as a series of high-level diplomatic missions aimed at convincing Trujillo to leave the island. US policy, though, relied primarily on support for an assassination attempt. US officials nurtured and established contacts with dissidents within the Dominican Republic. They provided weapons and support, assessing the feasibility of assassination plans. Trujillo was killed during a trip to one of his regular mistresses – one of the methods that had been discussed with US officials.

Trying to Divorce the Dictator: Eisenhower and Trujillo

In 1957, Robert Farland became US Ambassador to the Dominican Republic. He was told to start developing contacts within Trujillo's opposition. He did so through parties at the US Embassy and through his deputy, Henry Dearborn. The aim was to maintain a facade of cordial relations with the dictator, while nurturing candidates for a possible successor regime.[9]

Already in 1958, a group of dissidents told CIA Chief of Station Lear Reed that they intended to shoot Trujillo while he visited a local racetrack. While not opposed to assassination, Reed told them that – before proceeding – they should make sure to have someone ready to replace the dictator. Reed, who did not speak Spanish, started to develop contacts with Americans in the Dominican Republic who did. Among those recruited were individuals close to General Juan Tomas Diaz, the type of military figure the United States envisaged for the post-Trujillo regime.[10] Another important contact was the American Lorenzo Berry (also known as 'Wimpy').[11] Wimpy owned a grocery store which became a point of contact for the plotters. The store's bags were used to pass messages to and from US officials and, eventually, to deliver weapons to the plotters.[12] Over time, the dissidents divided into an 'action group' with the task of assassinating Trujillo, and a political group, with the task of taking over the government once Trujillo had been assassinated.[13] Compartmentalisation was far from perfect.

In February 1960, the Special Group started considering a programme of covert support for Dominican dissidents as well as an effort to increase intelligence coverage of the country.[14] The Administration also sent Democratic Senator George Smathers and William Pawley to the island, to convince the dictator to resign. Pawley had a track record of controversial activities in the region,[15] as well as extensive financial interests in the Dominican Republic.[16] To these emissaries, Trujillo unconvincingly promised to hold free elections, but made sure to use pictures of the visiting Smathers for propaganda.[17] A similar mission by General Edwin Clark, a good friend of Eisenhower, also failed.[18]

Rafael Trujillo: Assassination and Covert Regime Change

Updating Washington in the same weeks, Farland explained to Assistant Secretary of State for Inter-American Affairs Roy Rubottom that the dissidents were becoming restless, and they might look for support elsewhere – that is, from Castro. Farland specified that the dissidents were convinced that they were ready to do anything, except the 'ultimate step', the killing of Trujillo. For this, they required US assistance. Farland added: 'I think the time has come for certain agencies of our government, without attribution, to establish and implement a definitive constructive program to influence the course of events in the Dominican Republic.' Farland reassured Rubottom such an approach had been cleared with Secretary of State John Foster Dulles and his brother DCI Allen Dulles.[19] Farland also reported a plan – allegedly concocted by the dissidents themselves – codenamed Operation Lancet. The plan entailed the arrival of a Special US Envoy who would give Trujillo 12–18 hours to leave. The envoy would make clear that if Trujillo refused, a border incident would be created and used as a pretext for collective military intervention. If Trujillo accepted, a provisional government would be formed.[20]

At the start of April, the State Department asked Farland whether – if so instructed – he would be able, 'with appropriate civil and military dissident elements', to take over the government and – if so – what US aid was needed prior to take over. Farland replied that the dissidents were 'poorly armed, loosely organized' and lacked a working relationship with the military. A takeover was feasible if one or a combination of six developments were to emerge: clandestine shipment of weapons and sabotage materiel, an invasion, the implementation of Lancet, advanced psychological conditioning by radio, the development of a step-by-step plan preceding the coup, and 'the incapacitation or assassination of Trujillo'.[21]

On the 14th, in a meeting of the National Security Council attended by the President, the linkage between Trujillo and Castro, as well as the risk of another Castro in the Dominican Republic, was discussed.[22] After the meeting, Herter wrote to Eisenhower that there was no time 'quietly to encourage a moderate pro-United State leadership among the civilian and military dissidents'.[23] The President agreed and approved the request to foster the downfall of Trujillo. The Administration instructed the Embassy to identify military and civilian dissidents who would be ready to take power and ask for US support.[24]

In May, while in Washington, Farland reported the dissidents' request for a small number of high-powered rifles with telescopic lenses. In his view, there was no problem in the purchase and delivery of these weapons, but much depended on whether the US government wanted to be involved in this type of activity. J. C. King, Chief of the CIA's Western Hemisphere division, agreed. As Richard Bissell later recalled, everyone hearing about the type of weapons requested would have understood that they were meant for assassination.[25] Farland also made clear that the dissidents aimed to assassinate Trujillo and that one plan envisaged the detonation of a powerful bomb along the route of his nightly walk.[26] Having met Farland and other US officials working on the Dominican Republic, Eisenhower stated that Trujillo and Castro were proving equally problematic and he wished to 'see both of them sawed off'.[27] Dearborn had reached a similar conclusion. Trujillo would not voluntarily leave the island and would continue to dominate whether he was president or 'dogcatcher'.[28]

Towards the end of May, Farland left the Dominican Republic for good. One of the main reasons was the concern that Trujillo might arrange Farland's assassination and blame it on the opposition as a stratagem to stay in power. The President also approved a new policy of covert assistance to the dissidents.[29] Having met with the dissidents, Dearborn told Washington that for security reasons the dissidents had not planned much beyond the 'incapacitation of Trujillo'. Having heard from Dearborn, the CIA and the State Department agreed that US support should have extended to the provision of a 'small number of sniper rifles or other devices for the removal of key Trujillo people form the scene'.[30] This was the first agreed-upon transfer of weapons.

In mid-June, Trujillo's emissaries reported an alleged conversation between the dictator and Chief of Station Reed to Dearborn. Whether Reed had warned Trujillo of US plans as alleged, or whether it was a fabrication, his role was diminished. With Reed mistrusted by the opposition and Farland gone, Dearborn became the main channel of communication between the Agency and the dissidents. In his new role, Dearborn would start using two channels of communication: 'eyes only' memorandums to the State Department and a secret 'Roger channel' – not unlike Devlin's PROP channel – for CIA communication.[31]

On 1 July, senior CIA and State Department officials agreed to deliver twelve sterile US rifles Model 1903 (Springfield) with telescopic sights and 500 rounds of ammunition to be 'used against key members of the Trujillo regime'.[32] Two weeks after the approval of the rifle delivery, Dearborn reported that a group of dissidents had identified seven possible ways to achieve regime change. These included a rebellion by the armed forces, a revolution spearheaded by civilians, a palace coup, a land invasion of the country, assassination through a command assault, or assassination through an explosive device. The dissidents considered the latter two options plausible. The assault would require a small number of weapons and grenades, but it would be very difficult as all the plotters risked being killed in the process. The bomb plan would be likely to succeed and would require fewer men.[33] All options were beyond the dissidents' capabilities, except the last type of assassination.[34] During a NSC meeting on the 25th, Eisenhower stated that it had become necessary to 'solve the Trujillo situation'. 'Until Trujillo is eliminated,' the President lamented, US allies in the region would not reach a level of indignation sufficient to deal with Castro.[35]

In August, following the OAS, the United States interrupted diplomatic relations with the Dominican Republic due to the Dominican dictator's assassination attempt against Venezuela's Betancourt. While US Embassies closed, US consulates did not and Dearborn remained as Consul General and de facto CIA Chief of Station until February 1961.[36] In September, Rubottom was replaced by Thomas Mann. At State, Frank Devine became the main point of contact with Dearborn.

Dearborn told Devine that the best hope for the Dominican Republic, the United States and the OAS was for 'Dominicans to put an end to Trujillo before he leaves the island'. Even in exile, Trujillo would have been a threat to the region and US allies, using his wealth to cause trouble in the hemisphere. 'If I were a Dominican,' Dearborn wrote, 'I would favor destroying Trujillo as being the first necessary step in the salvation of my country.' He added: 'If you recall Dracula . . . it was necessary to drive a stake through his heart to prevent a continuation of his crimes.' The same was true of Trujillo.[37] In October, the CIA considered but ultimately rejected the delivery of the 300 rifles and other materiel requested by the dissidents,[38] but contacts with the dissidents intensified.

On 4 November, the CIA's Frank Thomas met Gianni Vicini, one of the leaders of the 'political group'.[39] Thomas and Vicini agreed that the dissidents' requests for 300 rifles indicated that they lacked support within the military, making the removal of Trujillo unlikely. The exchange showed the CIA's readiness to participate in a specific job (the assassination of Trujillo), but not in a broader covert paramilitary operation, a point Bissell confirmed in a Special Group meeting later in the month. The Group also approved a still obscure 'plan' for the island.[40]

On 3 January 1961, with his presidency coming to an end, Eisenhower reminded his associates that the United States had hoped to move against Castro and Trujillo simultaneously. He ordered his National Security Advisor to move as quickly as possible against Trujillo.[41] On the 12th, Mann wrote to Under Secretary Livingston Merchant noting that – at multiple times – the dissidents had asked to be supplied with '"hardware" of various types' (inverted commas in the original) including 'conventional arms' and 'more exotic devices'. The request was discussed in a Special Group meeting. Thomas Parrott argued that the weapons could be procured but the introduction of the weapons to Dominican territory depended on the dissidents' capabilities to receive them.[42] On the last day of the Eisenhower Administration, the Special Group agreed on the delivery.[43] Devine announced the decision and notified Dearborn of the arrival of a new CIA Chief of Station, Robert Edward Owen. Owen arrived on the 7th and maintained contact with Wimpy and others who worked with the dissidents' 'action group', while Dearborn remained the main point of contact for the political group led by Vicini.[44]

The Kennedy Administration and the Assassination of Trujillo

As the new administration took office, the Special Group approved the delivery of small arms and related equipment to the Dominican

Rafael Trujillo: Assassination and Covert Regime Change

Republic, and confirmed the 'operational proposal', that is, the mysterious plan discussed on 29 December.[45]

Assassination and the supply of weapons were the main topic of a meeting between the CIA and two of the leading Dominican dissidents from the 'political group' (Vicini and Donald Reid Cabral) on 11 February.[46] As Ned Holman – Chief of the Western Hemisphere Branch 3 (Caribbean)[47] – summarised, the dissidents agreed that 'the key to the success of the plot was the assassination of Trujillo'. Holman asked for more clarity on the assassination plans and was told that the plan had not yet been finalised, but the latest version envisaged the use of explosives in a drainage pipe along the path of Trujillo's nightly walk. To this end, dissidents asked if a US technician could be sent for training purposes. The dissidents also asked for an ex-FBI agent who could carry out the assassination but were told that FBI agents were not killers for hire. The dissidents then enquired about alternative methods of assassination including the use of cameras and other items that could fire projectiles, a slow-working chemical to be rubbed on Trujillo's hands through handshake, or the use of silencers for rifles. Asked for further ideas on assassination, the officer declined since – without instructions – he could not get directly involved in planning, but he did advise the two dissidents to avoid mob action.[48]

Holman held a second meeting with the two dissidents on the 15th. Vicini asked whether – since assassination was the agreed-upon objective of the delivery of weapons – other more exotic methods of assassination could be explored. These included a powerful bomb and detonating device, which he considered an easy method to eliminate Trujillo. Holman responded that such a plan had been considered by Agency experts who viewed the prospects of such a plot as very uncertain. An alternative was poison that could be put in capsules and added to the dictator's pills. The group agreed that it would be a good idea to explore how the dictator obtained his pills.[49] Holman's report of the meeting was passed to the Station which estimated that a plan to ambush Trujillo was almost certain to fail as it was precisely the type of assault bodyguards train for.[50]

* * *

As these meetings were taking place, new National Security Advisor McGeorge Bundy wrote to Secretary of State Dean Rusk setting the new President's policy on the Dominican Republic. Kennedy wanted to avoid a Castro-like regime on the island as well as 'political rap', the reputational costs domestically and internationally coming from too visible support for Trujillo.[51] On the 14th, Bundy also requested that Bissell prepare a report for 'higher authority' (the President) on the Agency's plans in the Dominican Republic.

Rusk briefed the President on the 15th. He pointed to the adverse effects of the US government's support for Trujillo's dictatorship. Rusk also touched upon US officials' contact with dissidents. 'Our representatives in the Dominican Republic,' Rusk stressed, 'have, at considerable risk to those involved, established contacts with numerous leaders of the underground opposition. These leaders look at the United States for assistance.' He also told the President that the CIA had been authorised to deliver a small quantity of weapons and sabotage equipment to the dissidents outside the Dominican Republic, a reference to the January 1961 Special Group decision.[52]

On the 17th, Bissell's report to Bundy – and presumably the President – confirmed that the CIA had been authorised to provide the weapons. It also suggested that the Agency was ready to provide further armaments if the dissidents developed the capabilities to receive them.[53] Bissell reported that due to the precarious situation in the Dominican Republic, the 'liquidation' of Trujillo or the rounding up of the opposition were likely. Bissell also notified the President of contacts with exile leaders who had disclosed 'their plan of action which they thought could be implemented if provided with arms for 300 men, explosives and remote-control detonation devices'.[54] Bissell's report failed to mention that the CIA was aware of – and heavily involved in – these assassination plots. Unsurprisingly, Bissell later did not recall why he had not been completely forthcoming in his report nor whether assassination was discussed with the President and in what terms.[55] At a minimum, from early February, the new Administration and the President were aware of an existing CIA authorisation for the delivery of weapons to dissidents and of the fact that the killing of Trujillo was likely. No effort was made to rescind that authorisation.

Rafael Trujillo: Assassination and Covert Regime Change

CIA officers continued their direct involvement in (and review of) assassination plans. The dissidents were told that their latest plan to place a bomb at a point on the path of Trujillo's nightly walk[56] was 'utterly out of question due to constant guard at that point'. Instead, the CIA recommended an alternative location for the bomb, underneath some drainage pipes. Photos of the precise location were sent back to headquarters for an assessment.[57] Days later, a dissident told Dearborn that a plan was being finalised to kill Trujillo by intercepting his car 'at a point near Wimpy's supermarket', and that the time of execution depended on Trujillo's travels. Headquarters cabled back that it was 'deeply interested' in the plan and requested additional information if it was to provide timely assistance.[58]

In mid-March, the dissidents sent additional requests to Dearborn. They needed fragmentation grenades, five rapid-fire weapons, and ten 64 mm anti-tank rockets. The dissident group had a short window of time in which to kill Trujillo since 'fringe' plotters with 'loose mouth' were endangering the plan.[59] In his report, Dearborn also insisted on the pouching of high-powered weapons since the plotters were losing momentum.[60] The request for weapons prompted Dearborn's 'picnic letter' to the State Department.[61] While the 'pineapple' request was rejected, Dearborn made an additional request for three .38 caliber Smith & Wesson pistols. Chief of Station Owen recommended the weapons be sent via diplomatic pouch. They were needed as a tangible show of support. Owen's telegram evidenced the close collaboration between dissidents, Dearborn and CIA Station. The security of the plotters had now become a US priority since the loss or arrest of one of the key dissidents could lead to the exposure of the US role.[62] After an initial reluctance, the pistols were pouched[63] and delivered to the dissidents, via Wimpy.[64]

Contacts with the CIA's Station helped the dissidents refine their plan, which now entailed attacking Trujillo while he visited one of his mistresses in the city. For such an operation, a Station officer reported, the dissidents needed five M3 or comparable machine guns and 1,500 rounds of ammunition for personal defence, while the deed itself would be done with quieter weapons. The Station officer had also offered concussion grenades to help with the job, but the dissident leader had refused, suggesting that most of his men were more acquainted with rapid-fire weapons. Both parties agreed on the urgency of the delivery and that pouches would be the preferable delivery method.[65]

Sharing the dissidents' sense of urgency, the Station officer reported back to headquarters (including the DCI) that the attitude of the opposition was that of 'drowning man reaching for straw. He wants straw and not offers of swimming lessons.' Three further elements demonstrated the tight collaboration between the CIA and the dissidents. First, the dissidents reviewed and approved a CIA draft for the leaflets to be dropped on the Dominican Republic. Second, the Station officer and the dissident leader agreed to share contacts in the military to avoid crossing wires. Finally, the Station officer reviewed and assessed the latest assassination plan and considered it better than those previously discussed.[66]

Dearborn was very much aware of and supportive of these developments. He was also aware of the risks in being too explicit in his communications, especially with Devine,[67] but disregarded his own advice. On the 22nd, Dearborn cabled State to report on developments among the dissidents. The small group of dissidents he had been working with had settled on assassination. 'Political assassination is ugly and repulsive,' Dearborn wrote, 'but everything must be judged in its own context.' Assassination was not too different from the US government's use of the atomic bomb which was also ugly and repulsive but ultimately saved lives.[68]

Meanwhile, at the CIA, the Station's report of the dissidents' request for pouching machine guns caused bureaucratic conflict over the propriety of the transfer.[69] On the 25th, Bissell intervened to settle the score. 'It is our objective,' he told the Station, 'to undertake and support program to replace the present regime with a government which is acceptable to the best of the internal dissidents and responsive to the immediate and long range interests of US government.' The Agency and the US government also wanted to avoid 'precipitous, uncoordinated' action by the dissidents that could lead to the emergence of a pro-Castro government, at least until 'opposition groups and HQs are better prepared to support assassination, effect a change in the regime, and cope with aftermath'. The mere disposal of Trujillo could create more problems

Rafael Trujillo: Assassination and Covert Regime Change

than it would solve. In the meantime, the Agency would continue to provide material support to the dissidents, 'in the event they should bring about effective change in regime prior to date fixed by CIA'. As a sign of support, HQ was ready to 'deliver machine guns and ammunition to opposition leader when he develops capability to receive same'. Bissell cautioned that – if further clarification were needed – the State Department could arrange for a return of the Chief of Station to Washington for consultation.[70]

* * *

Back in the Dominican Republic, Dearborn had a long meeting with Vicini on 27 March which centred on the discussion of 'Project Plutarch'. Plutarch was the codename of Angel Severo Cabral – one of the conspirators Dearborn had met – and his project was the assassination of Trujillo.[71] Vicini pushed Dearborn for a more active role by the US government in support of the dissidents, especially to avoid the risk that other groups, less aligned with US interests, killed Trujillo first.[72]

One day after Bissell's telegram, with Dearborn's concurrence – and perhaps based on the dissidents' complaints – the Station asked Headquarters to provide the dissidents with three .30 calibre M1 carbine rifles that had been left behind in the Consulate after the break of diplomatic relations between the United States and the Dominican Republic. The Station also requested additional ammunition for the carbines. Headquarters agreed.[73] The carbines' serial numbers were filed off to assuage HQ's concerns that their use could expose CIA involvement. Nine magazines were also pouched.[74] Eventually, the carbines were passed to Wimpy, with 'no complications', on 7 April.[75]

With the Chief of Station in Washington for a debriefing, intermediaries had told Dearborn of the dissidents' insistence on the need for the requested machine guns. The not-so-subtle message read that the 'Leica Cameras Model M-1' (the carbines that had been received by the dissidents) were not enough. Only Leica Cameras Model M-3 (the machine guns) would help in completing the 'photographic job' (assassination) safely.[76] On the 7th, the provision of machine guns was agreed upon – through a 'pouch restriction waiver request' made by the Chief of the Western Hemisphere Division and approved by Bissell. It was understood as a way of ensuring the dissidents' continued cooperation as well as maintaining their confidence in the 'Agency's determination to live up to its earlier commitments to the group', including promises of weapon delivery.[77]

By mid-April, developments in the Dominican Republic coincided with the final preparations and launching of the Bay of Pigs invasion. The failure of the invasion threw the Administration's policy towards Trujillo as well as the Agency into chaos.[78] Headquarters told the Station that due to the 'unsettled conditions in the Caribbean', the machine guns that had been passed to the Station should be kept there. At such a tense moment, the vacuum created by the assassination of Trujillo only risked further instability.[79] Perhaps cautioned by the Bay of Pigs failure, or perhaps prodded by family connections, Kennedy also seemed ready to review his policy towards Trujillo. Contingency plans for a full invasion were being readied[80] and Kennedy decided to send another diplomatic mission to the island to assess the situation and convince the dictator to leave.[81] This mission, like the others before it, failed, and already on the 20th the plotting restarted.

The Station notified Langley of the safe arrival of the machine guns and of the intention to keep them there. Dearborn reported the dissidents' anger at the refusal to pass these weapons to them.[82] A few days later, the Station told Headquarters that Antonio de la Maza planned to assassinate Trujillo between 29 April and 2 May, and that he planned to use the carbines 'plus whatever else he could get'. De la Maza also requested access to the machine guns. On the 30th, Dearborn reported that the dissidents' plan was to kill Trujillo via a roadside ambush. Again, the machine guns were requested.[83]

Finally, Bissell relented, writing to the Station that he shared Dearborn's view as to the role of the machine guns as a demonstration of US support, but Bissell's telegram was allegedly never sent. The machine guns – or so it seems – did not move.[84] One day later, in a meeting between a CIA officer and Adolph Berle, Chairman of the Interagency Task Force on Latin America, the latter refused any requests to become involved in the delivery of weapons. He stated

Rafael Trujillo: Assassination and Covert Regime Change

that he could not care less for Trujillo and agreed with the 'general sentiment', but that the United States could not get involved in assassination anywhere in the world.[85] There was more than a hint of Powers's 'assassination spiel', especially since Berle did not seem to play an active role in the plotting, and he might have been excluded from key decisions.

During a NSC meeting on the 5th, the President cautioned that the United States should not 'initiate' the overthrow of Trujillo if no plans for a clear succession emerged.[86] Three days later, in guarded, but unmistakeable, language, the Agency stressed that the best outcome for the Dominican Republic would be Trujillo's death, since 'his continued existence, even outside the country, will pose a serious threat to the establishment of a properly elected government'. Dominicans would also live in fear of his return.[87]

Having travelled back to Washington for consultation, Dearborn met with officials in the State Department, as well as Richard Goodwin and Arthur Schlesinger at the White House. Predictably, Dearborn was later unsure as to the content of these conversations, but he had the impression that Goodwin had been reviewing the cable traffic from the Dominican Republic,[88] which would have included his explicit discussions of assassination plots and of the US government's role in them.[89]

With Dearborn engaged in policy discussions in Washington, Devine shared a list of eight points that should guide the US position. The first of these points stated: 'The USG should not lend itself to *direct* political assassination' (emphasis added). The second lamented that the US moral posture (presumably after the Bay of Pigs) was already tarnished. The third highlighted contradictions in US policy: 'we would be encouraging the action, supplying the weapons, effecting the delivery, and then turning over only the final execution to (unskilled) local triggermen', a complaint that seemingly called for more US involvement.[90]

Having reviewed the situation, Goodwin learnt that the CIA held in custody at the Ciudad Trujillo Station a limited number of weapons and grenades and that it had passed three revolvers and three carbines to dissidents for their 'projected efforts to neutralize Trujillo'.[91] Goodwin recalled that he found 'neutralize' to be 'one of the most brilliant euphemisms' he had ever seen and that he discussed the CIA and assassination with the President.[92] Goodwin was also notified that the CIA had in its custody machine guns and ammunition and that these could be delivered securely to the dissidents if so desired, but no decision to transfer them was made.[93]

On the 16th, Dearborn asked for further instructions on how to deal with the dissidents. The State Department replied – under Goodwin's instruction – that Dearborn needed to follow the President's wish (expressed at the NSC meeting on the 5th) that the United States should not initiate a coup if a political solution was not available. Incredulous, Dearborn replied on the 21st that State Department representatives had been involved for over a year in efforts to overthrow Trujillo and that it was too late to consider whether the US should initiate the overthrow. He asked for further guidance from State.[94]

While awaiting guidance from State, Dearborn's close contact with the dissidents continued. The timing of the assassination – they told Dearborn – now only depended on Trujillo's pattern of behaviour. They also asked for further confirmation regarding support for a post-Trujillo regime. Dearborn replied that the speed of US assistance would be increased if the US had a clearer picture regarding the plan, the timing and the personalities involved, but the dissidents questioned whether this could be done for reasons of security.[95]

* * *

Back in Washington, Goodwin continued working on a draft for instructions to Dearborn. The final text recommended that he continue working with the dissidents, without associating the United States with 'political assassination since US as a matter of general policy cannot condone assassination'. It continued, 'In actual fact we feel that the transfer of arms would serve very little purpose and expose the United States to great danger of association with assassination attempt.'[96]

The cable received mixed reactions. Dearborn did not interpret it as a change in US policy. He interpreted the cable as saying, 'we don't care if the Dominicans assassinate Trujillo, that is all right. But we don't want anything to pin this on us, because we aren't doing it.'[97] The Chief of Station disagreed. He understood that the United States risked being exposed, especially since weapons had been transferred to one of the dissident leaders. The cable seemed like a 'retreat' from previous policy, but he warned: 'HQs aware extent to which US government already associated with assassination. If we are to at least cover up tracks CIA personnel *directly* involved in assassination preparation must be withdrawn' (emphasis added).[98]

In a dynamic not dissimilar to the one we saw in the case of Raul Castro's attempted plane crash, the cable was too late to make much of a difference and those involved in the drafting knew it. Years later, Bissell confirmed the point, adding that 'an important purpose of the cable was for the record to minimize or to counter charges of US association with the assassination attempt'. It was a 'save your ass' cable, Bissell conceded.[99]

This view is confirmed by several pieces of evidence. First, a pristine copy of the telegram has survived, while much of the documentary record of the last two weeks of May 1961 is unavailable.[100] This is not entirely surprising. Dearborn had extensively discussed with Devine the need to 'destroy' their communication.[101] After the assassination of Trujillo, the State Department also ordered Dearborn, if he could do so 'most inconspicuously', to 'destroy any records concerning contacts with the plotters and any related matters',[102] except general contingency plans and this anti-assassination cable.[103]

Second, what has survived beyond the cable itself is its drafting history. Key changes can be identified throughout the drafting process. The draft expressed a concern that a transfer of arms might 'expose the United States to great danger of ultimate disclosure of participation in assassination'. As to association with assassination, the cable read: 'we must not permit *the danger of disclosing US association with* political assassination'.[104] Based on this drafting history, the US government's main concern was not assassination itself but the risk that its involvement in assassination might be exposed. Finally, the coordination and drafting of the cable took two weeks and, in this time, the US government made no practical effort to stop assassination plotting.[105]

On 30 May, Trujillo was ambushed and assassinated as he travelled to one of his mistresses' homes. The plan was the same that had been discussed with US officials. According to US officials, the weapons provided by the United States were not used on the night of the assassination, although they might have been at the scene.[106] This is contradicted by both key protagonists of the plot and Dominican historians. Severo Cabral, one of the plotters, admitted that the three M-1 carbines 'were used in the tyrannicide'. Dominican historian Emilio Cordero Michel also adds that two of the pistols were taken by the plotters to the scene of the assassination.[107]

Conclusion

During a post-assassination meeting at the White House, Dearborn recalled, as other officials were discussing the future of the Dominican Republic, he interrupted and said 'I think that . . .' Suddenly, the President cut him off and said, 'We already know what you think.'[108] Dearborn interpreted this as evidence that the President had been reading his cables. At the end of the meeting, Kennedy reportedly took Dearborn aside and told him: 'You did a good job for us down there.'[109] The point is confirmed by former CIA Inspector General Scott Breckinridge, who wrote that 'the highest levels of the government in two administrations supported the coup group and . . . believed the objective could be achieved only by killing Trujillo'.[110]

Contacts with the dissidents had started under Eisenhower. By the summer of 1960, it was clear that the capabilities of the dissident group were limited, and that assassination was their preferred path to removing Trujillo. With few intermissions, support for the dissidents remained the backbone of US policy. Both Dearborn and the CIA's Chief of Station established 'direct contact' with dissidents whose 'sole aim . . . was to bring about the assassination of General Trujillo'.[111] Awareness of these contacts and their purpose reached the White House. Breckinridge recalled that 'there was daily correspondence and communication and consultation between the State, the CIA, and the White House, and that there were . . . dozens of people involved in a constant consultation', with 'no compartmentation'. It was a 'joint effort'.[112]

Rafael Trujillo: Assassination and Covert Regime Change

The Trujillo case, while indirect, showcases a high degree of US government involvement in and support for assassination. Weapons were delivered on at least two occasions and US officials at times acted as spokesmen for the dissidents in Washington, emphasising their requests for more support.[113] CIA officials also acted as advisers reviewing and assessing assassination plans. Debates within the US government also covered assassination in explicit terms. The term 'assassination' often featured in telegrams and memorandums. US officials (overall) showed little compunction at being involved in assassination. A perfunctory effort was made to distance the US government from assassination, but the objective was to massage the historical record and to avoid controversial disclosures. There were no moral qualms and many actors reflected on the appropriateness of assassination as an attempt to save lives.

In later years, Dearborn suggested that the killing of Trujillo would have happened even without US support. This is disingenuous. Yes, the killing itself would have happened without the US material support (the three carbines and the three pistols). The US government's posture and its support for Trujillo's assassination, though, provided an invaluable psychological and political boost to the plotters. Combined with the material and logistical support, this made the assassination inevitable.[114] In the following years, another US ally started to be perceived as a threat to US interests, Ngo Dinh Diem of South Vietnam. The picture is somewhat more complex, but the conclusion was the same: he had to go.

Notes

1. Senate Select Committee to Study Governmental Operations with Respect to Intelligence Activities (SSCIA), Interim Report: Alleged Assassination Plots Involving Foreign Leaders (Interim Report) (Washington, DC: US Government Printing Office, 1975), 199.
2. Stephen Rabe, *The Most Dangerous Area in the World* (Chapel Hill: University of North Carolina Press, 1999), 35.
3. Rabe, *The Most Dangerous*, 35; Joseph Farland, Oral History Interview, Association for Diplomatic Studies and Training (ADST), available at https://adst.org/OH%20TOCs/Farland,%20Joseph%20S.toc.pdf (accessed 23 October 2023), 20.

4. Farland, Oral History Interview, 20.
5. David Talbot, *The Devil's Chessboard* (New York: William Collins, 2016), 322.
6. Alex von Tunzelmann, *Red Heat* (New York: Simon & Schuster, 2011), 92–3; Bernard Diederich, *Trujillo: The Death of the Dictator* (Princeton, NJ: Marcus Wiener, 1990), 9.
7. 'Carta dejada por Octavio de la Maza', Colección Bernardo Vega, Archivo General de la Nación, Republica Dominicana, available at http://consulta.agn.gob.do/cbvnode/app.html#/details (accessed 23 October 2023).
8. Trujillo had tried to solve the problem by arranging the failed invasion of Cuba, discussed in the previous chapter.
9. Farland, Oral History Interview, 19.
10. Diederich, *Trujillo*, 48.
11. Bernardo Vega (former Dominican Ambassador to the United States), Skype interview with the author, 5 May 2022.
12. Bernardo Vega, 'Wimpy por fin habla', *Imágenes de nuestra historia*, 24 February 2015, available at https://www.facebook.com/imagenes-denuestrahistoriard/photos/wimpy-por-fin-habla-por-bernardo-vega-lorenzo-berry-mejor-conocido-como-wimpy-nu/826193817415990/ (accessed 23 October 2023).
13. William Colby, 'Assassinations' Memorandum to Philip Buchen, 16/6/1975, JFK Assassination Records (JFKAR) 178-10003-10377.
14. CIA, Inspector General Report – Trujillo (IG Report), 1967, 16. In December 2022, a less redacted version of the same report was released. CIA, IG Report December 2022 is used below when information is taken from this later version. SSCIA, Interim Report, 192.
15. Anthony Carrozza, *William Pawley* (Washington, DC: Potomac Books, 2012); Max Holland, 'Private Sources of U.S. Foreign Policy: William Pawley and the 1954 Coup d'État in Guatemala', *Journal of Cold War Studies*, 7.4 (2005), 36–73.
16. Telegram, Chief of Station, Ciudad Trujillo to Chief WH division, 12/6/1958, JFKAR 104-10049-10375.
17. Michael Hall, *Sugar and Power in the Dominican Republic* (London: Greenwood Press, 2000), 94.
18. CIA, IG Report, 18.
19. Memorandum Farland to Rubottom, 22/3/1960, General Records State – Decimal File 739.00 – Dominican Republic, Box 1636, Folder 739.00/3-160, NARA; CIA, IG Report, 19. See the version of the report released in JFKAR 104-10214-10034, 21.
20. Memorandum Farland to Rubottom, 22/3/1960.

21. CIA, IG Report, 20–1.
22. Bernardo Vega, *Los Estados Unidos y Trujillo: los días finales, 1960–1961* (Santo Domingo: Fundación Cultura Dominicana, 1999), 190.
23. Herter, Memorandum for the President, 14/4/1960, General Records State – Decimal File 739.00 – Dominican Republic, Box 1636, Folder 739.00/3-160, NARA.
24. Vega, *Los Estados Unidos*, 193.
25. Richard Bissell, SSCIA Testimony, 22/7/1975, DNSA, Covert Operations II, 77.
26. CIA, IG Report, 22–3.
27. Stephen Rabe, 'Eisenhower and the Overthrow of Rafael Trujillo', *Conflict Quarterly*, 6 (1986), 39.
28. Carrozza, *William Pawley*, 284.
29. Vega, *Los Estados Unidos*, 246.
30. CIA, IG Report, 25; SSCIA, Interim Report, 193.
31. Vega, *Los Estados Unidos*, 317.
32. CIA, IG Report, 26.
33. Vega, *Los Estados Unidos*, 306.
34. Henry Dearborn, Oral History Interview, ADST, 24/4/1991, available at https://www.adst.org/OH%20TOCs/Dearborn,%20Henry.toc.pdf?_ga=2.78585044.1552135724.1558425638-1442121572.1558425638 (accessed 23 October 2023), 41.
35. Vega, *Los Estados Unidos*, 311.
36. Ibid., 360; SSCIA, Interim Report, 195.
37. SSCIA, Interim Report, 195.
38. Diederich, *Trujillo*, 53.
39. Vega, *Los Estados Unidos*, 449.
40. SSCIA, Interim Report, 196.
41. Stephen G. Rabe, 'The Caribbean Triangle: Betancourt, Castro, Trujillo, and US Foreign Policy 1958-1963', *Diplomatic History*, 20.1 (1996), 70.
42. Memorandum, 'CIA Covert Activities Dominican Republic', 13/5/1961, DNSA Covert Operations III.
43. Summary of CIA intelligence operations, undated, DNSA – Covert Operations III.
44. Vega, *Los Estados Unidos*, 510, 529; Vega, Interview with the author.
45. Summary of CIA intelligence operations; SSCIA, Interim Report, 197.
46. Vega, *Los Estados Unidos*, 525.
47. Marvin Gray, 'Interview with Frank Devine', Memorandum for the file, 26/4/1975, DNSA Covert Operations II; Philip Agee, *Inside the Company: CIA Diary* (New York: Stonehill, 1975), 366.

48. Conference with Source 1 and Source 2, 13/2/1961, DNSA, Covert Operations III.
49. Memorandum C/WH3 for the record, Meeting with [redacted] and his cousin, 16/2/1961, DNSA Covert Operations III.
50. CIA, IG Report, 32.
51. Memorandum, Bundy to Secretary of State, 13/2/1961, DNSA, Covert Operations III.
52. Memorandum for the President, 'The Dominican Republic', 15/2/1961, DNSA, Covert Operations III.
53. SSCIA, Interim Report, 204.
54. Richard Bissell, Memorandum for Bundy, 17/2/1961, DNSA Covert Operations III.
55. Lindsey O'Rourke, *Covert Regime Change* (Ithaca, NY: Cornell University Press, 2018), 197; Bissell, Testimony, 92.
56. A plan not unlike the one discussed by Vicini with Holman.
57. Telegram from Ciudad Trujillo to Director, 15/2/1961, DNSA Covert Operations III.
58. CIA, IG Report, 32–4, December 2022.
59. Ibid., 34.
60. Ibid., December 2022 release, 35.
61. SSCIA, Interim Report, 199.
62. CIA, IG Report, 35
63. SSCIA, Interim Report, 199.
64. Summary of CIA intelligence operations, undated, DNSA Covert Operations III; SSCIA, Interim Report, 200.
65. Vega, *Los Estados Unidos*, 562.
66. Telegram, Station to Director, 20/3/1961, DNSA, Covert Operations III.
67. A February 1961 State Department's decision had made the Dearborn–Devine personal correspondence a matter of official record. Vega, *Los Estados Unidos*, 541.
68. Telegram, Dearborn to State, 22/3/1961, Colección Bernardo Vega.
69. CIA, IG Report, 35–6.
70. Telegram Bissell to Dominican Republic, 25/3/1961, DNSA, Covert Operations III.
71. Frank Moya Pons, 'El 30 de mayo: a 60 años de la gesta', *Precision*, 24 May 2021, available at https://precision.com.do/archivo-general-de-la-nacion-invita-a-panel-el-30-de-mayo-a-60-anos-de-la-gesta/ (accessed 24 October 2023); Vega, *Los Estados Unidos*, 564.
72. Vega, *Los Estados Unidos*, 573.
73. The telegram agreeing to the transfer was signed by Bissell himself. CIA, IG Report, 38; SSCIA, Interim Report, 200.

74. CIA, IG Report, 39.
75. Vega, Interview with the author; CIA, IG Report, 39; CIA, IG Report, December 2022, 40, 61.
76. CIA, IG Report, 42.
77. Memorandum for Chief, RI, 'Pouch restriction waiver request and certification', 7/4/1961, DNSA Covert Operations III; SSCIA, 'Testimony of Richard Bissell', Subject: 'Question 3 of 4 questions developed during SSC Hearing of Mr Richard Bissell on 12 June 1975', 23/6/1975, JFKAR 157-10011-10017, 2.
78. Von Tunzelmann, *Red Heat*, 259.
79. CIA, IG Report, 44.
80. Memorandum for Earle Wheeler to Clifton, 5/5/1961, DNSA, Covert Operations, III.
81. Von Tunzelmann, *Red Heat*, 228–9.
82. CIA, IG Report, 44.
83. CIA, IG Report, 45–6.
84. Allegedly the telegram, while signed by Bissell and released by Dulles, was never sent. SSCIA, Interim Report, 207; Richard Bissell, Memorandum from Director to [redacted], 2/5/1961, DNSA Covert Operations III.
85. Memorandum, Subject: Dominican Republic, 3/5/1961, DNSA Covert Operations III.
86. SSCIA, Interim Report, 209.
87. JFK Digital Collection, Dominican Republic General, 1/61-6/61, 9 (of document), 57 of folder, available at https://www.jfklibrary.org/asset-viewer/archives/JFKNSF/066/JFKNSF-066-001 (accessed 24 October 2023).
88. SSCIA, Interim Report, 210. Thomas Hughes later confirmed Dearborn's hunch, saying that Goodwin and Schlesinger certainly read the cable traffic. Thomas L. Hughes, Interviewed by Charles Stuart Kennedy, 7/7/1999, ADST Oral History Project, available at https://adst.org/OH%20TOCs/Hughes,%20Thomas%20L.toc.pdf (accessed 24 October 2023), 125.
89. Richard Goodwin, *Remembering America* (New York: Little, Brown, 1988), 210.
90. SSCIA, Interim Report, 206.
91. Ibid., 211.
92. Richard Goodwin, Testimony to SSCIA, 18/7/1975, DNSA Covert Operations II, 49.
93. SSCIA, Interim Report, 211.
94. CIA, IG Report, 50.

95. Ibid., 50–1.
96. Telegram for CIA officer from State, 29/5/1961, DNSA Covert Operations III.
97. SSCIA, Interim Report, 213.
98. CIA, IG Report, 52; SSCIA, Interim Report, 214.
99. SSCIA, Bissell Testimony, 138.
100. Sections of the CIA Inspector General report dealing with the Trujillo assassination remain redacted. CIA denied the author's FOIA (Freedom of Information Act) request for further disclosure.
101. Letter Dearborn to Devine, 2/5/1961, Coleccion Bernardo Vega.
102. Rockefeller Commission 'Summary of Facts: Investigation of CIA involvement in plans to assassinate foreign leaders', 5/6/1975, National Security Archives, available at https://nsarchive.gwu.edu/document/21512-document-19 (accessed 24 October 2023), 84.
103. SSCIA, Interim Report, 214.
104. Draft version of memorandum of 29 May to Dearborn, DNSA Covert Operations III.
105. O'Rourke, *Covert*, 206.
106. William Colby, Testimony to SSCIA, 4/6/1975, DNSA Covert Operations II, 26.
107. Vega, *Los Estados Unidos*, 656.
108. Dearborn, Oral History Interview, 40.
109. Hanry Dearborn, Letter to Senator Frank Church, 29/11/1975, Frank Church Papers, Series 2.6, Select Committee 1966–1975, Folder 2/2, Albertson Library, Boise State University.
110. Scott Breckinridge, *CIA and the Cold War: A Memoir* (London: Praeger, 1993), 117.
111. 'Review of Station Santo Domingo, Operations 1 January 1961 to present', 22/1/1962, NSAr, CIA File, Robert Borosage Collection, Washington, DC.
112. Colby, Testimony, 111.
113. See contradictions in Colby testimony to SSCIA, 39, 65.
114. Vega, Interview with the author.

5 Ngo Dinh Diem: Preparing the Ground for Assassination

On 1 November 1963, explosions filled the air in Saigon. A coup had started in the early hours of the morning. Mutinous troops had taken over buildings and key points in the city; many troops loyal to the regime had surrendered. South Vietnamese President Ngo Dinh Diem had refused to answer calls from the mutinous generals throughout the day. At 4 p.m. (Saigon time) he had finally answered the phone but had refused the generals' offer of safe passage in exchange for surrender.[1] He still held out hope that the United States could come to his rescue.

At 4.30 p.m., Diem called US Ambassador Henry Cabot Lodge. 'Some units have made a rebellion and I want to know what is the attitude of the U.S.', Diem asked.

Lodge, one of the key figures in orchestrating US support for the coup, evaded the question:

> I do not feel well enough informed to be able to tell you. I have heard the shooting but am not acquainted with all the facts. Also, it is 4:30 a.m. in Washington and the U.S. Government cannot possibly have a view.

Diem did not buy it. 'But you must have some general ideas,' he said. 'After all, I am a Chief of State. I have tried to do my duty.'

Lodge conceded the point: 'You certainly have done your duty.' He also expressed his concern for Diem's physical safety: 'I have a report that those in charge of the current activity offer you and your brother safe conduct out of the country if you will resign. Had you heard this?'

Diem lied: 'No . . . You have my telephone number.'

The call concluded with Lodge pledging help for Diem's safety.[2] In a matter of hours, Diem and his brother Ngo Dinh Nhu were dead, shot in the back of an armoured vehicle by the bodyguard of General Duong Van Minh, the coup's leader.

* * *

In the early 1960s, US government involvement in South Vietnam increased. The survival of the South Vietnamese regime as well as its continuation of the conflict against the North became US priorities. Like Trujillo, Diem had been a staunch ally of the United States, but many had started to see him as an obstacle to the pursuit of the US government's foreign policy goals.

The Kennedy Administration, through its ambassador and the CIA, established contact with a group of disgruntled generals. It nurtured their efforts and provided encouragement for their coup. The US government established a system of incentives and sanctions for the generals, never making the survival of Diem part of the deal – far from it. While discussions of assassination were less explicit than in case of Trujillo, the assassination of Diem (and his brother Nhu) was always understood as a likely outcome of the US-sponsored coup. Despite having several officials on the ground during the coup, including one at the mutinous generals' headquarters, the United States refused opportunities to save Diem. Having made assassination a possible – and likely – outcome, the US left Diem and Nhu in the hands of the plotters. In 1975, the Church Committee's investigation of the assassination of Diem concluded that it was carried out 'without United States involvement or support'.[3] The episode showcases a more indirect level of US involvement in assassination, but the committee's timid conclusion must be revised.

Trouble Begins: Diem and the Buddhist Protests

On 7 May 1963, Lucien Conein was in Hue, in central Vietnam, as liaison between the CIA and the South Vietnamese Ministry of Interior, inspecting the progress of the Strategic Hamlets programme. Based on his previous experience in Vietnam,[4] Conein had come to know the generals gathering in Hue but was told

Ngo Dinh Diem: Preparing the Ground for Assassination

that he could not stay. According to Conein, at the meeting the generals decided to crack down on Buddhists.[5] On 8 May, as Buddhists gathered to celebrate the 2,527th birthday of Buddha, government forces fired on the gathering. The pretext was that the ceremony had violated a ban on flying religious flags. The ban had not been enforced a week earlier, when Catholics were permitted to fly papal banners to celebrate the 25th anniversary of Ngo Dinh Thuc's (Diem's brother) ordination.[6]

The government initially blamed the Viet Cong and refused to accept responsibility even after it became clear that the Army was to blame. Widespread protests followed, soon turning political and increasing throughout the summer. The protests culminated in the martyrdom of Buddhist monks, famously met with contempt by Nhu and his wife Madame Nhu.[7] On 16 June, the Buddhists and the government seemed close to reaching an agreement on a set of measures proposed by the monks, but the government gave no sign of interest in implementing its provisions.[8]

In Washington, the news of the protest did nothing to bolster Diem's cause. Some US officials, particularly in the State Department and White House, already saw with irritation Diem's resistance to American proposals for suppressing the communist-led insurgency[9] and his reluctance to seriously engage with US officials in Saigon.[10] Diem's detractors in Washington told President Kennedy that the US government needed to press him harder and that any future support had to be made conditional on political, economic and military reforms.[11]

As the protests escalated, US officials identified Nhu as the main culprit, but recognised that Diem was unlikely to separate himself from Nhu. After a meeting in which the possibility of a coup against Diem was raised for the first time, Secretary of State Dean Rusk cabled the US Embassy in Saigon stating that Diem had to 'unequivocally meet Buddhist demands', otherwise the United States would have to 're-examine' the 'entire relationship' with his regime.[12] Three days later, Rusk followed up with a more specific instruction: 'Suggest you consider steps gradually increase covert and overt contacts with non-supporters of GVN.'[13] The aim was to improve US intelligence and the US government's position in case of a coup.[14]

In early July, the CIA stressed the possibility of a palace coup which was likely to involve the assassination of Nhu and his wife and, potentially, the 'elimination' of Diem through less forceful means.[15] On the 10th, a CIA Special National Intelligence Estimate (NIE) concluded that if Diem did not fulfil his 16 June commitments, 'chances of a non-communist assassination or coup attempt against Diem will be better than even'.[16] Meanwhile, Nhu was able to nip in the bud any potential coup by arranging an almost 'psychoanalytic' meeting with South Vietnam's leading generals, discussing with them how to carry out a successful coup. Spooked and confused, the generals dropped any plan.[17]

By mid-August, Vietnam had become a priority for the Administration.[18] Kennedy decided to recall Ambassador Fritz Nolting, seen by many as too aligned with Diem. As a replacement, Kennedy settled on Henry Cabot Lodge, a former Republican Senator, US Ambassador to the UN under Eisenhower, and former vice-presidential candidate defeated by Kennedy and Johnson in 1960. The possibility of a coup against Diem was front and centre in Lodge's pre-departure meeting with Kennedy on 15 August. 'The time may come,' Kennedy told Lodge, 'Though, we've gotta just have to try to do something about Diem.' Lodge agreed. He reported that he shared the views of Madame Chuong, mother of Madame Nhu and wife of the Vietnamese Ambassador to the United States Tran Van Chuong. The ambassador had resigned in protest at the violence against the Buddhists. Madame Chuong had told Lodge that unless the Nhus left the country, there was 'nothing on earth' that could prevent their assassination and that of Diem.[19]

To Kennedy, a coup seemed likely. He told Lodge: 'I don't know how well prepared you are for that out there, or who we would sort of support, or who we would – and – I think that's going to be the key – your key problem this year.' Having heard Lodge's references to the possibility of assassination, the President seemed unperturbed. He added: 'It may be that they ought to go, but it's just a question of how quickly that's done, and if you get the right fellow . . .' Assassination, or so it seems, was not only a likely policy outcome, but also an acceptable policy option. As in the case of Trujillo, Kennedy seemed more concerned about the political aftermath of the assassination than about the assassination itself. The President concluded the meeting by stressing his full confidence in

Ngo Dinh Diem: Preparing the Ground for Assassination

Lodge: 'I think we have to leave it almost completely in your hands and your judgment.' Lodge, again, stressed the possibility that 'they all' might get assassinated, and the President simply moved on, inquiring whether Madame Nhu was a lesbian.[20]

In Vietnam, Diem correctly saw the change of ambassador as an ominous development. Still dealing with the protests, Vietnamese generals had proposed imposing martial law to bring the Buddhists back to their pagodas and restore order. While Diem agreed,[21] Nhu decided to use the generals' initiative as a ploy. On 21 August, he deployed his US-trained special forces to raid the pagodas and arrest 1,400 Buddhists. The aim was twofold: put the blame on the Army, thus turning the people against it, and present incoming Ambassador Lodge with a fait accompli.[22] The plan backfired.

On the 22nd, Lodge's first day on the job, Vietnamese generals contacted Conein and a former CIA official, Rufus Phillips, then working at the economic aid mission. They wanted to make clear that the Army was not responsible for the raid on the pagodas. They also sent out feelers regarding a possible coup. Having been briefed on these meetings, Lodge cabled Washington: 'Suggestion has been made that US has only to indicate to "Generals" that it would be happy to see Diem and/or Nhu go, and deed would be done.' The cable added a note of scepticism: 'Situation is not so simple, in our view.'[23] The reply to Lodge's request for instructions became one of the most controversial telegrams of the Vietnam War.

The cable stated that the United States could not 'tolerate' Nhu in a position of power, that the new ambassador should give Diem a chance to 'rid himself of Nhu', but if he refused the US was prepared to accept that it could 'no longer support Diem'. The telegram expressed full confidence in Lodge and encouraged him to explore alternative leadership options and to tell the generals that a new government would receive direct support in case of breakdown of the central government.[24] It was a green light for a coup.

With principals out of town on vacation, the drafting of the cable fell to (more) junior and – crucially – anti-Diem officials including Roger Hilsman, Director of Intelligence and Research at State, and Michael Forrestal at the White House. Officials at all levels of the US government, though, including Rusk, McNamara and the President, were involved in the policy decisions. They knew (and approved) of the cable.[25] The instructions, after all, weren't too dissimilar to those Kennedy had given Lodge in their first meeting.

In Vietnam, having received the cable, Lodge refused the suggestion that the United States should try one last time to convince Diem and, instead, went straight to the generals to express US support. At the White House, Forrestal told Kennedy that while the US might prefer to retain Diem in office, this seemed increasingly unlikely. As Forrestal concluded: 'we should leave to the Vietnamese military leaders the decision whether Diem can be preserved'.[26] This was an early indication that the US government was keen to support a coup and ready to wash its hands of Diem.

On the 26th, Conein was authorised to outline the new American policy to two of the generals. In line with Forrestal's memorandum to Kennedy, the policy was that Nhu had to go, but it was up to the generals what they did with Diem. Furthermore, the United States established a series of sanctions and incentives for the generals to proceed. The incentives were such that – after the coup had succeeded – the US would help the generals and provide material and financial support to the new government. As to the sanctions, as Luke Nichter wrote, 'if the Nhus did not go and the Buddhist situation was not addressed as indicated, the United States would no longer continue military or economic support'.[27] US support for the coup was made contingent on certain political measures, but not on the safety of Diem.

In the following days, debate emerged in Washington about the appropriateness of the 24 August telegram, but it was never withdrawn. The Administration, though, appeared divided on how to proceed.[28] Intelligence pointed to an unclear balance between pro-coup and anti-coup forces. The United States, the President warned, should not 'go into a coup' merely because it felt it had to. The President also commented that 'he assumed some form of exile would be best for Diem and Nhu and he assumed that we would not want any harm to happen to either if we had anything to do with it',[29] a stronger position for the record than the one expressed in the secret meeting with Lodge.

From Saigon, Lodge cabled that 'the game had started'. The generals mistrusted the United States and any further request to Diem to abandon the Nhus would be taken as a sign of US indecision.[30]

Even John Richardson, the CIA Station chief who had traditionally aligned with Diem and Nhu, agreed that the US had reached a 'point of no return' and the coup had a good chance of succeeding.[31] Rusk asked Lodge whether a final attempt could be made to detach Diem from the Nhus. Lodge was opposed; the best option to remove the Nhus was 'by the Generals taking over the government lock, stock, and barrel'.[32]

On the 29th, Hilsman reminded the President that the US government's 'approach to the Generals specified that the decision on whether or not Diem should be retained was up to them'.[33] Throughout the process, Kennedy was very much in charge, and he took every opportunity to confirm his confidence in Lodge.[34] While making clear that he reserved the right to withdraw support at the last minute – perhaps a lesson learnt in the Bay of Pigs – he also wrote to Lodge: 'I have approved all the messages you are receiving from others today, and I emphasize that everything in these messages has my full support. We will do all that we can to help you conclude this operation successfully.'[35]

In the last days of August, the coup petered out. The generals had requested a halt in economic aid to the Diem regime as a sign of support. The White House had refused; instead Lodge had only provided some intelligence. As Lodge had warned, the generals interpreted this half-hearted measure as a sign of wavering US support. The collapse of the coup – based on a less than ironclad US support – showed the extent of the generals' reliance on the US government's approval and support, and, consequently, the US government's ability to stop the coup if it wanted to.[36]

From Reset to Assassination

In the aftermath of the coup's collapse, the US government reassessed its policy towards Diem. In a NSC meeting on 17 September, two options emerged: an effort to re-establish a modus vivendi with the Diem government, or a policy of increased economic pressure to weaken the regime. The second policy option was approved. The President also decided to send Secretary of Defence Robert McNamara and General Maxwell Taylor on a mission to

Vietnam to assess the political and military situation in the country. Lodge was opposed to the mission. He had adopted a stance of ignoring the regime and such a high-profile mission would have required renewing engagement with Diem.[37]

On the topic at hand, the McNamara–Taylor report included the recognition that – with the tense situation in Saigon – the assassination of Diem and Nhu was always a possibility.[38] The report recommended that no active measures be taken to encourage a coup but added that US officials in Saigon – while keeping the pressure on Diem – should 'urgently . . . identify and build contacts with alternative leadership if and when it appears'.[39]

In Washington's eyes, the position of the South Vietnamese government had become even more untenable. First, the government was increasing its repression and police state tactics.[40] Second, rumours started to spread that Nhu had been talking to emissaries of North Vietnam. These contacts, allegedly developed through French and Polish diplomats, aimed at reaching a provisional agreement on the future of the country, which would include the departure of US advisers.[41]

On 2 October, coup rumours resurfaced. During an 'accidental' meeting with Conein at Saigon airport, General Tran Van Don told the CIA official that the generals were planning another coup for the end of October or start of November, and that they should talk. Having received permission from William Truehart (Lodge's deputy), Conein attended a follow-up meeting with Don on the same day. The generals, Don stated, had a real plan, and only required a signal of US moral support. Conein should meet with General Duong Van Minh, known as 'Big Minh', who oversaw the coup plotting. Lodge authorised the meeting.[42]

In the meantime, Lodge had moved to strengthen his control of US policy in Vietnam. He had obtained the removal of CIA Chief of Station Richardson. The generals interpreted Richardson's departure as a sign of support for a coup. They had always considered Richardson a close ally of Nhu.[43] Lodge had asked the President to replace Richardson with Edward Lansdale.[44] After Lodge's request, Lansdale reportedly met with Kennedy. The President asked whether he would be willing to return to Vietnam and convince Diem to get rid of Nhu. Lansdale agreed. According to

Ngo Dinh Diem: Preparing the Ground for Assassination

Seymour Hersh, the President went further. He asked whether – if he (Kennedy) changed his mind – Lansdale would help in also getting rid of Diem himself, a proposal Lansdale refused.[45]

On the 5th, Conein met with Minh who presented three possible coup options: the assassination of Nhu and Diem's other brother, Ngo Dinh Can; a military encirclement of Saigon; and a direct confrontation in Saigon between the generals' troops and units loyal to the regime.[46] On the same day, the Station reported the meeting to Washington. Minh, the telegram read, did not need US material support to carry out the coup, but he wanted 'American assurances that the USG will not attempt to thwart this plan'.[47] Supportive of Conein's endeavours, Lodge wrote to Rusk asking for instructions. He proposed that the US government assure Minh that it 'will not attempt to thwart his plans'. The government should also 'offer to view his plans, other than assassination plans' – a difference with the Trujillo plots – and confirm that economic aid would continue under a new regime that promised to gain the support of the people and win the war.[48]

Having heard from Conein about the three options proposed by Minh, David Smith, acting CIA Chief of Station, sent a message to Lodge and Trueheart. Smith recommended against setting the US government 'irrevocably against the assassination plot, since the other two alternatives mean either a bloodbath in Saigon or a protracted struggle which would rip the Army and the country asunder'.[49] In this sense, assassination was distasteful but could be effective in limiting the amount of violence. Informed of Smith's recommendation, CIA Director McCone sent a cable to Saigon recommending a hands-off approach:

> Believe assassination discussion need most careful handling ... We certainly cannot be in a position of stimulating, approving or supporting assassination, but on other hand, we are in no way responsible for stopping every such threat of which we might receive even partial knowledge. We certainly would not favour assassination of Diem.[50]

The message left unsaid what the US government thought about the assassination of Nhu and Can. Furthermore, it clearly gave the impression that Washington and Langley were washing their hands of the matter.

To clarify US policy, McCone met with the President and the Attorney General. While circumlocutory language was used, it seems that assassination was discussed. The President agreed with McCone's stand-off position.[51] Sceptical about the chances of success of a coup, McCone told the President: 'if I was the manager of a baseball team and I had one pitcher, I'd keep him in the box whether he was a good pitcher or not'.[52] The following day, McCone sent a stronger message on the topic of assassination. He directed that Smith's recommendation be withdrawn because the US government 'cannot be in position actively condoning such course of action and thereby engaging our responsibility'.[53]

McCone later testified that – in the case of Vietnam – his opposition to assassination was not moral, but strategic. He understood the situation in Vietnam as a war, and, hence, assassination to be permissible. However, he was concerned about the risks of US exposure and of instability in the country. Such instability could affect the conduct of the war. Furthermore, William Colby, then Chief of the CIA's Far East Division, who had been drafting McCone's cables to Saigon, also wrote that the assassinations of Nhu and Can were to continue.[54] Back in Saigon, Conein reported the handwringing over assassination to the generals, who were unimpressed. As he recalled, they simply responded: 'You don't like it like that? Well, we'll do it our own way anyhow . . . we won't talk about it anymore.'[55] This was enough for Conein.

On 5 October, the White House cabled Saigon to warn against any initiative that might be understood as covert encouragement for a coup, but the same telegram also asked the Ambassador to build contacts with 'possible alternative leadership'.[56] On the 9th, the CIA restated the US position to the Station in Saigon: 'While we do not wish to stimulate a coup, we also do not wish to leave the impression that US would thwart a change of government or deny economic and military aid to a new regime.' The cable also instructed the Station to request more detailed information regarding the individuals involved and the conduct of the coup, to assess its chances of success.[57]

Through the linguistic gymnastics typical of covert operations, the Administration had settled on an ambiguous policy of 'not thwarting' a coup. The US government needed to stay as far away

Ngo Dinh Diem: Preparing the Ground for Assassination

as possible from the details of the plan to preserve plausible deniability, but, at the same time, it wanted to gather information, to be able to advise the generals and guarantee the coup's success. Of course, the distinction between not thwarting a coup and supporting one was feeble, especially since, as in the August plot, the United States had established a system of incentives for the generals. Richardson (mistrusted by the generals) had been recalled. The US had pledged economic and military aid to the generals if the coup was successful. Lodge had also cut off from the decision-making process General Paul Harkins, Commander of the Military Assistance Command – Vietnam, who had generally opposed a coup.[58]

In the following days, contacts between Conein and Don continued.[59] Having been warned against a coup by the unwitting Harkins, Don bombarded Conein with questions regarding the US government's position and support. Conein reassured Don: the policy of 'not thwarting' the coup had not changed. The risks for all involved were clear. 'Mon vieux,' Conein told Don, 'I love my lily-white skin as much as you love your yellow skin, and I'm not going to take any chances. They can bump me off and call it a Vietcong incident, and nobody'll know the difference.' Harkins was simply unaware of US policy. As leading Vietnam historian Stanley Karnow has written, Don's questions are emblematic: 'they suggested, once again, that the conspirators were desperately anxious for U.S. approval and might cancel the coup were it not forthcoming'.[60] As in August, while the US government was in no position to guarantee the ultimate success of the coup, it had the power to turn the coup on or off at will.

On the 28th, having received further assurances from Lodge, Don told Conein that the coup was imminent and to stay at home starting on 30 October. Don said that the US Ambassador would be given plans of the coup, though not forty-eight hours in advance as the two had previously agreed, but only four hours in advance.[61]

The Station reported to headquarters that – at such a late stage – 'no positive action' from the US government could have prevented a coup, except, perhaps betraying the coup plotters to Diem and Nhu. The Station expected requests from the generals for materiel and financial support.[62] On the 29th, last-minute doubts started to

143

emerge in Washington.⁶³ Lodge made sure that, this time, US support did not waiver. He warned the White House that the plotters might ask for funds 'to buy off potential opposition' and that the US should oblige if it could be done discreetly.⁶⁴ A 4 p.m. meeting at the White House recognised the odd position of Lodge. A trip back to Washington would have raised alarm bells, but his presence in the country during the coup would have made a mockery of 'plausible denial'.⁶⁵

In Saigon, rumours of a pending coup started swirling. Adding to the confusion and to the slow reaction from Diem, Nhu had been scheming to preserve the regime, engineering a fake coup that would reinstall Diem and Nhu in power.⁶⁶ On 1 November, the real coup struck.

* * *

At 1.15 p.m. Saigon time, an aide-de-camp to General Don went to Conein's house to let him know that the coup was in progress. The United States had been given four minutes', not four hours', notice.⁶⁷ Conein was ready. Surely, he had in his mind Lodge's recent warning that if the coup failed, 'he would see to it that Conein never worked another day for the US government'.⁶⁸ The Ambassador, or so Conein recalled, would have denied that he even existed.⁶⁹ He changed into his uniform, asked Phillips to take care of his family, grabbed a .38-caliber revolver, and hopped on a jeep. Conein also took with him 3 million piastres from his house's safe.⁷⁰ In the preceding days, following guidelines from Lodge, the CIA had also stored 5 million piastres (equivalent to US$68,000) in a safe at the Station. The money was used to reward military units who joined the coup and to buy their loyalty, a sign that US officials in Vietnam had moved past the stand-offish policy of not thwarting the coup.⁷¹ Conein travelled to the Joint General Staff (JGS), the coup plotters' headquarters. He remained there throughout the coup. Conein was able to communicate via radio and through a telephone line to the Embassy. The line had been spared when the generals had cut telephone lines.⁷²

With the fighting in Saigon escalating, Diem and Nhu remained in the presidential palace. Nhu was initially convinced that his

Ngo Dinh Diem: Preparing the Ground for Assassination

countercoup would soon commence. By the time the two brothers realised that this was a real coup, it was probably too late. When one of the units involved in the coup got bogged down, Conein took the initiative and told the generals: 'Once you are into the attack you must continue. If you hesitate you are going to be lost.'[73] At 1.40, the generals called the palace. They promised safe passage for the two brothers if they surrendered. Otherwise, they warned, the palace would be attacked at 3.30 p.m. By 1.45, the palace was surrounded. The stand-off continued for the rest of the afternoon, with Diem either refusing to pick up the phone or rejecting the generals' request to surrender. Diem called Lodge at 4.30.

At 4.45, the generals – with Conein at the compound – called Diem again. This time, they asked Colonel Le Quang Tung – head of the Special Forces and Diem loyalist – to speak to Diem. The Colonel told the President that the rebels had captured key civilian installations and that there was nothing left to do but surrender. As soon as he hung up, the Colonel and his brother, deputy head of the Special Forces, were driven to a different area of the JGS compound and shot by troops loyal to General Minh.[74]

At 5.15, Minh called the palace again, but Diem hung up. One hour and 30 minutes later, Minh ordered his troops to move on the palace. With no sign of surrender and struggling to contain his fury, Minh again called Diem. If he refused to surrender, the General told the besieged President, he would be 'blasted off the face of the earth'. With no response, at 9.40 p.m. Minh launched the first air assault on the palace. The forces at the palace soon surrendered but Minh felt humiliated when he travelled to the palace in full pomp to discover that the brothers weren't there. Diem and Nhu had fled the palace by using a system of secret tunnels. They had reached the safe house of a regime loyalist. The house had been fitted with a phone line hooked to the presidential palace, giving the impression that Diem was still there and in control.[75] At 6.20 a.m. on 2 November, Diem called Don, pledging to surrender in exchange for safe conduct to the airport and free departure from Vietnam. Half an hour later, he called again to surrender unconditionally.

At this stage, Don and Minh asked Conein to secure an aircraft that could take the brothers to safety. Conein passed the request to Acting Chief of Station Smith, who replied that the Agency would prefer if the aircraft could fly the brothers directly to the first country that would offer them asylum. For this reason, or so Smith reported, it would take up to twenty-four hours to secure an adequate aircraft.[76] Various versions exist of Minh's reply when Conein told him about the twenty-four-hour wait. According to Nichter, Minh was non-committal, replying 'Twenty-four hours? Fine.'[77] According to historian William Rust, who interviewed Conein, Minh replied that the generals could not possibly hold the brothers that long.[78] The generals were eventually informed that Diem and Nhu had moved into a church in Cholon. Minh ordered a convoy to pick them up. In the convoy was Captain Nhung, Minh's bodyguard, responsible for the execution of Tung and his brother the previous day. As the group departed, Minh raised two fingers, an agreed-upon signal telling Nhung to kill the brothers.[79] The brothers were picked up outside the church, handcuffed, and put in the back of an armoured vehicle. They were shot on the way back from the church to JGS.

According to an early version of events by Conein, as the convoy departed, at JGS the generals started preparing the stage for a peaceful transition of power. For this reason, Conein decided to go home before the media got there. This contradicts evidence that the generals, in a series of meetings throughout the day, had agreed to kill the brothers. The issue was put to a vote and the majority voted in favour. Conein later confirmed the veracity of this account.[80] No peaceful transition of power was on the cards. General Tran Van Don admitted in later years that the generals feared holding Diem prisoner. The people's support for him might return and the US government might decide to abandon the generals and restore Diem.[81]

Once home, Conein received a message from the Embassy telling him to go back to inquire about the safety of the two brothers. When he did so, he was told by Minh that they had committed suicide, something Conein could not and did not believe. Minh also invited Conein to view the bodies. Conein called out Minh's lie but refused to see the bodies to avoid further implicating the United States.[82] And yet, he also had time to provide more money (1.6 million piastres) to Don, this time to pay for the families of those injured in the coup. The brothers were dead. The Diem regime was no more.

Conclusion

On the afternoon of 2 November, Lodge reported the death of the brothers to Washington. According to General Maxwell Taylor, Kennedy was famously shocked by the news, he turned pale and left the room in aguish.[83] On the 4th, while still professing his shock at Diem's death, Kennedy reasoned that the United States 'must bear a good deal of responsibility'[84] for the coup. In a note to Kennedy on the 6th, Lodge provided a candid assessment of US responsibility. While the coup would have happened without the United States, 'it is equally certain that the ground in which the coup seed grew into a robust plant was prepared by us, and that the coup would not have happened [as] it did without our preparation'.[85] The same conclusion can be reached for the assassination of Diem.

Certainly, compared to the cases of Castro and Lumumba, the US government's role was more indirect. Even compared to the case of Trujillo, assassination was a less explicit policy choice. Assassination was clearly considered a possible – even probable – policy outcome. US officials, in Saigon and in Washington, including Kennedy, were clearly aware that assassination was a likely outcome of US support for a coup. They had been debating the consequences of an assassination of the two brothers since August.[86] The President also kept a tight grip on US policy and coup plotting.

As the coup developed, US policy towards the generals never made the safety of the brothers or (at a minimum) of Diem a priority. While establishing various political conditions, such as the release from prison of Buddhist activists, the US government never made US support for the coup contingent on the survival of Diem. As Taylor – who had opposed the coup – put it later, the system of sanctions – such as the cut-off of aid – against the Diem regime contributed to the outcome: 'by seeing that we disapproved of Diem's actions we certainly encouraged the elements that eventually overthrew him and assassinated him'.[87] The generals' questions to US officials at the time and later admissions show how the US government had – at various points – been in a position to stop the coup. This might have entailed saving Diem (politically and otherwise), something that was not a US government priority. As General Tran Van Don later put it, if the Administration had 'stipulated as condition' the safety of the brothers, the coup would not have gone ahead. The plotters expected to find them in the palace, and they could not guarantee their safety in the attack.[88]

When the November coup got under way, US officials had privileged access to its development but did not make Diem's survival a priority. As the Agency later admitted, during the coup, through Conein and other officials in Saigon, the station was able to 'report almost minute-by-minute progress of the coup'.[89] The Kennedy Administration's limited confidence in the generals and Conein's level of preparation and presence at JGS throughout the coup suggest that he acted – on instructions from Lodge and the rest of the US government– as an adviser to the generals rather than as a simple bystander.[90] At JGS, Conein might have known of Tung's killing. He was aware that at least one of the generals wanted Diem dead,[91] and he had witnessed Minh's increasing rage at Diem for dragging the process on for too long. He also provided extensive financial rewards to the generals, making them almost 'hired hands'.[92] Even the CIA later admitted that the passing of these funds was a 'sensitive matter'.[93] The accounting for those funds was never 'frank or complete'.[94]

Finally, and perhaps more importantly, despite months of plotting, the US government did not develop 'contingency arrangements' to safely take the brothers out of the country.[95] As Nichter wrote, it is true that if the brothers required to travel to the first country that would offer them asylum – possibly France – a long-range aircraft such as KC-135 was needed. But plenty of planes were available to – at least – take the brothers to safety. The US government had prepared aircraft to extract the generals, Lodge and Conein's family in case the coup failed and the situation turned ugly.[96] Conein's interpretation was that the US was taken by surprise since the generals, who had insisted on no US support, now requested a US aircraft.[97] Even if this were true, the US prioritised (im)plausible deniability over Diem's safety. Whatever the rationale, the two brothers were abandoned 'to the post-coup mercies of the coup plotters'.[98]

Ngo Dinh Diem: Preparing the Ground for Assassination

Compared to the Trujillo case, the language of decision-making was more guarded. When the risk of assassination became impossible to ignore, some reticence and opposition did emerge. There was a certain opposition towards the assassination of Diem personally. The fact that Diem was a US ally at the time might have acted as a contributing factor. This opposition never extended to Diem's brothers Nhu and Can. Furthermore, US officials expressed some opposition to more explicit and direct involvement in assassination, but not in abandoning Diem to his fate, a fate the US government had done much to seal. Coup plotting, weapons' transfer, and the US government's openness to assassination – especially if it helped achieve US objectives – often characterised the US government's covert foreign policy. While the administration in charge did change, they also defined the next episode, this time in Chile.

Notes

1. Tim Weiner, *Legacy of Ashes* (New York: Doubleday, 2007), 219.
2. David Halberstam, *The Best and the Brightest* (London: Pan Books, 1974), 355.
3. Senate Select Committee to Study Governmental Operations with Respect to Intelligence Activities (SSCIA), Interim Report: 'Alleged Assassination plots against foreign leaders', (Interim Report) (Washington, DC: US Government Printing Office), 1975, 5.
4. William J. Rust, 'CIA Operations Officer Lucien Conein', *Studies in Intelligence*, 63.4 (2019), 47–8.
5. Lucien Conein, SSCIA Testimony, 20/6/1975, Digital National Security Archives (DNSA), Covert Operations II, 16.
6. Stanley Karnow, *Vietnam: A History* (London: Pimlico, 1994), 295.
7. Lindsey O'Rourke, *Covert Regime Change* (Ithaca, NY: Cornell University Press, 2018), 177.
8. Pentagon Papers, 'The overthrow of Ngo Dinh Diem: May – November 1963', IV B5, 5–6.
9. Thomas Powers, *The Man Who Kept the Secrets: Richard Helms and the CIA* (New York: Pocket Books, 1979), 159.
10. Memorandum for Hilsman, Conversation with Diem, January 1963. Saigon. FRUS, 1961–1963, vol. III Vietnam, January–August 1963 (FRUS vol. III), doc. 6.

11. Memorandum from Hilsman and Forrestal to President Kennedy, 'A report on South Vietnam', 25/1/1963, FRUS vol. III, doc. 19; Memorandum from Bowles to President Kennedy, 'Subject: Recommendations for a fresh approach to the Vietnam impasse', 17/3/1963, FRUS vol. III, doc. 52.
12. Telegram from Rusk to Embassy Vietnam, 11/61963. FRUS vol. III, doc. 167.
13. Government of Viet Nam.
14. Telegram Rusk to Embassy Vietnam, Subject: Contingency Plan enclosed in May 23 letter, 14/6, FRUS vol. III, doc. 175.
15. CIA Information Report, 'Subject: Situation Appraisal of the Political Situation as of 1200 hours on 6 July', 8/7/1963, FRUS vol. III, doc. 212.
16. Special National Intelligence Estimate, 'Subject: The situation in South Vietnam', 10/7/1963, FRUS vol. III, doc. 217.
17. CIA Telegram/Information Report, 'Subject: Nhu comments on Buddhist infiltration by VC', 24/7/1963, National Security Archives (NSAr), 'New Light in a Dark Corner: Evidence on the Diem Coup in South Vietnam, November 1963', November 2020, available at https://nsarchive.gwu.edu/briefing-book/vietnam/2020-11-01/new-light-dark-corner-evidence-diem-coup-november-1963 (accessed 24 October 2023).
18. Fredrik Logevall, *Choosing War* (Berkeley: University of California Press, 1999), 5.
19. Luke Nichter, *The Last Brahmin: Henry Cabot Lodge Jr. and the Making of the Cold War* (New Haven, CT: Yale University Press, 2020), 129.
20. Transcript of JFK and Lodge Meeting, 15/8/1963; Doc. 3 NSAr, 'New Light'.
21. Pentagon Papers, 'The overthrow',12.
22. George Herring, *America's Longest War* (Boston, MA: McGraw Hill, 2002), 116.
23. Telegram Embassy Vietnam to the Department of State, 24/8/1963, FRUS vol. III, doc. 276.
24. Telegram from George Ball to Embassy in Vietnam, 24 August, FRUS vol. III, doc. 281; Pentagon Papers, 'The overthrow', 15.
25. Halberstam, *The Best*, 322–3. Thomas L. Hughes, Interviewed by Charles Stuart Kennedy, 7/7/1999, Association for Diplomatic Studies and Training (ADST) Oral History Project, 99, available at https://adst.org/OH%20TOCs/Hughes,%20Thomas%20L.toc.pdf (accessed 24 October 2023); NBC News, 'Vietnam Insight, Part II: The Death of Diem', George McTurnan Kahin Papers, Box 33,

Folder 56; Thomas Hughes, Notes of conversations with Hilsman and Forrestal, 24–28 August 1963, NSAr, 'New light'.
26. Memorandum Forrestal to President, 'Subject: Vietnam', 27/8/1963, NSAr, doc. 4, NSAr, 'JFK and the Diem Coup', 5/112003, available at https://nsarchive2.gwu.edu/NSAEBB/NSAEBB101/index2.htm (accessed 24 October 2023).
27. Nichter, *The Last*, 142.
28. Memorandum of conference with President, 'Subject: Vietnam', 28/8/1963. FRUS, 1961–1963, vol. IV, Vietnam, August–December 1963, doc. 1.
29. William Colby, 'Presidential Meeting on South Vietnam', 28/8/1963, US National Archives, Records of the Central Intelligence Agency, Miscellaneous Files, Box 6 JFK-M-7 F1 to F3. I thank William Rust for providing a copy of this document.
30. Telegram from Henry Cabot Lodge to Department of State. 29/8/1963, FRUS vol. IV, doc. 12.
31. Pentagon Papers, 'The overthrow', 19.
32. Larry Bassett and Stephen Pelz, 'American Goes to War in Vietnam, 1963', Discussion Paper No. 3, Workshop on the origins of the Vietnam War, Columbia University, 11 April 1980, George McTurnan Kahin Papers, Box 33, Folder 54, Cornell University Library.
33. Memorandum of conference with President, 'Subject: Vietnam', 29/8/1963, NSAr Document 11; NSAr, 'JFK and the Diem Coup'.
34. O'Rourke, *Covert*, 179.
35. Message From the President to Lodge, 29/8/1963, FRUS vol. IV, doc. 18.
36. Karnow, *Vietnam*, 300.
37. Pentagon Papers, 'The overthrow', 30.
38. Memorandum Taylor to McNamara, 'Subject: Report of McNamara–Taylor Mission to South Vietnam', 2/10/1963, FRUS vol. IV, doc. 167.
39. Pentagon Papers, 'The overthrow', 34.
40. Halberstam, *The Best*, 352–3.
41. Seymour Hersh, *The Dark Side of Camelot* (London: HarperCollins, 1997), 420–1. See documents on the topic in Box 33, Folder 55, George McTurnan Kahin papers.
42. Telegram from the CIA Station Saigon to Agency, 3/10/1963, FRUS vol. IV, doc. 171.
43. William J. Rust, *Kennedy in Vietnam* (New York: Da Capo Press, 1985), 148.
44. Letter Lodge to the Secretary of State, 13/9/1963, FRUS vol. IV, doc. 104.

45. Howard Jones, *Death of a Generation* (Oxford: Oxford University Press, 2004), 364; Hersh, *The Dark Side*, 3.
46. Nichter, *The Last*, 148.
47. Telegram CIA Station Saigon to Agency, 5/10/1963, FRUS vol. IV, doc. 177.
48. US Senate, Committee on Foreign relations, 'US involvement in the overthrow of Diem, 1963', Study No. 3, 20/7/1972, 13.
49. SSCIA, Interim Report, 217.
50. John McCone, Testimony to SSCIA, 6/6/1975, DNSA Covert Operations II, 60.
51. SSCIA, Miscellaneous records of the Church Committee, 'Diem', June 1975, JFKAR 157-10014-20227.
52. McCone, Testimony, 60.
53. SSCIA, Interim Report, 217.
54. SSCIA, Miscellaneous, entry for October 5–7.
55. Weiner, *Legacy*, 218.
56. CIA Inspector General Report, Unsanitized Copy Diem Report, (IG Report) 1967, available at https://www.archives.gov/files/research/jfk/releases/2018/104-10214-10036.pdf (accessed 25 October 2023), 30.
57. CIA, IG Report, 32.
58. Rust, *Kennedy*, 148.
59. IG Report, 33.
60. Karnow, *Vietnam*, 311.
61. CIA IG Report, 37.
62. Ibid., 38.
63. Thomas Ahern, *CIA and the House of Ngo*, NSAr, available at https://nsarchive2.gwu.edu/NSAEBB/NSAEBB284/2-CIA_AND_THE_HOUSE_OF_NGO.pdf (accessed 25 October 2023), 204.
64. CIA IG Report, 39.
65. The White House, Checklist for 4pm Meeting, 29/10/1963, Box 33, Folder 55, George McTurnan Kahin Papers.
66. Pentagon Papers, 'The overthrow', 54.
67. Rhett Dawson, 'Diem Assassination', Memorandum to Fritz Schwartz and Curt Smothers, 7/7/1975, JFKAR 157-10014-10152.
68. Ahern, *CIA*, 207.
69. NBC, 'The Death of Diem'.
70. Weiner, *Legacy*, 219.
71. CIA IG Report, 40.
72. Lucien Conein, Interview, *Vietnam: A Television History*, 7 May 1981, available at https://openvault.wgbh.org/catalog/V_17B091E22675449F9D3E61ABF070482F#at_2226.816_s (accessed 25 October 2023).

73. NBC, 'The Death of Diem'.
74. Nichter, *The Last*, 155; Rust, *Kennedy*, 169.
75. Weiner, *Legacy*, 220.
76. Rust, 'CIA Operations', 53.
77. Nichter, *The Last*, 157.
78. Rust, *Kennedy*, 171.
79. Max Hastings, *Vietnam: An Epic History of a Tragic War* (London: William Collins 2018), 152.
80. NBC, 'The Death of Diem'. Conein related the existence of a blood oath among those present regarding what happened that day.
81. Le Tu Hung, *Four Dalat Generals*, 74–6, in Box 34, Folder 6, George McTurnan Kahin Papers. See 'Dinner with general Tran Van Don', 24 March 1981, Box 34, Folder 6, George McTurnan Kahin Papers.
82. Conein, Interview, *Vietnam: A Television History*.
83. Editorial Note, FRUS vol. IV, doc. 274.
84. John Kennedy, Recorded Voice Note, 4/11/1963, Miller Center, White House Tapes, available at https://millercenter.org/the-presidency/educational-resources/jfk-memoir-dictation-assassination-of-diem (accessed 25 October 2023).
85. Karnow, *Vietnam*, 311.
86. Memorandum from George Carver to Acting DCI. 28 August. Subject: Alternatives to Ngo Family Regime in South Vietnam. CIA Reading Room, available at https://www.cia.gov/readingroom/docs/CIA-RDP79R00904A001000010007-5.pdf (accessed 25 October 2023).
87. General Maxwell Taylor, Interview, Oral History Collection, Lyndon Johnson Library, 9/1/1969, 22.
88. Seminar with General Trav Van Don, 23/3/1981, Cornell University, Box 33, Folder 55, George McTurnan Kahin Papers.
89. CIA IG Report, 42.
90. Rust, *Kennedy*, 164.
91. Conein, Testimony, 52.
92. Nichter, *The Last*, 153.
93. CIA, IG Report, 41.
94. Report Elder to Colby on 'Special Activities', 1/6/1973, JFKAR 104-10303-10007.
95. Hughes, ADST Interview, 102.
96. Nichter, *The Last*, 155.
97. Ibid., 157.
98. Hughes, ADST Interview, 102.

6 René Schneider: Removing the Main Obstacle to a Coup in Chile

On 24 March 1972, E. Howard Hunt and Gordon Liddy entered the Hay-Adams Hotel in Washington, DC. Hunt, a former CIA officer who had been involved in assassination plots against Fidel Castro, was then working for the Nixon White House in a squad called 'the plumbers'. Their task was, at least initially, to plug leaks of national security information that had plagued the Nixon Administration from its inception. Hunt and Liddy were meeting for lunch with Dr Edward Gunn, an officially retired CIA physician with a 'very substantial knowledge of the unorthodox application of medical science to Agency problems'.[1]

Ten days earlier, Hunt had met Charles Colson, Nixon's primary enforcer. Colson had relayed to Hunt how the President had decided to do something about the journalist Jack Anderson who had become a 'great thorn' in his side.[2] Over lunch, Hunt, Gunn and Liddy – without disclosing the name – tentatively explored options to disorient the target. As the discussion progressed, Liddy urged his companions to forget about discrediting Anderson. The 'logical and just solution' was to kill him.[3] The three agreed that the best option was – in Liddy's words – to use the same tactic used by the FBI when surreptitious entries go wrong. Anderson would be 'assaulted, his wallet and watch removed'. He would simply be 'the latest victim of the outrageously high rate of street crime in Washington'.[4] Initially, the task was given to Cuban exiles but they turned out to be on friendly terms with Anderson.[5] Eventually, Liddy agreed to do the deed himself, but with the Watergate scandal unfolding, the plan went nowhere.[6]

* * *

René Schneider: Removing the Main Obstacle to a Coup

Since the start of Nixon's career, Anderson had published several stories that had exposed his personal corruption and that of his Administration. In 1972, Anderson received documents detailing the US government's collusion with the International Telephone & Telegraph Corporation (ITT) to interfere in the 1970 Chilean elections.[7] The Nixon Administration had worked to prevent the socialist candidate Salvador Allende from being elected. The 40 Committee – tasked with managing covert operations[8] – had approved a 'spoiling' action against Allende. Going beyond the committee, the CIA had also worked with ITT to channel money directly to Jorge Alessandri, Allende's right-wing opponent.[9] This was the operation exposed by Anderson.

* * *

The 1970 Presidential elections in Chile took place on 4 September. Allende finished first with 36.6 per cent of the vote, Alessandri second with 35.27 per cent, and Radomiro Tomic – the Christian-Democrat – a more distant third with 28.1 per cent. With no candidate achieving an absolute majority, a vote of confirmation from Congress was due to take place on 24 October. After Allende's victory, the Administration followed two main paths, known in US documents as 'Track I' and 'Track II'. Track I aimed at convincing then President Eduardo Frei to intervene to prevent Allende's confirmation. Track II – the secret track – aimed at creating the conditions for a military coup. As a more constitutional solution proved unlikely, the distinction between the two tracks became harder to maintain.

As part of Track II, the US government also became involved in a plan to kidnap General René Schneider, the commander-in-chief of the Chilean Army, understood as the main obstacle to a coup. The Schneider case showcases interesting aspects of the CIA's indirect involvement in assassination. The Agency was in contact with (and provided weapons to) groups that – at a minimum – wanted to kidnap Schneider. Both the plotters and the CIA were aware that assassination was a likely outcome of such a course of action, and yet the collaboration continued. Schneider was killed during a botched kidnap operation. The assassination strengthened support for the constitution, and Allende was confirmed President on 24 October. The US government continued its overt and covert interference in Chile, until Allende fell in a coup led by General Augusto Pinochet on 11 September 1973.[10]

Election Results and Early Policy Options

'We have been living with a corpse in our midst,' US Ambassador to Chile Edward Korry wrote to Washington as the votes were being counted. 'Its name is Chile. The decomposition is no less malodorous because of the civility which accompanies it.' The 'stink of defeat' was evident from the mounting celebrations of pro-Allende forces.[11]

Already in August, as some uncertainty prevailed as to whether an Allende victory would have been detrimental to US interests, Korry had been adamant. Writing back to Washington, he had lamented that if Allende were to prevail, the United States would have demonstrated its 'impotence', and if he were to be inaugurated, the only option would have been to maintain minimal relations.[12] Furthermore, the only situation that could have pushed the army to act would have been the 'breakdown of law and order to a condition of chaos'. Crucially, any serious coup plotting needed to devise a method to overcome the opposition of General René Schneider. The commander-in-chief of the Chilean army had long expressed his view that the military should respect the constitutional process, the so-called Schneider doctrine. An intervention would also have needed the blessing of President Eduardo Frei. For this reason, Korry had been exploring – with Chilean contacts – the possibility of bribing Chilean members of parliament to prevent Allende's confirmation.[13]

Korry's coup scepticism notwithstanding, the CIA had started working on coup options. The US government's involvement with the Chilean military to overthrow Allende, the Agency envisioned, would have 'permanently' relieved the United States of any risks associated with an Allende regime.[14] In terms of likely candidates for a coup, the Agency had identified General Roberto Viaux who had been fired after leading the short-lived Tacnazo insurrection in 1969. Viaux was still a military figure of influence and prepared to 'incur considerable personal risk in preventing an Allende victory'.[15]

* * *

René Schneider: Removing the Main Obstacle to a Coup

Three days after the elections, an intelligence memorandum reported the possibility of a military power play, but the main obstacle remained Schneider,[16] who had restated his opposition to a coup during a meeting of Chilean high military officials on the 5th.[17] After a 40 Committee meeting took stock of the situation,[18] National Security Advisor Henry Kissinger asked Korry for a 'cold-blooded' assessment of the possibility of military intervention. Korry needed to explain how such an intervention would be organised, who would participate, whether all the leaders would work together, whether those in touch with General Camilo Valenzuela[19] would take part, what overt or covert role the US government would need to take, whether the troops would follow the leaders, what the reaction in the country would be (from the people and from Allende's forces), and finally, what the chances of success were. The same backchannel message also authorised Korry to expand his contacts to obtain the political intelligence needed to answer these questions. He was told to 'tread a fine line'. 'We are not inciting or organizing *at this point*' (emphasis added), the message read.[20]

William Broe, head of the CIA's Western Hemisphere Division, also asked the Chief of Station in Santiago, Henry Hecksher, to undertake the 'operational task of establishing those direct contacts with the Chilean military which are required to evaluate possibilities and, at least equally important, could be used to stimulate a golpe if and when a decision were made to do so'. The cable also recognised the difficulties in establishing high-level contacts with military officials in a surreptitious manner. An option was to send personnel that could establish these contacts without exposing the Agency. The station was made aware that the task was of the highest priority in Washington.[21]

On the 10th, Korry reported that Alessandri had just made a public statement announcing that he would not take office if selected by Congress. This conformed with the plan Korry had been working on since before the elections. The plan aimed at getting Alessandri enough congressional votes to be confirmed; he would then resign, thus leading to new elections in which Frei – having been formally out of office – could then compete. Korry did admit that those calling the plan a 'Rube Goldberg contraption' had a point, but with Alessandri's speech the prospects had improved.[22] One day later, Korry responded to Kissinger's request.

'Opportunities for further significant USG action with the Chilean military,' he wrote, 'are non-existent.' The military was already aware of the US government's position regarding the dangers posed by Allende, but Korry could see 'no group or individual within the armed forces around whom a coup effort with any real chance of success could be organized'. Only 'apocalyptic developments' in Chile might push the army to act.[23]

Towards Track I and Track II

'The big problem today is Chile.' Kissinger told Nixon in a phone conversation on the 12th. 'I am following it,' Nixon replied, 'and I want a personal note to State that I want to see all the cables on Chile.' Kissinger told Nixon that State wanted to let Allende 'come in and see what we can work out'. Nixon was beside himself: 'Like against Castro? Like in Czech? The same people said the same thing. Don't let them do that.' Kissinger also told the President that he was going to see Donald Kendall (CEO of Pepsi) and Augustin Edwards (owner of the CIA-subsidised *El Mercurio*, a newspaper staunchly opposed to Allende). Nixon counselled caution. 'We don't want a big story leaking or that we are trying to overthrow the government.' 'That's essential.' Kissinger agreed.[24] Half an hour later, Kissinger also spoke to CIA Director Richard Helms; the two agreed not to let 'Chile go down the drain'.[25] The two exchanges clarified both the high degree of Nixon's involvement in the decision-making surrounding Chile and his scepticism towards the State Department and possible diplomatic tracks. While maintaining a concern with plausible deniability, the CIA, Kissinger and Nixon set to work on the overthrow of Allende.

In Santiago, Korry initially continued working on his para-constitutional option to prevent Allende's congressional confirmation. Korry's plan, while dressed in prettier clothes, amounted to pure bribery. On the same day of the Nixon–Kissinger phone call, he had reported to the 40 Committee on a meeting with General Valenzuela. The general referred to the fact that President Frei had complained about Schneider's 'constitutionalism sickness'. The commander-in-chief of the army was the problem in any military solution.[26]

René Schneider: Removing the Main Obstacle to a Coup

The 40 Committee approved a $250,000 fund for Korry's plan. To nudge Frei to act, it also authorised the CIA to start a propaganda campaign on the risks posed by an Allende presidency.[27]

Kendall and Edwards had already warned DCI Helms that this scenario was unlikely to work. The key to a successful coup was, in their view, to get General Carlos Prats, Chief of the National Defence Staff, to act, which would 'involve neutralizing Schneider'. The Alessandri plan was quickly abandoned; the latter needed too many votes compared to the eighteen Allende required.[28] Officials in the State Department and the NSC continued to oppose more forceful measures. On the 14th, for example, Winston Lord of the NSC warned Kissinger of the reputational costs of a US intervention against a democratically elected government and its impact on the US government's negotiating position in Vietnam.[29] In his own warning against intervention, Viron Vaky, Kissinger's deputy at the NSC, stated that, 'moralism aside', a more explicit US intervention had 'practical operational consequences'; these included the risks of 'widespread violence and insurrection'. Allende was not a mortal threat; a more careful posture was needed.[30] These warnings were disregarded.

On the morning of the 15th, Kendall and Edwards met secretly with Nixon. After the meeting, Nixon called Kissinger, Helms and Attorney General John Mitchell into the Oval Office. It is here that Nixon gave his instructions to Helms. Helms's famous handwritten notes read:

> 1 in 10 chance, perhaps but save Chile
> Worth spending
> Not concerned risks involved
> No involvement of Embassy,
> $10,000,000 available, more if necessary
> Full time job, best men we have
> Game plan
> Make the economy scream
> 48 hours for plan of action.[31]

As Helms later recalled, with these instructions 'President Nixon had ordered me to instigate a military coup in Chile, a heretofore democratic country.' The President was used to the language of covert operations, and – based on his experience in government – certainly meant what he said. Helms felt he was in no position to question the President's order.[32] The Director ordered the establishment of a Task Force. Deputy Director for Plans Tom Karamessines, Broe and David Attlee Phillips were its key members. A secret channel of communication to Santiago was set up and additional personnel were sent to the Chilean capital.[33]

Working to sow chaos in Chile, on the night of the 16th, through an intermediary, Korry gave the green light for General Viaux to make an incendiary statement on the political situation in the country. The US Ambassador had persuaded Minister of Defence Ricardo Ossa – one of his main contacts – not to obstruct the statement. 'The Fatherland is not negotiable, nor liberty compromisable,' Viaux had declared, adding that he did not want to split the army, but he was ready to stand with others to defend the Fatherland. With the political temperature raised, Korry expected a plan to develop in five parts: a declaration from a minister of the government that the economic situation was desperate; the resignation of the cabinet; the replacement of most of the cabinet with military officials; the resignation of Frei and his appointment (envisaged by the Constitution) of an interim president selected from the armed forces commanders-in-chief; and a new military junta pledging to hold future elections. Korry did note several weak spots in the plan, especially whether Frei would agree to resign and whether Schneider would go along with such a plan. Korry also hinted that he was in full contact with General Valenzuela.[34] In a separate cable to the 40 Committee, the Santiago station confirmed Korry's news. Valenzuela was playing a 'key role in the planned takeover' and had reached a full understanding with Viaux. Frei remained uncommitted.[35]

One day later, at a 40 Committee meeting, while doubts and some opposition to the plan emerged, Kissinger stressed that – if a military action were to take place – the United States needed to be ready for 'contingencies' and to support the military.[36] Alexis Johnson of the State Department authorised Korry to pursue the plan that entailed the military 'takeover' of the government, the control of Unidad Popular militants, and the call for elections

René Schneider: Removing the Main Obstacle to a Coup

with Frei as candidate. Korry was also to assure Frei that – while such an option needed to be entirely Chilean – he could count on US financial support for his campaign and that the military could count on continued US support if they collaborated in preventing an Allende presidency.[37]

On the 21st, CIA headquarters wrote to the Station in Chile that a task force had been established and that the objective was to 'prevent Allende assumption of power'. It noted: 'parliamentary legerdemain has been discarded. Military solution is objective.' The insistence on a manoeuvre involving Frei was not out of a 'sense of legality' but because Frei might be more willing to act if a constitutional fig leaf could be found, and, if Frei were to run again for president, his chances would be improved by the appearance of legality.[38] The Agency launched a propaganda campaign to convince Frei to act.[39] The 40 Committee also considered exploiting the outgoing President's desire for a position in an international organisation.[40]

At this stage, the Agency reaffirmed the existence of two main tracks in the US covert operations in Chile. One was the more 'parliamentary' solution that Johnson had discussed with Korry. This also entailed a coup, albeit with a fig leaf of legality. The second was for the CIA only to work towards a direct military solution. The telegram stressed that the Agency and Korry were not working in tandem. If Korry decided to exceed his instructions and work for a direct military coup, that was his choice, but the Agency could not be seen as prodding him. Relations with the Ambassador had to be limited to those on Track I.[41]

In the following days, obstacles accumulated. In a meeting of Chilean generals, Schneider reiterated his constitutional position. He was also aware that something was going on behind his back.[42] Korry continued to ask his contacts within the Chilean government to warn the military of the 'drastic change' that would follow an Allende presidency.[43] And yet, he had to report to Washington that Chile remained 'calm'. The economy was damaged but business as usual continued, and the armed forces continued to act as 'sturdy guardian of the Constitution'. Schneider was unmovable. Korry raised the possibility again that Schneider could be 'displaced' by including him in a new military cabinet. This would remove the main obstacle to an eventual takeover. A catalyst for such a development, Korry suggested, could be an announcement about a dramatic economic situation.[44]

On this basis, Korry proposed a series of economic measures to undermine the Chilean economy. These included pressure on US companies to threaten to leave Chile in case of Allende's confirmation. In a message to Frei, Korry warned that 'not a nut or bolt will be allowed to reach Chile under Allende. Once Allende comes to power, we shall do all within our power to condemn Chile and the Chileans to utmost deprivation and poverty.'[45] But the President remained unmoved.

The Station shared Korry's frustration with Frei. It reported that Korry had worked to put the military and Frei on the same wavelength, but there wasn't much more that could be done. 'Amb and Station,' the cable continued, 'stopping barely short of issuing calls to open sedition.' The Station also recognised that for a coup to succeed, Frei needed to remove the 'main stumbling block': Schneider. The chance of a direct coup remained slim. 'That type of coup,' the telegram continued, 'simply not in cards.' Perhaps aware of machinations in Washington, the Station also cautioned: 'forget about black operations and propagandistic conditioning of the armed forces. They rarely read. Bear in mind that parameter of action is exceedingly narrow.'[46]

These warnings fell on deaf ears. On the 24th, Kissinger's deputy, Alexander Haig, lamented Korry's ineffectiveness and his excessive 'idealism'. The time had come to provide those working with the United States with more explicit guarantees, including money and safe havens. A real effort also needed to be made to 'work on the Chilean military'. Military representatives needed to be armed with the authority to promise a stepped-up support after a successful coup.[47]

On the same day, the CIA station in Santiago received its marching orders from Headquarters. 'We postulate that Frei will not move,' Headquarters wrote, and his willingness to move might only be influenced by the creation of a climate 'in which such a move can take place successfully'. 'We conclude,' the cable continued, 'that it is our task to create such a climate climaxing with a solid pretext that will force the military and the president to take some action in the desired direction.' Three main avenues needed to be pursued: convince Frei to act or go, create an atmosphere in which he or others can act successfully, and assist in creating the flashpoint or pretext for action. Inside Chile, the cable acknowledged, there was still no feeling that the election of Allende was 'evil'. In such a situation it would have been hard to justify a military coup. It was up to the Agency to 'gradually create a climate in which this conclusion becomes inevitable'. Therefore:

> The station should employ every stratagem, every ploy, however bizarre to create this internal resistance ... Funds should be expended liberally to stiffen, organize and hearten resistance from every individual or group that is willing to stand up and be counted ... If we are successful, the pretext in all likelihood will present itself.[48]

Two special agents – Anthony Sforza and Bruce MacMaster – joined the Station's operations under 'deep cover'. At times called 'false flaggers' for their 'ability to assume non-US nationality', they worked to establish contacts with high-risk individuals and to give the Agency further layers of deniability. MacMaster used a forged passport and presented himself as a Colombian businessman representing concerned US businesses. Sforza pretended to be Argentinian as well as a Mafia-connected smuggler.[49]

The CIA was not the only agency involved. On 28 September, the Defense Intelligence Agency sent a message to US Army attaché in Santiago Paul Wimert. The latter was instructed to 'work closely with the CIA chief ... in contacting and advising the principal military figures who might play a decisive role in any move which might, eventually, deny the Presidency to Allende'. He was also instructed to refrain from informing the Ambassador of his role and to keep up the appearance of taking orders only from Korry in his day-to-day activities.[50]

In Santiago, Frei was sending contradictory signals, talking tough with some military officials, but telling Schneider that he respected his constitutional position.[51] Frei had also failed to attend the Congress of his own party on 3rd and 4th of October, where a decision had been taken to pass Tomic's congressional votes to Allende. This was the last nail in the para-constitutional

163

option's coffin.[52] In a repeat of the Lumumba episode, as the paraconstitutional option fizzled out, the military remained the US government's main point of contact, and harsher measures – like assassination – the preferred policy option.

Overcoming the Main Obstacle: Schneider's Assassination

With this setback, the 40 Committee reconvened. Kissinger reminded those present that there were only eighteen days left before Allende's confirmation and some 'drastic action' to shock the Chileans into action was needed. Meyer and Korry expressed scepticism that an Allende presidency could be prevented. Kissinger, then, reasoned that the committee was 'faced with a problem since Higher Authority does not accept the fact that Allende is likely to be President'. The White House wanted every signal 'short of public insult' to stimulate the Chileans to act.[53] Kissinger also wanted to increase economic pressure. In the meeting, he was 'quite blunt'. 'If higher authority had the choice of risking expropriations or Allende's accession,' Kissinger reported, 'he would risk the dangers of expropriations.' An open posture of hostility should be adopted while taking care that it did not appear 'completely obvious'.[54]

This tough posture was reflected in an explicit cable from Helms to the Station. Helms instructed Chief of Station Henry Hecksher to 'contact the military and let them know USG wants a military solution and that we will support them now and later'. The cable also ordered the use of 'all available assets and stratagems including the rumor-mill to create at least some sort of coup climate'. The cable concluded, 'we want you to sponsor a military move which can take place . . . in a climate of economic and political uncertainty'.[55] In Santiago, the activity became more narrowly focused on the removal of Schneider.

On 7 October, Wimert – the army attaché in Santiago— spoke to General Valenzuela and other military officials at the War Academy. Valenzuela raised the effort to convince Frei to 'eliminate General Schneider . . . replace him [or] send him out of the country'. The army officers admitted that they had also studied a plan

René Schneider: Removing the Main Obstacle to a Coup

to kidnap Schneider since he remained the main obstacle to a military takeover. Headquarters was supportive: 'This would make it more important than ever to remove him and to bring this new state of events . . . anything we or Station can do to effect removal of Schneider? We know this rhetorical question but wish inspire thought on both ends on this matter.'[56] The Agency and its officials in the field were keen to cooperate on Schneider's removal.

Contact with Viaux also expanded to collaboration in engendering a coup.[57] A situation report recognised that he was the 'only leader of stature who is conspicuously prepared to act'. The Agency ordered one of the special agents (or false flagger) to offer Viaux 'moral, financial, and material (arms) support on behalf of an unidentified US group'.[58] Viaux told the contact that – to prove his bona fides – he should 'arrange an airdrop consisting of: 150 noise grenades, 150 paralyzing grenades, 50 submachine guns and ammo, 50 grenade launchers, 300 tear gas shells and 330 gas masks'.[59] In a series of follow-up meetings, special agents negotiated with Viaux on the extent of this material and financial support.[60]

Before an agreement could be reached, Korry became aware of these developments occurring behind his back. He wrote an angry telegram to Johnson at State and Kissinger warning that an attempt to foster a coup would be the Nixon Administration's Bay of Pigs. He was appalled to discover that the Agency was working on terrorist acts and coup plotting with Pablo Rodriguez, a member of the extremist group Patria y Libertad, and with Major Arturo Marshall who had expressed a desire to assassinate Allende.[61] Contact between the Agency and these groups, Korry continued, was dangerous and discredited his work since he had assured Chilean authorities that he was in charge.[62] But Korry wasn't in charge. He was cut out from the Track II decisions.

Communication on Track II was regular and intense between the Agency and the White House, as was the pressure bearing on the Agency from the White House.[63] Perhaps feeling this pressure, the Station showed that it was willing to go to extreme lengths. Chief of Station Hecksher and a contact well informed on the situation in the Chilean military 'jointly analyzed available means to remove Schneider as CINC army'. The contact stated that political considerations had prevented Frei from offering Schneider a cabinet position. The kidnapping of Schneider, again, was considered an available option. It was also explicitly recognised that this was likely to lead to Schneider's death. The contact presciently warned that an 'abduction attempt might lead to bloodshed' and that Schneider's accidental death 'would rally the army firmly behind the flag of constitutionalism'. Importantly, Hecksher showed no opposition to the kidnapping of Schneider nor any concern regarding the prospect that he might get killed. The contact also offered two additional warnings. First, he warned the Chief of Station that Viaux was unreliable. He was a 'man without an army'. Second, he cautioned against the risks entailed in the army's decision to abandon constitutionalism: 'all hell would break lose. Soldiers fighting soldiers. Was that desirable?' Once again, Hecksher seemed unfazed. He simply replied that 'USG did not really care as long as resulting chaos denied Allende the presidency.'[64]

In the meantime, Viaux, who had initially promised a coup between 9 and 10 October, stalled. Uncertainties surrounding the coup's prospects convinced CIA headquarters to ask the Station to try and stop this attempt.[65] In a clear sign of the Agency's influence, Viaux agreed to postpone the operation.[66] The Station reported that it had arrived 'at Viaux solution by process of elimination'. Under 'optimum circumstances', Viaux could hope to split the military between units loyal to the constitution and those loyal to him. Militants of Unidad Popular might also enter the fray. 'Carnage could be considerable and prolonged i.e. civil war.' Again unfazed, the Station recommended proceeding with increased support for Viaux, including the arms drop he had requested. The drop, the Station wrote, would demonstrate US interest in the survival of Chilean democracy, it would be a morale boost for the plotters within the armed forces, and finally it would be a strong signal to the Chilean high command that the US government was willing to condone civil war and all it entailed. The drop would certainly cause a violent showdown between Viaux and Schneider. The contradiction with the interest in the preserving the Chilean democracy did not register. In short, the Station concluded, 'You have asked us to provoke chaos in Chile. Thru Viaux solution we provide you with formula for chaos which unlikely to be bloodless. To dissimulate US involvement will clearly be impossible.'[67]

René Schneider: Removing the Main Obstacle to a Coup

On the 13th, the Station told Headquarters that Viaux would attempt to remove Schneider in the following forty-eight hours.[68] Viaux was the 'only figure in Chile who is now actively attempting to carry out a coup'.[69] The Station acknowledged that there still wasn't much of a coup climate. Furthermore, Viaux had failed to develop any plan to 'contain High Command, especially General Schneider' and to confront an eventual pro-Allende mob.[70]

Pressure from the White House also continued to be intense. Nixon reconfirmed his 'conviction that it was absolutely essential that the election of Mr. Allende to the presidency be thwarted'. The Agency invited the Station to continue contacts with Viaux.[71] On the 14th, communication arrived at Langley that Viaux was ready to kidnap Schneider, in a move that was coordinated with General Valenzuela – a further sign that the two generals were working together. Viaux had also requested weapons and other support.[72] Viaux's group would act on the morning of the 17th. 'First step will be to kidnap [redacted] Schneider.'[73] On the same day, in the Senior Review Group, Kissinger – who likely knew of the latest developments – stated: 'If I read the signs correctly, my client [Nixon] would like to bring him [Allende] down.'[74] The intelligence agencies were doing everything in their power to make that happen.

Lieutenant General Donald Bennett, Director of the DIA, sent a 'Top Secret; Sensitive; Destroy Immediately', message to Wimert. He was to identify two trusted Chilean generals and convey to them this message:

> High authority[75] in Washington has authorized you to offer material support short of armed intervention to Chilean Armed Forces in any endeavors they may undertake to prevent the election of Allende on October 24, his inauguration on 4 November, or his subsequent overthrow.[76]

At this point, the Agency's Task Force recommended the Station to contact Viaux and make clear that neither an air drop nor paralysing gas (one of the General's requests) were forthcoming. Instead, the Agency promised money for weapons as well as support in obtaining them. The Agency also promised $250,000 for the life insurance the retired general had requested for the members of his team, but it could not include written insurance policies. Once again, the main concern for the Agency was Schneider. 'What does Viaux intend to do to neutralize the Alto Mando?' Headquarters queried.[77]

In a conundrum not dissimilar to that confronted in the Diem case, Headquarters stressed its willingness to contribute to the coup by providing intelligence and financial support, primarily for the purchase of weapons. This, however, depended on having more information on how Viaux intended to carry out his coup. As Headquarters understood, 'the step we are taking now in getting closer to Viaux always carries with it the possibility of deeper involvement to protect our investment. That we could not do if operating in the dark.' Viaux's first move would have been the kidnap attempt, but the Agency remained keen to support the former general. It was important to keep Viaux's coup alive and his group 'financially lubricated'.[78]

Later, the same day, the situation seemed to change. It was reported that President Frei had asked Admiral Fernando Porta, the Chief of Naval Operations 'guilty' of talking to Allende, to take a leave of absence. Alongside Schneider and Prats, Porta was one of the leading military figures opposed to a coup. Porta realised that the move was intended to make a coup easier, something US observers also noted.[79] The Agency's contacts within active-duty officers were also bearing fruit. Chief of Station Hecksher told them of the US government's willingness to provide support before and after a coup. Based on these developments, a Track II report concluded that the odds of a coup had 'improved significantly'. Viaux was no longer the only plausible candidate to pull it off.[80]

* * *

In Washington, on 14 October, the 40 Committee met to discuss progress in Chile. The CIA's Chile Task Force lead, Karamessines, sounded a note of caution, telling those present that – as things stood – only the 'unpredictable Viaux' seemed ready to launch a coup and there wasn't much that could be done to prevent Allende's confirmation. Those in attendance seemingly agreed.[81]

René Schneider: Removing the Main Obstacle to a Coup

The following day, though, Karamessines had a separate secret meeting with Kissinger and his deputy Haig to discuss Track II. Karamessines told them that Viaux's plan was risky, and it might jeopardise moves then being prepared by better placed military officers, including Valenzuela.[82] The message the three agreed on aimed at warning Viaux against 'precipitate action':

> We have reviewed your plans and based on your information and ours, we come to the conclusion that your plans for a coup at this time cannot succeed . . . Preserve your assets. We will stay in touch. The time will come when you with all your other friends can do something. You will continue to have our support.

According to the Agency's minutes, the meeting concluded 'on Dr. Kissinger's note that the Agency should continue keeping the pressure on every Allende weak spot in sight – now, after the 24th of October, after 5 November, and into the future until such time as new marching orders are given'.[83] On the same day, Kissinger spoke to Nixon. 'I saw Karamessines today,' he told the President, 'That looks hopeless. I turned it off. Nothing would be worse than an abortive coup.'[84] Nixon agreed: 'Just tell him to do nothing.'[85]

Seemingly reflecting the discussion in the meeting, on the 16th, the Agency's telegram to the Station included the message for Viaux as agreed upon, but it also added that the Station needed to convey to Viaux:

> Our objectives are as follows: (A) To advise him of our opinion and discourage him from acting alone; (B) Continue to encourage him to amplify his planning; (C) Encourage him to join forces with other coup planners so that they may act in concert either before or after 24 October.

The telegram wished 'optimum good fortune' to other military officials involved in the plotting, including Valenzuela, and asked the Station to review all activities and contacts, including 'anything else your imagination can conjure which will permit you to continue to press forward toward' the objective.[86]

Much controversy surrounds the meeting between Karamessines, Kissinger and Haig and the follow-up cable. The controversy pits the Agency against the NSC, particularly Kissinger and Haig. Kissinger later testified that the minutes taken by Karamessines were – in essence – what had been agreed, albeit in a bit more detail than he would have liked. According to Kissinger, the spirit of the meeting had been that of 'turning off' Viaux and the coup plotting. The outcome of the decision – in Kissinger's view – should have been an end to Track II. Haig agreed. After the 15th, or so their argument went, the White House knew nothing about coup plotting; Track II was dead. If the Agency had continued plotting, it was without the White House's authorisation.[87] Until now, only CIA documents – including Karamessines's minutes and the Agency's message to Santiago – showed that the Nixon Administration's goal was not to end the plotting, but to take measures that could guarantee that – if a coup did happen – it could be successful. The point was confirmed by Phillips, also CIA, who testified that the contacts were not cut off and Viaux was encouraged to continue plotting and work with others, including Valenzuela.[88] Confronted with these opposing interpretations, the Church Committee was unable to take a side.[89]

We now know that Haig, Kissinger and the White House continued Track II plotting after the 15th. On the 16th, Haig wrote a memorandum[90] to Kissinger. He explained that Karamessines had called complaining about a 'little disconnect' in communication in Santiago. It continued, 'after CIA had, on track II, directed our Attaché to contact the various military personalities in the Chilean armed forces, he has received duplicatory instructions via General Bennett from Mel Laird', then Secretary of Defense. This, Haig worried, 'may result in some problems, especially in light of yesterday's decision to hold off *efforts towards a premature coup but continue to build assets*' (emphasis added). Haig recommended Kissinger to call Laird and let him know that 'the President had started this action a bit ago through Helms and that no one else was to know', and for this reason Laird should only liaise with Kissinger for any future Track II decision.[91] Track II was far from dead; the plots had not been turned off.

* * *

René Schneider: Removing the Main Obstacle to a Coup

As James Lockhart has shown, following Frei's decision to fire Porta, Admiral Hugo Tirado had become the new chief of the navy. Tirado's strong opposition to Allende meant that the navy was more likely to participate in a coup. On the 17th, Viaux, Tirado, Valenzuela, Huerta and other plotters met and agreed to execute Viaux's plan. The plan would start with the kidnap of Schneider. Huerta would then 'reveal' several caches of weapons allegedly belonging to the Movement of the Revolutionary Left (MIR), a left-wing extremist group. Frei would declare a state of emergency in Santiago which would put all forces in the city under Valenzuela's command. Tirado would then form a military junta with Viaux as Ministry of Defence, Frei would leave, and Schneider would be presented with a fait accompli and be released. The only obstacle remaining was Valenzuela's request that – as a matter of honour – Schneider should not be kidnapped by military officials. For this, Viaux could count on Patria y Libertad, as well as groups of extremist right-wing students and professionals.[92]

The generals' agreement to proceed, though, did not mean that the US government's role was diminished. In the late evening of the 17th, Wimert met with Tirado and Valenzuela. The latter requested eight to ten tear gas grenades, three 45 caliber machine guns and 500 rounds of ammunition. Tirado said that he had available three machine guns, but they could be identified and traced back to him due to their serial numbers. The transfer of weapons was approved.[93]

The following day, Viaux presented one of the Agency's special agents with a fifteen-point scenario for a coup, starting with the kidnapping of Schneider.[94] Valenzuela also confirmed to Wimert that he and Viaux were working together.[95] There was no separation between the two groups. He had arranged for Schneider to attend a stag party. The Commander-in-Chief would be abducted as he left the party and would then be flown to Argentina. The kidnapping would be blamed on Allende supporters and Frei would resign, thus opening the way for a military takeover.[96] According to Valenzuela's rosy picture, the junta would dissolve the parliament, but this was – in his eyes – the only unconstitutional act.[97]

The kidnapping on the 19th failed. Schneider had decided to leave the party in his private vehicle as opposed to his official car.

Furthermore, the police guard had failed to withdraw as agreed.[98] In the aftermath of the failure, concerned about the lack of activity, CIA Headquarters asked the Station to confirm whether the party had taken place and whether anything was moving.[99]

Wimert was told that a second kidnap attempt would be made on the 20th. This also failed. As Schneider was leaving the Ministry of Defence, the kidnappers got stuck in traffic and lost his car. As these first attempts faltered, the Station was requested to provide further information about a post-coup junta and its likely approach. In a reference to pressure from the White House, the Station was told, 'Headquarters must respond . . . to queries from higher levels.'[100] On the 20th, the Station responded that – thanks to the 'vigorous effort' of false flag officers – a coup was now likely as confirmed by Valenzuela's signalling of his intention to move.[101]

When the machine guns and ammunition finally arrived at Santiago airport, Wimert was there to collect them. At 2.00 a.m. on the 22nd he travelled to the outskirts of Santiago to deliver them to his contacts.[102] CIA Headquarters had also agreed to use Wimert to pass $50,000 to the kidnappers, as requested by Valenzuela.[103] A few hours after the passage of weapons, Schneider's car was intercepted on his way to work. The back window was smashed. Schneider was shot as he tried to reach for his gun.

The first reports of the shooting reaching the Station suggested that Schneider had been machine-gunned and that 'grease guns' had been used. Eventually, investigations concluded that Schneider was shot with handguns, but at least one of the CIA-supplied sub-machine guns was present at the scene, as were the tear gas masks. At Headquarters, having briefed Director Helms on the latest developments, the Task Force sent a congratulatory message back to the Station. A 'maximum effort', the telegram read, had been achieved. Any further move was left to the 'Chileans themselves', but the Station had done an 'excellent job of guiding Chileans to point where a military solution is at least an option for them' and it had done so, remarkably, under 'extremely difficult and delicate circumstances'. The Task Force concluded by asking whether a coup was still an option.[104] It wasn't.

With a coup failing to materialise, the Agency refused Viaux's last-minute plea to help in publicly blaming the botched kidnapping on leftists. The Station also reneged on its pledge to cover insurance for members of Viaux's groups.[105] On the 24th, Viaux turned himself in. Valenzuela ordered a media blackout to avoid any leaks and the disclosure of his cooperation with Viaux.[106] On the same day, the Chilean Congress confirmed Allende as President. There was nothing left for the CIA to do, except to cover its tracks.[107] Track II was temporarily put on ice.

Conclusion

The Church Committee's interim report was particularly lenient towards the CIA and the US government in its assessment of the Schneider assassination. It acknowledged that the CIA had financed and provided weapons to anti-Allende military figures. However, the report accepted Kissinger's version of events regarding the withdrawal of US active support to the group that eventually carried out the kidnapping one week before it happened: the famous 15 October decision. It also accepted the argument that the Viaux and Valenzuela groups worked separately, hence the transfer of weapons to one group had no effect on the kidnapping and assassination. Finally, the report found no evidence of a plan to kill Schneider, nor of awareness by any US officials that Schneider might be shot during the abduction.[108]

Most of these conclusions have been proven false or misleading. The division between the two groups of plotters was non-existent; just a last-minute facade to cover tracks. The Schneider abduction was discussed and prepared at the highest levels of the Chilean military and relied on the collaboration of terrorist groups like Patria y Libertad (also financed by the CIA). As to the 15 October decision to end support for the kidnappers/coup plotters, the NSC document discussed above confirms the Agency's version of events and Kissinger's continued involvement in Track II after the 15th. In terms of political control, then, the White House was clearly following developments closely, especially through contact with Karamessines, a key member of the CIA's Chile Task Force. Phone conversations between Kissinger and Nixon also seem to suggest that the President was following events closely.

In the Schneider case, the US government's involvement in assassination was clearly indirect. There is no explicit call for the assassination of Schneider, although, in more circumlocutory language, he is often identified as the main stumbling block and someone who should be 'neutralised'. Assassination – as a US objective – does not appear in the minutes of policy-making meetings. However, the CIA Station – and, one can assume, Langley, if not the White House – had been explicitly warned that any attempt to abduct Schneider could lead to his assassination and further violence. Through Track II, the CIA was involved in the planning and, at various stages, requested information on the development on these plans and pushed the plotters to act. Viaux and others often communicated their plans to the Agency and US officials spurred the plotters forward. Perhaps under pressure from the White House, the Station showed a complete disregard for the risk of violence in Chile.

Certainly, as several scholars have shown, Chilean officials were at the heart of the coup plotting and of Schneider's assassination. At times, they disregarded the US government and the CIA's instructions.[109] The fact remains that several agencies of the US government collaborated with the plotters, who often relied on the US government's advice. They also received weapons and financial and political support. More generally, the US government's overt and covert policies were essential in creating a coup climate. The conclusion reached by Thomas Powers in the late 1970s still rings true: 'If the CIA did not actually shoot General Schneider, it is probably fair to say that he would not have been shot without the CIA.'[110]

Notes

1. Howard Hunt, Testimony, Senate Select Committee to Study Governmental Operations with Respect to Intelligence Activities (SSCIA), 10/1/1976, Digital National Security Archives (DNSA), CIA Covert Operations II, 32.
2. SSCIA, Addenda to the Interim Report on Alleged Assassination plots, Book IV: Supplementary Detailed Staff Reports on Foreign and Military Intelligence (Washington, DC: US Government Printing office, 1976), 134.
3. Gordon Liddy, *Will* (New York: St. Martin's, 1980), 287.

4. Liddy, *Will*, 288.
5. Mark Feldstein, *Poisoning the Press* (New York: Picador, 2011), 287.
6. Howard Hunt, *American Spy* (New York: John Wiley & Sons, 2007), 199.
7. Feldstein, *Poisoning*, 275-276.
8. National Security Decision Memorandum 40. 'Responsibility for the conduct, supervision, and coordination of covert action', 17/2/1970, available at https://www.nixonlibrary.gov/sites/default/files/virtuallibrary/documents/nsdm/nsdm_040.pdf (accessed 25 October 2023).
9. Document undated, unnamed, DOCUMENTSPCIA300009080, State Department Chile Declassification Files (CDF); SSCIA, 'Covert Action in Chile' Report (Washington, DC: US Government Printing Office, 1975), 12–13.
10. Lubna Qureshi, *Nixon, Kissinger, and Allende* (Lanham, MD: Lexington Books, 2009); Peter Kornbluh, *The Pinochet File* (New York: The New Press, 2013); James Lockhart, *Chile, the CIA, and the Cold War* (Edinburgh: Edinburgh University Press, 2021); Jonathan Aslam, *The Nixon Administration and the Death of Allende's Chile* (London: Verso, 2005).
11. Telegram Embassy to State, FRUS 1969–1976, vol. 21, Chile, doc. 62.
12. SSCIA, 'Covert Action', 10, 23.
13. Cable, Korry to Crimmins, 11/8/1970, CDF.
14. Kornbluh, *Pinochet File*, 9.
15. CIA, Acting Chief of Western Hemisphere Division, 'Phase II Planning', 23/8/1970, HAK Office, Country File, Latin America, Box 128, Chile Wrap-up/Post-mortem 2/3, RNPL.
16. Intelligence Memorandum, 7/9/1970, FRUS, 1969–1976, vol. E-16, Documents on Chile, 1969–1973, doc. 18.
17. CIA Intelligence Information Cable, 8/9/1970, FRUS vol. 21, doc. 67.
18. Memorandum for the Record, Minutes of the Meeting of the 40 Committee, 8/9/1970, FRUS vol. 21, doc. 70.
19. Commander of the Santiago garrison.
20. Backchannel message to the Ambassador to Chile (Korry) and the Chief of Station, 9/9/1970, FRUS vol. 21, doc. 71.
21. Telegram CIA to the Station in Chile, 9/9/1970, FRUS vol. 21, doc. 72.
22. Telegram Embassy Chile to Department of State, 10/9/1970, FRUS vol. 21, doc. 75.
23. Memorandum Ambassador to Chile to 40 Committee, 11/9/1970, FRUS vol. 21, doc. 78.
24. Telephone conversation Nixon/Kissinger, 12/9/1970, FRUS vol. 21, doc. 82.

25. Telephone conversation, Helms/Kissinger, 12/9/1970, 12:00 noon, HAK Tel Con, Chronological File, Box 6 Jul–Sep 1970, Chronological File, 1/2, RNPL.
26. Backchannel message Korry to the 40 Committee, 14/9/1970, FRUS vol. 22, doc. 85.
27. Telegram Johnson to Korry, 14/9/1970, CDF.
28. CIA, Memorandum of conversation, 'Discussion of the Chilean Political Situation', 18/9/1970, National Security Archives (NSAr), Augustin Edwards: a declassified pobituary, 25/4/2017, available at https://nsarchive.gwu.edu/briefing-book/chile/2017-04-25/agustin-edwards-declassified-obituary (accessed 25 October 2023).
29. Memorandum Winston Lord to the Kissinger, 14/9/1970, FRUS vol. 21, doc. 87.
30. Kornbluh, *Pinochet File*, 11.
31. CIA notes, 'Meeting with President on Chile at 15:25 Sept 15 '70', 15/9/1970, NSAr, 'Extreme Option: Overthrow Allende', 15/9/2020, available at https://nsarchive.gwu.edu/briefing-book/chile/2020-09-15/extreme-option-overthrow-allende (accessed 25 October 2023).
32. Richard Helms, *A Look over My Shoulder* (New York: Ballantine Books, 2003), 399.
33. 'Report on CIA Chilean Task Force Activities, 15 September to 3 November 1970', 18/11/1970, CDF; Kornbluh, *Pinochet File*, 14.
34. Backchannel message Korry to the Kissinger, 17/9/1970, FRUS vol. 21, doc. 102.
35. Memorandum from the Station in Chile to the 40 Committee, 19/9/1970, FRUS vol. 21, doc. 105.
36. Minutes 40 Committee Meeting, 19/9/1970, CDF.
37. Johnson memo to Korry, 22/9/1970, FRUS vol. 21, doc. 113.
38. Telegram CIA to the Station in Chile, 21/9/1970, FRUS vol. 21, doc. 107.
39. Kornbluh, *Pinochet File*, 13.
40. Memorandum for the record, 40 Committee meeting 24/9/1970, CDF.
41. Message CIA to Station Chile, 21/9/1970, FRUS, 1969–1976, vol. E-16, doc. 22.
42. Telegram Station to Director 22/9/1970, CDF.
43. Backchannel message Korry to Meyer and Kissinger, 21/9/1970, FRUS vol. E-16, doc. 23.
44. Telegram Embassy Chile to State, 22/9/1970, FRUS vol. E-16, doc. 24.
45. SSCIA, Interim Report: 'Alleged assassination plots involving foreign leaders' (Interim Report) (Washington, DC: US Government Printing Office, 1975), 231.

René Schneider: Removing the Main Obstacle to a Coup

46. Telegram Station to HQ, 24/9/1970, CDF.
47. Memorandum Haig to Kissinger, 24/9/1970, FRUS vol. 21, doc. 119.
48. CIA Telegram to Santiago, 27/9/1970, in Kornbluh, *Pinochet File*.
49. Kornbluh, *Pinochet File*, 15, 21.
50. Editorial Note, FRUS vol. 21, doc. 151; 'Report on CIA Chilean Task Force Activities, 15 September to 3 November 1970', 18/11/1970, CDF.
51. Talking Paper on Track II, 6/10/1970, CDF.
52. 'Report on CIA Chilean Task Force'; Seymour Hersh, *The Price of Power* (New York: Summit Books, 1983), 272.
53. Informal report on 40 Committee meeting, 6/10/1970, CDF.
54. Minutes of the meeting of the 40 Committee, 6/10/1970, in 'Proposed Agenda for 40 Committee, Tuesday, October 6, 1970', CDF.
55. CIA, Cable HQ to Santiago, 7/10/1970, in Kornbluh, *Pinochet File*.
56. SSCIA, Interim Report, 241.
57. Track II, 7/10/1970, CDF.
58. Track II, 9/101970, CDF.
59. Chile Task Force Chronology, undated, CDF.
60. Kornbluh, *Pinochet File*, 23.
61. According to some accounts, the CIA had interrupted contact with Marshall once they had found him to be unstable. Ignoring pressure from Washington, Korry approached Allende directly to warn him of an assassination plot against him. Eventually, Allende convinced the Chilean police to arrest Marshall. Having resisted arrest, he was found in possession of a rifle with telescopic sight, thus providing confirmation of his secret mission. Hersh, *The Price*, 293; Kornbluh, *Pinoche* File, 16; SSCIA, Addenda, 127.
62. Backchannel message Korry to Johnson and Kissinger, 9/10/1970, FRUS vol. 21, doc. 144.
63. The channel of communication was Karamessines (head of the Chile Task Force) to Haig (Kissinger's deputy), Haig to Kissinger and (presumably) to Nixon.
64. Telegram Santiago to HQ, 9/10/1970, CDF.
65. SSCIA, Interim Report, 248.
66. Ibid., 252.
67. Telegram Station to CIA, 10/10/1970, CDF.
68. Telegram Santiago to HQ, 13/10/1970, CDF.
69. The document adds 'with the exception of' but the name is redacted.
70. Situation 13/10/1970, CDF.
71. Kornbluh, *Pinochet File*, 23.
72. Telegram Station to HQ, 14/10/1970, CDF.
73. One could speculate as to what the short redaction is hiding. It is a short one. 'Or kill', maybe?

74. Minutes of a Meeting of the Senior Review Group, 14/10/1970, FRUS vol. 21, doc. 150.
75. The President.
76. Editorial Note, FRUS vol. 21, doc. 151
77. Telegram from Phillips and Broe, 12/10/1970, CDF.
78. Ibid.
79. James Lockhart, *Chile, the CIA and the Cold War* (Edinburgh: Edinburgh University Press, 2021), 192–3; Track II, 14/10/1970, CDF.
80. Track II, 14/10/1970, CDF.
81. SSCIA, Interim Report, 250.
82. Lockhart, *Chile*, 201.
83. SSCIA, Interim Report, 242.
84. It should be noted that the phone conversation laments the risk of an abortive coup, not of a coup in general.
85. Telephone conversation, President/Kissinger, 15/10/1970, HAK Tel Con, Chronological File, Box 7 October 1970, 12–16 October 2/2, RNPL.
86. The precise nature of the objective is still redacted. Telegram CIA to Station – Chile, 15/10/1970, FRUS vol. 21, doc. 154
87. SSCIA, Interim Report, 227.
88. David Attlee Phillips, Testimony, SSCIA, 31/7/1975, DNSA Covert Operation II, 28.
89. SSCIA, Interim Report, 227.
90. Unearthed for the first time in the research for this book.
91. Al Haig, Memorandum for Henry Kissinger, 16/10/1970, Al Haig Chronological File, Box 972, Folder October 14–24, 2/2, RNPL. In a handwritten note on the document, Haig also tells Kissinger that he has spoken with Bennett and the latter will let Haig know if Laird issues new orders.
92. Lockhart, *Chile*, 202.
93. SSCIA, Interim Report, 243.
94. CIA, 'Special mandate from the president on Chile', undated, CDF.
95. Kornbluh, *Pinochet File*, 27.
96. SSCIA, Interim Report, 244.
97. CIA, Cable from Santiago Station, 19/10/1970; NSAr, 'The United States and Chile', available at https://nsarchive.gwu.edu/briefing-book/chile/2020-10-22/cia-chile-anatomy-assassination (accessed 26 October 2023).
98. SSCIA, Interim Report, 244.
99. Qureshi, *Nixon*, 63.
100. CIA, 'Special mandate from the President on Chile', undated, CDF.

101. Peter Kornbluh, 'The CIA and Chile: Anatomy of an Assassination', NSAr, 22/10/2020, available at https://nsarchive.gwu.edu/briefing-book/chile/2020-10-22/cia-chile-anatomy-assassination (accessed 26 October 2023).
102. CBS, *60 Minutes: Schneider v. Kissinger*, 2001, available at https://search.alexanderstreet.com/preview/work/bibliographic_entity%7Cvideo_work%7C2855887 (accessed 26 October 2023).
103. The latter, at times, put the amount of money at $250,000. See NSAr, Interview with Paul Wimert, Cold War Documentary Interviews, available at https://nsarchive2.gwu.edu/coldwar/interviews/episode-18/wimert1.html (accessed 26 October 2023).
104. Cable Phillips to CIA Station Santiago, 23/10/1970, available at https://nsarchive.gwu.edu/document/23593-cia-cable-santiago-station-headquarters-reaction-shooting-general-schneider-secret (accessed 26 October 2023).
105. As we have seen, this was part of the plan discussed with Valenzuela. Chile Task Force Chronology, undated, CDF.
106. Chile Task Force Chronology, undated, CDF.
107. Kornbluh, *Pinochet File*, 31–5.
108. SSCIA, Interim Report, 5.
109. Lockhart, *Chile*, 200–2.
110. Thomas Powers, *The Man Who Kept the Secrets: Richard Helms and the CIA* (New York: Pocket Books 1979), 303.

7 The 'Season of Inquiry' and the Fight over the Ban on Assassination

On 27 February 1975, the phone rang on the desk of journalist Daniel Schorr. The previous month, Schorr had requested a background interview with CIA Director William Colby. The request had finally been granted. The call could not have come at a better time.

Schorr had become aware that on 16 January, President Gerald Ford had hosted a luncheon for editors and journalists of the *New York Times*. During the luncheon, Ford had discussed his selection of commissioners for the recently appointed Rockefeller Commission tasked with investigating allegations of the CIA's improper activities within the United States. When journalists had pointed out the conservative character of the commissioners, Ford had responded that the inclusion of more liberal members might have led to the discovery of even more problematic CIA activities. At that, Abe Rosenthal, the *Times* managing editor, had asked: 'Like what?' and the President had responded, 'Like assassination', before belatedly stating that the conversation had been off the record.

Rumours of Ford's admission had made their way to Schorr, who had started investigating. Colby's call gave Schorr a chance to ask the CIA's spymaster directly.[1] After thirty minutes of general chat, he abruptly asked the question: 'Has the CIA ever killed anybody in this country?'

Colby was taken aback. It wasn't the first time he had been called to defend himself or the Agency against accusations of assassination.

* * *

In 1967, while stationed in Vietnam, Colby had been involved in the internal investigations of the Agency's role in the coup against

Diem. Later, as CIA Chief of Station in Vietnam and of Chief of the Far East Division, Colby had overseen the US government's pacification programme in Vietnam, known as Civil Operations and Rural Development Support (CORDS). CORDS included the controversial Phoenix Program, aimed at the 'neutralisation' of members of the Viet Cong Infrastructure (VCI), the civilian support network of the Viet Cong. 'Neutralisation' encompassed arresting, rallying or killing members of the VCI.[2] Colby had been called to explain and defend the programme in Congressional hearings and, at times, had struggled to defend Phoenix against accusations that it was an unruly campaign of assassinations.[3]

In 1971, after an article in *Parade* magazine suggested that the CIA was the only US government agency with a licence to kill, Colby had hoped to write a full public rebuttal. Instead, having investigated the Agency's files, he prepared an internal directive against assassination. Then Director Richard Helms had signed it.[4]

* * *

With Schorr, Colby retreated to what he called the CIA's 'long-time practice of answering only the specific question'.[5] 'Not in this country.' He replied. For Schorr, it was a shock. He continued:

'Who?'

When Colby replied that he could not talk about it, Schorr improvised.

'Hammarskjöld?' Referring to the UN Secretary General killed in mysterious circumstances during the Congo crisis. Colby denied.

'Lumumba?'

Colby told Schorr that he could not expand further. After the call, Schorr realised that – even without targets – he had a story, and he could go live with it.

The story of the 'season of inquiry' has been chronicled elsewhere.[6] Assassination and allegations that the US government had been involved in assassination plots against foreign officials played a prominent role in shaping the intensity and breadth of the inquiry. The Ford Administration established the Rockefeller Commission but worked to stymie its investigation of assassination. The Administration also worked to undermine the investigations of the Senate

Select Committee to Study Governmental Operations with Respect to Intelligence Activities (known as the Church Committee). The committee published an interim report on assassination plots against foreign officials which recommended the establishment of a statute to outlaw assassination. The recommendation was ignored. Instead, Ford published an Executive Order reforming the intelligence community. Executive Order 11905 included a ban on assassination. Contrary to the committee's recommendations, the ban was not enshrined into law and its meaning and remit remained vague. This ambiguity created an opening for contestation and (re) shaped the US government's conduct in the realm of assassination.

The Season Begins

In May 1973, the press had started highlighting connections between the CIA and the Watergate break-in. New CIA Director James Schlesinger, a Nixon loyalist, who had replaced Helms in February 1973,[7] asked Colby (then his deputy) what else was happening in the CIA that might lead to scandal. Colby had replied that he did not know.[8] On the 9th, Schlesinger signed an internal memorandum for all CIA employees, drafted by Colby. Schlesinger ordered CIA employees to report any activity past or present that might have violated the CIA charter.[9] Almost 700 pages of documents rolled in. The collection soon took the name of 'Family Jewels'.[10] The collection – as Henry Kissinger later conceded – was 'dynamite'.[11]

Colby and Schlesinger agreed that Congress had to be notified and reassured that the Agency had stopped similar activities. Leaders of Congressional committees and subcommittees agreed that the 'jewels' should not be made public.[12] Colby and Schlesinger also decided not to tell the Nixon White House about the collection. The CIA took additional protective measures such as new internal directives that prohibited illegal activities. Colby issued the directives on 29 August 1973, including a new internal prohibition on assassination: 'The CIA will not engage in assassination, nor induce, assist or suggest to others that assassination be employed.'[13]

On 20 December, Colby – by then CIA Director – agreed to meet with investigative journalist Seymour Hersh, who was working on a story on intelligence activities.[14] Hersh told Colby that he knew of a 'massive' CIA operation against the anti-war movement and other US citizens. Colby had hoped that by meeting with Hersh he could put the story to bed – or, at a minimum, put it into perspective. Despite later criticisms, Colby's expectation was not unreasonable. The year before, Colby had been able to convince Hersh not to publish a story on the expedition of the *Glomar Explorer*, a CIA–Howard Hughes venture to retrieve a sunken Soviet nuclear submarine.[15] Furthermore, the DCI was afraid that Head of Counter-intelligence James Angleton, whom Colby was about to fire, was behind the leaks to Hersh.[16]

In the meeting, Colby did not deny the existence of such an operation, but he told Hersh that he was confusing various pieces of the puzzle, and that the operation was not as massive as he implied. Far from dissuading Hersh, Colby's comments were taken as confirmation. On 22 December, the front page of the *New York Times* read: 'Huge CIA Operation reported in US against anti-war forces, other dissidents in Nixon years.' The White House was caught off guard. The 'season of inquiry' had started.

* * *

Early measures taken by the White House aimed at preventing the emergence of a full-blown scandal and of Congressional investigations.[17] Colby was told to write a report on the CIA activities for the President. Chief of Staff Donald Rumsfeld put Dick Cheney, Deputy Assistant to the President, in charge of all communications to the President regarding the crisis.[18] In this process, Colby was isolated. National Security Advisor Henry Kissinger despised him, saw him as too willing to reveal US secrets, and kept him away from the White House.[19]

On Christmas Eve, Colby presented his report to Kissinger. Assassination plots were excluded and Colby only briefed Kissinger orally. On Christmas Day, Kissinger – not Colby, who was kept at arm's length – briefed Ford, telling the President that beyond Hersh's revelations detailed in Colby's report, the CIA had been involved in other problematic activities. 'Some few of them clearly were illegal,' Kissinger wrote, 'while others – though not technically illegal – raise profound moral questions. A number, while neither illegal nor morally unsound, demonstrated very poor judgment.'[20] Ford started considering the appointment of a blue-ribbon commission to investigate the allegations. Kissinger expressed his 'strong recommendation' that this commission be limited to Hersh's allegations, thus excluding assassinations.[21]

The Rockefeller Commission and Assassination

Only in the afternoon of 3 January was Colby able to meet Ford. Citing Castro, Trujillo and Schneider, Colby told the President: 'We have run operations to assassinate foreign leaders. We have never succeeded.'[22] Such a stark revelation was quite the bombshell, especially the admission of 'running' the operation against Schneider. The minutes of the meeting do not record any of the attendees' reactions.

On the morning of the 4th, Ford met with Kissinger and his deputy, Brent Scowcroft. Kissinger appeared almost apoplectic. 'What is happening is worse than in the days of McCarthy,' he warned the President. 'You will end up with a CIA that does only reporting, and not operations.' This was preposterous. At the same time, the CIA was mounting a major covert operation in Angola and Kissinger was very much at the centre of it.[23] Kissinger also added that – according to former DCI Helms – Hersh's story was just the tip of the iceberg; other items were ready to emerge. 'If they come out,' Kissinger continued, 'blood will flow. For example, Robert Kennedy personally managed the operation on the assassination of Castro.'[24]

In an afternoon meeting with former DCI Richard Helms, Ford admitted that the situation threatened the existence of the CIA. Helms agreed: 'I don't know everything which went on in the Agency; maybe no one really does. But I know enough to say that if the dead cats come out, I will participate.'[25] By the evening of the 4th, Ford had decided to 'protect the functions of the Agency with a Blue-Ribbon group which will operate responsibly'.[26] The White House's priority was not to find the truth, but to obstruct the commission. As Vice-President Walter Mondale put it, 'they did not want to do much with it'.[27]

The Administration's selection of white, male and conservative commissioners reflected this aim;[28] as did the selection of Vice-President Nelson Rockefeller as Chairman. Rockefeller had a long affiliation with the intelligence community and with controversial covert operations.[29] As Colby recalled, Rockefeller also had very little interest in investigating the CIA's wrongdoings.[30] Commission staffers were also certain that Rockefeller's closeness to Kissinger would skew the investigation.[31] Beyond the personnel, the mandate of the commission also betrayed an interest in limiting the investigations. It asked the commission to evaluate solely activities the Agency conducted within the United States which might give rise to problems of compliance with the CIA's charter. This excluded foreign covert operations and broader questions of impropriety. The commission had the power to ask other agencies for relevant documents, and these agencies were encouraged to cooperate, but they were under no obligation to do so.[32] The commission had to rely on the CIA to reveal its own secrets.[33]

Early in the commission's investigation, David Belin, the commission's Staff Director, had asked the CIA for a copy of the 'Family Jewels'. The Agency had initially demurred.[34] The first copy of the document passed to Belin did not include the discussion of assassination since the CIA considered the material extremely sensitive and outside the scope of the commission's inquiry. Only at Belin's insistence was the material disclosed. The material, Belin wrote, was 'so horrible that there had to be a thorough investigation that would promptly bring the matter before the public'.[35]

After intense debate among staffers, and after a confrontation between the commission's staffers and the White House,[36] the Administration agreed to expand the commission's mandate to look at assassination attempts, but only those that had domestic connections. This limited the commission to the assassination plots against Fidel Castro and Rafael Trujillo. Belin took charge of the investigation of the former, counsel Marvin Gray of the latter. There were other attachments. White House Counsel Philip Buchen warned Belin that once the investigation was completed, it was up to the White House to decide what should be included in the final report.[37]

As the investigation got under way, it became apparent that several documents had been destroyed long before the commission. The staff of the commission also struggled to access those that had survived.[38] Assurances of cooperation, Belin concluded after a long fight with Kissinger's office, were 'garbage'. 'The real intent from the very beginning was to deny access.'[39] To supplement the historical record, the commission was able to call on witnesses, but it struggled to obtain valuable information. Amnesia was rampant in Washington, or so it seemed. Helms, for example, denied recalling any plan for the assassination of Castro, any other assassination plan, the name of the committee in charge of covert operations during his tenure, and even the date of the Cuban missile crisis.[40] Similarly, Secretary of Defense McNamara apologetically told investigators that he did not take notes of the meetings he attended and, try as he might, his memory of those years was 'very bad'.[41]

In several depositions, a distinction also emerged between ideas individuals involved might have talked about or brainstormed, and actual plans. Talk of assassination, several witnesses admitted, might have happened, but it did not mean that any actual plan was being pursued or that any authorisation had been given, by either the CIA or the White House.[42] Similarly, former members of the Kennedy Administration – even confronted with documentary evidence – could not or would not explain how assassination had emerged as a policy option.[43] The lines of authorisation were seemingly too blurred to trace.

If getting information out of witnesses was challenging, the investigators were often unwilling to press them. During Helms's deposition, for example, staffers seemed to buy the former DCI's timid performance. But the commissioners knew better. A few days before Helms's testimony, George Manfredi, counsel to the commission, had reported on his search of Helms's records, highlighting several memoranda and handwritten notes in which the former DCI talked about assassination plots, as well as other activities at the centre of the commission's inquiry. Manfredi included evidence that Helms had discussed with Nixon and Kissinger a series of topics including 'assassination (Diem, Trujillo, Castro)'. The document could have played a prominent role in Helms's cross-examination, but nothing happened.[44]

The Ban on Assassination

Despite these limits, the report and the sections dealing with assassination were not a complete whitewash. Belin's investigation contained extensive details of the various phases of the plots against Castro. It concluded that the CIA was 'directly involved' in plans to assassinate the Cuban leader but that evidence regarding lines of authority was conflicting.[45] Counsel Gray's less thorough investigation on Trujillo concluded that there was no direct American participation in the assassination itself, but extensive communication with the plotters and the US government's awareness of their 'lethal intentions'.[46] For investigators, it proved impossible to establish responsibilities beyond the CIA and a few characters within it. This result was preordained. In most cases, access to the files of the NSC and of other committees in charge of covert operations had been denied.[47]

Towards the end of the commission's investigation, Chairman Rockefeller and Commissioner Douglas Dillon let the media know that the report would soon be released, including a section on assassination.[48] In the last days of May, the White House requested that the commission turn over all the materials related to its investigation and the complete draft. Having received the draft report, Cheney heavily redrafted and edited several sections to reduce the criticism of the CIA and the impression that the CIA's activities had been illegal. Assassination plots were removed altogether. The complete draft of the commission's report submitted to the White House included twenty chapters. Chapter 20 contained Belin's and Gray's report on assassination. On 6 June, the report was released. The chapter on assassinations was nowhere to be found. The report also contained an explicit lie suggesting that investigation of assassination plots had been abandoned for lack of time.[49] The ball passed to Congress.

The Church Committee, the White House and Assassination

Watergate and the hearings that followed – including hearings on the US government's covert interference in Chile – had broken the wall of secrecy around the Agency.[50] At one point, in October

1974, Senator James Abourezk (D-SD) had even proposed to outlaw covert operations altogether, through an amendment to the Foreign Assistance Act.[51] The amendment had been voted down, but the mid-term elections of November 1974 brought further trouble for the Agency. Riding high on the wings of the Watergate scandal, the Democratic Party had won 9 seats in the Senate and 49 in the House. As historian Laura Kalman put it, these new Democrats were 'Watergate babies', and they 'did not sleep, they screamed'.[52]

In December 1974, the new Congress passed a momentous amendment, sponsored by Leo Ryan (D-CA) and Harold Hughes (D-IO). The Hughes–Ryan amendment changed the practice of covert operation. From then on, before a covert operation could be approved, the President had to 'find' that such operation served the national interest. The finding – or a Memorandum of Notification that aimed at providing a 'significant' expansion to an existing finding[53] – had to be communicated to the appropriate Congressional committees.[54] While far from perfect, as intelligence historian Loch Johnson has argued, such a measure was a strong attack against the doctrine of plausible 'presidential' deniability.[55]

* * *

On 15 January, Colby had been called to testify to a joint session of the Senate's Armed Services and Appropriations Committee. Colby had mentioned this request during his briefing to President Ford on 3 January.[56] Ford opposed the publication of Colby's report on the 'Family Jewels' but Colby used the report as the basis of his Congressional testimony and – to the White House's dismay – agreed to its release and publication. According to Robert McFarlane, then staff assistant to National Security Advisor Kissinger, Colby had revealed other 'gratuitous information' critical of the Agency which could lead to an expansion of the inquiry.[57]

Regardless of Colby's testimony, Congress was already too invested in the CIA scandals not to pursue a full-blown investigation. The Senate established a select committee 'to study governmental operations with respect to intelligence activities'. The committee was headed by Senator Frank Church (D-ID) with John

Tower (R-TX) as its vice-chairman.[58] Appointed chairman, Church told CBS *Face the Nation* that he expected his investigation to be 'much more broad-reaching than the President's commission'.[59] The investigation was 'imperative' but it would not entail a 'vendetta' nor a 'whitewash'. It would aim – where possible – to release information to the public and to proceed in a bipartisan manner.[60]

Having failed to prevent a Congressional investigation, the Executive moved to limit its depth and breadth. Although both Ford and his Press Secretary Ron Nessen later insisted that the White House was open to full cooperation and broadly agreed with the need for investigation,[61] the historical record tells a different story. The White House understood that – for domestic political reasons – it had to give the impression of cooperation.[62] It was just a facade which created a 'velvet stonewall' – an impression of amiability and cooperation which covered obstructionist tactics.[63] The White House did not hesitate to deploy the trappings of executive power to intimidate young (and at times inexperienced) investigators.[64] The manipulation of the committee also came to rely on the Republicans on the committee and their staff, often acting as a 'fifth column'. As the investigation intensified, so did partisan divisions.[65]

The CIA also prepared for battle. Under the direction of Colby, the Agency created a task force to deal with the committee's requests and a central index to track all documents requested by the committee. The Agency classified these documents according to a typology to determine whether and in what detail they should be released. Sensitive material would not be available to the committee in its 'raw form'. This category included memoranda to and from the President as well as other documents on sensitive matters where executive branch privileges are involved. This material could be used by the Agency to prepare oral briefs for the investigators, but the documents themselves would not be provided. Documents in a second category could be viewed only at the originating agency and might have been subject to restrictions from such agency.[66] Documents in a third category would be provided only in a sanitised form. Finally, only a small amount of (mostly generic) documents would be provided to the committee in their original form.[67] In dealing with requests, the CIA also made widespread use of 'abstracts'. These short summaries of much larger and potentially more controversial documents gave the impression of collaboration while revealing very little.[68]

In a meeting with Tower and Church, Ford made clear that he had no intention of letting the investigations get out of hand. Each controversy between the White House and the committee should be resolved on a case-by-case basis.[69] As policy, any request for documents or for testimonies needed to be cleared with the Counsel's office and with the White House.[70] The White House and Kissinger established channels and backchannels to influence witnesses and committee members.[71] Executive officials, including Colby, were asked to rehearse their testimonies at the White House, until they were sufficiently bland.[72] Having heard Colby's first testimony, Church was unimpressed. He told the media that he had learnt nothing new and expected the DCI to go back to the committee soon.[73]

Fighting over the Assassination Report

In the aftermath of Colby's testimony, as the fight over the release of documents continued, the committee started its official investigation of assassination plots.[74] As Loch Johnson has written, when it came to assassination documents, Colby was intransigent.[75] In the first week of June, the issue of assassination documents was made even more pressing by the release of the Rockefeller Commission report. The media and Congress (including Church) accused Ford of a cover-up.

Within the White House, debate emerged as to what material to transfer to the committee. Transferring only the material in possession of the Rockefeller Commission would have provided a skewed picture of covert operations.[76] Those documents only covered the CIA, and the committee was already aware of assassination plots and of the role of Special Groups.[77] Transferring all documents including NSC and Special Groups documents, in turn, was considered 'unprecedented' and detrimental to US foreign policy and diplomatic relations.[78] Kissinger initially advised Ford that no material be released. He eventually relented. Church, Kissinger thought, would find himself in the untenable position of either refusing to investigate or of dragging the Kennedys – and by extension his own party – through the dirt.[79] The material was transferred only after further pressure from the committee and its chairman,[80] but the transfer was conditional. An agreement had been reached with the committee that the documents would be passed 'on loan'. They could not be disclosed or released, and if the committee did want to release them, it would have to subpoena them as if they had not been transferred, unless the White House approved.[81] Even then, the release was very selective. 'Papers evidencing the approval process such as proposals or recommendations made to the President or to groups which advised the President, as well as deliberations within such groups', were to be excluded.[82] The CIA and the NSC were satisfied with the very conservative approach taken in the release.[83] This decision set the stage for two of the main problems encountered by the committee: first, the controversy surrounding the publication of the interim report on assassination plots; second, the impossible task of breaking the wall of secrecy around assassination and the presidency.

Throughout the summer, the Church Committee investigated assassination. On 10 October, Church reported to the Senate that the investigation into assassination plots was complete, and that the Senate would receive the report soon.[84] The news that the committee intended to publish an interim report on assassination pushed the White House back into crisis mode. 'I think this is a more highly sensitive area than any we have had,' Ford stated. 'I never assumed they had the right to publish this.' Warned by Attorney General Edward Levi that the White House had no legal option to prevent publication, Ford was still unsatisfied: 'I said they had to handle these assassination documents as we had and we released none of them.'[85] Buchen tried to put the problem into perspective: 'all we are fighting,' he told the President, 'is official confirmation of material which is already widely known. This is not a good issue on which to go to the mat.' Colby disagreed. 'Any document which officially shows American involvement in an assassination,' he told the group, 'is a major foreign policy disaster.' Ford concurred: 'I think we should review it and then say it is not in the national interest to release it at all.' The issue – Kissinger added – impinged on the power of the executive.[86]

The committee had agreed to let the executive review the interim report. Officials from State, Defense and the CIA reviewed it. All agreed that the publication would do 'irreparable damage' to both US national security and the reputation of the United States.[87] Having read the assessments, Colby urged Ford 'in the strongest terms possible' that the report should not be published.[88] The President and DCI started an all-out effort to prevent the publication. They wrote letters to all the senators on the committee explaining the dramatic national security implications of the release of information, and Colby even held a public press conference to convince the Senate not to publish the report.[89] Church responded with a letter to the President in protest[90] and made similar points publicly. The committee fractured, largely along partisan lines. The Senate refused to endorse its own committee's report. Only Church's insistence and his threat to resign led to the publication of the interim report on 20 November.

The Report and Its Findings

When it was published, the report presented a damning picture of US foreign policy. The committee understood the necessarily partial nature of its findings as several documents had been destroyed.[91] The controversial nature of the topic made it unlikely that explicit discussions would make it into historical records. For this reason, the committee had worked to corroborate documentary evidence with a painstaking search for testimonies.[92] Here, the committee had to confront unexpected difficulties such as the murder of witnesses – including Sam Giancana and Johnny Rosselli, the Mafia gangsters involved in the assassination plots against Fidel Castro.[93] Keeping in mind these difficulties, the committee was still able to hear – behind closed doors – from leading figures of the Kennedy and Eisenhower administrations, from current and former CIA officials, and from shady figures of the underworld, including Mafia dons and corrupt cops. Overall, the investigations collected 8,000 pages of sworn testimony from seventy-five witnesses, over sixty days of hearings.[94]

The report unveiled the US government's involvement in assassination plots and the development of general assassination

The Ban on Assassination

capabilities. The committee identified two cases (against Castro and Lumumba) initiated by the CIA. For Lumumba, the report came close to establishing a presidential order to assassinate. For Castro, the evidence established the conduct of assassination plots from 1960 to 1965. In the committee's view, lines of responsibility led (almost) all the way to the White House. It also identified another three cases of more indirect US involvement (Trujillo, Diem and Schneider). The US government was certainly aware of the local actors' lethal intent in the case of Trujillo, but, or so the committee thought, was not aware of – and perhaps was even opposed to – assassination in the case of Diem. In the case of Schneider, the committee accepted the view that contact with the group that kidnapped and killed Schneider had been interrupted before the plot.[95] Overall, the committee reached the narrow conclusion that no foreign leader had been killed in plots directly initiated by US officials.

Beyond these plots, the committee was also able to piece together some evidence on additional cases, which did not make it into the main body of the report, such as Sukarno of Indonesia and Duvalier of Haiti.[96] The committee's Interim Report also explored the CIA's development and institutionalisation of a general capability for the assassination of foreign officials.[97] Finally, a later addendum mentioned some brief consideration of assassination plots against Chiang Kai Shek in 1949 and Chou Enlai in 1955.[98]

Assassination in US Foreign Policy

In reflecting on assassination and its role in US foreign policy, the report established that – short of war – assassination is incompatible with 'American principles, international order, and morality' and it should be rejected as a 'tool of foreign policy'.[99] The committee did concede that the Cold War environment of heightened tension in which many of the plots took place could explain, but not justify, assassination.[100] The committee argued that at no point were the plots justified by an imminent danger posed by the foreign officials in question. Only Castro posed a 'physical threat'

193

to the United States, but only in the context of the missile crisis, and the assassination plots had started much earlier and continued afterwards.[101] Some scholars have argued that, from this observation, one should conclude that the killing of a leader posing an imminent threat would have been justified under the criteria established by the committee.[102] This is incorrect. The committee stressed that – even if the targets had posed an imminent danger – the US government should have refrained from assassination and from justifying its actions using the standards of totalitarian states, a point lost in later interpretations.[103]

The report did make a distinction between two activities. 'Targeted assassination instigated by the United States,' the report read, 'must be prohibited.'[104] The committee seemed more ambivalent regarding the US involvement in coups. The committee – recognising the history of US rebellion against tyranny – did not completely rule out involvement in coups or support for dissidents. But it did not provide a green light either. It warned that coups involved 'varying degrees of risk of assassination' and such risk should have featured prominently in any decision surrounding involvement. It also warned that support for dissidents and other groups created problems of control over these groups and their activities.[105]

Several CIA officials had stressed the practical and moral difference between the provision of weapons to certain groups and the initiation of an assassination plot.[106] There was a distinction to be made, Colby stressed, between 'supporting armed action' and 'committing assassination'.[107] At times, the CIA's David Attlee Phillips explained, in a 'pretty tough business' like coups, once you got involved, it often proves impossible to place 'stop and go buttons on the machinery that you have set in motion'.[108] At least some members of the committee, though, understood that this distinction often played an enabling role within the policy-making process. For example, during his questioning of Phillips, Senator Gary Hart stated:

> Nobody apparently sits down and decides that they are going to kill John Smith, the President of country A. That apparently is abhorrent. But more than once, they sit down and decide they will topple John Smith's government, and accidentally John Smith gets killed, but they feel that it is unfortunate, but apparently no culpability.[109]

In this sense, support for third parties and this type of indirect involvement made the killing of foreign officials more palatable.[110] This process of 'othering' – well understood within the literature on state terror and state crimes – both permitted policymakers to circumvent existing norms and provided them with a form of (moral) self-reassurance.[111] Government officials in these cases – such as Justin O'Donnell in his approach to Lumumba – were able to 'outsource' the conduct of controversial activities to local actors, protecting their reputation and self-image, and circumventing norms, while promoting their agenda.[112]

This point connects to another area of concern discussed in the report: communication. Bouts of amnesia, again, abounded, especially when it came to recollecting orders, authorisations and plans. Committee members proved less kind than their Rockefeller Commission counterparts with those who relied on the fine distinction between brainstorming ideas and actual plans. When one witness tried to make this argument, Senator Walter Mondale lost his patience:

> We know, in fact, orders were given to assassinate Mr Lumumba. Both the person who gave the orders and the person who received them testified to that effect . . . Similarly, we know in fact that orders were given to assassinate Mr Castro . . . So when you say it didn't get off the ground, it sure as hell did.[113]

The committee also highlighted the pernicious role of euphemisms, innuendos and circumlocutions. During testimonies, committee members and staffers heard from several witnesses how words that – to all intents and purposes – seemed to call for assassination, seemingly did not. Committee staffers were also told that many of these words were inherently ambiguous, and their meaning was clear only in the mind of those who pronounced them at the time.[114] The report eventually conceded that this ambiguity was so rife as to confuse even CIA directors.[115] In an environment combining high pressure and no clear statement of policy, the report argued, assassination could easily have appeared as an available policy option.[116]

Euphemisms and circumlocutions also served clear purposes. First, they helped in maintaining a sanitised historical record. This was particularly the case in documents that involved the NSC, the cabinet and the President. As Bissell told the committee, 'Especially when some kind of record is being kept', US officials 'talk around' a subject like assassination. This does not mean that the meaning is 'obscure or not understood by those present'. In his view, both Livingston Merchant's question regarding getting rid of the Cuban leadership, and Gordon Gray's report of Eisenhower's views on Lumumba clearly called for assassination (and were understood as such) regardless of the 'gobbledegook' used.[117] When this failed, the historical record could always be manipulated through the destruction of documents or the use of last-minute 'save your ass' telegrams aiming to distance the US government from assassination.[118]

Second, like outsourcing, euphemisms also shielded those using them from the immorality of what they were doing. In this sense, 'failing to call dirty business by its rightful name may have increased the risk of dirty business being done'. Finally, they also blurred the lines of authorisation and responsibility. They made authorisations to subordinates – at least those that made it into the official record – and witnesses' recollections inherently murky. The same applied to discussions with those at the top.[119] An iconic exchange between Senator Charles Mathias and Helms exposed the nature of presidential deniability:

> Senator Mathias: Let me draw an example from history. When Thomas Becket was proving to be an annoyance, as Castro, the King said 'who will rid me of this troublesome priest?' He didn't say, 'go out and murder him'. He said, 'who will rid me of this man,' and let it go at that.
> Mr. Helms: That is a warming reference to the problem.

Helms admitted that 'in the tradition of the time', he would have found it 'very difficult' to discuss assassination with a president; that was the type of topic to be kept away from the Oval Office.[120]

Euphemisms were not the only factor preventing the committee from establishing clear lines of authorisation and responsibility. The doctrine of 'plausible deniability' had gotten out of hand. Initially developed to protect the role and the overall reputation of the US government in the conduct of covert operations, the doctrine had soon been extended to 'mask decisions of the president and his senior staff', including CIA directors. Over time, US officials had also established decision-making fora, procedures and practices that could shield the President and his reputation, providing him with personal deniability.[121] The use of Special Groups for the discussion and approval of covert operations also contributed to shielding the President. These groups, the report concluded, acted as 'circuit breakers'.[122] Confronted with this problem, the committee was startled. Did the committee fail to establish presidential responsibility because there was no such thing and the CIA had been acting as a rogue elephant – as Church had famously hinted at the start of the investigations – or because there was such a thing, but it was successfully protected by obscure language and plausible deniability? Both prospects, the report argued, were disturbing.[123]

It also became apparent that beyond individuals' moral qualms, by and large questions of legality had not entered the picture when it came to assassination.[124] On this topic, the committee heard from Lawrence Houston, General Counsel of the CIA from its founding to 1973.[125] Houston testified that he had never been consulted on plans to assassinate foreign leaders and he only heard after the fact.[126]

From Church's Law to Ford's Ban

In his initial remarks to the Senate, Church had identified a pattern of 'lawlessness' in the CIA's activities and the need to restore the 'sanctity of the law'.[127] The report recommended the establishment of a law or statute that would prohibit assassination. It recognised the existence of internal CIA directives banning assassination, but concluded that these were not enough. They were purely internal measures that could be easily undone. 'Administrations change,' the report read, 'CIA Directors change, and someday in the future what was tried in the past may once again become a temptation.' The only way to resist this future temptation was a law that would prohibit assassination.[128]

As International Relations scholarship on norms puts it, with a law, a prohibition against assassination would have achieved 'legal' character. This would certainly have strengthened the prohibition. As part of judicial and court proceedings, the prohibition would have been better isolated from challenges, making contestation and the erosion of the norm harder.[129] A law would also have removed the ban from the sole control of the CIA or the White House.[130]

As envisioned by the committee, the law would have made it a criminal offence 'to conspire within or outside the United States against a foreign official . . . to attempt to assassinate a foreign official or . . . to assassinate a foreign official'. In this understanding, the success or failure of the assassination plot did not determine its illegality; the very attempt was prohibited. The report was also very clear as to the definition of 'foreign official'. In a prescient point, the report noted that – due to the 'reality of international politics' – the label of 'foreign official' applied not only to officials of a foreign government but also to officials of an insurgent force, an unrecognised government, or a political party. The killing of any of these officials would be punishable if 'politically motivated', that is, due to the official's 'political views, actions, or statements'.[131]

Furthermore, the committee established a clear binary distinction, between wartime and peacetime, as to when the prohibition applied. The prohibition did not apply in a state of declared war or during a use of force in accordance with the War Powers Resolution.[132] Finally, the committee recognised that in situations of extreme emergency, exceptions could be made to the prohibition. In the committee's view, these exceptions were justified only in extreme circumstances, such as 'a new Hitler' or a situation of 'grave national emergency' like the one President Abraham Lincoln confronted during the Civil War.[133]

For many in the Ford Administration, the establishment of a law prohibiting assassination represented the worst-case scenario. After one of his testimonies to the Church Committee, Colby had reported back that – to his dismay – 'All the questions were on assassination, and it was like "when did you stop beating your wife?"' In the same meeting, Kissinger was adamant: 'It is an act of insanity and national humiliation to have a law prohibiting the President from ordering assassination.'[134] While Ford's reaction to Kissinger's outburst isn't recorded, the President had similar concerns.

On 5 June, Ford explained that the White House should be 'careful' in making statements regarding assassination, since Church might decide to write them into law. A law would have constrained Ford's powers and those of future presidents.[135] Some of Ford's advisers disagreed. Attorney General Levi wrote that the 'state of the law' on several issues related to the intelligence community was 'unsatisfactory'. The lack of a federal law prohibiting assassination was a particularly glaring omission. The definitions and criteria developed by the committee, Levi wrote, were sensible and the Administration should have given 'enthusiastic . . . support' to the legislation proposed by the committee.[136] This view did not prevail.

To regain the initiative, protect the executive, and stymie Congressional legislation,[137] the White House published Executive Order 11905 in February 1976. In a Special Message to Congress accompanying the order, Ford stated that he would welcome legislative efforts 'making it a crime to assassinate or attempt to conspire to assassinate foreign official in peacetime'.[138] But the origins of the order as well as its tone and content told a different story. As John Oseth has argued, 'the order was by no means an act of executive contrition. Much of it reads, in fact, as if the major national concern in 1976 was to strengthen, rather than to constrain, our intelligence capabilities.'[139] The text of the order showed no sign that questionable (and illegal) activities had occurred. The order established oversight tools, but they were largely toothless and contained within the executive. The CIA Office of General Counsel,[140] for example, was tasked with submitting reports to the President's Intelligence Oversight Board regarding any activity that raised issues of legality and propriety.[141]

The order also contained a prohibition on assassination. The Interim Report (and Levi) had called for specific criteria and lack of flexibility. The ban contained in the order seemed to advocate the exact opposite.[142] It simply stated: 'No employee of the United States Government shall engage in, or conspire to engage in, political assassination.'[143] Several features of the ban are important in understanding the evolution of the US government's assassination policy. The ban was vague. It did not specify what activity amounted to assassination nor under what conditions the ban would apply. It also said nothing as to which targets were protected by the prohibition. In line with what Jacqueline Best has called 'strategic ambiguity', vagueness permitted future policy-makers to 'govern through ambiguity'.[144]

This had been the main concern of Ford and Kissinger. A vague ban preserved presidential powers and permitted future presidents to exploit the blurry boundaries of the prohibition to achieve their political objectives.[145] As IR scholarship shows, the character of a norm – in this case the ban – also influences the likelihood of efforts to contest it, that is, to challenge its meaning, its remit, and its appropriateness. A vague norm entailing 'complex undefined concepts' – like assassination – and an unclear remit makes contestation more likely.[146] Finally, contrary to a law, the ban could be amended, reinterpreted or revoked without the need for Congressional involvement and without legal proceedings. As former CIA and National Security Council official Bruce Riedel argued, the order represented an effort to 'avoid banning assassination. It was Ford-Administration-bound. This effort was very deliberate.'[147]

Conclusion

At various moments during the season of inquiry, the Ford Administration considered assassination a different ball game, an area that was supposed to stay secret and under the executive's control. The Administration effectively undermined the work of the Rockefeller Commission. As the investigation of assassination moved to the Church Committee, the White House and the CIA stepped up their effort to present a unified front and to obstruct the investigations. The Administration ultimately failed in its attempt to prevent the publication of the interim report, but – by publishing an Executive Order – was successful in stymieing Congressional legislation.

Between September 1976 and February 1980, Congress tried to put into law a prohibition on assassination. Many of these efforts aimed at an expansive understanding of assassination, in one case understood as the killing of 'any person' during the conduct of

The Ban on Assassination

intelligence activities, or more often as the killing of any 'foreign official'.[148] The main effort surrounded a new bill to reform the intelligence community, S. 2525, 'National Intelligence Reorganization and Reform Act'. The proposed bill contained a detailed and wide-ranging definition of assassination and a set of penalties (years to life in prison). It specified the meaning of 'foreign official' and established only an exception for wartime if the assassination had been conducted against an official of the country with which the US government was at war and if it had been authorised by a US official.[149]

By this time, the Carter Administration had come into office with the aim of restoring transparency and morality to the conduct of US foreign policy. Eventually, the Administration followed its predecessor's path. In 1978, Carter approved Executive Order 12036 which updated Ford's 11905. Carter's order was much more stringent. The overall language of the order highlighted the restrictions imposed on the intelligence community, the importance of morality and the rule of law, and robust internal and external procedures to report questionable activities.[150]

The order also contained a new ban on assassination: 'No person employed by or acting on behalf of the United States Government shall engage in, or conspire to engage in, assassination.'[151] Two differences emerge when the language of Carter's ban is compared with that of Ford. First, the order included individuals 'acting on behalf of the United States'. This change expanded the remit of the ban.[152] The prohibition now applied to both persons who are employees of the US government and those who are not employees but who act on its behalf.[153] This change also appeared to close a loophole surrounding US involvement in coups.[154] This conclusion is debated. As Michael Schmitt reports, Carter's National Security Advisor, Zbigniew Brzezinski, argued later that the President had never intended the order to extend to situations in which the assassination of a foreign leader is the indirect outcome of a coup supported by the United States. It remains unclear to what extent this view was shared within the Administration. Several episodes during the Carter Administration seemed to imply a certain reticence in supporting coups.[155]

Second, the order dropped the adjective 'political'. According to Carter's Attorney General, Griffin Bell, the decision simply reflected

Carter's attention to detail. The order was too wordy, and assassination already implied a political motivation. In contrast, Jonathan Fredman, a lawyer in the CIA's Office of General Counsel, and others have suggested that dropping 'political' expanded the remit of the ban to prohibit any killing, regardless of motivation.[156]

Carter himself, CIA Director Stansfield Turner, Vice-President Walter Mondale and Secretary of State Cyrus Vance were – at least initially – sceptical of covert action.[157] The policy experience of several members of the Administration had been shaped during the inquiries of the 1970s. Many had taken part in the Congressional inquiries as staffers or, in the case of Mondale, as members of the committee.[158] While this conclusion is necessarily provisional, it would seem that during the Carter Administration, and even in its tensest moments,[159] assassination was never considered an available option.[160] Assassination, some have pointed out, would have been 'anathema' to the President.[161] And yet, as the Church Committee had predicted, with a change in administration, the temptation of assassination returned. Challenges to the ban started as soon as Ronald Reagan took office.

Notes

1. It is likely that Seymour Hersh told Schorr. Daniel Schorr, *Clearing the Air* (New York: Berkley Medallion Books, 1978), 145.
2. Douglas Valentine, *The Phoenix Program* (Lincoln, NE: iUniverse, 2000); Mark Moyar, *Phoenix and the Birds of Prey* (London: University of Nebraska Press, 2007); Dale Andrade, *Ashes to Ashes* (Lexington, KY: Lexington Books, 1990).
3. US House of Representatives, 'US Assistance programs in Vietnam', 22nd report, Committee on Government operations, 17/10/1972, 46.
4. Randall Woods, *Shadow Warrior: William Egan Colby and the CIA* (New York: Basic Books, 2013), 338.
5. William Colby, *Honorable Men* (New York: Simon & Schuster, 1978), 410.
6. Loch Johnson, *A Season of Inquiry* (Lexington: University Press of Kentucky, 1985); Kathryn Olmsted, *Challenging the Secret Government* (Chapel Hill: University of North Carolina Press, 1996); Dafydd Townley, *The Year of Intelligence* (London: Palgrave Macmillan, 2021).

7. Christopher Moran, 'Nixon's Axe Man: CIA Director James R. Schlesinger', *Journal of American Studies*, 53 (2019), 117.
8. Moran, 'Nixon's Axe Man', 117; William Colby, Testimony at US Senate Select Committee to Study Governmental Operations with Respect to Intelligence Activities (SSCIA), 21/5/1975, Digital National Security Archives (DNSA): Covert Operations II.
9. James Schlesinger, 'Memorandum for all CIA employees', 9/5/1973, DNSA: Family Jewels.
10. Howard Osborn, 'Family Jewels', 16/5/1973, available at https://nsarchive2.gwu.edu/NSAEBB/NSAEBB222/family_jewels_full_ocr.pdf (accessed 26 October 2023).
11. Henry Kissinger, *Years of Renewal* (New York: Simon & Schuster, 2000), 312.
12. John Prados, *Lost Crusader: The Secret Wars of CIA Director William Colby* (Oxford: Oxford Universty Press, 2003), 264.
13. Colby, *Honorable*, 349.
14. John Prados, *The Family Jewels* (Austin: University of Texas Press, 2014), chapter 1.
15. Nicholas Dujmovic, 'Oral History: Reflections of DCI Colby and Helms on the CIA's "Time of Troubles"', *Studies in Intelligence*, 51.3 (2007), 41; Todd Bennett, *Neither Confirm nor Deny* (New York: Columbia University Press, 2023), 82.
16. Harold Ford, *William E. Colby as Director of Central Intelligence* (CIA: CIA History Staff, 1993), 103.
17. Memo Kissinger to Rumsfeld, 'Public handling of New York Times allegations of CIA domestic activities', 23/12/1974, Richard Cheney Files, Box 6, Intelligence Subseries, Folder 'Intelligence – General', Gerald Ford Presidential Library (GFPL).
18. Kissinger/Rumsfeld telephone conversation, 7:30a.m., 23/12/1974, in Cheney Files, Box 5, Intelligence Subseries, Folder Intelligence – Colby Report, GFPL.
19. Woods, *Shadow Warrior*, 362.
20. Kissinger to President, 'Colby Report', Memorandum to President Ford, 25/12/1975, Cheney Files, Box 5, Intelligence Subseries, Folder Intelligence – Colby Report, GFPL.
21. Kissinger to President, 'Colby Report'.
22. Memorandum of conversation, Ford, Colby, Buchen, Marsh, Scowcroft, 'Allegations of CIA Domestic Activities', 3/1/1975, Digital files, National Security Advisor – Memoranda of Conversations, 1973–1977, Box 8, GFPL.
23. John Stockwell, *In Search of Enemies* (New York: W. W. Norton, 1978), 55.

24. Memorandum of conversation, Ford, Kissinger, Scowcroft, 4/1/1975, Digital files, National Security Adviser – Memoranda of Conversations, 1973-1977, Box 8, GFPL.
25. Memorandum of conversation, Ford, Helms, Marsh, Buchen, Scowcroft, 4/1/1975, Digital files, National Security Advisor – Memoranda of Conversations, 1973–1977, Box 8, GFPL.
26. Memorandum of conversation, Ford, Rockefeller, Kissinger, Rumsfeld, Buchen, Marsh, Scowcroft, 4/1/1975, Digital files, National Security Advisor – Memoranda of Conversations, 1973–1977, Box 8, GFPL.
27. Walter Mondale, Skype Interview with the author, 26 May 2016.
28. John Oseth, *Regulating US Intelligence Operations* (Lexington: University Press of Kentucky, 1985), 77.
29. He was Undersecretary of Health, Education, and Welfare in 1953–4 under Eisenhower. At this time, the CIA had branched out in medical and academic institutions for the conduct of drugs, mind-control and hypnosis experiments (discussed in Chapter 1). Some of the funding to institutions was channelled through Rockefeller's department. Later, Rockefeller acted as Eisenhower's representative on the Operations Coordinating Board, the committee overseeing covert operations. Finally, Rockefeller had served on the President's Foreign Intelligence Advisory Board since 1969. Kenneth Kitts, 'Commission Politics and National Security: Gerald Ford's Response to the CIA Controversy of 1975', *Presidential Studies Quarterly* 26.4 (1996), 1085–6.
30. Colby, *Honorable*, 400.
31. David Belin Papers (DBP) (1961), 1963–1998, Box 55, Inside the CIA: The Belin Report, Book files, Draft Chapter 13, 'Confrontation with Kissinger', 9, GFPL.
32. Executive Order 11828, 4/1/1975, available at https://www.presidency.ucsb.edu/documents/executive-order-11828-establishing-commission-cia-activities-within-the-united-states (accessed 26 October 2023).
33. Luca Trenta, '"An act of insanity and national humiliation": The Ford Administration, Congressional Inquiries and the Ban on Assassination', *Journal of Intelligence History*, 17.2 (2018), 127.
34. John Prados and Arturo Jimenez-Bacardi, 'The Rockefeller Commission, the White House and CIA Assassination Plots', National Security Archives (NSAr) 29/2/2016, available at https://nsarchive.gwu.edu/briefing-book/intelligence/2016-02-29/gerald-ford-white-house-altered-rockefeller-commission-report#_edn2 (accessed 26 October 2023).
35. Belin, 'Inside the CIA: The Belin Report'; DBP (1961), 1963–1998, Box 55, Book files, Draft Chapter 7, "The 'Family Jewels'", 8–4 [*sic*], GFPL.

36. Gellhorn memo to Belin, 'CIA activities within the United States', 8/3/1975, NSAr, 'Gerald Ford White House Altered Rockefeller Commission Report in 1975; Removed Section on CIA Assassination Plots', 29/2/2016, available at https://nsarchive.gwu.edu/briefing-book/intelligence/2016-02-29/gerald-ford-white-house-altered-rockefeller-commission-report (accessed 26 October 2023).
37. Letter Buchen to Belin, 31/3/1975, DBP (1961), 1963–1998, Box 26, Rockefeller Commission Numbered files: C-20 Personal Notes on interviews and testimonies, Folder C-21 Correspondence, White House 1975.
38. Clapper to Belin, 'Public Affairs Considerations in Report', 2/5/1975, DNSA, 'The Rockefeller Commission', doc. 11.
39. Belin, 'Inside the CIA' DBP, Box 55, Book files, Draft Chapter 13, 'Confrontation with Kissinger', 13–22, GFPL.
40. Richard Helms, Deposition to Rockefeller Commission, 23/4/1975, DNSA Covert Operations II.
41. Rockefeller Commission 'Summary of Facts: Investigation of CIA involvement in plans to assassinate foreign leaders', 5/6/1975, NSAr, available at https://nsarchive.gwu.edu/document/21512-document-19 (accessed 26 October 2023), 48.
42. Rockefeller Commission, 'Summary of Facts', 55.
43. Ibid., 32.
44. George Manfredi, 'Examination of a portion of the record of Richard Helms', 19/3/1975, JFK Release, 178-10003-10439.
45. Rockefeller Commission, 'Summary of Facts', 69.
46. Ibid., 85.
47. Ibid., 5.
48. Ron Nessen, *It Sure Looks Different from the Inside* (New York: Simon & Schuster, 1978), 63.
49. Prados and Jimenez-Bacardi, 'The Rockefeller Commission'.
50. Britt Snider, *The Agency and the Hill* (Washington, DC: Center for the Study of Intelligence, 2008), 29; Thomas Powers, *The Man Who Kept the Secrets* (New York: Pocket Books, 1979), 331.
51. CIA, Employee Bulletin, 29 October 1974, CIA Reading Room, available at https://www.cia.gov/readingroom/docs/CIA-RDP79-00957A000100070033-7.pdf (accessed 26 October 2023).
52. Laura Kalman, *Red Star Rising* (New York: W. W. Norton, 2010), 38.
53. Arturo Jimenez-Bacardi, 'Speaking Law to War: International Law, Legal Advisers, and Bureaucratic Contestation in US Defence Policy', PhD dissertation, University of California, Irvine, 2015, 179.

54. US Senate, Intelligence Oversight Act of 1980, Report, 15 May 1980, CIA Reading Room, available at https://www.cia.gov/readingroom/docs/CIA-RDP85-00003R000300010007-3.pdf (accessed 26 October 2023), 3.
55. Loch Johnson, *The Third Option* (Oxford: Oxford University Press, 2022), 182.
56. Memorandum of conversation, Ford, Colby, Buchen, Marsh, Scowcroft, 'Allegations of CIA Domestic Activities', 3/1/1975, Digital files, National Security Advisor – Memoranda of Conversations, 1973–1977, Box 8, GFPL.
57. Notes, 25/1/1975, NSAr, Staff Assistant Robert C. McFarlane Files, 1974–1977, Box 3, Folder January 21–31, 1975, GFPL.
58. Another committee, eventually chaired by Otis Pike, had also been formed in the House. However, since the Pike Committee did not explore assassination, it is outside the remit of this chapter and book. For a detailed discussion of the Pike Committee, see Johnson, *Season of Inquiry* and Townley, *The Year*.
59. CBS, *Face the Nation*, 2/2/1975, Transcript, Frank Church Papers, Series 2.6, Select Committee 1966–1975, Folder 1/2, Albertson Library, Boise State University (AL/BSU).
60. Senator Frank Church, Press release, 27/2/1975, Frank Church Papers, Series 2.6, Select Committee 1966–1975, AL/BSU.
61. Nessen, *It Sure Looks*; Gerald Ford, *A Time to Heal* (London: W. H. Allen, 1979), 230.
62. Frederick Schwarz, Phone interview with the author, 11 May 2016.
63. Frederick Baron, Assistant to the Chief Counsel, 'Church Committee Oral History', Interview, US Senate Historical Office, 2016, 7.
64. Baron, 'Oral History', 9.
65. James Risen, *The Last Honest Man* (New York: Little, Brown, 2023), 235–9.
66. William Colby, Testimony to SSCIA 23/5/1975, RCF, Box 5, Intelligence Subseries, Folder Intelligence – Colby Testimony, GFPL.
67. CIA, 'Responsibilities and Support', 25/3/1975, DNSA 'White House', doc. 10.
68. John Prados and Arturo Jimenez-Bacardi, 'White House Efforts to Blunt 1975 Church Committee Investigation into CIA Abuses Foreshadowed Executive-Congressional Battles after 9/11', NSAr Briefing Book, 20/7/2015, available at http://nsarchive.gwu.edu/NSAEBB/NSAEBB522-Church-Committee-Faced-White-House-Attempts-to-Curb-CIA- Probe/ (accessed 26 October 2023).
69. Memorandum of conversation, Ford, Kissinger, Church, Tower, Buchen, Rumsfeld, Marsh, Scowcroft 5 March 1975, Digital files,

National Security Advisor – Memoranda of Conversations, 1973–1977, Box 9, GFPL.
70. Philip Buchen, 'Meeting with Secretaries Kissinger, Schlesinger, and Colby', 13/5/1975, in NSAr, 'White House Effort'.
71. Kissinger telephone conversations with Tower (Telcon 23 /7/1975) and McGeorge Bundy (Telcon 17/6/1975) in DNSA, Kissinger Conversations: Supplement II, 1969–1977.
72. Memo Buchen to the President, 'Request of the Senate Select Committee on Intelligence Activities for Information on Covert Actions', May 12, 1975, Remote Archive Capture (RAC), Box 36, Folder Philip Buchen Files, Intelligence Series (16), GFPL; Trenta, 'An act of insanity', 133–4.
73. Nicholas Horrock, 'Colby Reviews CIA Activities in Testimony at Senate Inquiry', *New York Times*, 16 May 1975, available at https://www.nytimes.com/1975/05/16/archives/colby-reviews-cia-activities-in-testimony-at-senate-inquiry.html (accessed 26 October 2023).
74. Prados, *Lost Crusader*, 320.
75. Johnson, *Season of Inquiry*, 43.
76. Philip W. Buchen Memorandum for President, 'U.S. Government Involvement in Plots to Assassinate Foreign Leaders', 7/6/1975, available at https://nsarchive.gwu.edu/document/21513-document-20 (accessed 26 October 2023).
77. Memorandum of conversation, 5/6/1975, Box 12, Memoranda of Conversations – Ford Administration, National Security Advisor Memoranda of Conversation, 1973–1977, GFPL.
78. Office of the Deputy Assistant to the President, 'Briefing Book List on Strategy for Dealing with Intelligence-Political Situation, c.' 4/6/1975, NSAr, 'The Rockefeller Commission'.
79. Townley, *The Year*, 172.
80. Loch Johnson, *A Season of Inquiry Revisited* (Lawrence: University Press of Kansas, 2015), 44.
81. Buchen, Memorandum for the record, 'Meeting in Situation Room on Friday, June 27 concerning pending requests of the Senate Select Committee on intelligence activities', Richard Cheney Files, Box 6, Intelligence Subseries, Folder 'Intelligence – Congressional Investigation 3', GFPL.
82. Ibid.
83. Henry Knoche, 'Ground Rules for Supplying SSC Staff', 30/6/1975, Richard Cheney Files, Box 6, Intelligence Subseries, Folder 'Intelligence–Congressional Investigation 3', GFPL; Memorandum, McFarlane to Kissinger, 13/5/1975, 'Church Committee Request for Documents

on Covert Operations', RAC, Box 27, Folder NSAr Staff Assistant Robert McFarlane Files (1), GFPL.
84. Frank Church, Report to the Senate, 10/10/1975, Frank Church Papers, Series 2.6, Select Committee 1966–1975, Folder 2/2, AL/BSU.
85. Memorandum of conversation, Ford, Kissinger, Schlesinger, Levi, Lynn, Colby, Buchen, Marsh, Rumsfeld, Scowcroft, Raoul-Duval, 13/10/1975, NSAr – MemCon, 1973–1977, Digital files, GFPL.
86. Memorandum of conversation, 13/10/1975.
87. See the three documents: Memorandum, Breckinridge to Colby, 'SSC Draft Report on Assassination', 20/10/1975; Memorandum for the Record, Thomas Latimer on Draft Report, 20/10/1975; William Hyland, Memorandum for the record, 20/10/1975, RCF, Box 7, Intelligence Subseries, Folder 'Intelligence – Report on CIA Assassination Plots (2)', GFPL.
88. William Colby, Letter to the President, 20/10/1975, America Since Hoover collection, 1929–1980, Box 11, Folder Investigations of the US Intelligence Community, GFPL.
89. Ford, *William E. Colby*, 152.
90. Frank Church, Letter to the President, 4/11/1975, America Since Hoover collection, 1929–1980, Box 11, Folder Investigations of the US Intelligence Community, GFPL.
91. SSCIA, 'Alleged Assassination Plots Involving Foreign leaders', Interim Report (Interim Report) (Washington, DC: Us Government Printing Office, 1975), 3.
92. Johnson, *A Season of Inquiry Revisited*, 52.
93. Thomas Maier, '"Mafia Spies: Sam Giancana Is Gunned Down before He Can Be Called before Senate', *Chicago Sun Times*, 6 April 2019, available at https://chicago.suntimes.com/2019/4/6/18343958/mafia-spies-sam-giancana-is-gunned-down-before-he-can-be-called-before-senate (accessed 26 October 2023). Rosselli was also found dead before his second testimony to the Church Committee. His dismembered and decomposing body was found in Miami in a 55-gallon steel fuel drum. Bryan Smith, 'How the CIA Enlisted the Chicago Mob to Put a Hit on Castro', *Chicago Magazine*, 23 October 2007, available at https://www.chicagomag.com/chicago-magazine/november-2007/how-the-cia-enlisted-the-chicago-mob-to-put-a-hit-on-castro/ senate (accessed 26 October 2023).
94. SSCIA, Interim Report, 2.
95. Ibid., 4–5.
96. Ibid., 4.
97. Howard Hunt, Testimony to SSCIA, 10/1/1976, DNSA Covert Operation II; SSCIA, Addenda, 128–30.

98. SSCIA, Addenda to the Interim Report on Alleged Assassination plots, Book IV: Supplementary Detailed Staff Reports on Foreign and Military Intelligence (Washington, DC: US Government Printing office, 1976), 131–3.
99. SSCIA, Interim Report, 1.
100. Ibid., 256.
101. Ibid., 258.
102. William Banks and Peter Raven-Hansen, 'Targeted Killing and Assassination: The US Legal Framework', *University of Richmond Law Review*, 37 (2003), 718.
103. SSCIA, Interim Report, 258.
104. Ibid., 258.
105. Ibid., 257.
106. Colby, Testimony, 84.
107. Ibid., 88.
108. David Attlee Phillips, Testimony to SSCIA, 31/5/1975, DNSA, Covert Operations II, 33.
109. Phillips, Testimony, 170.
110. This more ambivalent conclusion does not mean that the committee considered assassination only as the targeting of individuals through covert methods. The committee, after all, analysed three coups and reflected on the connection between coups and assassinations. Michael Schmitt, 'State-Sponsored Assassination in International and Domestic Law', *Yale Journal of International Law*, 17.2 (1992), 609–85.
111. Ruth Jamieson and Kieran McEvoy, 'State Crime y Proxy and Judicial Othering', *British Journal of Criminology*, 45 (2005), 504–27.
112. Rebecca Sanders, 'Norm Proxy War and Resistance through Outsourcing: The Dynamics of Transnational Human Rights Contestation', *Human Rights Review*, 17 (2016), 166.
113. Testimony of Thomas Parrott, SSCIA, 10/7/1975, DNSA Covert Operations II, 40.
114. See, for example, Testimony of Gordon Gray, SSCIA, 9/7/1975, DNSA, Covert Operations II, 9.
115. SSCIA, Interim Report, 266.
116. Ibid., 273.
117. Richard Bissel, SSCIA Testimony, 10/9/1975, JFK Assassination Record (JFKAR) 157-10014-10093 (December 2022), 34.
118. Richard Bissell, SSCIA Testimony, 22/7/1975, DNSA Covert Operations II, 138–9.
119. SSCIA, Interim Report, 278.
120. Ibid., 266.

121. Michael Poznansky, 'Revisiting Plausible Deniability', *Journal of Strategic Studies*, 45.4 (2022), 511–33.
122. SSCIA, Interim Report, 11.
123. Ibid., 261.
124. Jimenez-Bacardi, 'From Lawlessness to Secret Law', 127.
125. He had initially considered covert operations outside the CIA charter but had later changed his mind. Lawrence Houston, SSCIA Testimony, 2/6/1975, DNSA Covert Operations II, 80.
126. Houston, Testimony, 4–5. Perhaps, an exception here is the seashell plot against Castro.
127. Frank Church, Report to the Senate, 10/10/1975, Frank Church Papers, Series 2.6, Select Committee 1966–1975, Folder 2/2, AL/BSU.
128. SSCIA, Interim Report, 282–3.
129. Nicole Deitelhoff and Lisbeth Zimmermann, 'Norms under Challenge: Unpacking the Dynamics of Norm Robustness', *Journal of Global Security Studies*, 4.1 (2019), 10.
130. Deitelhoff and Zimmermann, 'Norms under Challenge', 10; Luca Trenta, 'Death by Reinterpretation: Dynamics of Norm Contestation and the US Ban on Assassination in the Reagan Years', *Journal of Global Security Studies*, 6.4 (2021), doi: 10.1093/jogss/ogab012.
131. SSCIA, Interim Report, 282–3.
132. Ibid., 283–4.
133. Ibid., 285–6; Michael Reisman, 'Some Reflections on International Law and Assassination under the Schmitt Formula', *Yale Journal of International Law*, 17 (1992), 691.
134. Minutes NSC Meeting, 15/5/1975, NSC Meetings File, 1974–77, Box 1, GFPL.
135. Memorandum of conversation, Ford, Kissinger, Scowcroft, 5/6/1975, National Security Adviser – Memoranda of Conversations, 1973–1977, Box 12, Digital Files, GFPL.
136. Memorandum from Levi to Ford, 30/1/1976, FRUS vol. XXXVIII, Part 2: Organization and Management of Foreign Policy; Public Diplomacy, 1973–1976, doc. 66, available at https://history.state.gov/historicaldocuments/frus1969-76v38p2/d66 (accessed 26 October 2023).
137. Cheney's memorandum to the President on 16/9/1975 'The Intelligence Community', Richard Cheney Files, Box 6, Intelligence Subseries, Folder 'Intelligence – Options Paper'; Richard Cheney Files, Box 6, Intelligence Subseries, Folder 'Intelligence – New York Times Articles by Seymour Hersh (2)', GFPL.

138. Elizabeth Bazan, 'Assassination Ban and E.O. 12333: A Brief Summary', *Congressional Research Service*, Report for Congress, 2002, 2.
139. Oseth, *Regulating*, 92.
140. Jimenez-Bacardi, 'Speaking', 124–5.
141. Oseth, *Regulating*, 93-4.
142. Charlie Savage, *Takeover* (New York: Little, Brown, 2007), 29.
143. Gerald Ford, 'Executive Order 11905: United States Foreign Intelligence Activities', 18/2/1976, available at http://fas.org/irp/offdocs/eo11905.htm#SEC.5 (accessed 26 October 2023).
144. Jacqueline Best, 'Ambiguity, Uncertainty, and Risk: Rethinking Indeterminacy', *International Political Sociology*, 2.4 (2008), 356.
145. Trenta, 'An act of insanity', 138.
146. Diana Panke and Ulrich Petersohn, 'Why International Norms Disappear Sometimes', *European Journal of International Relations*, 18.4 (2012), 725.
147. Bruce Riedel, Interview with the author, 4 August 2016, Washington, DC.
148. Boyd Johnson, 'Executive Order 12,333: The Permissibility of an American Assassination of a Foreign Leader', *Cornell International Law Journal*, 2.2 (1993), 409–10.
149. 'Chief of State or the political equivalent, President, Vice President, Prime Minister, Premier, Foreign Minister, Ambassador, or other officer, employee, or agent of (A) a foreign government; or (B) a foreign political group, party, military force, movement, or other association; or (C) an international organization', National Intelligence Reorganization and Reform Act of 1978, 899.
150. Jimmy Carter, Executive Order 12036: United States Foreign Intelligence Activities, 24/1/1978, available at https://irp.fas.org/offdocs/eo/eo-12036.htm (accessed 26 October 2023); Oseth, *Regulating*, 115–20.
151. An effort to revive S. 2525 in 1980 also failed. Johnson, 'Executive Order 12,333', 411.
152. It can be understood as 'applicatory contestation', that is, one targeted at reshaping the remit of a norm; Trenta, 'Death.'
153. Russell Bruemmer, 'The Prohibition on Assassination: A Legal and Ethical Analysis', in Hayden Peake and Samuel Halpern (eds), *In the Name of Intelligence* (Washington, DC: NIBC Press, 1995), 141.
154. Schmitt, 'State-Sponsored Assassination', 663.
155. See the Administration's approach to the possibility of a coup at the time of the Soviet interference in Afghanistan, Documents 38–45 in FRUS vol. XII, Afganistan, 1977–1980, 110–12.

156. Jonathan Fredman, 'Covert Action, Loss of Life, and the Prohibition on Assassination, 1976–1996', *Studies in Intelligence*, 1996, 16; Banks and Raven-Hansen, 'Targeted Killing', 721.
157. Christopher Andrews, *For the President's Eyes Only* (London: HarperCollins, 1996), 429.
158. Mondale, Interview with the author.
159. William Quandt described the mission of General Robert Huyser to Tehran in the last days of the Shah as one of the 'darkest pages' of the Administration, but this did not extend to assassination plots. William Quandt, Interview with the author, 19 July 2012, Charlottesville, Virginia.
160. Mondale, Interview with the author.
161. Riedel, Interview with the author.

8   Muhammar Qaddafi: The Return of Assassination during the Reagan Years

'International terrorism will take the place of human rights [in] our concern, because it is the ultimate abuse of human rights.' On 28 January 1981, eight days after Reagan's inauguration, Secretary of State Alexander Haig criticised the approach adopted by the Carter Administration. He called for a renewed focus on terrorism and for a policy of swift retribution against terrorist acts.[1]

Later in the day, Haig reported to Reagan that he had listed the President's foreign policy priorities. 'Finally,' Haig added, 'I stressed that we mean business in dealing with terrorism; we're very concerned about human rights and basic issues of human dignity, but international terrorism is the number one problem right now.'[2]

Key members of the Reagan Administration were obsessed with terrorism, which they understood through a Cold War lens.[3] When it wasn't blaming the Soviets, the Administration tended to identify a loose coalition of 'outlaw' states, including Iran, Libya and Syria, as a 'new international version of Murder, Incorporated', in Reagan's flamboyant rhetoric.[4] The Administration started to adopt the term 'state-sponsored terrorism'. This definition was broad enough and ambiguous enough to permit the conflation of a diverse set of activities as threats to the United States, and to facilitate the targeting of a diverse group of enemies.[5] Among these enemies, none played a more prominent role than Libyan leader Muhammar Qaddafi.

* * *

While multifaceted, the confrontation with Qaddafi was part of the Reagan Administration's effort to revamp the covert action capabilities of the CIA after the investigations of the mid-1970s. In this process, the Administration worked to weaken the restrictions imposed by the ban on assassination by reinterpreting its meaning and its remit in three main areas: counterterrorism, the CIA's involvement in coups and unconventional warfare, and the direct targeting of foreign leaders.

Building on these reinterpretations, in the case of Qaddafi, the Administration deployed both direct and indirect methods in what amounted to a campaign of assassination (attempts) against the Libyan leader. Relying on local friendly governments, it provided logistical and financial support, as well as training, to local groups that aimed at overthrowing Qaddafi. When these methods faltered, it used military force and took advantage of its technological superiority. The legal and political precedents set by the Administration shaped the US government's conduct in the realm of assassination in the following years.

Reagan's Cold Warriors and the Ban on Assassination

As the Reagan Administration took power, members in key positions to reshape the intelligence community looked with contempt at what they perceived as the timidity of the existing bureaucracy. They understood Reagan's mandate as one of restoring US power and taking the fight to the Soviet Union.[6] Reagan himself famously held strong views on communism and on America's role in the world. The United States was a force for good and so was the CIA.[7]

According to his biographer, Lou Cannon, Reagan had little understanding of the intricacies and practicalities of covert action.[8] But as a politician, he had shown a keen interest in intelligence matters.[9] Reagan had been an often-absent member of the Rockefeller Commission. Publicly, he had long acted as a staunch supporter of the intelligence community. He declared himself to be unimpressed by the scandals and media revelations of the mid-1970s, describing the Congressional and public outcry against the CIA as 'much ado about – if not nothing, at least very little'.[10]

Muhammar Qaddafi: Assassination during the Reagan Years

Having campaigned to revamp the intelligence community, Reagan offered the post of CIA Director to his former campaign manager, William Casey.[11] Casey's experience in the Office of Strategic Services (OSS), under 'Wild Bill' Donovan, provided him with clear views on the necessity of covert action. To him, the Cold War was no different than the fight against the Nazis. The enemy might have changed but the stakes and the rules had not; there were no rules.[12] As Ric Prado, one of Casey's most loyal covert warriors, put it: under Casey, the CIA would be 'engaged, aggressive, and daring, like the OSS'.[13]

After his career in the OSS, Casey had become rich in the private sector through financial investments and the publication of several books on business law. The books taught the reader how to exploit legal loopholes to pay less tax. Casey would apply this same approach in his conduct of covert operations. Casey also agreed with the President on the overblown and detrimental nature of the revelations and inquiries of the 1970s.[14] Furthermore, he – like Reagan – was also critical of the cuts and changes in regulations and personnel brought about by Carter and his DCI Stansfield Turner. They had, in Casey's view, 'neutered' the agency.[15]

Casey accepted the role of CIA Director only after receiving assurances from Reagan that the position would become, for the first time, a cabinet-level position. This change guaranteed Casey a position of power in the conduct of foreign policy and a stronger voice on budgetary matters.[16] The CIA's budget increased by 200 per cent to reach $30 billion between 1980 and 1987.[17] The DCI quickly started running his own foreign policy, often behind Congress's back.[18] This was especially true since Casey brought to the job a real contempt for Congress and Congressional oversight. During his confirmation hearings, while rejecting the accusation that he wanted to 'unleash' the Agency, he made clear that too much oversight could hinder the Agency's vitality and performance.[19]

Once at the helm of the Agency, Casey was free to reinvigorate covert, paramilitary and political action.[20] He decided to recall a high number of covert operatives and intelligence officers phased out or retired during the 1970s. He also replaced several officials who had acquired regional expertise with loyalists who shared his attitude.[21] His tenure also started with radical changes to internal regulations for the conduct of operations. As Casey took office, a 130-page book reportedly provided instructions on how to conduct operations. During an internal meeting in his early months, Casey held up the book and said: 'Here's the trouble. We're too timid. The attitude is "Don't stick your neck out. Play it safe." This kind of crap is smothering us. You practically have to take a lawyer with you on a mission. I'm throwing this thing out.' And he did. He replaced it with a memorandum that recommended the use of 'common sense'.[22]

Based on his business law experience, Casey also brought a new approach to interpreting legal provisions. As Admiral Bobby Ray Inman, for a short time Casey's deputy at the CIA, recalled, Casey's view was that 'anything not explicitly prohibited by law you could do'.[23] If the law compelled the President to present Congress with intelligence findings, the CIA would either ignore the requirement or present sweeping findings. With the arrival of Casey, lawyers in the Agency understood that they had to be ready to write much broader and more aggressive intelligence findings.[24]

Casey named Stanley Sporkin as the CIA's legal counsel. Sporkin was a Casey loyalist, having previously worked under him. He shared Casey's views on the need to shake the intelligence community from its torpor.[25] The Agency, according to Sporkin, was still haunted by the ghost of Frank Church and suffered from a 'no syndrome'.[26] Sporkin fits perfectly the figure of the permissive legal adviser detailed by legal scholar Charlotte Peevers. He was 'cherry-picked' for his loyalty and opinion. He acted as a facilitator, 'constructing intricate technical arguments which might reconstruct seemingly illegal policies as legal'.[27]

While Casey and Sporkin were political appointees, several career officials within the CIA held different views. The revelations and inquiries of the 1970s had left a deep scar on the Agency's institutional culture and memory. While some officials longed for a return to the good old days promised by Casey, others were now unwilling to be seen as bending the rules. Members of this faction included Deputy Director Inman and John McMahon who would replace Inman after his resignation.[28] Within the Administration these officials were an often powerless minority. Casey could rely both on loyalists in the Agency and on several allies within the rest of the Administration, such as the President, Secretary of State Haig (later George Shultz), and some aggressive NSC officials.

* * *

In the first few months of the Administration, a key obstacle to Casey's intelligence revolution emerged: the Carter Administration's Executive Order (hereinafter EO) 12036. The debates surrounding the approval of a new order for the intelligence community engendered the first confrontation between US intelligence officials wary of Casey's approach and others who wanted a return to a 'glorious' past.

After a draft of a new EO leaked, Congress challenged the Administration's aggressive plans for reform. During Congressional hearings, Inman warned that forces within the Administration were pushing for an almost complete relaxation of restrictions on operations, a comment that attracted criticism from Reagan's loyalists.[29] At the NSC, Ken DeGraffenreid and Donald Gregg, a former CIA official whose career had been obstructed by Turner, questioned the necessity of explicit restrictions. Carter's EO represented an 'attack on the intelligence agencies by an unholy alliance of smug, comfortable bureaucrats and those on the political left committed to radically curtailing our capabilities'. It was 'punitive, demeaning, and in some ways silly', with multiple layers of unnecessary oversight, 'long on "do nots" and short on what kind of performance is expected'; overall, a 'licence to loaf'.[30] Only a short and aggressive draft could show the country and the world that the CIA was 'out of the dog house'.[31]

During the review process, much of the bureaucratic battle focused on the need to remove 'demeaning language'. This became a euphemism to remove most of the restrictions Carter's order imposed on the Agency. The expression permitted policymakers to maintain a facade of legitimate concern for the morale of the intelligence community, while more accurately aiming at weakening the restrictions. As the drafting of a new order was under way, DeGraffenreid provided an annotated version of Carter's EO for internal deliberation. He challenged the prohibitions listed in the order since they unnecessarily constrained the intelligence community and presented the CIA as something that needed to be kept on a tight leash. Next to the ban on assassination, he wrote, 'RR [Ronald Reagan] doesn't have to say this. I believe he won't either.'[32] When Casey seemed unwilling to pursue a complete redraft,[33] National Security Advisor Richard Allen protested.[34]

Despite the NSC's protestations, the structure of EO12333, published in December 1981, is similar to that of Carter's order. The ban on assassination was also reconfirmed. On closer inspection, however, important differences with Carter's order emerge. The new ban on assassination in section 2.11 read: 'No person employed by or acting on behalf of the United States Government shall engage in, or conspire to engage in, assassination.' To this, section 2.12 added that 'No agency of the Intelligence Community shall participate in or request any person to undertake activities forbidden by this Order.'[35] Importantly, the Carter order had extended this second prohibition to all agencies of the US government. This change left the door open for agencies beyond the intelligence community to engage in prohibited activities. The change was also coupled with a blurring of the lines of authority and responsibility.[36] Under Reagan's order, the NSC could establish independent subgroups to carry out intelligence-related activities. Only the President's opinion – and not a broader policy review as envisioned under Carter – was needed to assign 'special activities' (covert action) to an agency other than the CIA.[37]

The language and tone of the order also showed crucial changes. The emphasis on restrictions and duties of Carter's order almost completely disappeared. The need for moral and ethical 'propriety' of intelligence activities also disappeared. The only requirement was the avoidance of explicit illegality. This conformed with Casey's approach. It opened the possibility of government officials asking for favourable legal opinions to circumvent the problem of explicit illegality.[38] In a memorandum to Reagan, Counsellor Edwin Meese described the new order as shorter and 'more flexible than its predecessors'. The order, Meese added, 'specifically authorizes you [Reagan] to initiate intelligence activities even if they are not mentioned in the Order'.[39]

Muhammar Qaddafi: Assassination during the Reagan Years

Assassination and Counterterrorism: The Plot against Fadlallah

With Carter's 'demeaning' order out of the way, the Administration moved to set a more assertive posture in the realm of counterterrorism. In April 1982, National Security Decision Directive (NSDD) 30 on 'Managing Terrorist Incidents' increased the power of the NSC. It established a Terrorist Incident Working Group, 'activated' by the National Security Advisor and chaired by a senior NSC member, as well as an Interagency Group on terrorism, responsible for overall US policy.[40] The directive built on provisions established in EO 12333 to enable the creation of less accountable subgroups beyond the CIA that, under the President's authority, could now be assigned covert operations. The directive also permitted an expansion of the NSC's power in the realm of counterterrorism.[41] As the Directive was being approved, Noel Koch (Assistant Secretary of Defense for International Affairs and the Pentagon's counterterrorism chief) had recommended Deputy Defense Secretary Frank Carlucci to discuss with Casey various counterterrorism measures, including the 'elimination of identifiable terrorist leaders'. Having read the recommendation – and in a repeat of Harvey's scolding of Lansdale's assistant – Carlucci went to Koch's office urging him 'never to put anything like that on paper'.[42]

* * *

On 18 April 1983, a suicide bomber drove a GMC pick-up truck packed with nearly 2,000 pounds (910 kg) of explosives into the US Embassy in Beirut. The whole front section of the Embassy collapsed. Among the victims, seventeen were Americans. Eight were CIA officers. Robert Ames, the Agency's Chief of the Near East Division, and Kenneth Haas, Beirut Chief of Station, died in the blast.[43] On 23 October, a second, much more deadly bombing occurred at the US Marines barracks in Beirut: 307 people were killed, including 241 Americans.

The evidence in both cases pointed to Hezbollah and Iran. Syria was also likely involved. Reagan signed NSDD 109 holding

Hezbollah and Iran responsible. At the Pentagon, plans started for a retaliatory strike, settling on the Sheikh Abdullah Barracks in Baalbeck, the main city in the Syrian-controlled Bekaa Valley.[44] Koch sent the super-secret military Intelligence Support Activity (ISA) to Beirut to collect intelligence.[45] ISA was reportedly given a 'hit list' of people the Administration would have liked to see eliminated. While the CIA helped in tracking those people, ISA refined the intelligence regarding their infrastructure and their support networks. Work focused on two main targets: Hussein Musawi, responsible for the bombing, and Sheikh Mohammed Hussein Fadlallah, understood as the spiritual leader of Hezbollah. To the dismay of Casey and other officials, no retaliation was conducted. ISA was withdrawn.[46]

With this meek response, tension started to mount within the Administration. Casey argued forcefully that the Administration should have abandoned high standards of evidence before retaliating against terrorists. He also pleaded with the Administration to abandon concerns regarding possible violations of the ban on assassination in the fight against terrorism: 'This is a rough business. If we're afraid to hit the terrorists because somebody's going to yell "assassination," it will never stop. The terrorists will own the world.'[47]

These two arguments found a receptive audience within the Administration, particularly from Secretary of State Shultz, who argued that the Administration should stop being afraid of 'technicalities' and should face the 'gut issue'. As he put it: 'We need to have an agreement that when we know where terrorists are, we will act against them.'[48] Similar arguments came from the NSC, where Steve Rosen, a RAND expert advising the NSC and the Pentagon, wrote to National Security Advisor Robert McFarlane that one of the main reasons for Soviet success in the Third World had been their ability to 'threaten political leaders'. 'While we do not wish to harm political leaders,' the memo continued, 'we do wish to kill terrorists.'[49]

By this time, the NSC – with the support of the CIA – had positioned itself at the forefront of the fight against terrorism. Through the creation of NSC subgroups, terrorism had largely been removed from the remit of the State Department. This was also a result of disagreements within the Administration as to the necessity and character of a military response against terrorism. This rivalry often pitted Shultz, who pushed for a more proactive posture and for a military response to terrorism, against Secretary of Defense Caspar Weinberger, at the helm of a still reluctant post-Vietnam Pentagon.[50] This rivalry also made covert operations more palatable as a method to split the difference and do something.[51]

In the NSC's bureaucracy, Oliver North had assumed a dominant position. Like Casey, North had a gung-ho attitude. He was willing to bend and circumvent the law and viewed with contempt more cautious CIA career officials.[52] North put forward the argument that 'surgical strikes' against known and identified terrorists could solve the problem while limiting civilian casualties.[53] North had also been working on the draft for a new National Security Decision Directive on terrorism.

The draft contained the suggestion that the Administration should adopt a policy of 'neutralization' of terrorists. During the drafting process, the CIA's McMahon protested: 'Did North have his head in the sand during the 1970s? Was he oblivious to the Reagan executive order banning involvement in assassination?'[54] On 2 March, Reagan suggested that a redraft was still an option if language was a problem but added that it was urgent to approve the directive since the steps detailed in it were the right ones.[55]

As internal debate continued, members of the Administration, including Casey and Shultz, launched a public relations campaign to justify a more assertive counterterrorism posture. In a series of speeches Shultz lamented that the United States was behaving like the 'Hamlet of nations', uncertain in its confrontation with terrorism. He called for an effort to educate the US public on the necessity to strike first.[56] These speeches stressed the need for pre-emptive (and preventive) uses of force against terrorism, including individual terrorists,[57] even if the United States could never muster the type of evidence that would 'stand up in a court of law'.[58] This process, while not explicitly mentioning assassination, combined quiet (and secret) policies that moved away from compliance with the norm, with a public framing of these policies as necessary. The aim was to progressively normalise the killing – neutralisation – of terrorists.[59]

When approved, NSDD 138 identified state-sponsored terrorist groups, terrorist organisations and individual terrorists as the main threats and defined terrorism as a threat to national security. It tasked the Secretary of Defense with 'develop[ing] a military strategy that is supportive of an active, preventive program to combat state-sponsored terrorism before the terrorists can initiate hostile acts'. The directive crystallised the understanding of terrorism as an act of war. This was something that the Long Commission – established to investigate the Marine barracks bombing – had already recommended.[60]

The document also asked the DCI to step up intelligence cooperation with friendly governments and 'develop, in coordination with other friendly security services, capabilities for the pre-emptive neutralization of anti-American terrorist groups which plan, support, or conduct hostile terrorist acts against U.S. citizens, interests, and property overseas'.[61] It required the drafting of a new intelligence finding which included 'lawful measures' to 'neutralize or counter terrorist organizations and terrorist leaders'.[62] The directive referred to Executive Order 12333 which of course included the ban on assassination, but the distinction between organisations and individuals seemed to suggest that the targeting of terrorist leaders was permitted.[63] McFarlane recognised that the directive's linguistic ambiguity sought to 'minimise the attention placed on pre-emptive covert activities in order to preclude adverse reactions which could constrain' the Administration's options.[64]

In the same days, Reagan also signed a second NSDD, still unnumbered and still classified. This directive provided 'legal protection' to covert operatives involved in pre-emptive and self-defensive actions against terrorists in case those actions violated US laws or executive orders.[65] As several IR scholars have suggested, the implementation of measures aimed at protecting norm violators clearly signals the reduced strength of the norm,[66] in this case the ban on assassination.

As the NSDD was being approved, the powers of the CIA also expanded with two new directives. One authorised the targeting of terrorists. The second, approved in 1985, gave the agency even more operational latitude. It established that aggressive and lethal covert operations against terrorists would be deemed legal if

Muhammar Qaddafi: Assassination during the Reagan Years

conducted in 'good faith'. As a source familiar with the directive put it, the directive aimed precisely at circumventing, or even rescinding,[67] the ban on assassination. A former White House official stated that, building on the two directives, the CIA had a 'go anywhere' and 'do anything' authority. It was, another source put it, 'an astounding blank check', a true 'licence to kill'.[68]

* * *

Based on these developments, North drafted a finding for a covert operation that called for the CIA to train teams hired by the Lebanese intelligence services who could hit targets inside Lebanon. Within the CIA, again McMahon opposed the plan. On strategic grounds, he argued that the Lebanese intelligence services could not be trusted. To them, intelligence operations simply meant 'tossing a bomb ... blowing up people'. More importantly, for McMahon, the targeting of individual terrorists violated the ban on assassination. 'You better go back and tell those cowboys they can't have it both ways.' He told Casey:

> If the president lifts the executive order banning assassination, we'll knock off terrorists. But if he keeps that one on the books, and we're bumping people off, do you know what happens when the shit hits the fan? It's the CIA's ass ... It's not administration policy, it is not an NSC idea – it's those crazy bastards at the CIA.[69]

Lifting or publicly modifying the ban on assassination was not something the Administration was willing to do, but the measures the Administration was taking also made such an open challenge redundant.

Robert Oakley, from the State Department, and Claire George, a CIA career official, came to agree with McMahon's view that the Lebanese teams could not be trusted. The Pentagon agreed to send two men from the newly formed Joint Special Operation Command (JSOC) to liaise with the teams and report back on them. Some accounts suggest that a negative report from JSOC and/or the opposition from State and from the CIA's old guard brought the operation to an end. It seems likely, though, that the cooperation and training continued.[70]

The CIA had been working on legal opinions and practical methods that would permit its involvement in assassination. As to the legal arguments, Casey could rely on the pliable Sporkin. As he reportedly told Sporkin, 'Don't tell me it can't be done . . . find me a legal way to do it.' Relying on the ambiguous text of the ban, Sporkin argued that targeting terrorists did not constitute assassination. The legal opinion stated that the ban on assassination only applied to heads of state. If the Administration took precautions to hit the right targets, minimise civilian casualties and inform the relevant Congressional committees, there were no legal constraints on the targeting of terrorists.[71] Combined with NSDD 138, Sporkin's legal opinion contested the remit of the ban. It started to set the argument that, as Robert Chesney has written, 'the use of lethal force for counter-terrorism purposes was a different kettle of fish'.[72]

On 1 November 1984, Reagan signed a still classified NSDD (149) supporting Lebanon in its efforts at counterterrorism, and an intelligence finding – shared with Congress – authorising the training of the Lebanese teams as suggested by North.[73] According to John Maguire, who rose through the CIA's ranks under Casey, the director liked the plan to train hit teams. 'It took a page from Mossad's book.'[74]

The main target for the hit teams was the Lebanese cleric Fadlallah. The CIA Directorate of Intelligence had suggested that 'the continued growth of the radical Shia movement in Lebanon' largely depended on the charismatic leadership of sheikhs like Fadlallah.[75] The CIA also considered him the ideational force behind the bombing of the Marine barracks and responsible for the kidnapping of its new station chief William Buckley, as well as other terrorist attacks.[76]

The hit teams already provided a certain level of deniability. They were, after all, third-party local actors. To further distance the Agency from the operations, Casey travelled to Saudi Arabia to discuss the operation with Prince Bandar. At a follow-up meeting at the Prince's Virginia estate, Casey asked him directly if he would consider financing a covert operation to kill Fadlallah. The Prince, who was bankrolling several of the Agency's ventures,[77] was happy to oblige.[78] He would not only finance the operation but also help with the selection and training of the Lebanese hit teams. Politically as well as tactically, Saudi support permitted the CIA to further distance itself from the operation, and to act more indirectly. It permitted Casey to undermine Congressional oversight as well as internal criticism.[79]

The Agency and the Saudis reportedly worked with a Lebanese team, a special force named Foreign Works and Analysis Unit which aimed at retaliatory strikes against terrorists.[80] In this instance, retaliation took the form of a car bomb. The CIA provided the address of the garage where the car bomb was prepared, the addresses of Fadlallah's residences, as well as communication and equipment for the Lebanese teams. As Martin and Walcott put, in a throwback to an earlier era of assassination plots, CIA officers had 'complained to their Lebanese counterparts that Sheikh Fadlallah was a meddlesome priest, which deliberately or not left some of the Lebanese with the impression that Washington, or at least Langley, Virginia, wanted Fadlallah eliminated'.[81]

On 8 March 1985, a truck stopped outside Fadlallah's residence in the West Beirut suburb of Bir al-Abed. As the cleric's SUV approached, the bomb exploded, demolishing a section of the building. The attack missed the sheikh but killed eighty civilians. After the bombing, Fadlallah inspected the smouldering ruins: his life intact, his reputation enhanced. A banner with the inscription 'Made in USA' was lifted over the destroyed building, making clear that the Lebanese population and America's enemies in Lebanon disregarded the finer points of plausible deniability.[82] Reagan rescinded the finding after the bombing. By the time of the Fadlallah plot, the CIA had fully re-entered the assassination business. Controversies in the mid-1980s also helped in setting legal and political precedents for the confrontation with Qaddafi.

Assassination and Unconventional Warfare: The Contras and the Mujahideen

With the 1984 presidential elections just around the corner, the press obtained a training manual that the CIA had prepared for the 'Contras'. The Contras were an insurgent force the CIA had formed and trained to overthrow the Sandinista government in Nicaragua. Casey, the CIA and North had become the main backers of the 'contra war' against the Sandinistas, while Congress had grown increasingly opposed. One section of the training manual, titled 'Selective use of violence for propagandistic effects', became an immediate object of controversy. It read: 'It is possible to neutralize carefully selected and planned targets such as court judges, justices of the peace, police and state security officials, CDS [Sandinista Defence Committee] chiefs' and other targets.'[83] These targets, the manual suggested, should be chosen on the basis of their popularity and of the difficulty in replacing them.[84]

The language of the manual clearly exposed the Administration and the CIA to a potential violation of the ban on assassination. The use of the euphemism 'neutralization' – made (in)famous by the Phoenix Program in Vietnam – seemingly called for the assassination of foreign officials. The role and position of these officials made their 'neutralization' a 'political' act, and, hence, an assassination. Through the order, the CIA was asking third parties (the Contras) to be involved in assassination – a criminal activity – thus violating section 2.12 of the EO. As the manual leaked to the press, it was immediately christened the 'Contras murder manual'.[85]

The controversy surrounding the manual was taken up in the second 1984 presidential debate between Reagan and Democratic candidate Walter Mondale. Syndicated columnist Georgie Anne Geyer asked Reagan whether the recommendations made in the manual amounted to the US version of state-sponsored terrorism. Reagan stumbled but eventually admitted that 'CIA men' in Nicaragua recognised that the 'manual was a direct contravention of my own executive order in December of 1981, that we would have nothing to do with regard to political assassinations'.[86] Reagan reassured viewers that he had ordered an investigation and one was already being conducted by the CIA's Inspector General. The two investigations, though, were only tasked to assess whether the episode had highlighted any 'managerial deficiencies',[87] a very narrow mandate.

Confronted with further criticism, the White House seemed to adopt two strategies. First, it tried to argue that the manual did not impinge on the ban on assassination at all. Reagan reneged

Muhammar Qaddafi: Assassination during the Reagan Years

on the statement he had made in the debate: neutralisation simply meant that 'you just say to the fellow who's sitting there in the office, "You are not in the office anymore."' When completed, the CIA Inspector General's report reached a similar conclusion. This strategy was disingenuous, and it did not work.[88] Already in 1982, after the Contras' first major operation, the Defense Intelligence Agency had reported that the insurgents' modus operandi included 'the assassination of minor government officials'.[89] Furthermore, members of Congress had been receiving briefings and reports regarding contra killings. Individuals recommended by the manual constituted the bulk of the victims, which implied not simply wanton violence, but a campaign of political and targeted assassination.[90]

The second, and more successful, White House strategy relied on establishing layers of deniability. Several high-level officials argued that the manual was the work of an 'overzealous freelancer'.[91] This proved false. The author, it soon became apparent, was John Kirkpatrick. Kirkpatrick – an eccentric former US army major, with experience in Vietnam and Phoenix – was on the books of the CIA paramilitary branch, the International Activities Division (IAD). He had been contracted by the then CIA's chief of the Latin American Division, Dewey Clarridge – a Casey loyalist – to train the Contras.[92] Officials then argued that the author of the manual, while not a freelancer, was a low-level employee and nobody within the Agency had vetted the manual. This was also false. It did not matter.

Through these justifications, the Reagan team suggested that the ban expected the direct control of the US government over the conduct of its employees and local allies. The CIA and the Administration, the argument went, did not have enough control over the drafting, vetting and publication of the manual. Since US agencies were not directly responsible for the manual, they did not intentionally violate the ban.[93] This also conformed with a Department of Justice opinion suggesting that the US government needed to 'directly instigate or commission the action' before it would fall within the Executive Order's prohibition.[94] The House Intelligence Committee's investigation largely accepted the White House's conclusion.[95]

Congress's acquiescence has convinced several observers that this was a minor, largely partisan controversy, confirming the resilience of the assassination ban,[96] but behind the scenes, the Agency was developing arguments and justifications aimed at expanding its power. Contradicting the White House's arguments, in a secret two-page letter to members of the House and Senate Intelligence Committees, Casey took full responsibility for the manual. He wrote that the discussion on 'neutralisation' referred to situations in which the guerrillas occupied a new town and resistance remained. The letter's language and its references to 'guerrilla', 'occupation' and 'potential resistance' make clear that, in Casey's view, the situation in Nicaragua was one of unconventional warfare and insurgency. This was a context – Casey implied – in which the ban on assassination did not apply, or – at a minimum – needed to be interpreted differently.[97] Gone was the Church Committee's clear-cut distinction between peace and war. Casey's letter aimed at creating a grey area of quasi-war in which the CIA could engage in lethal paramilitary activities like assassination.

Clarridge went even further. In a secret briefing to Congress, he made three main points. First, he stated that he had control of the activities of the Contras. He argued that the Contras were 'his' rebels and they had been killing civilians as well as Sandinista officials. Clarridge's clarification about the CIA's control of the Contras contradicted the White House's line regarding a lack of control and violated section 2.12 of the EO. Second, restating Casey's argument, Clarridge also argued that these killing were normal. The Contras were involved in a war and these things happened. Third, Clarridge added that the killing of these officials was political, but it did not violate the ban on assassination since – in his view – the ban only applied to heads of state.[98] Another of the Agency's ventures in the mid-1980s further weakened the ban.

* * *

From its inception, the Reagan Administration had supported the mujahideen in their effort to repel the Soviet invasion of Afghanistan. Initially, and based on the precedent set by Carter, the volume and type of weaponry had been limited in order to maintain a veneer

Muhammar Qaddafi: Assassination during the Reagan Years

of plausible deniability. By 1985, the US government had completed a major review of its Afghanistan policy. Restrictions on US covert support for the mujahideen were relaxed. For Casey, as historian Peter Schweizer noted, 'operations against Soviet leadership . . . were an important step up in the escalation of the war. So long as the Soviet elite were immune to attacks . . . they would continue to back the war in Afghanistan.' Casey concluded that the way forward was the targeting of sons of senior party officials, then deployed in Afghanistan.[99] This claim finds little confirmation, but several sources agree that one key element of this new strategy was the targeting of specific and high-level Soviet officials and generals with sniper rifles. As the journalist Steve Coll wrote, '"The phrase 'shooting ducks in a barrel' was used," one participant recalled. The sniper programme's advocates wanted to "off Russian generals in series".'[100]

Such proposals renewed the controversy surrounding a potential breach of the ban. The United States was not involved in a declared war or in a use of force sanctioned under the War Powers Resolution. Soviet generals were certainly foreign officials. They were not random Soviet officers but high-level officials precisely identified, and they were being targeted for political reasons, including demoralising the Soviet Union.[101] Furthermore, while assassination does not impinge on the type of weapon used, the proposed weapons for these operations (explosives, sniper rifles and night vision goggles) facilitated the covert targeting of specific individuals and, hence, made assassination the weapons' 'most likely use', and this is how they were understood at the time.[102] The actual killing was not done by the CIA itself, but by its local allies, the mujahideen, violating section 2.12 of Reagan's order.[103]

As in the Nicaragua case, Casey and like-minded officers pushed for the delivery of weapons. In the field, Gust Avrakatos argued that, in the context of paramilitary operations, the ban on assassination did not apply. The CIA, he argued, was involved in a war; therefore, supplying sniper rifles and explosives was no different than supplying other weapons of war. Michael Vickers, the Agency's head of the Afghanistan Covert Action Program, also pushed for the rifles. Some lawyers within the CIA, as well as officials who had lived through the inquiries of the 1970s – like John McMahon – challenged such a permissive interpretation.[104]

Confronted with internal opposition, Casey requested a legal opinion from both CIA and NSC lawyers regarding what made the provision of certain weapons different from the provision of others. CIA lawyers replied that the main difference was intent.[105] While other weapons could have multiple uses, they suggested, it was difficult to argue that sniper rifles had any other use but assassination. This legal opinion enabled Casey and Avrakatos to adopt a permissive and influential interpretation of the ban based on intent. Casey replied to the CIA's lawyers: 'if anyone asks don't tell them these are sniper rifles for assassination; tell them they are hunting rifles: that's our intent. What they choose to hunt is their decision, not ours.'[106] Based on this interpretation, weapons were provided to the mujahideen with only cosmetic changes (i.e. night vision goggles and scopes were removed). They were officially (re)labelled as 'individual defensive devices', and the CIA promised that it would not share intelligence on the location of Soviet generals and officials with the mujahideen, a promise soon broken.[107] The 'intent' argument also permitted the CIA to conspire with other actors in the Afghan theatre who were engaging in assassination, as long as no specific directives or demonstration of intent emerged.[108] The CIA's relationship with the British MI6 reportedly provided the Agency with additional options. Avrakatos, or so he recalled, could not explicitly suggest to the British the use of car bombs, but he could say, '"Fadlallah in Beirut was really effective last week. They had a car bomb that killed three hundred people." I gave MI6 stuff in good faith. What they did was always up to them.'[109] A similar debate surrounded the so-called 'buffalo gun', a '14.5 mm heavy machine gun' modified into a long-range sniper rifle. After a successful prototype, even McMahon this time relented as long as the weapon was included in the mujahideen arsenal as an 'anti-material' weapon, another play on intent.[110]

Beyond the particularities of the Afghan case, the 'intent argument' to circumvent the ban can be understood as a form of plausible deniability. The government was not denying the existence of the operations, nor the US government's involvement in them, nor (at times) the President's knowledge of them.[111] Instead, the government denied that the operations amounted to assassinations or assassination attempts. This manoeuvre conforms with what Stanley Cohen has called 'interpretive denial'. In interpretive denial, the 'raw facts' are not denied but given a different – and less problematic – interpretation.[112]

The 'mad dog of the Middle East': Reagan, Qaddafi and El Dorado Canyon

The legal and political precedents set in the realm of assassination combined in one of the toughest battles of Reagan's 'war on terrorism', that against Qaddafi. On 21 January 1981, the day after Reagan's inauguration, Qaddafi and Libya were on the agenda of the National Security Council.[113] The Administration developed a multi-pronged approach to Libya: support for internal and international opposition, economic sanctions, an embargo on the imports of Libyan oil, and military exercise in and around Libya's territorial waters to provoke and challenge the Libyan dictator.[114]

From the very start, the Reagan Administration had identified the removal of Qaddafi as one of its main priorities. As Richard Allen, Reagan's first National Security Advisor, put it, Qaddafi 'was a dangerous snake, and we had decided to cut his head off'.[115] In March, Haig wrote to the President that among the defining decisions of his presidency was what to do with Qaddafi, who – Haig wrote – represented a threat to the stability of the West. The United States was not alone. 'Here, too, we must act. But in this case, we have others who will act with us.' 'Our objective,' Haig continued, 'would be to remove Qadhafi from power.' The US government, Haig believed, only needed to provide limited material support.[116]

According to French investigative journalist Vincent Nouzille, the Reagan Administration had agreed to take part in a coup against Qaddafi as early as 1981. The plan built on open discussions between the French and American secret services on the need to eliminate Qaddafi. It was arranged with Egyptian president Anwar Sadat following a visit by Alexander De Marenches, Director of French Secret Services, to the White House. On 10 May 1981, however, Giscard d'Estaing, the French president, who had given the green light for the operation, was defeated by François

Mitterrand in the presidential elections. Mitterrand decided to stop the operation.[117] Despite the cancellation of the plot, the US confrontation with Qaddafi escalated.

The US government started funding and supporting the National Front for the Salvation of Libya (hereinafter NFSL). The group – founded in 1981 – conducted armed opposition against Qaddafi and hoped to remove him from power. In December 1983, Sudanese President Jaafar Nimeiri visited Washington. During the visit, and at Casey's suggestion, he met with the leaders of the NFSL. Casey had been unconvinced that the group could achieve the removal of Qaddafi on its own, but he supported it as a low-risk option. The Sudanese president agreed to let the NFSL train on Sudan's territory to conduct attacks and raids across the border in Libya. On 8 May 1984, with the CIA's knowledge and support, the NFSL carried out an effort to assassinate Qaddafi and overthrow his regime. The coup failed, but Casey was impressed with the effort and interpreted it as a sign of Qaddafi's vulnerability.[118]

After the failed coup, the Administration initially worked to establish and consolidate a 'credible political opposition' that might be ready to exploit the situation. In this effort, the Administration was willing to 'force [the] pace to the maximum extent possible'.[119] A new propaganda campaign worked to convince the Libyan people to rise against Qaddafi, as well as to convince Qaddafi himself that military leaders around him were plotting to remove him from power. The aim of this propaganda campaign was to exploit the dictator's paranoia and flaws in his security network.[120] The CIA also started compiling a series of reports and assessments on security at Qaddafi's residences, on the consequences of his ousting, and on his prospects for survival. A CIA 'Vulnerability Assessment' concluded that 'disaffected elements in the Libyan military could be spurred to assassination attempts or to cooperate with the exiles against Qaddafi'. The NSC supported this view and asked for 'lethal aid' to be provided to Libyan opposition groups.[121]

Vincent Cannistraro and Donald Fortier at the NSC were also working on a broader plan for the removal of Qaddafi. They lamented the reactive posture of the Administration and called for a more aggressive stance.[122] The plan – codenamed FLOWER – consisted of two main options. Initially defined as 'bold' and 'broad', they later took the name of 'Rose' and 'Tulip'. Tulip included a series of covert operations to overthrow Qaddafi relying on anti-Qaddafi groups, as well as the support of neighbouring countries. Rose envisioned a surprise attack with conventional military force by Egypt supported by US power.[123] Egyptian president Hosni Mubarak refused to be involved in Rose. At the US Embassy in Cairo, Edmund Hull, then working on political-military affairs, also expressed scepticism and convinced US Ambassador Nicholas Veliotes to oppose the plan. Rose was abandoned.[124]

Tulip went ahead. Casey presented the finding to Congressional Intelligence committees. Some members of Congress, including David Durenberg (R-MN) and Patrick Leahy (D-VE), opposed the arming of anti-Qaddafi groups and suggested that it was preposterous to imply that Qaddafi would survive an attempt to overthrow him. The Administration was, again, in potential breach of the assassination ban. Building on the intent argument developed in the Afghanistan case, Casey told the senators that the purpose of the plan was to support those groups that wanted Qaddafi removed. 'They might try to kill him, but that was not the objective of the plan.' Assassination was not the explicit intent of US support and, hence, this kind of support did not violate the ban. The Reagan Administration withdrew the finding only after the controversy leaked to the press.[125]

During the internal debate over Tulip and Rose, two terrorist incidents – the hijacking of a TWA flight and attacks at Vienna and Rome airports – convinced the Administration to step up its counterterrorism efforts and its covert operations against Qaddafi.[126] Reagan had concluded that 'decisive measures' had to be taken to stop Qaddafi and he was ready 'to go much further' than any Administration had ever gone.[127] NSDD 205 confirmed this change of policy. Beyond establishing a series of punitive sanctions on Libya, the directive also declared a state of national emergency giving the President special powers to respond to the 'extraordinary threat to the national security and foreign policy of the United States' said to be presented by Libya.[128]

At this stage, Casey asked Clarridge to reassess the Agency's counterterrorism posture. Clarridge pushed for a new legal and institutional structure for the CIA – one that would permit offensive strikes against terrorists – and for the creation of super-secret 'action teams' that could track, attack and capture terrorists globally (one composed by Americans, one by foreign nationals). Clarridge also recommended the fusion of the intelligence counterterrorism capabilities. The Administration largely accepted Clarridge's recommendations, especially since they conformed with the conclusion reached by a task force led by Vice-President George H. W. Bush. The Task Force on Combating Terrorism had recommended an increased centralisation of the US government counterterrorism operations. It had also called for a more robust response, including covert operations.[129]

On 1 February 1986, Reagan established a new Counter-Terrorism Center.[130] As the Center was being created, Clarridge penned a new, highly classified, presidential finding on terrorism. The finding, building on the precedent set by North and Clarridge's earlier recommendations, authorised covert action by the CIA against terrorist groups worldwide. As CIA official Robert Baer recalled, Clarridge interpreted the finding as an authorisation to do anything he wanted anywhere against terrorists.[131] The finding was signed by Reagan along with a broader policy document, NSDD 207, signed in January 1986, 'The National Program for Combating Terrorism', classified Top Secret.[132]

* * *

On 14 March during a National Security Planning Group meeting, Shultz forcefully argued that Qaddafi was 'an enemy and a terrorist'. 'We should be ready to undertake action to hurt *him*, not just fire back,' Shultz continued, 'Our forces should *plaster him* and his military targets' (emphasis added). As other members of the Administration raised concerns regarding targets, Shultz replied that a better option would be if Qaddafi was 'put in a box'.[133] Reagan also seemed ready to step up efforts against Qaddafi. He promised that he would take the heat – coming from Congress – if Qaddafi was killed, another effort to protect potential norm violators. As Reagan wrote in his diary, in case of another terrorist attack by 'Libya's top clown', the United States had clear targets

Muhammar Qaddafi: Assassination during the Reagan Years

in its sight and would have replied with a 'hell of a punch'.[134] Another attack did come.

On 5 April 1986, a bomb exploded at the La Belle Discoteque in West Berlin. The club was often frequented by US servicemen. The bombing killed three people (two Americans) and injured 229 (79 Americans). The National Security Agency (NSA) had intercepted telegrams from Tripoli to the Libyan Embassy in West Berlin. The telegrams stated: 'We have something planned that will make you happy' and 'an event occurred. You will be pleased with the result.' The telegrams were 'raw' intelligence and NSA officials were unsure about their credibility. Yet, they were seized upon by White House and NSC officials.[135] Reagan, or so it seemed, had his 'smoking gun'.

On 8 April, North and other members of the NSC argued that the US government had to be ready to take advantage of the likely political vacuum created by US air strikes.[136] On the 11th, the CIA's Directorate of Intelligence identified a strike on Qaddafi's residences as the only measure that could convince the Libyan leader that the US was serious about 'his removal'.[137] During the policy debate over Libya, North had also proposed a series of methods to kill the Libyan leader. These included the use of a Special Forces (SEAL team) landing, the use of a conventionally armed Tomahawk missile, and the use of the ultimate bomber in the US arsenal, the Stealth. Admiral William Crowe, Chairman of the Joint Chiefs of Staff, had shot down as impractical all of North's proposals.[138] US policy settled instead on a conventional air strike.

When it came to the selection of targets, the Joint Chiefs of Staff initially opposed the inclusion of the Bab al-Azizia Barracks Compound, which hosted Qaddafi's residences, due to concerns regarding civilian casualties.[139] In a memorandum to Reagan, National Security Advisor John Poindexter swept aside these concerns. He argued that the high risk of 'collateral damage' for some targets was worth the potential reward. The reward was regime change.[140] Casey reportedly also intervened: 'don't just bomb the building, bomb the damn tent. That's where he lives.'[141] Reagan overrode the JCS objections.[142]

The air strike – codenamed Operation El Dorado Canyon – took place on 14 April. The operation, initially planned for the 12th,

235

was delayed due to North's effort to get up-to-date information on Qaddafi's location. The NSC had already stepped up its intelligence collection efforts to obtain 'near real-time data on Gaddafi whereabouts'.[143] The US government was also able to rely on local allies. After the TWA hijacking, during which the Israeli and US governments had worked together, a secret channel of communication and intelligence sharing had been established, something that NSDD 138 had recommended. Mossad started charting and sharing Qaddafi's movements 'hour-by-hour' at the time of the raid. The raid started at 2 a.m., clearly aiming to hit Libyan officials in their sleep. The nine F-111s deployed carried four 2,000-pound bombs each. According to reporter Seymour Hersh, Air Force officials considered the raid to have a 95 per cent PK (probable kill). As an Air Force officer reported. 'There's no question that they were looking for Qaddafi. It was briefed that way. They were going to kill him . . . the assassination was the big thing.'[144] Former Senator Gary Hart confirmed the aim of the operation. 'The bombing raid on Libya,' he argued, 'was a clear effort to assassinate Qaddafi.'[145]

Qaddafi survived the bombing, but one of his daughters was reportedly killed. In the 1980s, investigative journalists attributed Qaddafi's survival to technical difficulties in the bombing raid, with only a few of the nine F-111s deployed against the barracks placing their bombs on target.[146] While technical difficulties might have occurred, Libyan and Italian authorities have more recently confirmed that then Italian prime minister Bettino Craxi – opposed to the US government's policy towards Libya – used an intermediary to warn Qaddafi of the impending raid. Italian authorities understood the bombing as an assassination attempt and notified Qaddafi accordingly.[147]

After the raid, members of the Reagan Administration launched a concerted public relations campaign to deny that the strike violated the ban on assassination. A Senior White House official put forward the unconvincing argument that, regardless of the precision of the bombing, Qaddafi was not the target. The White House had also prepared a statement describing the possible death of the Libyan leader as 'a fortuitous by-product of our act of self-defence'.[148] Clarridge's account of the episode was caustic:

Muhammar Qaddafi: Assassination during the Reagan Years

Were we trying to kill him? You be the judge. Nine F-111Bs, each carrying four two-thousand-pound bombs, were tasked with attacking Al Azzyziyah. At six hundred miles per hour, a pilot could not be certain of hitting Qaddafi's command bunkers and avoiding his residence.[149]

At a Congressional hearing, Representative Norman Dicks (D-WA) questioned Secretary of Defense Weinberger, asking how the attack on Qaddafi's 'living quarters' could be defined in any other way but an attempt to assassinate a foreign leader. Weinberger suggested that 'living quarters' was a 'loose term' and that the United States had targeted the leader's command and control building. The Pentagon later confirmed this view: 'inasmuch as the entire complex was, in one way or another, related to Qaddafi's command and control of terrorism, the entire complex was considered targetable.'[150] Similarly, Schultz argued that Qaddafi 'was not a direct target ... we have a general stance that opposes direct efforts of that kind, and the spirit and intent was in accord with those understandings'.[151] Again, Cohen's interpretive denial and the intent argument are germane here.

Behind these public statements, the Administration was working on broader and far-reaching legal and political precedents. Abraham Sofaer, White House Legal Counsel, was critical of the War Powers Resolution (WPR) and of the constraints it imposed on the power of the President.[152] In Congressional hearings after the strike, he argued that a counterterrorism strike in (pre-emptive) self-defence was excluded from WPR notification requirements. These strikes did not entail a risk of confrontation with other states and the need for 'swiftness and secrecy' made consultation impossible.[153] These deployments of force did not amount to (nor pose a risk of) war, and they were a prerogative of the President. A grey area between peace and war was being crystallised.

This was particularly consequential because Sofaer and the Reagan Administration adopted an expansive view of self-defence. Sofaer defined the strike against Libya as a legitimate self-defensive and pre-emptive military measure. While referring to Article 51 of the UN Charter, Sofaer also admitted the US government adopted a more expansive notion of self-defence, one based on the imminence of the threat and customary international law, and not one based on an armed attack that had already occurred, as envisioned by the UN Charter.[154] Sofaer went beyond this. He cited approvingly a speech by Shultz that suggested that a state which supports terrorism or the preparation of terrorist activities from within its own territory 'is responsible for such attacks. Such conduct can amount to an ongoing armed aggression against another state under international law.'[155] In other words, the US government could use force to repel imminent, future and ongoing threats.

Finally, at a public lecture in 1989, Sofaer lamented the press's and Congress's tendency to call 'assassination' any action taken in self-defence.[156] He made clear that – as the Administration had concluded – the ban was not meant to apply to 'lawful killings undertaken in self defense against terrorists'.[157] But he also added a new dimension. Even if policymakers were aware that some of the targets the operation had hit were places in which Qaddafi lived, this did not make the strikes an assassination. According to the Reagan Administration's reasoning, reported approvingly by Sofaer, Qaddafi's position as head of state did not guarantee him 'legal immunity' from being attacked when present at a proper military target.[158]

This view implied that – as long as the United States portrayed a strike as an attack against a military target, infrastructure, and/or command and control centre, and not as a direct attack against a specific leader present at those targets – the policy was legitimate and did not violate the ban.[159] In this sense, even in peacetime, the ban on assassination did not protect foreign leaders if they constituted a threat that warranted action in self-defence.[160] In fact, the targets of self-defensive operations could be terrorists themselves, states, and leaders of states harbouring them.[161] As legal scholar Boyd Johnson noted, this line of argument showed 'the ease with which presidents can shroud assassination under the cloak of Article 51 self-defence'.[162]

A few days after the raid, Senators Robert Dole (R-KS) and Jeremiah Denton (R-AL) proposed a bill to expand the President's power to strike against terrorists without prior Congressional consultation, and outside WPR requirements. The bill authorised the assassination of a head of state personally involved in terrorism.[163]

It superseded the ban and gave the President blanket authority in counterterrorism. The bill was discussed in Congressional hearings but did not go past the committee stage. Its emergence, though, showed how effective the Administration had been – through its public discourse and (covert) foreign policy practice – in, at least momentarily, shifting the public debate in the context of assassination and counterterrorism.

Conclusion

In late 1986, the Iran–contra scandal erupted.[164] On 15 December, as he was about to testify on Iran–contra before the Senate Intelligence Committee, Casey collapsed in his office. After surgery and a long stay in hospital, Casey signed a letter of resignation brought to him by his deputy Robert Gates on 29 January. On 6 May, back at his home, Casey died, as Congress was about to begin public hearings on the scandal.[165]

By the time of Casey's death, and largely due to his aggressive view of covert operations, assassination had re-emerged – albeit under disguise – as an available policy option. The US government and the CIA became involved in direct and indirect efforts to assassinate foreign leaders as well as charismatic political figures. The case of Fadlallah is particularly instructive here for the Agency's extensive effort to act indirectly and behind Congress's back, relying on both regional governments (Saudi Arabia) and local allies. The campaign against Qaddafi also combined both indirect and direct efforts. Through the NFSL and the partnership with Sudan, the United States hoped to contribute to the overthrow of Qaddafi, which was likely to lead to his killing. When this failed, with El Dorado Canyon the US government took matters into its own hands, while relying on Israeli intelligence support.

Slowly but surely, euphemisms ('neutralisation', 'put in a box') re-emerged in the language of policymaking and so did plausible deniability for both the President and the US government. Compared to pre-ban cases, legal advisers in the CIA and other agencies had worked to develop legal rationales for the legitimation of assassination. This process amounted to what Duncan Kennedy has called 'legal work'. It is an effort to transform an 'initial apprehension' of what a system of law requires into a 'new apprehension' which better corresponds to the strategic 'extra-juristic preferences' of the actor.[166] This work was conducted in three main areas: coups and insurgencies, counterterrorism, and strikes against foreign leaders.

Through arguments regarding control over local actors and regarding the need for explicit intent to assassinate, the CIA could become involved in assassination in the context of insurgencies and coups. The need for an explicit directive signalling an intent to assassinate was confirmed in the Tulip case. Furthermore, secret directives gave the CIA the power to target terrorists globally, as long as this was done in 'good faith'. When controversy erupted, Sporkin and other CIA officials argued that the ban only protected heads of state. The attempt(s) on Qaddafi showed the US government's willingness to abandon its own (re)interpretation of the ban. Here, an expansive argument developed surrounding the permissibility of striking at foreign leaders in self-defence, if the strike was couched in terms of targeting infrastructure and/or command-and-control centres. Again, if no explicit indication of an intent to target an individual leader emerged, the United States could strike at will.

In the aftermath of Casey's death, the Administration eventually settled on FBI Director William Webster as new DCI. As Chris Whipple put it, 'if you set out to create the antithesis of Bill Casey, you might end up with William Webster'.[167] This applied above all to Webster's strict view of the rule of law. Not unlike the Congressional investigations of the 1970s, the backlash of Iran–Contra dampened the CIA's outreach and shaped its institutional culture. This new approach influenced the US government's approach to its next target, Panamanian leader Manuel Noriega.

Notes

1. Philip Taubman, 'US Tries to Back up Haig on Terrorism', *New York Times*, 3 May 1981, available at https://www.nytimes.com/1981/05/03/world/us-tries-to-back-up-haig-on-terrorism.html (accessed 27 October 2023).

2. Memorandum Haig to Reagan, FRUS, 1981–1988, vol. 1: Foundations of Foreign Policy, doc. 23.
3. Joseph Persico, *Casey* (New York: Viking, 1991); Chris Whipple, *The Spymasters: How the CIA Directors Shape History and the Future* (London: Simon & Schuster, 2020).
4. George De Lama, 'Reagan condemns 5 outlaw nations', *Chicago Tribune*, 9 July 1985.
5. Carol Winkler, *In the Name of Terrorism* (Albany: State University of New York Press, 2005), 70.
6. Seth Jones, *A Covert Action: Reagan, the CIA, and the Cold War Struggle in Poland* (New York: W. W. Norton, 2018), 63.
7. Betty Glad, 'Black-and-White Thinking: Ronald Reagan's Approach to Foreign Policy', *Political Psychology*, 4.1 (1983), 33–76.
8. Lou Cannon, *President Reagan* (New York: Simon & Schuster, 1992), 349.
9. Nicholas Dujmovic, 'Reagan, Intelligence, Casey and the CIA: A Reappraisal', *International Journal of Intelligence and Counterintelligence*, 26 (2013), 9–10; David Priess, *The President's Book of Secrets* (New York: Public Affairs, 2016), 150.
10. Rick Perlstein, *The Invisible Bridge* (New York: Simon & Schuster, 2014), 522.
11. Bob Woodward, Interview on *60 Minutes*, 27 September 1987, available at https://www.cia.gov/readingroom/docs/CIA-RDP90-00965 R000807540049-8.pdf (accessed 27 October 2023).
12. Robert Gates, *From the Shadows* (New York: Simon & Schuster, 1996).
13. Ric Prado, *Black Ops* (New York: St. Martin's, 2022), 86.
14. Herbert Meyer, *Scouting the Future: The Public Speeches of William Casey* (Washington, DC: Regnery Gateway, 1989), 12.
15. Doyle McManus, Interview with the author, 3 August 2016, Washington, DC.
16. John Ranelagh, *The Agency* (Cambridge: Sceptre, 1987), 676.
17. Steven Emerson, *Secret Warriors: Inside the Covert Military Operations of the Reagan Era* (New York: Putnam, 1998), 36.
18. Gates, *From the Shadows*, 286.
19. US Senate, 'Nomination of William J. Casey', Hearing before the Select Committee on Intelligence of the US Senate, 18/1/1981, available at https://www.intelligence.senate.gov/sites/default/files/hearings/97casey.pdf (accessed 27 October 2023), 25–6, 41.
20. Bruce Riedel, Interview with the author, 4 August 2016.
21. John Prados, *Presidents' Secret Wars* (Chicago: Elephant Paperbacks, 1996), 374.

22. Persico, *Casey*.
23. Whipple, *Spymasters*, 117.
24. John Rizzo, *Company Man* (London: Scribner, 2014), 79.
25. Constantine Menges, *Inside the National Security Council* (New York: Simon & Schuster, 1988), 363.
26. Bob Woodward, *Veil* (New York: Simon & Schuster, 1986), 161.
27. Charlotte Peevers, *The Politics of Justifying Force* (Oxford: Oxford University Press, 2013), 201.
28. Tim Weiner, *Legacy of Ashes* (New York: Doubleday, 2007), 364.
29. Charles Mohr, 'CIA Aide Clarifies Stand on Restraint', *New York Times*, 12 March 1981; John M. Oseth, *Regulating U.S. Intelligence Operations* (Lexington: University of Kentucky Press, 1985), 149–51.
30. Ken DeGraffenreid, Undated. 'Son of EO 12036', Memorandum to Allen. DeGraffenreid Kenneth Files, RAC Box 4, Box 3, Folder EO12036 Revision (2/12), Ronald Reagan Presidential Library (RRPL).
31. Donald Gregg, 'Points to make with Senator Goldwater,' Memorandum to Allen, 1/6/1981, DeGraffenreid Files, RAC Box 4, Box 4, Folder EO12036 Revision (Working File) (2), RRPL.
32. Ken DeGraffenreid. 1981. Revision to Executive Order 12036, DeGraffenreid Files, RAC Box 4, Box 7, Folder Intelligence Executive Orders drafts (1/6), RRPL.
33. William Casey, 'Revisions of Executive Order 12036', Memorandum to Allen, 2/6/1981. DeGraffenreid Files, RAC Box 4, Box 3, Folder EO12036 Revision (4/12), RRPL.
34. Memo Allen to Casey, 'Revisions of EO12036', Undated. DeGraffenreid Files, RAC Box 4, Box 4, Folder EO12036 Revision (Working File) (4), RRPL.
35. Ronald Reagan, Executive Order 12333: 'United States Intelligence Activities', 4/12/1981, available at https://www.archives.gov/federal-register/codification/executive-order/12333.html (accessed 27 October 2023).
36. Oseth, *Regulating*, 156.
37. Ibid., 153.
38. Ibid., 156.
39. Edwin Meese, Undated. 'Executive Orders on Intelligence and on Intelligence Oversight Board'. Memorandum to the President. DeGraffenreid Files, ND006, Casefiles 049964 1/6, RRPL.
40. National Security Decision Directive 30, 10/4/1982, available at https://fas.org/irp/offdocs/nsdd/nsdd-30.pdf (accessed 27 October 2023).

Muhammar Qaddafi: Assassination during the Reagan Years

41. Christopher Simpson, *National Security Directives of the Reagan and Bush Administration* (Boulder, CO: Westview Press, 1995), 441.
42. David Martin and John Walcott, *Best Laid Plans* (New York: Simon & Schuster, 1988), 66.
43. Whipple, *Spymasters*, 124.
44. Philip Taubman, *In the Nation's Service* (Stanford, CA: Stanford University Press, 2023), ebook, chapter 16.
45. Emerson, *Secret Warriors*, 194.
46. Michael Smith, *Killer Elite* (London: Cassell, 2006), 100–1.
47. Persico, *Casey*, 428.
48. National Security Planning Group (NSPG), Summary of Meeting. NSPG Meeting on Combating terrorism, 2/3/1984. Executive Secretariat NSPG, Box 3, NSPG 86 – 109, Folder NSPG 84, RRPL.
49. Steve Rosen, Undated. 'Low-level conflict and the US'. Draft Memorandum for Robert McFarlane. Donald Fortier Files Series 1 Subject File – Libya, RAC Box 7, Box 4, Folder Libya 1981–1984 6/6, RRPL.
50. Neil Livingstone, *The Cult of Counterterrorism* (New York: Free Press, 1989), 235.
51. Gates, *From the Shadows*, 224.
52. Ben Bradlee Jr., *Guts & Glory* (London: Grafton Books, 1988), 189.
53. Emerson, *Secret Warriors*, 194.
54. Woodward, *Veil*, 412.
55. Mattia Toaldo, *The Origins of the US War on Terror* (London: Routledge, 2013), 105.
56. George Shultz, *Turmoil and Triumph* (New York: Scribner, 1993), 648.
57. Timothy Naftali, *Blind Spot* (New York: Basic Books, 2005), 150.
58. Jeffrey D. Simon, *The Terrorist Trap* (Bloomington: Indiana University Press, 2001), 182.
59. Ryder McKeown, 'Norm Regress: US Revisionism and the Slow Death of the Torture Norm', *International Relations*, 23.1 (1999), 14–15.
60. Simon, *Terrorist Trap*, 178.
61. Ronald Reagan, NSDD 138 – Combatting Terrorism, 3/4/1984, available at https://fas.org/irp/offdocs/nsdd/nsdd-138.pdf (accessed 27 October 2023), 4.
62. Reagan, NSDD 138, 4.
63. Mark Gunneflo, *Targeted Killing* (Cambridge: Cambridge University Press, 2016), 113.
64. Toaldo, *The Origins*, 103–4.
65. David C. Wills, *The First War on Terrorism* (Lanham, MD: Rowman & Littlefield, 2003), 87.

66. Averell Schmidt and Kathryn Sikkink, 'Breaking the Ban? The Heterogeneous Impact of US Contestation of the Torture Norm', *Journal of Global Security Studies*, 4.1 (2019), 119.
67. William Banks and Peter Raven-Hansen, 'Targeted Killing and Assassination: The U.S. Legal Framework', *University of Richmond Law Review*, 37 (2003), 726.
68. Bob Woodward and Walter Pincus, '1984 Order gave CIA latitude', *Washington Post*, 5 October 1988.
69. Persico, *Casey*, 429.
70. For the former view, see Mark Mazzetti, *The Way of the Knife* (New York: Penguin 2014), 55; Robert Oakley, Interview, *Target America*, PBS Frontline, 2001, available at https://www.pbs.org/wgbh/pages/frontline/shows/target/interviews/oakley.html (accessed 27 October 2023); Naftali, *Blind Spot*, 148. For the latter, see Kai Bird, *The Good Spy: The Life and Death of Robert Ames* (New York: Crown Publishers, 2014), 334; Whipple, *Spymasters*, 120–1.
71. Christopher Fuller, *See It, Shoot It: The Secret History of the CIA's Lethal Drone Program* (New Have, CT: Yale University Press, 2017), 44.
72. Robert Chesney, 'Beyond the Battlefield, beyond al Qaeda: The Destabilizing Legal Architecture of Counterterrorism', *Michigan Law Review*, 112 (2013), 198.
73. Naftali, *Blind Spot*, 148.
74. Annie Jacobsen, *Surprise, Kill, Vanish: The Secret History of the CIA Paramilitary Armies, Operators and Assassins* (New York: Little, Brown, 2019), 530.
75. CIA Directorate of Intelligence, 'Near East and South Asia Review', 1/3/1985, CIA CREST.
76. Winkler, *In the Name*, 73.
77. Such as the mujahideen in Afghanistan and the Contras in Nicaragua; Whipple, *Spymasters*, 127.
78. Whipple, *Spymasters*, 127.
79. Woodward, *Veil*, 152.
80. Bird, *The Good Spy*, 334.
81. Martin and Walcott, *Best*, 222; Emerson, *Secret Warriors*, 194. According to Baer, this was even more explicit. Casey himself met with Lebanese military officials then training in the United States and told them: 'This guy Fadlallah's a goddamned problem . . . Isn't there something we can do about him?' Robert Baer, *The Perfect Kill* (New York: Plume Books, 2014), 308.
82. There is a debate as to the US degree of involvement. See Whipple, *Spymasters*, 128. Kai Bird also reports that a reliable source – Mustafa

Zein, friend of Robert Ames – told him that while the civilian casualties were not expected, the assassination operation had been ordered by Casey. Bird, *The Good Spy*, 334; Kai Bird, Phone interview with the author, 26 August 2022. Other accounts stress that it was a team of rogue agents from the Lebanese intelligence services, or the Lebanese intelligence services themselves who had been 'trained and provisioned' by the CIA. For the former, see Lt. Col. Bill Cowan, 'Interview', PBS, Target America, available at https://www.pbs.org/wgbh/pages/frontline/shows/target/interviews/cowan.html (accessed 27 October 2023). For the latter see, Vincent Cannistraro (then at the NSC), 'Interview', PBS Target America, available at https://www.pbs.org/wgbh/pages/frontline/shows/target/interviews/cannistraro.html (accessed 27 October 2023); Fred Burton, *Beirut Rules* (New York: Berkley, 2018), 178. Finally, Robert Baer blames the Lebanese military. Baer, *The Perfect Kill*, 71.

83. Michael Morisy, 'CIA releases full Contras manual on "Psychological Operations in Guerrilla Warfare"', MuckRock, 18/122017, available at https://www.muckrock.com/news/archives/2017/dec/18/cia-contras-manual/ (accessed 27 October 2023).
84. William Leogrande, *Our Own Backyard: The United States in Central America, 1977–1992* (Chapel Hill: University of North Carolina Press, 2000), 364.
85. Editorial team, 'The CIA Murder Manual', *Washington Post*, 21 October 1984, available at https://www.washingtonpost.com/archive/opinions/1984/10/21/the-cias-murder-manual/4cacbc42-1790-46db-baaa-02186a755758/ (accessed 30 October 2023).
86. *New York Times*, 'The Candidates Debate', 22 October 1984.
87. Joanne Omang and Lou Cannon, 'Reagan Orders Investigation of Controversial CIA Manual', *Washington Post*, 19 October 1984.
88. Leogrande, *Our Own Backyard*, 365.
89. Ibid., 413.
90. Ibid., 365–6.
91. Christopher Dickey and Joanne Omang, 'Alleged Author of CIA Manual Said to Be Ex-GI', *Washington Post*, 20 October 1984.
92. Persico, *Casey*, 417.
93. Ibid., 418.
94. Russell Bruemmer, 'The Prohibition on Assassination: A Legal and Ethical Analysis', in Hayden Peake and Samuel Halpern (eds), *In the Name of Intelligence* (Washington, DC: NIBC Press, 1995), 141.
95. US House of Representatives, *Report on the Activities on the Permanent Select Committee on Intelligence*, 98th Congress, Second Session, House Report 98–1196, 2 January 1985 (Washington, DC: US Government Printing Office, 1985), 16.

96. Michael Schmitt, 'State-Sponsored Assassination in International and Domestic Law', *Yale Journal of International Law*, 17.2 (1992), 665.
97. William Casey, Letter to Daniel P. Moynihan. 25/10/1984. Executive Secretariat NSC Agency File Records, RAC Box 1, 2 Box 3 – CIA, Folder CIA 10/17/84 – 12/10/84, RRPL.
98. Christopher Dickey, *With the Contras* (New York: Touchstone, 1987), 257.
99. Peter Schweizer, *Victory* (New York: Atlantic Monthly Press, 1994), 153.
100. Steve Coll, *Ghost Wars* (London: Penguin, 2005), 136.
101. Kirsten Lundberg, Philip Zelikow and Ernest May, 'Politics of Covert Action: The US, the Mujahedeen, and the Stinger Missile', *Kennedy School of Government*, Case Program (1999), 25.
102. Coll, *Ghost Wars*, 135–7.
103. George Crile, *Charlie Wilson's War* (London: Atlantic Books, 2002), 166.
104. Michael Vickers, *By All Means Available* (New York: Knopf, 2023), ebook, chapter 6.
105. Fitzhugh Brundage, *Civilizing Torture: An American Tradition* (Cambridge, MA: Harvard University Press, 2018), 157.
106. Schweizer, *Victory*, 208.
107. Coll, *Ghost Wars*, 136, 221.
108. Ibid., 136.
109. Crile, *Charlie Wilson's War*, 201, 277.
110. Vickers, *By All Means*, chapter 6. The purpose of these 'buffalo gun sniper rifles' became clearer in later years when the CIA became concerned that Pakistani Intelligence Services might divert the same weapons to Kashmir and use them for the assassination of local officials. See Coll, *Ghost Wars*, 221.
111. Michael Poznansky, 'Revisiting Plausible Deniability', *Journal of Strategic Studies*, 45.4 (2022), 511–33.
112. Stanley Cohen, *States of Denial: Knowing about Atrocities and Suffering* (Cambridge: Polity, 2001), 7–8.
113. Seymour Hersh, 'Target Gaddafi', *New York Times*, 22 February 1987; Priess, *The President's Book*, 155.
114. Brian Davis, *Qaddafi, Terrorism, and the Origins of the US Attack on Libya* (London: Praeger, 1990), 47.
115. Vincent Nouzille, *Les Tueurs de la Republique* (Paris: J'ai Lu, 2016), 111.
116. Memorandum Haig to Reagan, Undated, FRUS 1981–1988, vol. 1, Foundations of Foreign Policy, doc. 36.

117. Nouzille, *Les Tueurs*, 111; Vincent Nouzille, Skype interview with the author, 2 October 2020.
118. Joseph Stanik, *El Dorado Canyon: Reagan's Undeclared War with Qaddafi* (Annapolis: Naval Institute Press, 2003), 85.
119. Elements of an action plan, Donald Fortier Files Series 1 Subject File – Libya, RAC Box 7, Box 4, Folder Libya Jan-June 1985 4/4, RRPL.
120. Memorandum Next Steps to be taken on Libya, 8/8/1986, Folder Next Steps 2/2, Box 3, Box 91747, James Stark Files, RRPL.
121. Bob Woodward, 'CIA Anti-Qaddafi Plan Backed', *Washington Post*, 3 November 1985.
122. Donald Fortier and Vincent Cannistraro, 'The Qaddafi problem', Memorandum for McFarlance, 15/2/1985, Digital National Security Archives, CIA Covert Operations: From Carter to Obama, 1977–2010.
123. Stanik, *El Dorado Canyon*, 89.
124. Charles Stuart Kennedy, 'Interview with Ambassador Edmund James Hull', Library of Congress, available at https://www.loc.gov/item/mfdipbib001566 (accessed 30 October 2023), 148.
125. Stanik, *El Dorado*, 103.
126. Davis, *Qaddafi*, 70.
127. Inserts on Reagan's views on Libya, Undated, DNSA, Covert Operations.
128. Simpson, *National Security Directives*, 631.
129. Hank Crumpton, *The Art of Intelligence* (New York: Penguin, 2012), 122.
130. Coll, *Ghost Wars*, 139.
131. Ibid., 141.
132. Christopher Fuller, 'Reagan and the Evolution of US Counterterrorism', in Jonathan Hunt and Simon Miles (eds), *The Reagan Moment* (Ithaca, NY: Cornell University Press, 2021), 73.
133. Memorandum of conversation, NSPG on Libya, 14/3/1986, DNSA, Covert Operations.
134. Ronald Reagan, *The Reagan Diaries* (New York: HarperCollins, 2007), 381.
135. Hersh, 'Target Gaddafi.'
136. Memorandum from North et al. to Fortier, 'Next steps re Libya', 8/4/1986, available at http://www.thereaganfiles.com/19860408-next-steps-re.pdf (accessed 30 October 2023).
137. CIA Directorate of Intelligence, 'Libya: Gaddafi's likely response to a US military strike', 11/4/1986, CIA CREST.
138. Hersh, 'Target Gaddafi'.

139. Hersh, 'Target Gaddafi'; Christopher Andrews, *For the President's Eyes Only* (London: HarperCollins, 1996), 483.
140. Memorandum Poindexter to Reagan, 'Next steps Libya', undated, James Stark Files, Box 3, Box 91747, Folder El Dorado Canyon 6/10, RRPL.
141. Russell Riley, 'Interview with R. James Woolsey', William J. Clinton Presidential Library History Project, 13 January 2010, 90.
142. Andrews, *For the President's*, 483.
143. Elements of an action plan, Folder Libya Jan–June 1985 4/4, Donald Fortier Files Series 1 Subject File – Libya, RAC Box 7, Box 4, RRPL.
144. Persico, *Casey*, 498; Livingstone, *The Cult*, 271; Hersh, 'Target Gaddafi'.
145. Gary Hart, Skype interview with the author, 20 May 2016.
146. Jane Mayer and Doyle McManus, *Landslide* (Boston, MA: Houghton Mifflin, 1988), 222–3.
147. Qaddafi either left the barracks or found refuge in a bunker. Italy's then foreign minister, Giulio Andreotti, reportedly considered the assassination operation 'inappropriate'. 'Bobo' Craxi, Exchange with the author, 7 September 2023; Sergio Romano, 'Lettere al Corriere', *Corriere Della Sera*, 9 March 2011; *La Stampa*, 'Così Bettino salvò Gheddafi', 31 October 2008; Silvio Labbate, 'Italian Mediterranean Policy in the Early 1980s in the Light of National Archive Documents', *International History Review*, 42 (2020), 1009.
148. Martin and Walcott, *Best*, 296; Stanik, *El Dorado Canyon*, 153.
149. Duane Clarridge, *A Spy for All Seasons* (New York: Scribner, 1997), 339.
150. Davis, *Qaddafi*, 136.
151. Roger Herbert, 'Bullets with Names', thesis, Naval Postgraduate School, 1992, 59.
152. Memorandum Abraham D. Sofaer to Fred Fielding (Counsel to the President) 'War Powers Resolution and Military Action against Libya', 9/1/1986, Howard Teicher Files, Box 5, Box 91668, Folder Libya Sensitive 1986 (2/7), RRPL.
153. Abraham D. Sofaer, 'War Powers, Libya, and State Sponsored Terrorism', US House of Representatives, Hearings Before the Subcommittee on Arms Control, International Security and Science of the House Committee on Foreign Affairs, 1986, 7, 36.
154. Gunneflo, *Targeted Killing*, 141.
155. Abraham Sofaer, 'Terrorism, the Law, and National Self-Defense', *Military Law Review*, 1989, 126, 104.

156. Sofaer, 'Terrorism', 126, 117.
157. Ibid., 119.
158. Ibid., 120.
159. Mark Vlasic, 'Cloak and Dagger Diplomacy: The US and Assassination', *Georgetown Journal of International Affairs*, 1.2 (2000), 101.
160. Gabriella Blum and Philip Heymann, 'Law of Policy of Targeted Killing', *Harvard National Security Journal*, 145 (2010), 155; Nathan Canestaro, 'American Law and Policy on Assassination of Foreign Leaders', *Boston College International & Comparative Law Review*, 26.1 (2003), 25.
161. Gunneflo, *Targeted Killing*, 143.
162. Boyd Johnson, 'Executive Order 12,333: The Permissibility of an American Assassination of a Foreign Leader', *Cornell International Law Journal*, 25.2 (1992), 423.
163. Anti-terrorism Act of 1986, 17/4/1986, available at https://www.congress.gov/bill/99th-congress/senate-bill/2335/cosponsors?r=13&s=1&q=%7B%22cosponsor-state%22%3A%22Alabama%22%7D (accessed 30 October 2023); Sofaer, 'War Powers', 105.
164. Whipple, *Spymasters*, 129–30; Malcom Byrne, *Iran–Contra* (Lawrence: University Press of Kansas, 2014).
165. Whipple, *Spymasters*, 134.
166. Duncan Kennedy, *Legal Reasoning, Collected Essays* (Aurora, CO: Davies Group, 2008), 158; Noura Erakat, *Justice for Some: Law and the Question of Palestine* (Stanford, CA: Stanford University Press, 2019), 4.
167. Whipple, *Spymasters*, 138.

9 Manuel Noriega: Coups, Failed Coups and the Ban on Assassination

'America's public enemy number one in the United States is drug abuse,' President Richard Nixon intoned at a press conference on 17 June 1971. The press conference represented a foundational moment in the so-called 'war on drugs'.[1] As Nixon delivered these lines, Panama was becoming a hub for worldwide drug trafficking. In March 1971, a couple of months before the press conference, Nixon, John Ehrlichman and Egil Krogh – who had already arranged for the creation of the 'plumbers' – had agreed to secretly set aside $100 million for the Bureau of Narcotics and Dangerous Drugs (BNDD) to organise a secret kidnap and assassination programme. 'This decision action,' officials agreed, 'is our only hope for destroying or immobilizing the highest levels of drug traffickers.' BNDD officials started exploring the creation of hit squads. One hundred and fifty assassinations, or so the argument went, would have been enough to destroy the heroin trafficking operations.[2] In May 1971 the White House asked the BNDD's director, John Ingersoll, to draft a plan for 'clandestine law enforcement in the realm of counter-narcotics'. The plan allegedly included assassinations.

In January 1972, following pressure from the White House, Ingersoll asked his staff to devise a plan to deal with Omar Torrijos, leader of Panama, and his right-hand man Manuel Noriega. The plan contained four possible options: linking Noriega to a plot against Torrijos; leaking information to the press; linking Noriega's removal to the then ongoing Panama Canal negotiations; or the 'total and complete immobilization' of Noriega, a clear euphemism for assassination.[3] The plan seemingly went nowhere, but Ingersoll did travel to Panama to try and convince Torrijos to drop Noriega, and detrimental information was leaked to the press.[4]

Manuel Noriega: Coups and the Ban on Assassination

The plumbers continued to explore the option of assassinating Torrijos. Howard Hunt allegedly recontacted Manuel Artime. The two had worked together in plots against Fidel Castro in the early 1960s. Hunt introduced Artime to Gordon Liddy, in charge of the plumbers. The plan was supposed to coincide with Nixon's re-election. With the Watergate scandal breaking, this plan also went nowhere.[5] Once released from prison in 1977, Hunt admitted that, at the time, 'the feeling was that if Torrijos didn't shape up and cooperate, he was going to be wasted', and that the plumbers had assassination as part of their brief.[6]

* * *

The US government's relationship with Noriega is rife with assassinations and assassination plots: plots proposed, and plots pursued, plots only imagined, and plots eventually dropped. Noriega rose through the ranks of Panama's National Guard, a rise marred by violence against political opponents, corruption and controversy. Noriega had attended the (in)famous School of the Americas, where he focused on intelligence and counterintelligence. Based on Noriega's cooperation with US intelligence and its strategic needs, for much of the 1960s and 1970s, the US government turned a blind eye to the Panamanian's crimes, to his involvement in drug trafficking,[7] and to Noriega's double-crossing in the realm of intelligence and narcotics.[8] Throughout this time, he worked with the Drug Enforcement Administration (DEA)[9] and some of its enemies. He was also on the CIA's payroll.[10] By 1983, Noriega had become the de facto leader of Panama. While not abandoning his drug smuggling ventures and double-dealings he had also become a stable – if at times duplicitous – ally in the Contra war. He supported the United States by financing and training the Contras behind Congress's back. He had also proposed to Oliver North, Noriega's main contact in the National Security Council, to assassinate the Sandinista leadership – an offer North had refused, with the NSC settling instead on cooperation in sabotage operations.[11]

Towards the end of the Reagan years, Noriega's fortunes changed with a shift in US priorities. After Iran–Contra, the Reagan Administration moved its attention to the 'war on drugs'.

In February 1988, indictments against Noriega from courts in Florida and denunciations in the media[12] added to an already complicated relationship. The Reagan Administration started working overtly and covertly to remove Noriega from power. The Administration's covert measures engendered a debate as to the permissible role of the US government in supporting a coup. One of the main questions dealt with whether such support could amount to involvement in assassination.

Noriega remained in power and operations against Panama became one of the first ventures in the realm of covert operations of the incoming George H. W. Bush Administration. In October 1989, the Administration's failure to support a coup in Panama renewed debate regarding the power of the CIA and of the US government to support emerging coups. With the ban becoming the object of public debate, the Bush Administration and CIA Director William Webster worked with Congress on a permissive reinterpretation of the ban, one that more explicitly permitted the CIA's involvement in coups, even if they entailed a risk of assassination. This outcome coincided with the culmination of a broader review of the meaning of the ban on assassination.

Panama 1 to 4: Covert Operations under Reagan and Bush

In total, the US government launched five rounds of covert operations against Noriega. The first two, known as Panama 1 and Panama 2, even after more than thirty years remain shrouded in secrecy.[13] They seemingly entailed political action and the financing of opposition candidates.[14]

On 16 March 1988, the Chief of Police, Colonel Leonidas Macias, had tried to start a coup which was easily quashed. Noriega had taken advantage of the collapsed coup to purge the Panamanian Defence Forces (PDF) of disloyal officers.[15] In the United States, the setback convinced the Reagan Administration to do more. William Walker, a senior State Department official, decided to travel to Tel Aviv to meet Eduardo Herrera Hassan. Herrera, who was then Panama's Ambassador to Israel, travelled to the US to discuss plans with US officials. Noriega soon became aware of his travels and dismissed him.[16]

In the United States, Herrera – while on the US government's payroll – continued developing a plan for a coup. As he put it, 'What we wanted to do was enter Panama with a force and stage a coup. We would have seized him, arrested him [Noriega], maybe burned him ... We didn't know what would happen.' The plan envisaged the surreptitious entry of Herrera's group into Panama and the use of safe houses in US territory and/or US military bases to launch a campaign of increasing pressure on Noriega. The CIA would coordinate with Herrera and provide his group with communications equipment to incite the Panamanian population to rise against Noriega. The plan was opposed by the US military which imposed two main constraints: no use of US bases and no use of US troops.[17]

In mid-July, Reagan signed a presidential finding for the covert operation Panama 3. According to Administration officials, the authorisation involved activities falling short 'of a paramilitary operation to remove Gen. Noriega, such as kidnapping him'. The finding was also devised to help 'non-lethal' sabotage, distribute leaflets, disrupt PDF communications and distribute anti-Noriega propaganda.[18]

By this time, Noriega remained in power in Panama and Solis Palma was Acting President, a largely honorary title. But the Reagan Administration still recognised Eric Delvalle as President of Panama. The former president had been initially handpicked by Noriega when his predecessor Nicolás Barletta refused to drop an investigation into the murder of Hugo Spatafora. Spatafora, a leader of the opposition, had been killed by Noriega's henchmen. In office, Delvalle had quickly started working with the Reagan Administration in an attempt to legally remove Noriega from power. When the attempt failed, the president found refuge in the United States. On 15 July, Reagan phoned Delvalle to notify him of the new finding.[19]

After the phone call, US officials met with Delvalle who showed an interest in the plan and discussed various non-violent economic, diplomatic and psychological measures. None of these, according to Delvalle, had a chance of toppling Noriega; only the use of force did. Delvalle also suggested that the Panamanian population was unlikely to rise against Noriega 'unless it was in support of some outside action'. Arthur Davis, US Ambassador to Panama, and NSC officials informed him of the coup plans and Delvalle stressed the importance of a high-powered radio and a quick, visible success to raise morale.[20]

On the same day, the Administration presented a condensed version of the plan to Congressional oversight committees. This happened just before Congress's recess. A full briefing occurred on 26 July. During the briefing, two main sources of criticism emerged. According to some senators, the quality of the plan was poor, and it seemed more an effort to pacify Delvalle than to do anything against Noriega.[21] Others questioned whether the plan risked violating the existing ban on assassination. The US government and the CIA were covertly supporting third parties in their efforts to overthrow a foreign government. 'What assurances could the briefers give that Noriega wouldn't be killed during the kidnap attempt? . . . Wouldn't the covert action be as likely to bring about the assassination of Noriega as his arrest,' one senator asked.[22] Administration officials adopted the argument first proposed by Casey two years earlier. Killing Noriega was not the intent of the operation, but they couldn't guarantee that it would not happen.[23] The senators were unconvinced. One day later, a story in the *Washington Post* exposed the 'covert' plan. The White House and the Senate exchanged recriminations over the leak, with the Senators able to highlight that the news story contained references to the Delvalle phone call, something that had not been discussed with the Committee.[24] No further action was taken against Noriega as new policy initiatives were postponed pending the presidential elections. Ambassador Davis held a series of frustrating meetings with leaders of the Panamanian opposition in which he tried to explain Washington's silence.[25]

On 22 November, with Bush's victory secured, DCI William Webster met with Secretary of State George Shultz and other State Department officials. Webster lamented the 'fuzziness' of the US government's position. He admitted that there was scepticism within the CIA as to what policy might succeed against Noriega. The DCI stressed pressure from Bush and Donald Gregg (of Bush's staff) to get the issue resolved before the inauguration. Shultz concluded that US policy should continue to increase pressure on Noriega while not necessarily abandoning a negotiating track.[26] One month later, after a meeting between Reagan, Bush and Delvalle, a spokesperson for President-elect Bush confirmed his tougher stance: 'There must be no misunderstanding about our policy . . . Noriega must go.'[27]

In February, Bush, now President, authorised his first covert operation against Noriega, Panama 4, to support the opposition to Noriega in the upcoming elections of May 1989. The CIA had predicted that a peaceful election, even if blatantly stolen, would have strengthened Noriega's support with the military.[28] Bush reportedly lobbied Congressional committees personally. His request of $20 million was criticised since the plan included no indication of what to do with Noriega. The committees cut Bush's budget to $10 million. The covert plan involved primarily an effort to support opposition candidates in the upcoming National Assembly election, as well as preventing electoral fraud.[29]

The plan unravelled almost immediately. With the help of a Cuban team, Noriega was able to jam the radio transmitters provided by the CIA. The PDF also arrested Kurt Muse, an American citizen hired by the CIA to manage the communications of the opposition. To add insult to injury, Carlos Eleta Alamarán, the man in charge of the transfer of funds to the opposition groups, was arrested by US authorities on conspiracy to import cocaine into the United States.[30]

In the aftermath of Muse's arrest, members of the NSC went back to the drawing board. NSC officials recognised that the public support for a strong anti-drugs policy gave the Administration 'a virtually free hand' to move against Noriega. Three main options were considered: abrogation of Panama Canal Treaty rights, accommodation with Noriega, or a pressure track. The latter included three sub-options: a US military operation to remove Noriega and neutralise the PDF, a snatch operation to seize Noriega, or the organisation of a coup using covert and other means. The snatch operation was preferred since a coup posed risks of penetration by Noriega forces and a failed coup might increase repression.[31] On 5 May, Secretary of State James Baker stressed the Administration's objective 'that the Noriega dictatorship end and that democracy be restored in Panama'.[32]

The elections – rigged from the start – took place on 7 May 1989. When exit polls seemed to give a clear (3 to 1) victory to the opposition candidate Guillermo Endara, Noriega's forces intervened. The official result gave Carlos Duque – Noriega's candidate – a 2 to 1 margin of victory. Protests started almost immediately and former US President Jimmy Carter – in charge of one of the many missions observing the elections – publicly exposed their fraudulent nature. Protesting members of the opposition were attacked by Noriega's 'Dignity Battalion', a paramilitary group. The beatings were broadcast on live television. Noriega responded to the international outcry by nullifying the results of the elections.[33]

On the 11th, Bush publicly announced: 'the days of the dictators are over'.[34] He presented a seven-point plan to remove Noriega through a combination of threats and incentives, including the dispatch of additional US troops to the Panama Canal zone and the delineation of preventive security measures to protect US citizens.[35] On the 13th, Bush further escalated his rhetoric, publicly encouraging the PDF to carry out a coup. He told reporters, 'I would love to see them get [Noriega] out.'[36] The explicit call for a coup was moderated by the suggestion that if the PDF did carry out a coup, they should be able to do it on their own since they were a well-trained force.[37] The State Department favoured the use of force, but Secretary of Defense Dick Cheney opposed the deployment of US forces. Responding to the stalemate, Bush took advantage of a provision within the Panama Canal Treaty to authorise US troops to carry out unlimited training exercises in the country. Some took place in areas that Panama considered its exclusive domain. As Secretary of State Baker admitted, this was 'psychological warfare'.[38] In the summer of 1989, Bush again called on Panamanians to 'do everything they can to get Mr. Noriega out of office'.[39] When a coup did come, however, the Administration was woefully unprepared and unwilling to commit.

The Giroldi Coup and the Ban

Major Moises Giroldi was a loyal member of Noriega's inner circle. He had been promoted to major after helping Noriega put down the

Manuel Noriega: Coups and the Ban on Assassination

Macias coup in 1988. Progressively, he had become disenchanted with the regime and its increased repression. In September 1989, he had planned to meet with CIA officers, but had changed his mind at the last minute. After attending a baptism ceremony in which Noriega gave the order to shoot down any American aircraft, he settled on a coup.[40] His wife was able to contact personnel at the US Southern Command (SOUTHCOM). General Maxwell Thurman – who had just replaced General Frederick Woerner as head of SOUTHCOM – sent a colonel to vet Mrs Giroldi and a meeting was later arranged. As journalist Fred Kempe reported, Mrs Giroldi had two main requests. First, the United States should send aircraft to fly over the three airports in Panama to avoid reinforcements reaching Noriega from the air. Second, the United States should block roads to the Comandancia, Noriega's headquarters, to avoid land reinforcements.[41]

During the preparations, Giroldi himself met with CIA officials. They listened and took notes on the plan but did not provide any sign of explicit US support. Reportedly, they also warned Giroldi against killing Noriega, as the US government's involvement in a coup that led to the death to a foreign leader could have violated the ban on assassination.[42] CIA officials reported the meeting with Giroldi, putting his chances of success at less than even. The plan did not appear particularly well developed.[43]

At SOUTHCOM, Thurman was suspicious of Giroldi. He feared that the plot was Noriega's ploy to humiliate him just as he was starting in his new post. Thurman reported Giroldi's requests to General Colin Powell who had also just taken over as Chairman of the Joint Chiefs of Staff. Having spoken to Cheney, Powell agreed that the United States could block one of the roads requested by the plotters, since the movement could be masked as an exercise, but not the Bridge of the Americas since it would take US forces too close to the Comandancia.[44] The coup was supposed to take place on 2 October, but it was delayed at the last minute. This delay further increased US suspicions.[45]

On 3 October, at 6.30 a.m., Mrs Giroldi and her children were given protection at Fort Clayton. The coup commenced and Giroldi's forces were able to seize the Comandancia and capture Noriega. Giroldi – his wife later admitted – had no clear idea of what to do with Noriega and had naively expected that the Panamanian leader would agree to retire. Instead, from a room in the Comandancia, Noriega was able to call reinforcements, allegedly by calling one of his mistresses and explaining the situation.[46] Giroldi had initially rejected the idea of delivering Noriega to the United States. During the coup, though, and for a few hours, the Panamanian leader was a prisoner of Giroldi's forces and defenceless. This presented an opportunity for the United States to act.[47]

A few hours after Noriega's capture, Giroldi had finally accepted the need to deliver him to US forces. A delegation of plotters travelled to Fort Clayton to meet with Major General Marc Cisneros, Commander of the Army component of SOUTHCOM to arrange the delivery of Noriega. Cisneros replied that he would have accepted Noriega only if the plotters were able to deliver him to a US base. Having consulted Giroldi, the plotters seemingly rejected the offer.[48]

For the US government, communications to and from Panama were problematic. There was also uncertainty as to whether anyone in the area had the power to arrest Noriega. The Embassy mentioned an FBI agent on the Atlantic side of Panama, but they weren't reachable. At 12.30, the Department of State asked the Embassy whether there were any landing pads for helicopters at the Comandancia. The Embassy replied that there were three but also that heavy firing was occurring there.[49]

The heavy firing likely had to do with the fact that by 12.30 Noriega's reinforcements had arrived. Around the same time, Powell had finally been able to send three options to Thurman as to how to apprehend Noriega. Thurman could take Noriega into custody if he was delivered; he could provide covert support to the plotters to take Noriega to a US base; or he could also use a small US force, but this would require further presidential authority.[50] By then the coup was over. Noriega had regained control. Noriega's troops had arrived from one of the roads US forces had not blocked. The unit that came to Noriega's rescue was the US-trained Battalion 2000. Giroldi and other coup plotters were arrested, tortured and killed.[51]

* * *

The failed coup caused a political storm in Washington. Congress criticised the Administration for failing to support a coup after months spent calling for one.[52] In the Senate, William Cohen (D-MA), Vice-Chairman of the Intelligence Committee, faulted the Administration's ambiguous posture:

> On the one hand, we are encouraging them to revolt and to rebel, to overthrow, with perhaps some implied understanding that we will be there in the wings waiting to help, if necessary. Then when a revolt occurs, we have a policy of not helping.

Senator David Boren (D-OK), Chairman of the same Committee, concurred.[53]

To defend against the political onslaught, members of the Administration adopted several strategies. An internal post-mortem had concluded that the coup had failed 'because the organisers underplanned, overestimated their support, and misread the intentions and the ability of Noriega loyalists to react'.[54] The point was repeated publicly by Administration officials at the time and later in their respective memoirs.[55] The Administration also had to defend itself against the criticism that communication during the crisis was shambolic. They attempted to strike a balance between admitting communications problems – which, in part, excused the Administration's inaction – and presenting the President and his advisers as fully in control of the situation.[56]

One of the main lines of defence to emerge had to do with the ban on assassination. During Congressional hearings on 6 October, only three days after the failed coup, Cheney argued that the Senate Intelligence Committee's refusal to support the July 1988 finding and the letter the senators had written to the President about it had stymied US covert action. Part of the exchange with the senators is still redacted, but the outrage from the senators at this accusation is palpable. Cohen and Boren defended the Senate Select Committee's opposition to the July 1988 plan. Cheney replied that the plan had been shot down by the committee and this had created uncertainty about the authorities given to the Administration. Boren countered that the letter to the President had been written before the presidential elections since the committee did not want to tie the hands of the incoming President. Cohen – who had been one of the main critics of the July 1988 finding – hinted that the finding and the ensuing controversy had to do with the assassination of Noriega. Cheney insisted: 'The doubts about Noriega, the doubt about our ability to get Noriega if we did intervene, was one of the major reasons why we did not intervene.' Boren contested the argument, suggesting that the committee had not challenged any authority for covert operation proposed by Bush. He also hinted that some authorities had been reinstated after July 1988, but that the Administration had still walked away from supporting the coup. Cheney did not relent: 'the only reason I brought it up is I think it is an interesting parallel. The President, of course, has been criticized for his decision not to use lethal force, to topple Noriega, in this case.'[57] According to Deputy CIA Director Robert Gates, key members of Administration had been in a 'huge twist over the question of helping this major and the proscription against assassination'.[58]

A week later, the controversy went public. National Security Advisor Brent Scowcroft justified the Administration's lack of response to the coup as follows:

> The Congress in its micromanagement of the executive branch going clear back as far as the executive order prohibiting assassinations, which was forced by the Congress, has . . . certainly leaned us against the kinds of things now they're saying we should have done.[59]

President Bush also took the unprecedented step of releasing the July 1988 letter discussed in the hearings. The letter stated that the committee had indeed opposed the US government's involvement in assassination. According to the interpretation of some Administration officials, the letter could even be understood as requiring the CIA to notify Noriega if he risked being killed in a coup by CIA-supported third parties.[60]

The controversy focused even more narrowly on the ban. DCI Webster told reporters: 'The United States does not engage in selective, individual assassination . . . But the United States has other important overriding concerns . . . when despots take over, there has to be a means to deal with that short of making us to be hired killers.' He continued: 'We all need to look at that and say, "Have we pushed this beyond a practical effectiveness? Have we extended the executive order beyond its intended original meaning by both the White House and Congress?'"[61] According to Webster, the language of the ban had created confusion. Webster did not openly challenge a prohibition on an American-devised plot for assassination, but lamented the ban's ambiguity:

> Now the next thing is, hire a guy to kill Noriega or fund a group who wants to kill Noriega ... Our executive order would have in the past been construed at least that we could not do that ... Now it begins to get a little tighter when you say, 'Here's a group that says it doesn't plan to kill him, but they're going to have to play rough and it could happen'.

Webster recognised that past attempts to reinterpret the order had been challenging, but, in his view, the mood had changed.[62] Webster was right. The Administration's calls found a receptive audience in Congress. Senator Cohen, for example, opposed a complete abolition of the ban; as he put it, 'I don't want it to be open season on political enemies.' But he accepted the Administration's argument for an assessment of whether 'unreasonable shackles' had been imposed on the intelligence community.[63] In an article for the *Washington Post*, Cohen further explored some of the ban's contradictions:[64]

> After all, Executive Order 12333 would appear to ban placing a poison pen in one of Col. Moammar Gadhafi's jump suits, but permit the release of a gravity bomb from several thousand feet onto his desert compound ... Does the law turn upon whether a bullet or bomb carries a victim's name?

It was time to do away with these ambiguities.[65] At the same time, senior CIA officials – while admitting that the ban had not been a hindrance in the Agency's conduct during the Giroldi coup – did ask similar questions. Deputy Director for Operations Richard F. Stoltz, for example, argued that questions like 'what is assassination?' and 'what level of guilty knowledge amounts to a violation of the ban?' remained.[66]

Part of the controversy came down to the politics of blame shifting,[67] but the ban had clearly entered a phase of intense contestation, both regarding its meaning – what is assassination? – and its validity – was the ban a hindrance? Did it obstruct the conduct of (covert) foreign policy and the pursuit of US interests? Was it immoral?[68] As Cohen's reaction suggested, doing away with the ban would have been difficult for the Administration, even in the more permissive mood of the late 1980s. Instead, the Administration settled for a reinterpretation.

The (re)interpretation was finalised by William Barr at the Office of Legal Counsel (OLC) of the Department of Justice. Six Justice Department lawyers and four CIA lawyers worked on it, reviewing files on assassination, the Executive Orders starting with Ford's, as well as documents from the Ford, Carter and Reagan years. As Russell Bruemmer, the CIA's General Counsel at the time, put it, the aim was to assess:

> Whether the prohibition on assassination bars United States officials and agents from encouraging and supporting a coup against a foreign regime when there is a likelihood of violence and a possibility that the regime's leader and supporters will be killed during the violence.[69]

While the interpretation is still classified, reports at the time agree that it permitted the CIA to help coup plotters even if the coup entailed the risk of a foreign official's death, as long as US officials and agents had no 'specific intent' to kill a leader. The opinion built on the precedents established under Casey. Having seen the opinion, Bruemmer argued that such an exception would be true even in cases in which US officials and agents know that 'coup leaders intend to use whatever force necessary to subdue opponents'. Only if US government officials and agents become explicitly aware of the coup plotters' intention to assassinate a foreign official should they desist from helping the plotters. If no explicit intent emerged, US officials would be excused even if they had shared intelligence and technical assistance with the plotters.[70] While US officials saw the opinion as a 'clarification' more than a reinterpretation,[71] it provided a very permissive environment. As an OLC opinion, it also provided legal immunity to US officials and agents involved in a coup that might lead to assassination, as long as no specific intent or directive to kill emerged, a particularly unlikely scenario in the realm of covert action.

Manuel Noriega: Coups and the Ban on Assassination

Armed with this new interpretation, the Bush Administration adopted a new covert approach to Panama and Noriega: Panama 5. US officials in Panama had made clear to the State Department that a new approach was needed. If a meeting were to occur between US officials and (new) coup plotters, US officials needed to be able to 'suggest improvements to the plotters and offer expert US assistance . . . In short, we must be prepared to see this coup succeed.'[72] Under Panama 5, the US government would support a coup if one were to develop, even if it entailed Noriega's death. The CIA was granted a budget of $3 million.[73] A cartoon from Gerry Trudeau satirised the new approach:

'Okay, let me see I understand the ground rules for "accidental" loss of life.'
'Shoot amigo.'
'We're permitted to use violence to overthrow the government . . .'
'Correcto!'
'So I can enter Noriega's office forcefully with a weapon . . .'
'Right again!'
'But if I blow his head off?'
'You have to be on the record as having said "Oops"!'[74]

The plotting went nowhere, and Noriega was eventually arrested after a military invasion, Operation Just Cause. The Giroldi controversy, though, coincided with the culmination of a broader process of reinterpretation of the ban.

The Parks Memorandum and Assassination

Between the end of the Reagan Administration and the early Bush years, the Office of the Army Judge Advocate General had started working on a redefinition of assassination. According to Lt. Col. Dick Bridges, the JAG office led an inter-agency review which involved lawyers from the State Department, the CIA and other agencies. In October 1988, a provisional draft was circulated to the CIA and State.[75] A new memorandum was ready one year later.

Penned by Hays Parks, who had served as a legal consultant for the strike against Qaddafi in 1986,[76] the Memorandum of Law – titled 'Executive Order 12333 and Assassination' – reviewed international legal definitions of assassination. It defined assassination as 'an act of murder for political reasons, its victims are not necessarily limited to persons of public office or prominence'.[77] It recognised the role of the Executive Order in banning assassination and confirmed the distinction between peacetime and wartime operations. Peacetime assassination, the memorandum read:

> Would seem to encompass the murder of a private individual or public figure for political purposes, and in some cases . . . also require that the act constitute a covert activity, particularly when the individual is a private citizen. Assassination is unlawful killing and would be prohibited by international law even if there were no executive order proscribing it.

The use of force, the memorandum recognised, is regulated by article 2(4) and by the self-defence provision in Article 51 of the UN Charter. Reflecting the US government's position, though, the memorandum went beyond the internationally recognised right of self-defence. First, the memorandum found historical precedents for the use of force to 'capture or kill individuals' who pose a direct threat to US citizens or US national security. Second, it recognised the existence of a right to self-defence against an actual use of force, against an imminent threat, or against a 'continuing threat', a position that went back to Sofaer's argument in the case of Libya. The natural conclusion, then, was that the pre-emptive use of force by the US government is legal against a conventional enemy, and, by the same token, it was also legal against an individual terrorist who posed a threat. The terrorist had to be part of a well-structured and well-financed organisation. But a president's determination of an imminent threat blurred the distinction between peace and war. The memorandum concluded:

> Assassination constitutes an act of murder that is prohibited by international law and Executive Order 12333. The purpose of Executive Order 12333 . . . was to preclude unilateral actions by individual agents or agencies against selected foreign public officials and to

establish beyond any doubt that the United States does not condone assassination . . . Its intent was not to limit lawful self defense options against legitimate threats to the national security of the United States or individual U.S. citizens. Acting consistent with the Charter of the United Nations, a decision by the President to employ clandestine, low visibility or overt military force would not constitute assassination if U.S. military forces were employed against the combatant forces of another nation, a guerrilla force, or a terrorist or other organization whose actions pose a threat to the security of the United States.[78]

Such an interpretation, albeit with the caveat about terrorist organisations, is far reaching. It conflates different standards for the use of force in international law. It applies international humanitarian law (a standard reserved for relations among states) to the use of force against individuals, which should instead be regulated by international human rights law.[79] In line with Sofaer's earlier opinion, while recalling Article 51 it adopts an expanded notion of self-defence. Finally, the memorandum implies that if a use of force can be justified as a (pre-emptive) act of self-defence, by its very nature it cannot constitute assassination, regardless of the manner (overt or covert) in which it is carried out, and regardless of the target (a conventional enemy or an individual terrorist).

Conclusion

The Administration of George H. W. Bush engaged in covert operations against Noriega. In this process, it crystallised many of the precedents set during the Reagan years. In the aftermath of the Giroldi coup, the Administration successfully challenged the meaning and appropriateness of the ban on assassination.

Through public and secret exchanges, members of the Administration and of Congressional committees came to agree on a reinterpretation of the ban, one that permitted an expanded role for the CIA in the contexts of coups. In this new understanding, the ban permitted the CIA to become involved in a coup if no explicit directive and no explicit intent to assassinate emerged. This interpretation clearly built on Casey's argument and on his push for expanded CIA powers. The development also took advantage of a seemingly changed mood in Congress, with combative Congressmen joining the Administration in deploying the ban on assassination for partisan purposes.

Building on Sofaer's opinion, the Parks memorandum crystallised interpretations of the meaning of the norm that had first emerged in the Reagan years. It represented an explicit effort at both meaning and applicatory contestation. It redefined assassination and it excluded counterterrorism from the remit of the ban. It also confirmed Sofaer's view of the permissibility of strikes against imminent, continuing and more speculative threats, even when they targeted foreign leaders and officials. These innovations and reinterpretations became a staple of the US government's approach to targeted killing in the aftermath of 9/11. The onset of the confrontation with Saddam Hussein, though, revealed the persistence of ambiguities surrounding the ban.

Notes

1. Richard Nixon Foundation, 'Public Enemy Number One', 29 June 2016, available at https://www.nixonfoundation.org/2016/06/26404/ (accessed 30 October 2023).
2. Jonathan Marshall, 'The White House Death Squad', *Inquiry*, 5/3/1979, CIA-RDP90-00845R000100460002-5-2.
3. Seymour Hersh, 'US Aides in '72 Weighed Killing of Officer Who Now Leads Panama', *New York Times*, 13 June 1986.
4. Marshall, 'Death Squad'; Howard Hunt, *American Spy* (New York: John Wiley & Sons, 2007), 146.
5. Frederick Kempe, *Divorcing the Dictator* (New York: Putnam, 1990), 61.
6. Marshall, 'Death Squad'.
7. Eytan Gilboa, 'The Panama Invasion Revisited', *Political Science Quarterly*, 110.4 (1995–6), 541.
8. Robin Wright and Ronald Ostrow, 'Noriega's U.S. Intelligence Ties Could Vex Prosecution', *Los Angeles Times*, 16 January 1990.
9. Letter to Noriega from DEA Peter B. Bensinger, 2/10/1978, William Price Files, NSC Files, Subject Files, Folder Panama, George H. W. Bush Presidential Library (GHWBPL), College Station, TX.
10. The exception was the Turner era. Stansfield Turner, *Burn before Reading* (New York: Hyperion, 2005), 146.

11. Note from Oliver North, Subject: Iran, 8 May 1986, and Note from John Poindexter, Subject: Iran, 23 August 1986, in National Security Archives (NSAr), Electronic Briefing Book, 2, 'The Contras, Cocaine, and Covert Operations, available at https://nsarchive2.gwu.edu/NSAEBB/NSAEBB2/index.html (accessed 8 November 2023).
12. Seymour Hersh, 'Panama Strongman Said to Trade in Arms, Drugs, and Illicit Money', *New York Times*, 12 June 1986.
13. The Reagan Library does not have declassified files on covert operations against Noriega. Email exchange with the author, 1 August 2022.
14. Margaret Scranton, *The Noriega Years* (Boulder, CO: Lynne Rienner, 1991), 153.
15. Linda Robinson, 'Dwindling Options in Panama', *Foreign Affairs*, 68.5 (1989), 193.
16. William Buckley, *Panama* (New York: Touchstone, 1991), 158.
17. Scranton, *Noriega Years*, 154.
18. Ibid.
19. Lou Cannon and Joe Pichirallo, 'Covert Action on Noriega Is Cleared', *Washington Post*, 27 July 1988.
20. Memorandum for CIA, Summary of Report, Meeting with President Delvalle of Panama, 25/7/1988, CIA Reading Room, CIA-RDP90G01353R001200060008-9.
21. Cannon and Pichirallo, 'Covert Action'.
22. Kempe, *Divorcing*, 341.
23. Ibid.
24. Helen Dewar, 'Senators Accuse Administration of "Setup" on Panama Leak', *Washington Post*, 29 July 1988; Buckley, *Panama*, 164–5.
25. Ambassador Arthur Davis, Interview with Charles Stuart Kennedy, The Association for Diplomatic Studies and Training Foreign Affairs Oral History Project, 24 May 1991, 47–9.
26. Robert Gates, Memorandum for the record, DCI/DDCI Meeting with Secretary of State Shultz, 22/11/1988, CIA Reading Room, CIA-RDP89G01321R000500140006-7.
27. Gilboa, 'The Panama', 552.
28. CIA, DOI, 'Panama: the post-election political landscape', 24/4/1989, NSC Panama, April 1989 (2), GHWBPL.
29. Scranton, *Noriega Years*, 157.
30. Ibid., 158.
31. Opportunities and Vulnerabilities, Undated, Unnamed, NSC Panama, April 1989 (2), GHWBPL.
32. James Baker, 'Panama: post-election action plan', 5/5/1989, NSC Panama, April 1989 (2), GHWBPL.

33. Robinson, 'Dwindling', 197.
34. James Baker (with Thomas De Frank), *The Politics of Diplomacy* (New York: Putnam, 1995), 182.
35. Gilboa, 'The Panama', 554.
36. Christopher Andrews, *For the President's Eyes Only* (London: HarperCollins, 1996), 513.
37. Buckley, *Panama*, 183.
38. Baker, *The Politics*, 182.
39. Buckley, *Panama*, 166.
40. Ibid., 198.
41. Kempe, *Divorcing*, 374.
42. Ibid., 378.
43. Buckley, *Panama*, 199.
44. Bob Woodward, *The Commanders* (New York: Touchstone, 1991), 122.
45. Scranton, *Noriega Years*, 187.
46. Buckley, *Panama*, 202.
47. Ibid., 202.
48. Ibid., 205.
49. Cable American Embassy Panama to unspecified posts RE: events in Panama – 10/6/1989, National Security Council Files, Pryce, William T., Files, Latin American Directorate Staff Files, Box 1, Folder Panama October 1989 (2), GHWBPL.
50. Woodward, *The Commanders*, 123.
51. John Dinges, *Our Man in Panama* (New York: Random House, 1990), 305.
52. Gilboa, 'The Panama', 555.
53. US Senate, '1989 Events in Panama', Joint Hearings before the Committee on Armed Services and the Select Committee on Intelligence, 101st Congress, 6/10/22 and 17/12/22, 1989, available at https://babel.hathitrust.org/cgi/pt?id=pst.000017422093&view=1up&seq=2&skin=2021 (accessed 30 October 2023), 4.
54. Telegram for Pryce, 6/101989, Post-mortem on Giroldi coup, NSC Files, Pryce, William T., Files, Latin American Directorate Staff Files, Box 1, Folder Panama October 1989 (1), GHWBPL.
55. Thurman's testimony, in US Senate, '1989 Events', fn. 79; Colin Powell, *My American Journey* (New York: Ballantine Books, 1996), 418; Baker, *The Politics*, 186.
56. The Administration did take measures to improve crisis communication in the aftermath of the failed coup. Draft memorandum on Information flow during crises, NSC Panama, October 1989 (1), GHWBPL.
57. US Senate, '1989 Events in Panama', 36–53.

58. Tim Naftali, 'Robert Gates', Miller Center, Oral History Interview, 23–24 July 2000, 29.
59. David Hoffman and John Goshko, 'Administration Sought Funds Last Spring for Covert Action', *Washington Post*, 11 October 1989.
60. David Hoffman and David Ottaway, 'Guidelines on Noriega Set Last Fall', *Washington Post*, 24 October 1989.
61. Stephen Engelberg, 'C.I.A. Seeks Looser Rules on Killings During Coups', *New York Times*, 17 October 1989.
62. Engelberg, 'C.I.A. Seeks Looser Rules'.
63. Ibid.
64. While obliquely admitting the US effort to assassinate Qaddafi.
65. William S. Cohen, 'Noriega Not Worth American Killing', *Washington Post*, 17 October 1989.
66. David Ottaway, 'CIA Aides Call Hill Rules No Hindrance', *Washington Post*, 18 October 1989.
67. In later years, Cheney did not recall any concern over assassination at the time of the Giroldi coup; see Philip Zelikow et al., 'Richard Cheney', Miller Center, Oral History Interview, 16–17 March 2000, 53.
68. Nicole Deitelhoff and Lisbeth Zimmermann, 'Norms under Challenge: Unpacking the Dynamics of Norm Robustness', *Journal of Global Security Studies*, 4.1 (2019), 11. See also Luca Trenta, 'Death by Reinterpretation: Dynamics of Norm Contestation and the US Ban on Assassination in the Reagan Years', *Journal of Global Security Studies*, 6.4 (2021), doi: 10.1093/jogss/ogab012.
69. Russell Bruemmer, 'The Prohibition on Assassination: A Legal and Ethical Analysis', in Hayden Peake and Samuel Halpern (eds), *In the Name of Intelligence* (Washington, DC: NIBC Press, 1995), 152
70. Bruemmer also added that the OLC found that in some cases the death of a foreign official is so immediate and certain that the US government would be 'deemed to intend' their death. The OLC gave no explicit pronouncement on this but called for a case-by-case assessment. Bruemmer, 'The Prohibition', 153.
71. David Ottaway and Don Oberdorfer, 'Administration Alters Assassination Ban', *Washington Post*, 4 November 1989.
72. Cable Embassy Panama to Secretary of State, Proposed Scenario for Coup Approach, 17/10/1989, NSC Files, Pryce, William T., Files, Latin American Directorate Staff Files, Box 1, Folder Panama October 1989 (1), GHWBPL.
73. US House of Representatives, 'Congress and Foreign Policy 1989', available at https://babel.hathitrust.org/cgi/pt?id=umn.31951p00 864899y&view=1up&seq=74&skin=2021 (accessed 30 October 2023), 83.

74. Jonathan Fredman, 'Covert Action, Loss of Life, and the Prohibition on Assassination, 1976–1996', *Studies in Intelligence*, 1996, 20.
75. Associated Press, 'Army Official Says Military Strikes on Terrorists Legal', 11 April 1989.
76. Arturo Jimenez-Bacardi, 'From Lawless to Secret Law: The United States, the CIA and Extra-judicial Killing', in Alison Brysk and Michael Stohl (eds), *Contracting Human Rights* (Cheltenham: Edward Elgar, 2018), 127.
77. Hays Parks, 'Executive Order 12333 and Assassination', Memorandum of Law, *The Army Lawyer*, 1989, available at https://sites.duke.edu/lawfire/files/2019/01/ParksMemo1989.pdf (accesed 30 October 2023), 1.
78. Parks, 'Executive Order 12333 and Assassination', 8.
79. On this point and its consequences after 9/11, see Nils Melzer, *Targeted Killings in International Law* (Oxford: Oxford University Press, 2008), 51–3.

10 Saddam Hussein: Assassination and the Long Confrontation between the US Government and Iraq

On 2 August 1990, Saddam Hussein's Iraq invaded Kuwait. The US government spearheaded UN Security Council Resolution 660 condemning Iraq's aggression. In a National Security Council (NSC) meeting on the 4th, military and economic options were discussed. National Security Advisor Brent Scowcroft suggested that 'covert operations needed looking at'. Similarly, Secretary of State James Baker detailed a three-pronged strategy: 'to keep Saddam out, to make him pariah, and to topple him with covert action'.[1]

In the following weeks the Administration started building an international coalition.[2] Alongside the diplomatic track and preparations for the use of force, Bush signed a finding for the CIA: without violating the ban on assassination, the CIA's goal was to 'recruit Iraqi dissidents to remove Saddam from power'.[3] Thanks to William Barr's and the Office of Legal Counsel's opinion, the Agency now had more latitude to become involved in coups, even if they might lead to the assassination of the targeted foreign leader.

The Joint Special Operations Command was also working to eliminate Saddam more directly. As Sean Naylor reported, according to a Pentagon Special Operations source: 'There was an effort to just solve the problem by taking out Saddam Hussein.' The project was 'sanctioned by the White House, [but] that was one of those things where you provide enough cutouts you can't track it back to the president'. Several methods were considered, from shooting Saddam to calling in an air strike, but the project collapsed due to inadequate intelligence.[4]

One month later, during a visit to the Gulf, Air Force Chief of Staff General Mike Dugan explained the US government's strategy for the upcoming air war against Iraq:

> The Joint Chiefs of Staff have concluded that US military air power – including a massive bombing campaign against Baghdad that specifically targets Iraqi President Saddam Hussein – is the only effective option to force Iraqi forces from Kuwait if war erupts.

Since Saddam was a 'one man show' in Iraq, Dugan continued, 'if and when we choose violence he ought to be the focus of our efforts'. The comments sent the Administration into damage control mode. Scowcroft stated on *Face the Nation* that Dugan was not part of the chain of command, and he had no say in selecting targets.[5]

In response to Dugan's remarks, Secretary of Defense Dick Cheney compiled a list of 'problems' to justify firing Dugan. Among the reasons, point 6 read: 'You said we would violate the executive order banning participation in assassination.'[6] Cheney fired Dugan.[7] And yet, a line from Cheney could be understood as a throwback to the CIA's William Harvey's complaint about keeping requests for assassination off the historical record. Cheney told CBS, '*We never talk* about the targeting of specific individuals who are officials of other governments' (emphasis added).[8]

When the war started, the Administration made every possible effort to target Saddam personally. As in Operation El Dorado Canyon, targets were euphemistically defined as 'command and control centres'. As Scowcroft later admitted, 'We don't do assassinations, but yes, we targeted all the places where Saddam might have been.' The Administration, Scowcroft conceded, had deliberately set out to kill him if they possibly could.[9] Since the use of force had been approved by Congress (and sanctioned by the UN Security Council), and since Saddam commanded the Iraqi armed forces, the targeting of Saddam during wartime – in the absence of treachery – would not have constituted assassination.[10]

The CIA's authority to engage in a coup to overthrow Saddam, Dugan's firing, and the targeting of Saddam showcase the continued relevance of the ban on assassination in informing and shaping the boundaries of US foreign policy discourse and practice. The episodes also showcase the continued ambiguity surrounding the ban. The ban's ambiguity and its relevance continued during the Clinton Administration. In Clinton's first term, the Administration's relationship with the CIA was famously fraught with difficulties and controversies.[11] On Iraq, the Administration – like its predecessor – hoped that a combination of economic pressure and covert operations might create the conditions for a coup and for the removal of Saddam. When it became known that the Administration had refrained from supporting one such coup, rumours emerged that the decision was, at least in part, shaped by concerns regarding the ban on assassination. Once again, albeit with less intensity than during the Noriega controversy, the ban became an object of public scrutiny, and Congressional debate. While Saddam continued to defy the US government, the Administration made a final effort to kill him more directly in Operation Desert Fox.

The Failed Iraqi Uprising and the CIA's Lethal Finding

On 11 August 1990, confronted with Saddam's unwillingness to withdraw from Kuwait, President Bush told reporters: 'I hope that the Iraqi people do something about it so that their leader will live by the norms of international behavior that will be acceptable to other nations.'[12] The statement highlighted a nascent ambiguity surrounding US policy towards Iraq. If a war did come, what would constitute victory? If Saddam were to withdraw – voluntarily or under duress – with his arsenal and his regime intact, such an outcome would hardly give a sense of victory.[13] Bush feared that Saddam, if he remained in charge, 'might be viewed as a hero'.[14]

In January 1991, as the confrontation with Saddam escalated, the Administration issued National Security Directive 54 setting the aims of the war. The directive established a set of conditions for the United States to pursue regime change. These included Saddam's use of weapons of mass destruction (WMDs), his support for terrorist attacks against the United States or the coalition partners, and the destruction of Kuwait's oil fields.[15] Bush recognised the difficulties in getting Saddam. The security around him was tight and he moved constantly. The US government, he reflected, had struggled to find Noriega in Panama, where intelligence was solid; Iraq would have been even harder. In the President's view, the 'Iraqi people ought to take care of him'.[16]

In mid-February, one month after the start of Desert Storm, the President twice went public to remind the Iraqi military and the Iraqi people that they could stop the bloodshed if they took matters into their own hands and forced Saddam to 'step aside'.[17] According to Scowcroft, the message was unfairly understood as a presidential call to action.[18] Within the Administration, the goal was not for the Iraqi people to rise, but for a military official – perhaps someone close to Saddam – to hear the message and decide to get rid of the dictator. In Iraq, the message was broadcasts via international televisions and radios. Leaflets were dropped calling on Iraqi soldiers and civilians to bring down Saddam.[19]

The uprising started in Basra and spread into other major cities. One month after Bush's call to action, the rebels controlled fourteen of Iraq's eighteen provinces. Despite this success, the movement was unable to establish a presence in Baghdad where the regime was entrenched. As the uprising progressed, the rebel movement was taken over by better organised pro-Iranian groups.[20] The dominant position of Shia, pro-Iran groups permitted Saddam to portray himself as the saviour of the Iraqi Sunni minority. The largely Sunni Iraqi military rallied around the regime.[21]

Military and political decisions taken in Washington also contributed to the collapse of the uprising. On 3 March, at the ceasefire agreement for Operation Desert Storm, General Norman Schwarzkopf – while grounding Iraqi fixed-wing aircraft – accepted the Iraqi authorities' request to fly helicopters, even armed ones. Iraqi negotiators presented this request as necessary to move Iraqi officials due to the destroyed road infrastructure. Instead, helicopters were used to transport troops, which helped in quashing the uprising.[22] The quick ceasefire also contributed to the military defeat of the uprising. While twenty-nine Iraqi divisions had been destroyed, it soon became apparent that the better equipped and better trained Republican Guard divisions had been withdrawn and had survived.[23]

Beyond these military choices, the Bush Administration also made a political decision not to intervene. The likely opposition of members of the international coalition and concerns regarding the splintering of Iraq certainly played a part. But an intervention did not fit the Administration's plan; the aim of the Administration was 'to get rid of Saddam, not his regime'. The Administration's preference was for another military dictator, more compliant with Washington's wishes.[24] For this reason, the Administration ignored the pleas for help of both Kurdish and Shia groups during the ensuing repression and massacres.[25]

While shocked by the suffering of large segments of the Iraqi population, the Administration came to see the uprising as counterproductive. It was understood that a military coup had been in the offing, but the uprising pushed the Iraqi military to protect the regime. By mid-April the uprising was over, the United States and coalition partners had established a no-fly zone to protect the Kurdish population in the north of Iraq,[26] and the United Nations Security Council had passed Resolution 687, confirming sanctions on Iraq and imposing an inspection mission (UNSCOM) to assess Iraqi compliance and cooperation in the realm of WMDs.[27] The no-fly zone, the economic sanctions and the inspections regime came to define US policy towards Iraq for the following decade, often intersecting with covert operations and (alleged) assassination attempts against the Iraqi leader.

* * *

The brutal and controversial end of the Gulf War undermined the domestic political coalition that had supported it. Some members of Congress and (then emerging) neoconservatives ('neocons') in the media started to criticise the Administration's weak response to the uprising.[28] In a repeat of the debate surrounding the failed Giroldi coup in Panama, criticism soon touched upon the ban on assassination. Contestation, once again, challenged the ban's appropriateness for the conduct of US foreign policy.

Even before the end of the conflict, Senator Richard Lugar (R-IN) had stated that Saddam 'ought to be a target', adding that the ban on assassination needed to be re-examined. In certain situations, 'government-sanctioned killing of foreign leaders might be appropriate'.[29] In the House, Dana Rohrbacher (R-CA) expressed similar sentiments. 'There is nothing immoral about killing a bloodthirsty tyrant,' he stated, adding that deciding who was a tyrant was a prerogative of the President.[30] A few months later, former president Richard Nixon also joined the fray. 'If I could get him out of there,' the former President argued in a CBS *60 Minutes* interview, 'even putting a contract out on him, if the CIA still did that sort of thing, assuming it ever did, I would be for it'. Nixon's guarded statement on the Agency did not escape its Director. 'The CIA cannot intentionally set out to cause the death of a public figure,' CIA Director William Webster stated in a public airing of the intent argument, 'but may have dealings with groups seeking the overthrow of a despot.'[31]

By May, the Administration's posture had hardened. The State Department instructed US embassies in the capitals of US coalition partners on the new position: 'US/international community continues to support Iraq's sovereignty and territorial integrity but wants a new Iraqi leadership.' 'All possible sanctions,' the message continued 'will be maintained until he is gone. Any easing of sanctions will be considered only when there is a new government.'[32] While the telegram and the Administration's public posture stressed that this objective had to be reached via negotiation and not force, the Administration also stepped up its covert efforts.

Bush signed a presidential finding, shared with Congress, directing the CIA to create the conditions for the removal of Saddam. It was reportedly a 'lethal' finding. A later exchange between journalist Peter Jennings and Scowcroft explained the nature of the finding. 'Is it fair to say from a layman point of view that it is the nearest thing you can do to try to kill a foreign leader without saying you are going to set out to kill a foreign leader?' Jennings asked. 'That's right,' Scowcroft conceded. But he added that – for the Administration – that meant someone within the military.[33] The Administration still hoped for a 'silver bullet coup' with members of Saddam's family or one of his bodyguards pulling the trigger, or a 'palace coup' carried out by disgruntled Republican Guards.[34] In both cases, the Administration's policy envisaged – and worked to create the conditions for – the assassination of Saddam.

Saddam Hussein: Assassination and Confrontation with Iraq

Frank Anderson, chief of the Near East Division in the CIA's Directorate of Operations, was unimpressed by the finding. 'I don't like this,' he scribbled on his copy. His opposition was both philosophical and practical. On the philosophical side, he lamented the excessive reliance on covert operations as a token demonstration that the US government was 'doing something'. On the practical side, he agreed that the removal of Saddam was a laudable objective, but the resources put in place were not sufficient.[35] The US government and the CIA 'didn't have a single mechanism or a combination of mechanisms with which I could create a plan to get rid of Saddam at the time'.[36]

This policy also underestimated the strength and resilience of Saddam's regime. In the same months, Saddam foiled two military-led, palace coups.[37] The failure of these coups pushed the Administration towards more indirect methods, getting acquainted with – and starting to support – the existing Iraqi opposition. By this time, Ahmad Chalabi had emerged as one its leaders and, certainly, the most effective in getting Washington's attention.

The Rise of the INC

Chalabi came from a prominent Shia family. He had spent most of his life in the United States. He received a degree from MIT and later moved to Jordan, where he became chairman of the Petra Bank. Accused of embezzlement and false accounting, he quickly escaped Jordan to take the mantle of Iraqi opposition leader. In March 1991 he visited Washington with a delegation of Iraqi opposition members. They attended meetings at the Council for Foreign Relations and at the House International Affairs Committee, but the State Department refused to meet them.[38]

This rebuttal notwithstanding, the Administration was growing increasingly frustrated at Saddam's non-compliance with the terms of Resolution 687. In September, Haass detailed four main options to respond to Iraq's pattern of 'cheat and retreat': attack a single WMD site, attack multiple sites, attack all known WMD facilities, or conduct a large-scale military effort against all known WMD-related sites, military sites including Republican Guards and industrial facilities, and Command, Control, Communication and Intelligence sites. Some Arab states, according to Haass, preferred the latter option as they were 'worried about tweaking Saddam's tail without cutting off the head'.[39] Bush expressed his frustration in dealing with Saddam during a call with British prime minister John Major: 'We have public opinion saying we ought to get Saddam – I would love to see it – but it may not be achievable,' the President admitted.[40]

Eventually, Chalabi wrote a letter to President Bush detailing a programme for democratic change in Iraq. In response, Haass held a meeting with Chalabi and his delegation.[41] Having listened to their proposal, Haass told Chalabi that the Iraqi opposition had given the Administration 'something to think about'.[42] In the aftermath of the meeting, the Administration started supporting Chalabi's group, working to establish a more stable and cohesive coalition among the many anti-Saddam groups. The CIA became involved in the process, receiving financial support from Congress.[43]

The operation was further supported by an additional presidential finding towards the end of 1991. The finding still aimed at exploiting potential cracks within Saddam's inner circle, but this time it expanded to political action. New anti-Hussein activities came to include propaganda broadcasts and renewed contacts with the opposition.[44] The finding also authorised CIA officers to shift from 'intelligence collectors to active organizers working with dissidents' in Iraq and abroad.[45]

Renewed hopes of a military coup were dashed in early 1992. The plot promised to be exactly what the Administration envisaged. Led by Saad Jabr (son of former Iraqi prime minister Salih Jabr) and his London-based Free Iraq Council, the plot included the general who had first commanded the Republican Guard in 1963 and a former Iraqi ambassador. Both were Sunni and from Saddam's Tikrit region. In February, Jabr travelled to Washington to ask the Administration to bomb Baghdad for forty-eight hours and hit garrisons loyal to Saddam. In Jabr's view, this would have created sufficient confusion to permit the plotters to take over. In April, the regime foiled the plot, arresting and executing many army officers.[46]

Two months later, the CIA paid for a summit of the Iraqi opposition in Vienna. The groups agreed to work together, and the Iraqi National Congress (INC) was born. 'The INC,' its statement of

Saddam Hussein: Assassination and Confrontation with Iraq

intent read, 'endeavors to become the nucleus of an actual provisional government that will extend its authority over parts of the territory of Iraq and seek to expand it to cover all the territory of Iraq and to overthrow Saddam Hussein and his regime.'[47] To strengthen the organisation's appeal, the CIA hired a PR firm, the Rendon Group, which conducted a broad propaganda campaign against Saddam both in Iraq and internationally.[48]

In the summer of 1992, following the pleas of INC leaders regarding the dire situation of Shia fugitives in the south and due to stalemate at the UN Security Council, the United States and Britain agreed to establish a second no-fly zone in the south.[49] In the meeting with the INC, Scowcroft and Baker had assured the INC of America's support, but many in the Administration remained sceptical of its chances of success. 'We assumed,' one US official recalled, 'that we better view Chalabi a bit like people looked at someone in the 1950s running for statewide office in the South on the Republican ticket. Everyone knew he didn't have a chance. His job was to act like he had a serious chance.'[50] In October, the INC moved to the US-protected enclaves in northern Iraq and added Shiite groups to its ranks.

Based on the INC, and on Chalabi's campaign, a third option started to emerge to remove Saddam: a 'rolling coup'. The idea was for the INC and the Kurds to consolidate their control in the north and attract the defection of Iraqi military officers. With US support, these forces would 'roll' south and either take over the government or create sufficient chaos for someone to get rid of Saddam.[51] During Bush's last weeks in office, Iraq moved anti-aircraft missiles into the southern no-fly zone and an Iraqi government official reiterated Iraq's claims over Kuwait, in breach of Resolution 687. The US government and three other coalition allies responded with a limited airstrike. Approved by the incoming Clinton Administration, the strike left the Iraqi regime largely untouched.[52] Saddam had survived Bush.

Clinton vs Saddam: Round I

Clinton took office at a time of deep geopolitical uncertainty for both the US government and the CIA.[53] Intelligence and covert operations were not a priority for the new president and the first CIA Director, James Woolsey, was an outsider in Clinton's team.[54] Selected late, Woolsey had little clout with the President and he did not ingratiate himself with the rest of the National Security team by insisting on setting policies, as opposed to providing assessment. National Security Advisor Anthony Lake was particularly strict in enforcing the distinction. In addition, repeated crises, the lack of a clear mission and the constant battle for funding meant that the CIA was in trouble. Morale plummeted, many resigned, and risk aversion became the order of the day in certain quarters of the Agency. The budget for covert operations went as low as less than one per cent of the intelligence community resources.[55]

In Iraq, the problems identified by the CIA's Frank Anderson had not subsided. The Agency had no valuable sources close to Saddam, nor adequate intelligence. Within the Administration, some officials, including Vice-President Al Gore, held hawkish views regarding Iraq. They hoped that a combination of coercive measures (primarily sanctions) and covert operations would lead to a fracturing of the regime. Like its predecessor, the Administration was keen to see the end of Saddam's regime, but no one really knew how to achieve it.[56] The State Department worked to ratchet up pressure on Saddam at the UN. The no-fly zones, sanctions and inspection regime continued, as did covert operations. Through this policy of 'aggressive containment', the hope was that with enough pressure the regime would collapse.[57]

The Administration's problematic relationship with Saddam started with an attempted assassination. In April 1993, during a visit to Kuwait, former president George H. W. Bush allegedly escaped an assassination attempt concocted by the Iraqi government and its intelligence service. After a CIA and FBI investigation, the Clinton Administration decided to respond with a bombing. Based on Secretary of State Warren Christopher's recommendation, the bombing targeted Iraq's intelligence services headquarters and was carried out at night, to limit civilian casualties.[58]

Discussing the strike, Chairman of the Joint Chiefs of Staff Colin Powell argued: 'you can't go around bombing an entire country hoping to hit one individual'. The Administration, he continued, had shown a willingness to 'smack him whenever it's necessary'.

Powell's remarks implied that the Administration was hoping to get Saddam. The strike did deter Saddam from engaging in further terrorism,[59] but the CIA and its director were reportedly left with a 'sour taste' in their mouths. As Woolsey recalled, the decision to strike the intelligence headquarters was taken while he was out of town and without inviting his deputy, William Studeman, to the meeting. The CIA had 'people looking at the vulnerabilities of Saddam's regime and what one could do in order to really punish the regime without damaging the population'. The principals, in Woolsey's view, refused to listen to the 'equivalent to Casey's intervention on the Libya bombing', that is, to options to strike Saddam personally.[60] Instead, they carried out a limited strike, an effective retaliation 'against Iraqi cleaning women and night watchmen', as he later put it.[61]

Sailing to the 'Bay of Kurds'

The Administration maintained its predecessor's support for the Iraqi opposition and the 'lethal finding' against Saddam. The hope was still that a military coup would dislodge the Iraqi dictator.[62] As in the Bush years, the Administration's rhetoric often outpaced its capabilities and its intentions. In April 1993, Gore met with Chalabi and the INC. In August, the Vice-President wrote a letter complimenting Chalabi's leadership and giving the INC 'solid assurances that the United States will do whatever it can to assist you, to overthrow Saddam and establish democracy in Iraq'.[63] Chalabi interpretated the letter as his ticket to a US-supported regime change. This was not how most of the Administration interpreted it. Many viewed the INC with scepticism, especially its plans to overthrow Saddam. The Administration was happy to support Chalabi's and the INC's plan to weaken the regime from Iraqi Kurdistan by encouraging defections. This was, after all, a relatively cost-free covert political action. The Administration, though, was initially reluctant to go much beyond that.[64]

An initial step was the decision to expand the US government's and CIA's activities in northern Iraq. At Langley, Steve Richter oversaw the Iraqi Operations Group. In September 1994, his deputy, Robert Baer, visited the enclaves in northern Iraq with a Congressional delegation from the Senate Intelligence Committee. In Iraq, Baer met with leaders of the two main Kurdish groups, as well as with Chalabi.[65]

In early October, the CIA's Ted Price, Deputy Director for Operations, held a briefing for senior members of the Clinton Administration. Price knew that – like its predecessor – the Administration preferred a 'silver bullet' option. The centrepiece of his presentation was a chart depicting CIA contacts with officials within Saddam's network. The presentation gave the impression that Saddam was surrounded. Anderson, then on his way out of the Agency, pointed out that most of the connections were based solely on rumours and that many of these rumours were likely fabricated by double agents. Nonetheless, George Tenet, then the Director for Intelligence Affairs at the NSC, and others were impressed by Price's presentation. Administration officials reportedly became intrigued by the possibility of arranging a coup.[66]

While the confrontation with Saddam continued, between the end of 1994 and the start of 1995 the CIA dispatched Baer and a team of CIA officials, including Warren Marik, to Salahuddin in northern Iraq, to establish a base of operations. Once in Iraq, secret communications back to Langley were established. Chalabi became DB (the digraph code for Iraq) PULSAR 1. Masud Barzani, leader of the Kurdish Democratic Party (KDP), became DB EWOK (from the Star Wars creatures) and Jalal Talabani, leader of the Patriotic Union of Kurdistan (PUK), DB YETI.[67]

According to Martin Indyk, then special assistant to Clinton and senior director for Near East and South Asian affairs at the NSC, the CIA had explicit orders not to take any action without seeking the White House's approval.[68] Indyk had made sure of this by warning Baer during a meeting before the latter moved to Iraq.[69] For the White House, the rationale for the base was primarily intelligence collection and political operations to destabilise Saddam. Then National Security Advisor Anthony Lake did admit that while a 'lethal finding' is the wrong way of portraying the Administration's understanding of the CIA's role, 'this does not mean that the CIA was not given every chance or even encouraged to plan covert operations that could lead to Saddam's

Saddam Hussein: Assassination and Confrontation with Iraq

removal from office'.[70] Indyk also confirmed that while there was no explicit order to kill Saddam, the Administration's covert aim was overthrow. If that led to the assassination of Saddam, legally it was a different matter.[71]

On the ground, Baer and Marik interpreted their instructions liberally. According to Baer, the purpose of the mission, shared with the NSC, was to '[redacted] the Iraqi dissidents overthrow Saddam'.[72] Marik further recalled: 'Nobody said we should provide military training and provide weapons to the [National Congress] force. But when we did that and reported it back to Washington, nobody said stop it, either.'[73] In a matter of weeks, Baer established a working relationship with General Wafiq Samarrai, Saddam's former chief of military intelligence who had defected to the north in November 1994.[74]

Samarrai shared with Baer his intention to start a coup and asked for Washington's support. Baer replied that – before providing any support – Washington needed to know details of who was involved. Baer mentioned the outline of the plan to Langley and received a snappy cable in return: 'This is not a plan.' Baer did not share Langley's response with the general and gave a very liberal interpretation to the message: 'Washington hadn't rejected the coup; it just needed more details, such as the names of the officers involved.' In Baer's account, the general shared the details of the plan with him, and, in turn, he passed them on to Langley. Over time Baer has changed his story of what Samarrai's plot entailed. In one version, the plot necessitated creating a violent diversion in Baghdad which would convince Saddam to take refuge in Awjah, the area where he retreated when the regime was in danger. A source inside Saddam's security detail would notify the plotters of Saddam's arrival and one of the units loyal to the plotters would hold him there, giving the other units time to take over.[75] In another version, the plot entailed suborning twelve tanks and driving to Tikrit to 'pulverize Saddam in his palace'.[76]

What is certain is that, on 12 February 1995, the Badr Brigades, Iraqi Shiites supported by Iran, attacked and defeated a brigade of the Iraqi forces in the south of the country. Their success seemed to confirm the weakness of the Iraqi army. It also gave some credit to a plan Chalabi had long been selling to US officials and anyone

283

who would listen in Washington. The so-called 'two-cities' plan[77] relied on working on the generals commanding Iraqi garrisons in the cities of Mosul and Kirkuk, south of the northern zone. If they could be convinced to give the INC free rein, this could lead to the desertion of more and more Iraqi forces. If they were to refuse, they would suffer attacks from the INC and its forces. These attacks would be effective enough to embarrass the generals, demoralise them, and make them reluctant to return to Baghdad for a performance review.[78] Now, with forces rebelling in the south, or so the argument went, in a pincer movement, the Iraqi army would have no choice but join the rebellion.[79] The timing of the plan did not depend solely on strategic choices. Chalabi was under intense scrutiny for his misuse of CIA funds and the two main Kurdish factions were, as often the case, at loggerheads.

At this juncture, Chalabi reportedly asked Baer whether Washington would support an uprising and Baer replied that it was better to start one and then ask. Chalabi told Baer to inform Washington that he intended to start an uprising on 4 March as the only opportunity to prevent a split between the Kurdish factions. Baer, who initially had not disclosed Samarrai's military coup plan to Chalabi, decided to fold together the two plots.[80] Iran also got involved. Chalabi had long-established contacts with Iranian officials. As the time of the coup approached, Chalabi reportedly played a trick on his Iranian contacts. During a meeting, he allegedly left the room to give them time to read a letter. The US government letter, on NSC stationery, assured Chalabi that the United States had decided to assassinate Saddam and had sent a 'direct action' team to northern Iraq led by 'Robert Pope' for that purpose. The letter was likely a forgery from Chalabi,[81] but Baer took part in the ruse. Chalabi told him that the Iranians needed further proof of US support. Baer could not meet personally with the Iranians but could walk by just prior to the meeting. Baer agreed. He reasoned that, if Iran fell for it, it was their problem, not his. According to Chalabi's biographer Richard Bonin, Baer went further. He met personally with representatives of the Badr brigades, and when asked whether the United States supported Chalabi's plan, he replied, 'Any plan . . . We can't live with this fucker anymore.'[82]

Saddam Hussein: Assassination and Confrontation with Iraq

On 2 March, two days before the planned uprising, the White House became aware that Saddam was mobilising his Republican Guards and moving them towards the north to crush a suspected coup plot. According to Lake, the CIA reported on these developments, something confirmed by Indyk.[83] Acting DCI William Studeman told NSC officials that someone within the CIA named 'Bob' had been plotting with Samarrai – who was known to the CIA – to arrange a coup, but the CIA didn't know much beyond that.[84] It was unclear where the breakdown of communication had occurred.[85]

When NSC officials told Lake, the latter arranged a meeting with Secretary of State Warren Christopher, Secretary of Defense William Perry, and Gore. The plan was discussed but it appeared to all involved a terrible idea. Lake recalled how the plan reminded him of the Bay of Pigs. Kennedy had not explored what would happen next if the invasion failed. If the plotters had gotten bogged down, it was very unclear whether the US would have been able to help them. Bruce Riedel was less philosophical but found the same parallel: 'We called it the Bay of Kurds,' he recalled.[86] Moreover, the Administration, according to Lake, had very little confidence in either Chalabi or Samarrai.[87] The Joint Chiefs also made NSC officials aware that Iranian and Turkish forces were mobilising, thus raising the prospects of a regional war. Ultimately, Lake shared the views of the principals with the President, but to preserve presidential deniability took charge of turning off the plan, even if he knew that it meant taking a hit from critics of the Administration.[88] A message was sent to Turkey not to move and to Iraqi officials not to threaten the north. Lake also sent a message to Baer for Chalabi: 'The action you have planned for this weekend has been totally compromised. We believe there is a high risk of failure. Any decision to proceed will be on your own.'[89]

Baer was reportedly shocked by Lake's reaction. In his view, this was not (at least not entirely) a rogue operation. He had communicated details of the plan in telegrams to Langley, although, as he admitted, he had received no reply. Baer told Chalabi of Lake's telegram, but the latter decided to go ahead anyway. At the last minute, Barzani withdrew his faction's support.[90] Without Barzani's and the US government's support, the revolt quickly collapsed.

285

The story is not finished, though. Samarrai's plan seemingly included a direct assassination attempt against Saddam. The plan was for units loyal to Samarrai to take advantage of a trip by Saddam to the city of Samarra, Samarrai's hometown. Having blocked his convoy, units loyal to Samarrai would destroy Saddam's vehicle and anyone in it.[91] Baer seemingly communicated the assassination plot component to Headquarters and he was told to immediately desist. It remains unclear whether there was an assassination component and whether it was dropped, while the rest of the planning had continued.[92] NSC officials do not recall assassination being an issue during decisions surrounding the plot.[93] While one plot failed, another one was in the offing.

The Jordanian Coup and Operation Desert Fox

Built around former Baathist military officers, the Iraqi National Accord (INA) aimed to overthrow Saddam. A leading figure in the Accord was Iyad Alawi – codenamed PANTHER 1.[94] Sometime in 1994, Alawi had convinced Britain's MI6 that he had extensive contacts inside the Iraqi army who were ready to remove Saddam in a relatively bloodless coup. MI6 passed the information to the CIA's London Station which, in turn, passed it to Richter. This information had formed the backbone of Ted Price's October briefing to Clinton Administration officials.[95]

Richter needed little convincing. He had already been working with Muhammad Shawani, former brigadier general in the Republican Guards who was also in exile in London. Shawani had three sons in the Republican Guards. He told Richter that he would be able to recruit a high number of Iraqi officers and – with his sons' help – would launch a coup. All he needed was the CIA's help in creating the right conditions and in providing technical support and communication equipment.[96]

These developments coincided with a change of leadership at the CIA and surprising defections from Iraq. In mid-August 1995, the defection to Jordan of Hussein Kamel, Saddam's son-in-law and chief of Iraq's WMD programme, was interpreted as a sign that Saddam's regime was weakening.[97] At the Agency, the new

Saddam Hussein: Assassination and Confrontation with Iraq

Director, John Deutch, seemingly favoured a much narrower effort, one targeted specifically at eliminating Saddam. According to Christopher Whipple, Deutch admitted: 'the Iraqi situation kept me up at night . . . We were having trouble dealing with Saddam and didn't know what to do next to make him go away – *really* go away.'[98] George Tenet, who had been pushing for a coup while at the NSC, was now Deputy DCI.[99] The newfound intensity in the Agency reportedly reflected President Clinton's willingness to get rid of Saddam 'by fair means or foul'.[100] At one point, according to intelligence officials, 'Deutch came back from a meeting at the White House, all fired up, stating words to the effect of "Bring me the head of Saddam Hussein."'[101]

In January 1996, Richter and the Directorate of Operations Deputy Director David Cohen travelled to Riyadh, where they discussed the coup plans with Saudi intelligence, MI6, and Jordanian and Kuwaiti intelligence officials. They all agreed that they would support the Accord in its plot against Saddam, using Jordan as a base for psychological warfare – including a radio station – and training of INA personnel.[102] The CIA reportedly provided Alawi with $20 million over the course of their collaboration.[103] The coup – codenamed DBACHILLES – was planned for June 1996.[104] The promise of (and higher degree of confidence in) this coup contributed to Lake's decision to withdraw US support for the Chalabi–Samarrai plot.[105] US officials saw this coup as a much more serious effort, one with higher chances of success, and with better contacts in the Iraqi military.[106]

Instead, from the start, the operation was infiltrated. Even before the plot could commence, Saddam started rounding up those connected with it. After the failed coup, a phone rang at INA's headquarters in Amman and Shawani's sons told their father that they had been captured and were about to be executed.[107] In alliance with Barzani, in August 1996, Saddam proceeded to invade part of the north, crush Kurdish forces, destroy the INC infrastructure and seize its files and computers. The entire US covert operation and INC infrastructure were destroyed.[108] The Administration responded with a limited cruise missile strike only in the south of the country.[109]

* * *

In the following months, Chalabi – who had been sidelined by the Agency and the Administration – found new allies in the increasingly partisan Washington. Leading Republicans in Congress were happy to help.[110] Chalabi's allies also came to include Marik who had retired from the CIA shortly after the Iraq debacle, intellectuals from neoconservative circles, former Cold Warriors and former military officials. With the help of retired CIA operator Dewey Clarridge and former commander-in-chief of US special operations Wayne Downing, Chalabi developed a 'roll back plan for Iraq', the name itself a critique of the Clinton Administration's alleged preference for containment.

The plan entailed the training of 200–300 Iraqi exiles who, in turn, would become trainers for a much larger army. Eventually a 'liberation army' of 3,000–5,000 soldiers would include commando as well as anti-tank units. These would not engage Saddam's forces directly but would spread out from 'liberated zones', enticing Iraqi army officers to defect.[111] There were two main problems. First, the plan was expensive, costing $200–400 million to start. Second, the plan still needed a US show of force. As Clarridge admitted, '[US] Support for an insurgency will send a signal to Saddam that we're getting serious.'[112] The plan was ridiculed for its strategy and understood as posturing by several members of the Administration, former CIA officials and intellectuals.[113]

And yet, domestically, the Administration was coming under increased pressure – especially from Republicans within Congress and neocons without – to get rid of Saddam.[114] This pressure included several Congressional hearings where Chalabi presented himself as the only hope for a democratic Iraq and (neocon) experts pushed the Administration to do more. As part of this campaign, former DCI Woolsey warned of the threat of Iraqi WMDs but counselled against assassination or a coup. Assassination was prohibited by an Executive Order and, even if it wasn't, finding Saddam would be impossible and, if killed, he might be replaced by someone similar.[115] This campaign coalesced in a new think tank, the Project for the New American Century, which published a series of memoranda addressed to President Clinton and calling for regime change in Iraq.[116] The crowning achievement of this public

Saddam Hussein: Assassination and Confrontation with Iraq

campaign would famously come with Congress's approval of the Iraq Liberation Act (ILA) in the autumn of 1998.[117] At the time, though, while Chalabi's arguments continued to gain public traction in Washington, he had lost credibility with the Administration as well as with the rest of the Iraqi opposition.[118]

Alongside this pressure, talk of assassination emerged within policy debates. In a conversation with British prime minister Tony Blair – already a staunch US ally in the confrontation with Saddam – Clinton and Gore lamented the lack of progress. Gore made clear that the Administration was under pressure from Capitol Hill to 'go after Saddam's head'. Clinton concurred and lamented, 'that approach is nowhere near as simple as it sounds on the surface'.[119]

Confirming Gore's point, bipartisan calls did emerge to review the ban on assassination. Senator Diane Feinstein (D-CA) told CNN that – while she was not prepared to explicitly revise the ban on assassination – she couldn't help but think that 'the problem was Saddam'. Similarly, Senator Arlen Specter (R-PA) – former Chairman of the Senate Intelligence Committee and, hence, in a position to know about the ban and covert operations – argued that the Administration needed to work with Congress to formulate a policy to 'topple Saddam, to get rid of him'. The war-like state between the United States and Saddam made the targeting permissible. He added: 'When the attack was made against Libya back in April of 1986, it was acknowledged that there was an effort to target Qadhafi.'[120] Sam Brownback (R-KS) concurred, arguing that he was ready to sponsor legislation to review the ban on assassination in a manner that would allow Saddam to be targeted. 'I see no problem with us bombing very close and personal to Saddam.' Senator Richard Lugar (R-IN) also suggested that Saddam would 'have to be killed', if he could not be removed from office in other ways.[121] At the time, these calls intersected with another effort to review the ban on assassination in the context of the Administration's hunt for Osama Bin Laden (Chapter 11). In Iraq, the next main confrontation seemingly entailed a direct assassination attempt.

* * *

By the end of 1998, the international coalition was unravelling and was limited to the United States and the United Kingdom. Saddam had been repeatedly challenging the sanctions and the inspections regime. The sanctions were taking their toll on the Iraqi population and the population's plight, in turn, was weakening international support for them, as reflected in the Oil for Food Programme. Domestically, having signed the ILA, the Administration was under constant pressure to do something about Iraq. The Administration had responded to the critics by renewing its intent to work 'with the Iraqi opposition to bring about a change of leadership in Iraq'.[122] In national security deliberations, as Indyk recalled, Iraq was becoming a constant item on the agenda, and the Administration struggled to see an endgame.[123]

On 4 December, National Security Advisor Sandy Berger notified Clinton that UNSCOM Chairman Richard Butler had decided to conduct a series of no-notice inspections at Iraqi facilities. Berger offered several options for a US response depending on the extent of Iraq's obstruction. In case of some obstruction, the US government – in Berger's view – needed to point to the pattern of Iraqi behaviour since 1991. Since the United States had already 'done the pivot calling for Saddam replacement', no new declaratory posture was needed, but the US could expect international opposition to any use of force combined with domestic pressure to do more.[124] The onset of this UNSCOM round of inspection is particularly controversial, since it intersects with accusations surrounding the US government's and the CIA's exploitation of the UN mission for intelligence and – some argue – regime change purposes.[125]

An emphasis on a change of leadership was reflected in the internal discussion of the political objectives of the US raid. Operation Desert Fox aimed at punishing Saddam for his obstruction of the inspections and lack of compliance with UN resolutions. The operation's objective, though, went beyond the destruction of WMD-related facilities. The Administration hoped that the strike would weaken the WMD threat but also Saddam's 'command and control over his military and his people, increasing the chance that those Iraqis who want a different future for Iraq can change their leadership, and lead to an Iraq that complies with UNSCRs'.[126]

Saddam Hussein: Assassination and Confrontation with Iraq

The bombing took place between 16 and 19 December 1998. In the same days, the Clinton Administration confronted the President's impeachment trial – the House voted to impeach on the 19th – as well as preparation to strike at al-Qaeda's training camps in Afghanistan and other targets in Sudan (discussed in the next chapter). The bombardment was the heaviest since the Gulf War. The target list included 100 sites, twelve of which related to ballistic missiles and WMD facilities.[127] As the Administration's political objectives had implied, though, the bombing went beyond these facilities. In the aftermath of the strikes, Secretary of Defense William Cohen and Chairman of the Joint Chiefs of Staff General Henry Shelton admitted that – alongside bombs – US forces had also dropped 2 million leaflets targeting Iraqi army units in southern Iraq. The leaflets called for the army to rebel against the regime, highlighting the disparity of treatment with the better paid Republican Guards.[128] Sunni military officials did launch a coup one month later, but it failed.[129]

The choice of targets also suggested that the Administration might have aimed for a regime change strategy that included Saddam's assassination. The core of the bombing (49 out of 100 targets) aimed at weakening the regime itself. These targets included facilities connected to supporters of the regime. As Shelton put it, 'We know who protects the center of gravity.'[130] Saddam's Secret Police, Republican Guards facilities and units, as well as transportation and communication infrastructure were targeted. Some of these sites had been bombed during the Gulf War when they had been designated as 'L01' targets, that is, the first target in the leadership category. The office of Saddam Hussein's chief of staff was also attacked, 'albeit under the innocuous target name of "Secretariat Presidential Building"'.[131] According to Seymour Hersh, based on the work of US technicians as part of the inspection teams, US intelligence was also able to define a pattern to Saddam's movements. It became evident that Saddam would often visit two of his mistresses, one near his hometown of Tikrit and the other in suburban Baghdad. Both sites, Hersh writes, were targeted 'in the hope of assassinating him'.[132] Saddam and his regime survived the bombing.

Conclusion

As the plot he had helped develop crumbled, Baer was recalled to Washington. He was ushered into a meeting with the CIA General Counsel. Reportedly, he was told that he was in breach of Executive Order 12333 banning assassination and that the FBI had started an investigation for conspiracy to commit murder. On 22 March, Baer passed a polygraph test and one year later the Justice Department dropped the investigation for lack of evidence.[133] According to former CIA official Melissa Boyle Mahle, Baer's ordeal was understood by CIA officials as a demonstration of the risk-averse nature of the Agency and the White House in the mid-1990s: 'The risk of removing a designated enemy of the US by lethal force was just too much for the White House to accept.'[134] This argument gained particular traction in the aftermath of the 9/11 terrorist attacks, when apportioning blame for the tragedy became one of the primary concerns for intellectuals as well as (then) current and former US officials.

Certainly, in the early 1990s, and in the post-Cold War context, the Agency was less gung-ho than during the Casey years. It is also certain that the place of covert operations and the position of the ban on assassination in the 1990s are more complicated than this interpretation centred on risk aversion implies. By the end of the Bush Administration the ban had been reinterpreted to both permit the CIA's involvement in coups that might lead to assassination, and the targeting of foreign officials if they posed an imminent threat to US interests. William Barr's OLC opinion and Hays Parks's memorandum on assassination had crystallised these views emerging from the Reagan years.

In the language of decision-making, euphemisms reappeared as policymakers expressed a guarded interest in removing and killing Saddam. On the ground, whether support for the Samarrai/Baer/Chalabi coup was ended due to concerns regarding the Agency's involvement in assassination or more general concerns regarding the risks the plan entailed remains unclear.[135] The CIA and the White House might not have been opposed to an assassination attempt, but, as the intent argument implied, they were

Saddam Hussein: Assassination and Confrontation with Iraq

certainly opposed to one with US fingerprints all over it. While Baer must be taken with more than a pinch of salt, he seems to imply as much when he hints that the US government was fine with Samarrai's plan and the controversy surrounding assassination was a by-product of Chalabi's fake letter and its promise of a US government-sponsored 'hit team' under Robert Pope to kill Saddam.[136]

This position did not entail an unwillingness on the part of the US government to kill Saddam nor a crippling risk aversion. Throughout its confrontation with Saddam, the US government became involved in direct and indirect assassination attempts. Under Bush, efforts to assassinate Saddam emerged even before the start of Desert Storm. In its aftermath, the Administration approved a 'lethal finding' for the CIA. Some of the coup options (e.g. palace coup and silver bullet) were premised on the assumption that Saddam would be assassinated by someone close to him, something former US officials have confirmed. The CIA supported these operations and had also been authorised by the White House to support acts of sabotage inside Iraq to sow chaos in the country.[137] Under Clinton, the lethal finding remained on the books. The CIA provided funds and – if Marik is to be believed – training to groups, with a full understanding that they aimed to kill Saddam. While the Samarrai coup was abandoned, the INA one was pursued, precisely because it had better chances of removing – and killing – Saddam. More indirectly, the US government, as in previous episodes, combined economic sanctions, international pressure and covert psychological operations to create the conditions for regime change and, potentially, assassination.

Finally, if Operation Desert Fox explicitly targeted the residences of Saddam's mistresses and command and control centres, it represented a direct assassination attempt, a throwback to the earlier strike against Qaddafi's compound. If it didn't, many of the targets selected and the use of leaflets still suggest a willingness to kickstart a process of violent regime change. In any case, the US government was preparing the ground for (and comfortable with a policy of) assassination. By the time of the strike, though, the Administration was fully focused on another target, Osama Bin Laden.

Notes

1. Minutes of NSC Meeting on Iraqi invasion of Kuwait, 4/8/1990, NSC, Richard Haass Files, Working Files, OA/ID 01478-029, George H. W. Bush Presidential Library (GHWBPL).
2. Bartholomew Sparrow, *The Strategist: Brent Scowcroft and the Call of National Security* (New York: Public Affairs, 2015), 391–2.
3. Bob Woodward, *The Commanders* (New York: Touchstone, 1991), 282.
4. Sean Naylor, *Relentless Strike* (New York: St. Martin's Griffin, 2015), 51.
5. Woodward, *The Commanders*, 290–1.
6. Ibid., 294.
7. Peter Pringle, '"Bomb Baghdad" General Sacked', *The Independent*, 18 September 1990.
8. CBS News, 'Top Air Force Officer Is Fired over Remarks', CBS News Transcript, 17 September 1990.
9. Andrew Cockburn and Patrick Cockburn, *Out of the Ashes: The Resurrection of Saddam Hussein* (New York: HarperCollins, 1999), 34.
10. Mark Vlasic, 'Cloak and Dagger Diplomacy: The Use of Assassination', *Georgetown Journal of International Affairs*, 1.2 (2000), 102.
11. Chris Whipple, *The Spymasters* (London: Simon & Schuster, 2020), 153–60.
12. Joseph Stieb, *The Regime Change Consensus: Iraq in American Politics, 1990–2003* (Cambridge: Cambridge University Press, 2021), 66.
13. Stieb, *Regime Change Consensus*, 22–4.
14. George Bush and Brent Scowcroft, *A World Transformed* (New York: Doubleday 1998), 463.
15. Stieb, *Regime Change Consensus*, 37.
16. Bush and Scowcroft, *A World*, 464.
17. Reuters, 'Bush Statement', *New York Times*, 16 February 1991, available at https://www.nytimes.com/1991/02/16/world/war-gulf-bush-statement-excerpts-2-statements-bush-iraq-s-proposal-for-ending.html (accessed 31 October 2023).
18. Bush and Scowcroft, *A World*, 472.
19. Micah Zenko, 'Who Is to Blame for the Doomed Iraqi Uprisings of 1991?' *The National Interest*, 7 March 2016, available at https://nationalinterest.org/blog/the-buzz/behind-the-doomed-iraqi-uprisings-1991-15425 (accessed 31 October 2023).
20. John Simpson, *The Wars against Saddam* (London: Pan Books, 2003), 222.

21. Cockburn and Cockburn, *Out of the Ashes*, 20–1.
22. Lawrence Freedman, *A Choice of Enemies* (London: Phoenix, 2008), 251.
23. Simpson, *The Wars*, 221.
24. Dilip Hiro, *Neighbors Not Friends: Iran and Iraq after the Gulf Wars* (London: Routledge, 2001), 37.
25. Helga Graham, 'Hopes of Coup Led US to Ignore Shia Plea for Support', *The Observer*, 19 May 1991.
26. Zenko, 'Who Is to Blame.'
27. UN Security Council Resolution 687, 1991, available at https://www.un.org/Depts/unmovic/documents/687.pdf (accessed 31 October 2023).
28. Stieb, *Regime Change Consensus*, 55.
29. PR Newswire, 'Assassination Ban Should Be Revoked, Says Sen. Richard Lugar', 22 February 1991.
30. Associated Press, 'On Capitol Hill, Broad Support for Pursuing Saddam', 26 February 1991.
31. James Wensits, 'CIA Chief Denies Assassination Claims', *Chicago Tribune*, 18 February 1991; CIA Reading Room, CIA-RDP99-01448R000401660117-3.
32. Telegram, Secretary of State Washington, to Embassies London, Paris, Riyadh, Cairo, Ankara, Damascus, 4/5/1991, NSC, Richard Haass Files, Working Files, Folder Iraq, May 1991 [2], CF01585, GHWBPL.
33. Peter Jennings, 'Unfinished Business: The CIA and Saddam Hussein 1997', available at https://www.youtube.com/watch?v=lZHHAIeq2I (accessed 31 October 2023).
34. Cockburn and Cockburn, *Out of the Ashes*, 44.
35. Frank Anderson, CIA's Near East Division Chief from 1991 to 1994, PBS Frontline, The Survival of Saddam, Interviews, available at https://www.pbs.org/wgbh/pages/frontline/shows/saddam/interviews/ (accessed 31 October 2023).
36. Jennings, 'Unfinished Business'.
37. Hiro, *Neighbors*, 46.
38. Ahmad Chalabi, PBS Frontline, The Survival of Saddam, Interviews.
39. Memorandum Haass to Scowcroft, 'Options for dealing with Iraqi non-compliance', 24/9/1991, NSC, Richard Haass Files, Working Files, Folder Iraq, September 1991 [2], GHWBPL.
40. Memorandum of telephone conversation: Bush – PM Major, 25/9/1991, NSC, Richard Haass Files, Working Files, Folder Iraq, September 1991 [1], GHWBPL.

41. Michael Mazarr, *Leap of Faith* (New York: Public Affairs, 2019), ebook, chapter 2.
42. Cockburn and Cockburn, *Out of the Ashes*, 54.
43. Ibid.
44. John Broder and Robin Wright, 'CIA Authorized to Target Hussein Iraq', *Los Angeles Times*, 8 February 1992.
45. Patrick Tyler, 'Congress Notified of Iraq Coup Plan', *New York Times*, 9 February 1992.
46. Hiro, *Neighbors*, 60.
47. Mazarr, *Leap*, chapter 2.
48. Michael Gunter, 'The Iraqi Opposition and the Failure of U.S. Intelligence', *International Journal of Intelligence and CounterIntelligence*, 12.2 (1999), 150; James Bamford, 'The Man Who Sold the War', *Rolling Stone*, 17 November 2005, available at https://web.archive.org/web/20060612234417/http://www.rollingstone.com/politics/story/8798997/the_man_who_sold_the_war/ (accessed 31 October 2023).
49. Hiro, *Neighbors*, 66–7.
50. Cockburn and Cockburn, *Out of the Ashes*, 57.
51. Elaine Sciolino, 'A Failed Plot to Overthrow Hussein Is Reported in Iraq', *New York Times*, 14 March 1995.
52. Barton Gellman, 'US Delivers Limited Airstrike on Iraq', *Washington Post*, 14 January 1993.
53. Luca Trenta, 'Clinton and Bosnia: A Candidate's Freebie, a President's Nightmare', *Journal of Transatlantic Studies*, 12.1 (2014), 64–5; Madeleine Albright, *Madame Secretary* (New York: Macmillan, 2003), 139; Amy Zegart, *Spying Blind* (Princeton, NJ: Princeton University Press, 2007), 69.
54. Some have written that he was selected as an afterthought; Whipple, *Spymasters*, 154–5. Others have claimed that Woolsey's political orientation was similar to the then emerging 'neocons' and the Administration wanted to have a neocon within the tent. Ambassador Martin Indyk, Zoom interview with the author, 12 October 2022.
55. Loch Johnson, *The Threat on the Horizon* (Oxford: Oxford University Press, 2011), 266.
56. Mazarr, *Leap*, chapter 2.
57. Martin Indyk, *Innocent Abroad* (New York: Simon & Schuster, 2009), ebook, chapter 2.
58. Richard Clarke, *Against All Enemies* (London: Free Press, 2004), 81.
59. Indyk, *Innocent Abroad*, chapter 8.

60. Russell Riley, Interview with James Woolsey, 13/1/2010, William J. Clinton Presidential History Project, Miller Center, 89–90.
61. Tim Weiner, *Legacy of Ashes* (New York: Doubleday, 2007), 444.
62. Indyk, *Innocent Abroad*, chapter 2.
63. Chalabi Interview, PBS.
64. Cockburn and Cockburn, *Out of the Ashes*, 166; Freedman, *A Choice*, 290.
65. Richard Bonin, *Arrows of the Night* (New York: Doubleday 2011), ebook, chapter 9.
66. Cockburn and Cockburn, *Out of the Ashes*, 170–1.
67. Aram Roston, *The Man Who Pushed America to War* (New York: Nation Books, 2008), 103.
68. Mazarr, *Leap*, chapter 2; Indyk, *Innocent Abroad*, chapter 8.
69. Indyk, Interview with the author.
70. Anthony Lake, Phone interview with the author, 16/6/2022.
71. Indyk, Interview with the author.
72. It is unclear how many words the CIA has redacted before publication. Robert Baer, *See No Evil* (New York: Broadway Paperbacks, 2003), 174.
73. Jim Hoagland, 'How CIA's Secret War on Saddam Collapsed', *Washington Post*, 26 June 1997.
74. Baer, *See No Evil*, 181.
75. Ibid., 181–3.
76. Robert Baer, *The Perfect Kill* (New York: Plume Books, 2014), 131.
77. The plan is sometimes called 'three cities'. See Hoagland, 'How CIA's Secret War'; Bonin, *Arrows of the Night*, chapter 9.
78. Cockburn and Cockburn, *Out of the Ashes*, 182.
79. Baer, *See No Evil*, 192.
80. Ibid.
81. Something he denies; Bonin, *Arrows of the Night*, chapter 9.
82. Ibid., chapter 9.
83. Russell Riley, Interview with Anthony Lake, pt. 2, William J. Clinton Presidential Library History Project, Miller Center Oral History, Interview, 6; Indyk, Interview with the author.
84. Lake, Interview with the author.
85. Riley, Interview with Lake, 7.
86. Whipple, *Spymasters*, 169.
87. Lake, Interview with the author.
88. Ibid..
89. Baer, *See No Evil*, 173.

90. Evan Thomas, Christopher Dickey and Gregory L. Vistica, 'Bay of Pigs Redux', *Newsweek*, 23 March 1998; Hiro, *Neighbors*, 40.
91. Thomas et al. 'Bay of Pigs Redux'; Gunter, 'The Iraqi Opposition', 158; Cockburn and Cockburn, *Out of the Ashes*, 185.
92. Cockburn and Cockburn, *Out of the Ashes*, 185; Steve Coll, Zoom interview with the author, 22 February 2021.
93. Lake, Interview with the author; Indyk, Interview with the author; Indyk, *Innocent Abroad*, chapter 8.
94. Roston, *The Man Who Pushed*, 118.
95. Scott Ritter, *Iraq Confidential* (London: I.B. Tauris, 2010), 152.
96. Ritter, *Iraq Confidential*, 152.
97. Jeffrey Smith and David Ottaway, 'Anti-Saddam Operation Cost CIA $100 Million', *Washington Post*, 15 September 1996.
98. Whipple, *Spymasters*, 169.
99. Cockburn and Cockburn, *Out of the Ashes*, 218.
100. Whipple, *Spymasters*, 169.
101. Both Deutch and the White House deny this. Cockburn and Cockburn, *Out of the Ashes*, 221.
102. Hiro, *Neighbors*, 105.
103. Jon Lee Anderson, 'A Man of the Shadows', *New Yorker*, 16 January 2005, available at https://www.newyorker.com/magazine/2005/01/24/a-man-of-the-shadows (accessed 31 October 2023).
104. David Ignatius, 'The CIA and the Coup That Wasn't', *Washington Post*, 16 May 2003.
105. Hiro, *Neighbors*, 102.
106. Indyk, Interview with the author.
107. Roston, *The Man Who Pushed*, 118.
108. Gunter, 'The Iraqi Opposition', 148.
109. Indyk, *Innocent Abroad*, chapter 10.
110. Ibid.
111. Jim Mannion, 'Iraq US Insurgency', *Agence France Presse*, 25/November 1998; Warren Strobel, Thomas Omestad, Richard J. Newman, Bruce B. Auster and Thomas Gros, 'America's Plan to Get Saddam', *US News and World Report*, 30 November 1998.
112. Hiro, *Neighbors*, 154.
113. Milt Bearden, 'Lessons from Afghanistan', *New York Times*, 2 May 1998; Daniel Byman, Kenneth Pollack and Gideon Rose, 'The Rollback Fantasy', *Foreign Affairs*, 78.1 (1999), 24–41.
114. Stieb, *Regime Change Consensus*, 136; Kenneth Katzman, 'Iraq: U.S. Efforts to Change the Regime', Congressional Research Service, 22/3/2022, 4.

Saddam Hussein: Assassination and Confrontation with Iraq

115. US Senate, 'Iraq: Can Saddam Be Overthrown?' Hearing, Sub-Committee on Near East and South Asian Affairs, Committee on Foreign Relations, 2/3/1998, available at https://babel.hathitrust.org/cgi/pt?id=pst.000033083094&view=1up&seq=1&skin=2021 (accessed 31 October 2023), 5, 7, 23, 25.
116. Derek Chollet and James Goldgeier, *America Between the Wars* (New York: Public Affairs, 2008), 193.
117. Stieb, *Regime Change Consensus*, 158–68.
118. Dana Priest and David Ottaway, 'Congress's Candidate to Overthrow Saddam Hussein; Ahmed Chalabi Has Virtually No Other Backing', *Washington Post*, 21 April 1999.
119. Memorandum of conversation, Meeting with Tony Blair, 5/2/1998, Clinton Digital Presidential Library (CDPL), Declassified documents concerning Tony Blair (532 pages).
120. CNN, 'Showdown with Iraq: The World Watches', Late Edition with Wolf Blitzer, 15 November 1998.
121. Lee Michael Katz, 'Clinton Vows to Focus on Saddam's Ouster Assassination, Opposition Groups and Propaganda among Options', *USA Today*, 16 November 1998.
122. Summary, NSC Principals Committee Meeting, 18 December 1998, Declassified Documents Concerning the National Security Council (2 pages), CDPL.
123. Indyk, Interview with the author.
124. Samuel Berger, Memorandum for the President: 'Update on Iraq: the next several weeks', 3/12/1998; Samuel Berger, Memorandum for the President: 'Update on Iraq: the next several weeks', 4/12/1998, Declassified Documents on Desert Fox (200 pages), CDPL.
125. Ritter, *Iraq Confidential*; Robert Fisk, *The Great War for Civilisation* (New York: Knopf, 2006), 724–5.
126. 'Political Objectives of Strike against Iraq', Declassified Documents on Desert Fox (200 pages), CDPL.
127. Stieb, *Regime Change Consensus*, 155.
128. Barton Gellman and Vernon Loeb, 'One Aim: Kill Saddam's "Palace Guard"', *Washington Post*, 19 December 1998.
129. Indyk, *Innocent Abroad*, chapter 10.
130. Dana Priest and Bradley Graham, 'Airstrikes Took a Toll on Saddam, U.S. Says', *Washington Post*, 9 January 1999.
131. William Arkin, 'The Difference Was in the Details', *Washington Post*, 17 January 1999.
132. Seymour Hersh, 'Saddam's Best Friend', *New Yorker*, 5 April 1999.

133. Baer, *See No Evil*, 217.
134. Melissa Boyle Mahle, *Denial and Deception* (New York: Nation Books, 2006), 217.
135. Riley, Interview with Lake, 7.
136. Baer, *The Perfect Kill*, 134.
137. Smith and Ottaway, 'Anti-Saddam Operation'.

11 Osama Bin Laden: Assassination and Counterterrorism on the Road to 9/11

'Do you think you did enough sir?' Chris Wallace of Fox News asked former President Bill Clinton in a televised interview on 22 September 2006. 'No, because I didn't get him,' Clinton replied. 'But at least I tried.' Perhaps the most interesting bit of the interview came with Clinton barely able to remain composed. 'What did I do?' the former President asked, now almost screaming at Wallace, 'I worked hard to try to kill him. I authorized a finding for the CIA to kill him. We contracted with people to kill him. I got closer to killing him than anybody has gotten since.'[1]

While not a state official, Bin Laden could be understood as the leader of a dangerous and politically motivated movement. To paraphrase the memorandum penned by Hays Parks on assassination, he was also the leader of a structured, hierarchical and well-funded terrorist organisation. By the time of Bin Laden's appearance on US radars, while no explicit assassination orders were likely to appear, the US government had become involved in direct and indirect assassination attempts against foreign officials and it had often worked to create the conditions for assassination. Some ambiguity did remain – within and outside the executive – as to what type of operation was permitted under the ban and what type of presidential authorisation was needed to conduct such operations.

As the threat posed by al-Qaeda grew, the Administration developed a series of military and intelligence operations against Bin Laden. In certain cases, the aim of the operation was clearly to kill him. In others, more ambiguous kill or capture authorities were provided to the CIA and its local allies. Many of these decisions engendered public debate and contestation regarding the

301

meaning, remit and appropriateness of the ban. The pre-9/11 hunt for Bin Laden – the subject of this chapter – ultimately failed. The debates, claims and contestation surrounding the targeting of Bin Laden play a prominent role in the history of assassination and in ushering in the era of institutionalised targeted killings.

Bin Laden: From Financier to Mastermind

Two terrorist attacks in 1993 – the shooting of CIA officials outside the Agency's headquarters and the first bombing of the World Trade Center – rocked the Clinton Administration. At this time, if he was noticed at all, Bin Laden was considered more a financier of terrorism than a terrorist mastermind. A 1993 secret and classified State Department paper – 'The Wandering Mujahidin: Armed and Dangerous' – highlighted both Bin Laden's role as a donor and the transnational character of his financial network. The warning – raised by junior staff at the State Department – failed to alert the Administration,[2] but awareness of non-state terrorist groups was increasing. The 1995 Aum Shinrikyo group attack on the Tokyo subway using sarin showed the world the danger of non-state terrorist groups acquiring chemical and biological weapons.[3]

This increased attention was crystallised in a series of measures taken in 1995. In January, Executive Order 12947 declared terrorist acts that could undermine the Middle East Peace Process 'an unusual and extraordinary threat to the national security, foreign policy, and economy of the United States', and declared a state of national emergency to deal with them.[4] In June, the Administration approved Presidential Decision Directive (PDD) 39 titled 'U.S. Policy on Counterterrorism'. Building on Reagan-era counterterrorism efforts, the directive established a policy of no concessions towards terrorists.[5] It stressed deterrence and pre-emption of 'individuals who perpetrate or plan to perpetrate such acts'.[6] The directive emphasised the role of law enforcement and the 'punishment of terrorists for violation of criminal law'. Contrary to later criticisms, it was not all about law enforcement. The directive made clear that the US government reserved 'the option to act unilaterally, when necessary, to preempt, or punish terrorist attacks'.[7]

One month later, a National Intelligence Estimate (NIE) predicted that future terrorist attacks would be carried out by groups of 'transient' individuals who only had 'loose affiliations'. It also warned that these terrorist groups might target symbols of US economic and financial power.[8] The NIE did not mention Bin Laden or al-Qaeda.[9] Al-Qaeda also did not appear in DCI John Deutch's Worldwide Threat Assessment delivered to Congress in the same year.[10]

In Washington, a task force of former government officials assembled by the Council for Foreign Relations called for a more assertive CIA, particularly in the areas of pre-emption against terrorism and support for coups.[11] In presenting the task force's report, the Council's chairman, Richard Haass, stressed that 'rules that work to discourage or even prohibit preemptive attacks on terrorists or support for individuals hoping to bring about a change of regime in a hostile country should be repealed'. According to Haass – seemingly forgetful of Barr's opinion developed while he was in the Bush Administration – the ban on assassination inhibited work with non-Americans to overthrow dangerous governments in a cost-effective manner.[12]

Congress held similar views, especially in the realm of counterterrorism. In April, it passed the Anti-terrorism and Effective Death Penalty Act of 1996. In section 324, Congress warned that terrorism was 'among the most serious transnational threats faced by the United States'. The findings section of the bill read:

> President should use all necessary means, including covert action and military force, to disrupt, dismantle, and destroy international infrastructure used by international terrorists, including overseas terrorist training facilities and safe havens.[13]

By 1996, those connecting the dots of terrorist activities kept encountering the name of Bin Laden. The Agency decided to innovate its approach to counterterrorism. David Cohen, the head of the CIA's Directorate of Operations, decided to test the idea of creating a 'virtual station' based at the Agency's headquarters to track terrorism. He was supported by Clinton's National Security Advisor Anthony Lake. According to a CIA official who worked with him, as early as 1996, 'Tony was foaming at the mouth about Bin Laden.'[14] The aim of the station and of the officer in charge – Michael Scheuer – was to keep track of Bin Laden. This Bin Laden Issue Station (or Bin Laden unit) – also known as 'Alec Station' (the name of Scheuer's son)[15] – became a very dedicated group with a high awareness of the threat posed by al-Qaeda.[16] Most of the officers in the unit, though, were analysts who had never run operations. This created some mistrust between the Station and the Directorate of Operations.[17] Furthermore, many of the analysts Scheuer hired for the unit were women, which some in the Agency still saw as a drawback.[18]

* * *

Bin Laden had moved to Sudan in 1989, at the end of the Afghan war. From Sudan, he had launched a series of fatwas and declarations against both Arab governments in the region and the United States and its citizens. In Sudan, the Agency reported, Bin Laden had established a mutually beneficial relationship with the National Islamic Front then ruling the country.[19] For this reason, both the Saudi and the US government started exercising pressure on Sudanese authorities to do something about Bin Laden.[20]

US officials in Sudan faced a barrage of threats and harassment. Cofer Black, the CIA's chief of station in the country, was targeted for assassination by al-Qaeda operatives, as was Lake. At the time, Richard Clarke of the NSC complained that despite requests from the White House, the CIA proved unable to move beyond intelligence collection in Sudan and to arrange snatch operations against al-Qaeda operatives.[21] In turn, CIA officials in Sudan such as Black and Billy Waugh lamented that they were prevented from killing Bin Laden by both the Administration's legalistic approach and the lack of resources.[22]

Bureaucratic infighting aside, the CIA did conduct some daring collection operations. Ric Prado, for example, wore a mask that made him look like a black African and together with Black and Waugh collected intelligence on al-Qaeda in Khartoum.[23] The Agency had reportedly also acquired a secret document detailing

Osama Bin Laden: Assassination and Counterterrorism

al-Qaeda's request for help from the Sudanese government to acquire chemical weapons that could be used against US targets.[24] Based on the threats received by US officials, though, the Administration decided to close the US Embassy in Khartoum and to withdraw US personnel in February 1996.

In March, the US government communicated a series of measures that Sudan could have taken to improve relations with the United States; this included the provision of information on Bin Laden and other al-Qaeda operatives. No such information was provided. This tense relationship is likely to have contributed to the Administration's mistrust of a Sudanese government official's proposal to arrest or expel Bin Laden and – if needed – to send him home to Saudi Arabia.[25] Some reports also suggested that the same official had offered to hand him over to the United States, a view discounted by the 9/11 Commission.[26] The United States was not in a position to take hold of Bin Laden. Beyond his declarations of war, it was thought that Bin Laden had not (yet) attacked Americans – which ruled out any measure in self-defence – and there was no indictment against him.[27] Bin Laden was able to travel to Afghanistan.[28]

After his transfer to Afghanistan in 1996, Bin Laden settled in a decrepit former Soviet compound named Tarnak Farms.[29] Scheuer welcomed the move. A recent operation had rekindled the CIA's activities in the region.[30] Mir Aimal Kansi – the terrorist guilty of shooting CIA employees outside Langley – had fled to the border area between Afghanistan and Pakistan. With support from the Pakistani Intelligence Service and funds from headquarters, the CIA's Counter-Terrorism Center (CTC) recruited and equipped local tribal men. As the journalist Steve Coll reported, the tribals received 'mobile beacons that could be used to pinpoint the exact location of buildings by connecting to satellites hovering miles overhead. The technology would allow an American counterterrorism team to swarm an obscure location quickly once it was lit up by the Afghan agents.' Codenamed FD-TRODPINT, the tribals became 'lethal, exceptionally well-paid CIA bounty hunters'.[31] The tribals were not responsible for Kansi's capture,[32] but they were soon turned against Bin Laden.[33]

The Hunt Begins

In August 1997, Black updated George Tenet, who had by then replaced Deutch as DCI, on progress against Bin Laden. He told Tenet that the Agency and its assets had improved intelligence on 'his local movements, security arrangements and business activities'. '[Redacted]' (presumably the tribals' group) was 'near to providing real time information about Bin Laden's activities and travels in Afghanistan'.[34]

Working with Agency personnel, the tribals developed a capture plan. It entailed a surreptitious entry into the compound, the capture of Bin Laden, and his transfer to a cave where they could hide for some time with the prisoner. The time spent in the cave would permit them to calm the prisoner before he was taken in by US officials or friendly Arab governments.[35] The CIA was able to map the compound, identify the buildings where Bin Laden slept and those where his wives and children did. It conducted two early rehearsals of the plan in late 1997. The Agency also modified a shipping container to fit into a C-130 aircraft. Inside the container, the Agency placed a dentist's chair to hold Bin Laden during the transport. A retired Special Forces medic was also recruited to act as Bin Laden's doctor during the transport.[36]

In early 1998, with a federal grand jury in New York working on an indictment against Bin Laden, the CTC was confident enough to seek Tenet's and the White House's approval of the plan.[37] In February, Tenet briefed National Security Advisor Sandy Berger. The CTC noted the potential risks: people might be killed and/or US citizens in Kandahar might be taken hostage. But the Center stressed the importance of getting Bin Laden and the risks of inaction. In March, Bin Laden helped the CTC's case with a fatwa, signed by the World Islamic Front for Jihad Against Jews and Crusaders, which incited Muslims to kill Americans anywhere, 'to "shoot down their planes," "burn their corporations," and "sink their ships"'.[38]

After an additional rehearsal in the same month, disagreements started to appear. Having been briefed on the plan, Clarke expressed scepticism.[39] At the Bin Laden unit, Scheuer considered

Osama Bin Laden: Assassination and Counterterrorism

the plan 'the perfect operation'. It required minimal US presence and infrastructure and the tribals had also updated their plan, now keeping Bin Laden in a cave for up to a month, thus increasing the deniability of US government involvement.[40] Gary Schroen, the CIA Chief of Station in Pakistan, reported more mixed views in an email to Scheuer. Planning for the operation was going well. The plan was 'detailed, thoughtful, and realistic'. The team working on it was 'enthusiastic', but the odds of success were 'iffy'. The message concluded: 'Odds the op will get green light 50-50; odds it will succeed 40-60 (if we define success as ubl[41] either in custody or dead).'[42] Similarly mixed views emerged from the military.[43]

With the plan allowed to proceed, concerns started to appear among the Agency's leaders. On 18 May, the Agency reviewed the draft of a new Memorandum of Notification (MON) authorising the capture operation. The Reagan-era finding authorising global counterterrorism operations was still on the books and some viewed a new MON as unnecessary. Senior CIA managers – sensitive to charges of operating as a 'rogue elephant' – wanted something explicit on paper to authorise the operation.[44] In May 1998, John Rizzo drafted a MON authorising the CIA to provide support and funding for the tribals to capture Bin Laden and bring him to justice.[45] James Pavitt – assistant head of the Directorate of Operations – worried that the whole operation had 'at least a slight flavor of a plan for an assassination'. Pavitt's concerns regarding assassination were set aside. The Agency's leaders cleared the MON and sent it to the NSC.[46] In May, further rehearsals were successful. Clarke arranged meetings at the White House to discuss the plan, but the CIA's briefings reportedly left those in attendance unpersuaded.[47]

Three main sets of concerns seemingly sank the plan: a potential violation of the ban, civilian casualties and the nature of the mission. As to assassination, reflecting the views of those in the field, Schroen suggested that the death of Bin Laden was an acceptable outcome of the operation. CIA officials in the field seemed to operate under a version of the 'intent argument' that had informed the Agency's operations since the 1980s. As Coll writes, tribals and officials in the field knew that Bin Laden's compound was well protected. Any assault on the compound or kidnap attempt

307

would have likely caused a firefight. This was fine for CIA operatives – including the Islamabad case officer who briefed the tribals – if weapons were used during a 'reasonable effort to capture Bin Laden alive'. Officials at Langley in agreement with those in the field made sure to develop a paper trail that would document meetings with the tribals, and the instructions transmitted, thus providing legal cover. Everyone, including Schroen, expected that the tribals would kill Bin Laden during the operation.[48] But it was important to deny specific intent and have legal cover.

The senior leadership might have seen the situation differently. In the same years, these high-risk decisions had become more centralised, as the politically more sensitive CIA senior leadership wanted better control over operations.[49] Senior officials were reportedly worried that despite the Agency's personnel's best efforts 'a shootout could be seen as an as assassination'.[50] And yet, concerns about assassination had emerged within the leadership team at an earlier stage of the plan and had been set aside. A more pressing issue was potential collateral damage. Bin Laden's and his operatives' wives and children lived in the compound and an uncontrolled firefight might have caused an unacceptable level of civilian death, especially in case of failure. Attorney General Janet Reno – whose baptismism by fire had occurred with the FBI raid on the Branch Davidians in Waco, Texas which had killed several, including children – among others expressed this concern.[51]

The main showstopper was the nature of the operation itself, its chances of success, and its implications for the safety of the tribals, one of the Agency's prized assets. During a meeting with the US Attorney for the Southern District of New York, the head of CTC Jeff O'Connell had reduced the chances of success from Schroen's 40 per cent to 30 per cent.[51] Tenet recalled how all Agency officials in the chain of command counselled against the raid.[52] The Agency's Covert Action Review Group also counselled against it. They saw it – Michael Morell, then Tenet's Executive Assistant, recalled – as a 'poorly conceived plan . . . implausible'.[53] White House officials were similarly unconvinced. One expressed surprise at the amateurish nature of the plan. Clarke also remained unpersuaded: 'Am I missing something? Aren't these people going to be mowed down on their way to the wall?'[54] Tenet made the final call to cancel the raid,[55] something Clarke confirmed. The decision to call off the plan was a matter of practicalities, not legalities.[56]

* * *

With the plan shelved, on 22 May 1998 the Administration approved Presidential Decision Directive 62 , 'Protection Against Unconventional Threats to the Homeland and Americans Overseas'. The directive stressed the importance of counterterrorism and the global role of law enforcement in the apprehension and trial of terrorists. It also identified the CIA as the 'lead agency' for the disruption and pre-emption of terrorists 'consistent with US laws'. With the directive, the Administration established a new 'National Coordinator for Security, Infrastructure Protection, and Counter-Terrorism'. Having worked to push the directive through, Clarke reserved the role for himself. The Counter-terrorist Security Group (CSG) was already in existence, but the directive crystallised its role as the Administration's main policy and coordination group for counterterrorism.[57] Alongside this, a 'Small Group' chaired by National Security Advisor Sandy Berger, took a leading role in final counterterrorism decisions.[58]

On 5 August, a CSG meeting was convened to discuss Bin Laden; seemingly no one knew how to move forward.[59] Two days later, US officials were jolted into action. Almost simultaneously, bombs exploded outside the US embassies in Nairobi and Dar-es-Salaam: 224 people died in the blast, including 12 Americans, and more than 4,500 people were wounded.[60] As Berger recalled, the bombings were a real 'wake-up call'.[61]

Bombing Bin Laden: The Administration's View on Assassination and the Use of Force

On 8 August, one day after the bombings, Tenet notified Clarke that Bin Laden, his lieutenants and other terrorists were soon to gather at a training camp in Khowst, Afghanistan. Clarke related to Berger that Bin Laden was 'planning terrorist conference on August 20'.[62] In a follow-up Principals meeting, Tenet and the CIA

309

described the Khowst camp as primarily a jihadist target, thus easing the concerns about civilian casualties. Sitting next to Tenet, Clarke passed him a handwritten note: 'You thinking what I'm thinking?' Tenet replied: 'You better believe I am.'[63] On the 14th, Tenet confirmed that Bin Laden was among the prime suspects for the Embassy bombings. In secret briefings, Tenet also explained how several leading extremists were expected to be at Khowst. A strike at the camp would disrupt Bin Laden's organisation. In case of his death, the organisation might splinter, but retaliation against US citizens could ensue.[64]

On 20 August, under the name Operation Infinite Reach, Navy vessels in the Arabian Sea fired cruise missiles against the training camp and – controversially – against al-Shifa, a pharmaceutical facility in Sudan. The factory was destroyed. The missiles struck the training camp at 10 p.m. but missed Bin Laden – reportedly warned by the Pakistani Inter-Services Intelligence (ISI) – by a few hours.[65] In a televised speech, Clinton provided four main justifications for the strike: the targeted groups had played a role in the Embassy bombings, they had attacked Americans in the past, they were planning additional terrorist attacks, and they were seeking to acquire weapons of mass destruction.[66] When it came to admitting whether the strike had personally targeted Bin Laden, US officials initially hesitated.

On the 21st, Chairman of the Joint Chiefs of Staff Hugh Shelton declared that the training camp could be considered the equivalent of military headquarters, 'a command-and-control node'.[67] In a throwback to Operation El Dorado Canyon, and to the intent argument, Defense Secretary William Cohen stated that the United States had no specific knowledge of Bin Laden's whereabouts. Killing him was 'not our design', he added.[68] And yet, asked whether Bin Laden was personally targetable, he replied: 'To the extent that he or his organization have declared war upon the United States or our interests, then he certainly is engaged in an act of war,' and thus he was targetable.[69]

One day later, Berger publicly admitted that the strike had been timed to coincide with a gathering of terrorists and that the expectation was that Bin Laden would attend such a meeting. The strike, Berger explained, was legal. The training camp was a military target.

Osama Bin Laden: Assassination and Counterterrorism

The strike could be justified as a use of force in self-defence, following Article 51 of the UN Charter, and it also complied with Congress's 1996 law asking the President to take 'all necessary measures' against terrorists.[70] Clinton had followed War Power Resolution requirements, sharing intelligence with Congress and notifying members of Congress of the strike.[71]

In Washington, the early support Clinton had gathered for the strikes quickly vanished. Some asked whether attempting to strike at Bin Laden and failing might contribute to radicalising more individuals. Questions started to emerge as to the quality of intelligence regarding the targeting of al-Shifa.[72] Finally, the strike, like Operation Desert Fox (discussed in the previous chapter) coincided with the President's impeachment trial. Building on the then popular movie *Wag the Dog*, Republicans started to accuse the President of inflating the threat posed by al-Qaeda and using military force to distract from his impeachment proceedings. These criticisms influenced the Administration and contributed to its unwillingness to conduct further strikes.[73] A series of follow-on strikes developed by Shelton under the name Operation Infinite Resolve never took place.[74]

* * *

In this partisan atmosphere, the ban on assassination became – once again – an object of public debate and secret (re)assessment. This contestation was – in part – a partisan tool to criticise the Administration's alleged weakness. But by this stage, the contestation of the ban had also become more explicit. Intellectuals and former policymakers engaged in validity contestation, challenging the appropriateness of the ban for the conduct of US foreign policy, as well as the ban's morality. After the strike at Khowst, former military intelligence official Ralph Peters lamented that the United States had been crippled in the fight against terrorism and it should have abandoned legal niceties.[75] Paul Bremer similarly warned that the US needed to plan for a 'dirty war'. Among the measures to take, he listed revoking the ban on assassination.[76] Friendly fire was also in the air when George Stephanopoulos, who had just left the Clinton Administration, asked whether bombing wasn't an immoral solution risking unnecessary loss of life when the objective was to kill an individual.[77]

Bipartisan calls to review the ban also started coming from Congress. Towards the end of August, Orrin Hatch (R-UT), Chairman of the House Judiciary Committee, claimed that: 'There should be nothing that should not be on the table when it comes to fighting terrorists.'[78] In September, a bipartisan group of lawmakers questioned whether the restrictions imposed by the ban should have been reviewed. Senator Joseph Biden, then ranking minority member of the Senate Foreign Relations Committee, wrote to Attorney General Reno asking for clarifications about the ban. Republican Representative Bob Barr of Georgia, then sitting on the House Banking, Judiciary, and Government Reform Committee, tried to go further, pushing for new legislation that would revoke the ban. With the threat of terrorism increasing, he argued, the surgical 'removal of terrorist or hostile foreign leaders' was a weapon the United States needed in its arsenal.[79] The bill went nowhere.

While this debate was playing out publicly, within the Administration a group of lawyers had started to meet regularly to discuss counterterrorism operations.[80] Before the strike on Khowst, an internal legal review was conducted on the ban on assassination and on the permissibility of targeting Bin Laden. In a largely overlooked episode, an inter-agency group led by Assistant Attorney General Randy Moss produced a secret and still classified Memorandum of Law on assassination. The memorandum concluded that presidents like Reagan and Bush had been unnecessarily cautious in targeting enemy headquarters even when the actual objective was to kill an individual. Article 51 of the UN Charter and the inherent powers of the President under the Constitution (Article 2 Section 2) permitted the President to kill an enemy of the United States in self-defence, regardless of who the enemy was.[81] For this reason, there was no need to suspend, waive or revoke the ban on assassination.[82]

As the review took place, US officials started airing some of its findings in the press. One official – on condition of anonymity – revealed the bottom line, going back to the Parks memorandum. 'Lawful use of force in self-defense,' the official stated, 'is not assassination.'[83] In November 1998, investigative journalist James Risen revealed more details of the review. US officials were quoted stating that – based on an internal review – they had concluded that the United States had a right to strike at terrorist leaders in self-defence. Building this time on Sofaer's precedents, NSC spokesman David Leavy also stated that the 'Command and control of an enemy is a justifiable target.' And a top US counter-terrorism official stated – unironically – that in the case of terrorist groups the infrastructure is mostly 'human'.[84]

Like previous reinterpretations, this review represented an effort at contesting the ban to permit the preferred policy option. It also represented a case of secret law reshaping the conduct of US foreign policy. The partial public disclosure of information that followed the review provided US officials with the opportunity to legitimate their foreign policy choices without fully revealing the reasoning behind them.[85] Certainly, thanks to the legal review, few doubts remained that the US military was authorised to kill Bin Laden with a missile strike. According to Risen, based on the same legal review Clinton had also authorised intelligence agencies to use 'lethal' force as they carried out covert operations against Bin Laden.[86] The extent of these authorities became the object of endless recriminations.

A Game of MONs: Bin Laden, Covert Operations, and Assassination

In August 1998, as the Administration was reviewing the ban on assassination and firming up the justifications for a strike on Bin Laden, Clinton had signed a Memorandum of Notification (MON) authorising the CIA to work with the tribals to capture Bin Laden. The memorandum authorised them to use force, but only in self-defence. According to Rizzo, the Agency official drafting the MONs, such a requirement had a place in criminal law, but not in a MON.[87] The White House viewed it differently. Having conducted its internal review, the Administration aimed at utilising the same language in the MONs. As National Security Advisor Berger later put it, this MON, like all others, was 'authorized under the Law of

Armed Conflict', and this is how the Administration understood its confrontation with Bin Laden.[88]

From the field, the tribals reported that they had tried several ambushes, but CIA officials did not trust that any of the operations had taken place.[89] Since the tribals' difficulties and reciprocal mistrust were increasing, alternatives were developed. After the Embassy bombings, the White House had ordered the deployment of vessels and submarines armed with cruise missiles to the Arabian Sea. The White House hoped that the tribals – using technology the CIA had provided – could track Bin Laden and report to Langley his location, permitting the United States to strike. The aim of this type of operation was to kill Bin Laden, but the process was a time-consuming one. As former CIA official Mike Hurley put it, the 'TRODPINTS' (tribals) would spot Bin Laden and report with 'whatever method they were using' to Islamabad Station, who would cable into Headquarters on a FLASH basis; the message would make its way to the Director; the Director would notify the principals who would meet or gather by phone to decide. The missiles themselves would take time to get to Afghanistan.[90] The time that would elapse between notification and targeting was somewhere between four and six hours.[91]

With months passing, Clinton was reportedly becoming frustrated at the lack of progress against Bin Laden. At one point, he told Berger to put together a plan that went beyond retaliation. 'We gotta get rid of these guys once and for all . . . You understand what I am telling you?' he asked Tenet, Berger and Cohen in language encountered throughout this book.[92] Clarke started working on a broader plan – codenamed Delenda (to be destroyed) – which envisaged a series of economic, covert and military measures to eliminate Bin Laden and al-Qaeda.[93] Clarke's plan included the continuation of military strikes against al-Qaeda's infrastructure, beyond the narrow focus on Bin Laden. In September, he wrote to Steven Simon in the NSC that the aim was to 'keep the UBL network off base' and to show that the strike on 20 August was not a 'one-off'. Clarke recognised that there were so few targets connected to Bin Laden that Simon 'may also want to give some thought to planning, at least, strikes on Taliban high value targets to place pressure on them to give up UBL'. The US government should have moved away from any hope of another 'Appalachian conference'; a large gathering of terrorists was unlikely to happen again.[94]

* * *

In November 1998, the Agency recommended to 'revitalize [redacted][95] effort by providing more direct tasking which would allow them to directly assault his quarters'. This was better than a capture attempt on the road and would suit better the tribals' fighting expertise. A second option was to enlist Ahmed Shah Massoud and his Northern Alliance then fighting against the Taliban. Massoud seemed like a more competent partner.[96] A summary in the same weeks listed three declassified options to attack Bin Laden: an ambush using the tribals, a raid on one of his residences, and the use of the US military. Collateral damage featured as the main downsides of the raid and military options.[97]

At the start of December, Tenet sent a memorandum to CIA leaders: 'We must redouble our efforts against Bin Ladin himself, his infrastructure, followers, finances etc. with a sense of enormous urgency.' It continued: 'We are at war. I want no resources or people spared in this effort, either inside CIA or the Community.'[98] Tenet's call to action failed to make waves.[99] Later investigations found that Tenet failed to provide the additional funds and personnel required to fight such a war. Furthermore, in an era of tight budgets, the CTC had not even spent all its money and Tenet – despite calling for a war on al-Qaeda – often transferred money away from counterterrorism priorities.[100]

If the war memo failed to have an impact, the intelligence work of the tribals seemed to bear fruit. On 18 December, the CIA reported that Bin Laden was travelling to Kandahar. Two days later, intelligence confirmed that Bin Laden would be spending the night at the Haji Habash house, part of the governor's residence. Having heard that the principals were considering a strike, Schroen sent a strong message to Scheuer: 'Hit him tonight – we might not get another chance.' The principals met to discuss using cruise missiles to hit Bin Laden. Concerns about collateral damage quickly emerged; a nearby mosque could also be damaged. The principals agreed not to go ahead.[101] Perhaps exaggerating the number of casualties, Clinton later reflected on his decision: 'I nearly got him. And I could have killed him, but I would have to destroy a little town called Kandahar in Afghanistan and kill 300 innocent women and children, and then I would have been no better than him. And so, I didn't do it.'[102]

Once again, Tenet had been at the forefront of the decision not to go ahead. He had doubts about the reliability of the intelligence, which was based on a single source, and he recalled the risk of hitting a mosque.[103] When he reported to CIA officials in the Bin Laden unit and in the field, Tenet tended to blame the military and the White House.[104] This contributed to fostering mistrust between the Agency – especially its officials closer to the action – and the White House. Schroen wrote that he had expected the cancellation and that the increased security around Bin Laden now made a raid even harder.[105] Scheuer replied expressing similar discontent. 'I'm sure we'll regret not acting last night. This is the third time you and your officers have put UBL in this govt's sights and yet they have balked each time.' There was an element of 'unreality', according to Scheuer, in the 'out-of-Langley' deliberations. The principals spent too much time considering the risks of 'shrapnel' hitting the mosque and offending Muslims, but no similar concerns had emerged when it came to bombing Iraq.[106]

Perhaps due to a concern with collateral damage, the legal counsel to the National Security Advisor and Clarke worked on an additional MON for the Agency. This time, the MON reportedly permitted the Agency or the Pentagon to shoot down Bin Laden's helicopters or aircraft under certain circumstances.[107] Coll speculated that such an approach might have fitted with Clinton's preference for the use of 'lethal force' against Bin Laden and other key operatives, especially if it could be carried out in an 'immaculate' manner.[108] According to Shelton, the plan entailed shooting down a civilian aircraft carrying Bin Laden,[109] not a particularly immaculate proposition. It is unclear whether any step was taken pursuant to this MON.

Towards the end of December, Tenet and the White House started working on a new, more radical MON. The authority being developed initially envisaged that the tribals were authorised to capture Bin Laden and that they could use 'lethal force' in a capture attempt only if this increased the chances of success. An early draft on 21 December, restating this authority, included a disclaimer that the tribals would be paid only if they had correctly followed the instructions. Three days later, Tenet and Berger concluded that more expansive authorities were required.[110] On Christmas Eve 1998, Clinton signed a new one-page addition to the MON. This addition allowed the killing of Bin Laden if the CIA and/or the tribals assessed that capture was not feasible. The document was so secret that it was shared with only a few individuals. Berger asked the NSC legal adviser to only inform Albright, Cohen, Shelton and Reno; no one was allowed to keep a copy.[111]

In this context, Reno is often identified as one of the main obstacles the CIA confronted in the hunt for Bin Laden. According to Coll, Reno opposed broad 'lethal' authorities for the CIA and her opposition mattered both because Berger wanted a consensus on counterterrorism decisions and because the language the Administration was working in was in 'uncomfortable proximity' to the ban. News stories revealing Reno's opposition might also have damaged an already embattled president.[112] According to Rizzo, the CIA official behind the MONs, Reno's objections 'intimidated' CIA officials who took them as a sign that – if things went wrong – they were on their own. And yet, as Rizzo admitted, Reno's opposition to the plans was on policy grounds rather than about the ban.[113] Reno was not opposed to 'lethal' authorities if Bin Laden posed an 'imminent threat'. More broadly, the Justice Department expected that any operation would lead to a shoot-out in which Bin Laden would be killed. Congressional leaders were also briefed about this change of pace in the covert operations against Bin Laden.[114]

The President and White House officials – including Berger and Clarke – clearly understood the Christmas Eve MON as an authorisation to kill Bin Laden. As Clarke put it:

> We were able to get the President of the United States to change years of precedent, which said we couldn't do assassinations, wouldn't have hit lists, and he overcame all of that history and authorized CIA to establish a hit list with bin Laden's name on it.[115]

For CIA officials including Black and Scheuer, this was not the case.[116] The authorities were not as clear cut.[117] After all, the MON still contained the phrase 'if capture is not feasible'. It was unclear what feasibility implied and who would have to decide whether capture was feasible or not. In this view, the MON was 'fuzzy' in the most important area: the conditions for a kill.[118] As Scheuer later put it, 'We always talked about how much easier it would have been to kill him.'[119]

The text of the MON remains classified. And yet, during the 9/11 Commission investigation, staffers and the executive director, Philip Zelikow, hardly a Clinton sympathiser, had access to the text. According to Zelikow, the document provided 'kill authority'. 'It was one of the most sensitive and extraordinary documents signed out during President Clinton's time in office,' he admitted. Early drafts of the document had been amended precisely to remove any space for ambiguity. The MON clarified that if a capture operation was not feasible, the tribals could conduct an 'operation to kill' Bin Laden. 'There were no euphemisms in the language,' Zelikow concluded.[120]

Zelikow did question whether Clinton was fully committed to a kill operation. Perhaps Berger had persuaded him,[121] but Clinton had signed the MON giving the Agency and its assets kill authority. Having looked at the communications from the Agency to the Chief of Station in Islamabad and then to the assets, Alexis Albion, the Commission's chief investigator on the CIA and its activities, reached a similar conclusion. While the MON was read to the tribals word for word, it 'was the clearest communication that you may kill him, without being in the context of a capture operation'.[122] The authorities granted in the 1998 Christmas Eve MON became a moot point. Neither the CIA nor the tribals developed the capabilities or a plan to kill Bin Laden.[123]

The lack of progress with the tribals and the concerns with civilian casualties led various branches of the military to consider additional options for efforts targeted at Bin Laden. These included smaller aircraft and/or the deployment of Special Forces. For a mixture of political (military contempt for civilians),[124] intelligence (lack of actionable intelligence), cultural (Desert One and Black Hawk Down precedents) and strategic (basing rights and resources) reasons, no long-term planning or serious consideration to use Special Forces emerged before 9/11.[125]

* * *

Osama Bin Laden: Assassination and Counterterrorism

A new opportunity to hit Bin Laden with cruise missiles appeared in early 1999. The ban on assassination was no obstacle. The CIA shared intelligence that Bin Laden was visiting an area in the Afghan desert south of Kandahar. It soon became apparent that the isolated area was a high-tech, all-comforts bustard-hunting camp. The CIA was able to mark the camp with beacons and obtain GPS coordinates. On 8 February, intelligence confirmed the location of the camp. It also showed the presence of an official aircraft of the United Arab Emirates (UAE) near the camp. The Agency concluded that Sheikh Ali was the host.[126] On the ground, the tribals started observing Bin Laden from a distance. The Agency reportedly had an asset inside the camp itself and concluded that the best day to target Bin Laden was 11 February when the al-Qaeda leader would be visiting the camp for a few hours.[127] Based on this information, the military started preparing the strike.

CIA officials closer to the action were – as usual – sanguine about the opportunity to strike. 'Let's just blow the thing up,' Schroen claimed. 'And if we kill bin Laden, and five sheikhs are killed, I'm sorry. What are they doing with bin Laden? He's a terrorist. You lie down with the dog, you get up with fleas.' The CTC and the Bin Laden unit were also in favour.[128]

Tenet and Clarke were primarily behind the decision not to go ahead. Tenet came to have doubts regarding the quality of the intelligence. Clarke, who had visited the UAE only a few days earlier, worried about the risks of hitting targets connected to what he saw as one of the US government's best partners in the fight against terrorism. These justifications did not convince the CTC or the Bin Laden unit.[129] Far from it. Scheuer later accused Clarke of having hijacked the operation by talking to UAE authorities about Bin Laden's presence at the camp, which caused the camp to be quickly dismantled.[130]

A similar episode occurred in May 1999. Several sources of intelligence confirmed that Bin Laden would visit Kandahar for a few days. Once again the military prepared a strike and once again CIA officials in the Bin Laden unit and in the field pushed for it. The strikes were called off. CIA working-level officials were told that the military and the White House were concerned about the precision of the bombing (the United States had just hit the

Chinese Embassy in Belgrade) and about the quality of the intelligence. Scheuer expressed anger at the failure to hit Bin Laden despite having at least three opportunities in thirty-six hours. As he put it, Tenet was 'alone at the table' and the principals in the Administration were ready to blame him if something went wrong.[131] Ironically, though, Tenet was not at the table. He missed a crucial meeting in which the (potential) strikes were discussed. His assessment of the quality of the intelligence, a 50-50 chance of success, also helped sink the plan. This was the last time a cruise missile strike against Bin Laden was considered until after 9/11.[132]

* * *

This did not mean that plans against him stopped altogether. In mid-1999, Cofer Black became the new head of the CTC. At this juncture, the President also authorised a still obscure 'covert action under carefully limited circumstances which, if successful, would have resulted in Bin Ladin's death'.[133] In July, Clinton extended the Agency's authorities to work with other governments to capture Bin Laden. In particular, the US government had been exercising pressure on Pakistan to do something about the Taliban and Bin Laden.

Back in December 1998, during a meeting between Clinton and Pakistan's prime minister Nawaz Sharif, the latter raised the possibility of training a secret commando team to bring Bin Laden to justice. This would be composed of recently retired Pakistani Special Forces. The plan had initially been put on the back burner.[134] In July, during another meeting between the two, when Clinton pressed the Pakistani authorities to do more against Bin Laden, Sharif went back to his earlier proposal. This time, the plan received a green light. The CIA started training and equipping sixty commandos from Pakistan's intelligence agencies and special forces. By October, the forces were ready to go into action. US officials saw this as a real opportunity to kill Bin Laden. 'It was like Christmas,' one reportedly stated.[135] The plan conformed to previous indirect approaches to assassination adopted by the US government. The aim was for the US government to collaborate with a third party, in this case the government of Pakistan, and to have somebody else pull the trigger. The plan was hastily abandoned

Osama Bin Laden: Assassination and Counterterrorism

when Pervez Musharraf replaced Sharif in a military coup.[136] Once again, an assassination plan was seemingly undone by the changing political fortunes of US allies. The Pakistani commandos were not the only force the Agency had recruited to fight Bin Laden.

Massoud and the CIA: New Controversies Surrounding Assassination?

In February 1999, the Agency started working on a new MON to define the working relationship between the CIA and Massoud's Northern Alliance. In preparing a draft, Rizzo had used the same language of the last MON for the tribals: kill if capture is not feasible. The MON, though, became (in)famous due to Clinton's decision to personally make changes to the language of the Agency's authorities. According to Rizzo, Clinton's changes meant that the authorities were limited to using force only in self-defence. For Rizzo, again, this was the sign of a President willing to equivocate on the most sensitive part of the Agency's authorities. Clinton had given more authorities to a group (the tribals) that had no chance of getting Bin Laden, and stricter authorities to a group (Massoud's forces) that – or so some in the CIA thought – had better chances.[137] Tenet viewed the episode somewhat differently. He agreed that the language was closer to the August 1998 MON, that is, before a 'lethal' authority, and it expressed a preference for capture, but the authorities also accepted 'the possibility that Bin Laden could not be brought out alive'. 'We were plowing [sic] the same ground,' as he put it. Clinton later made the dubious claim that he did not recall why he made the change. The new, more conservative language, though, shaped the work of operatives on the ground.[138]

In the autumn of 1999 the Agency approved 'The Plan', a new strategy to revamp the effort against al-Qaeda. It included the recruitment of new assets and new – crucially, non-white and non-Western – officers, better training, better intelligence collection, and an increase in rendition operations.[139] In the same months, Black also received approval from Clarke to send a new team of CTC officials to liaise with Massoud. The team aimed at putting the collaboration – started in 1997 – on a stronger footing. Taking the name JAWBREAKER-5, the team worked to train, equip and expand Massoud's intelligence services and forces.[140] Tenet reported in November 1999 that the 'initial locational reporting' from Massoud's group was promising, and it offered the Bin Laden unit the opportunity of moving past single-threaded sources of intelligence.[141]

When they met Massoud, US officials stressed that – as much as they agreed with his view regarding the need to take the fight to the Taliban – that was not the US mission at the time. They had narrower instructions. The United States wanted Bin Laden captured or (if that proved impossible) dead. Massoud and his forces could kill Bin Laden but only as part of a capture operation.[142] Reportedly, this created difficulties for the case officers who had to report these instructions to the local allies.[143] After hearing these instructions, Massoud laughed. 'You Americans are crazy,' He told his briefers. 'You guys never change.'[144] These legal technicalities and fig leaves might have made sense in Washington and Langley, but they showed a detachment from the reality on the ground.

This was evidenced in an episode involving Massoud in late 1999 or early 2000. The Agency notified Massoud that Bin Laden had arrived at the Derunta military camp near Jalalabad. Having received the intelligence, Massoud sent out a commando team on mules, armed with Soviet-designed Katyusha rockets. According to Coll, the news of Massoud's commando team sent the Bin Laden unit at Langely into a state of frenzied concern.[145] Some thought that – by sharing intelligence with Massoud on Bin Laden's location – they were violating the ban on assassination.[146] A message was immediately sent to Massoud asking him to recall the mission. The Agency only had the authority to kill Bin Laden in the context of a capture operation. As a US official put it, Massoud's aides were incredulous. Their reply amounted to: 'What do you think this is, the Eighty-Second Airborne? We're on mules. They're gone.' Nothing came of the mule expedition, but the episode led Massoud to question the extent of US support.[147] While pressure from the CTC to improve collaboration continued[148] and while some planning did take place, no new operation was contemplated with Massoud's forces until after 9/11.[149]

Tenet did not recall any assassination controversy at the time. The Derunta episode coincided with a state of heightened tension and activity within the intelligence community surrounding the so-called 'Millennium plot', a thwarted multipronged attack by al-Qaeda operatives towards the end of December 1999.[150]

The Predator and the Prey

Despite successfully countering al-Qaeda during the 'Millennium plot', sometime between the end of 1999 and early 2000 Clinton expressed his frustration at the lack of progress against Bin Laden. In February, Berger sent a memorandum to the President detailing the progress made in the fight against terrorism. Clinton made notes expressing his dissatisfaction. Having seen the memorandum and Clinton's comments, Clarke made copies and used them to spur the bureaucracy into action.[151] One of the measures pushed by Clarke was the adoption and deployment of the Predator drone in the hunt for Bin Laden. The Predator had been used successfully for surveillance purposes in the Balkans and Iraq.[152] Clarke was also keen to establish a connection between the drone and the missiles deployed in the Persian Gulf. This would have reduced the time that elapsed between spotting and hitting Bin Laden. In the spring of 2000, a CIA–Pentagon project, codenamed 'Afghan Eyes', started to work on the deployment of the Predator drone in Afghanistan.[153]

After some initial bureaucratic rivalries regarding cost-sharing,[154] Berger wrote to Clinton noting the President's earlier frustration and identifying the lack of actionable intelligence as the main reason for failure. He notified him of the start of the Predator programme over Afghanistan and of the fact that he had asked Clarke to work on how to bring issues for decisions to Clinton in case the intelligence could establish Bin Laden's pattern of movement.[155] Berger made clear that he would have wanted more than a simple spotting of the terrorist leader; a pattern of life needed to emerge before a strike.[156]

On 7 September 2000, the first Predator flew over Afghanistan, out of a secret US base in Uzbekistan called K2.[157] Flights continued throughout September and October. Three times, the drone reportedly spotted a tall man in white robes surrounded by a security detail. CIA officials came to believe it was Bin Laden.[158] The drone, at this stage, was still solely a surveillance platform, and the CIA's insistence on deploying it on a 'proof of concept' basis meant that the Predator's intelligence could not be used to deploy missiles nor to inform the tribals.[159]

In late 2000, as the Predator development continued, the Agency expanded its networks on the ground and its intelligence collection capabilities when it came to Bin Laden's training camps. And yet, the conservative language of the authorities seemingly still shaped its activities. According to CIA Chief of Station in Islamabad Robert Grenier, CIA officials reportedly had to shut down a plan developed by one of their tribal networks to 'bury a huge quantity of explosives' at a road junction used by Bin Laden, to be set off as his motorcade travel through. This, Grenier argues, would have violated the CIA's authorities at the time and requirement to steer clear of any specific intent to assassinate.[160]

* * *

On 12 October 2000, al-Qaeda struck the USS *Cole* in the Gulf of Aden. Within the Clinton Administration, then approaching its last months in office, the attack engendered a heated debate regarding the nature of the response.[161] In a memo to Robert Cressey, Clarke tried to push for a more forcible response, suggesting that in the past the conclusion of intelligence investigations had been enough for a president to act, without waiting for evidence that satisfied a law enforcement approach.[162] Certainty of al-Qaeda's culpability would not be forthcoming. Like the hunt for Lumumba, the hunt for Bin Laden also intersected with domestic politics. The 2000 presidential campaign and the elections influenced the decision to delay any retaliation. A failed attack on Bin Laden would have affected Gore's chances of being elected. In the partisan atmosphere of the time, increased by the controversy surrounding the vote recount, the Administration also lacked the domestic (and international) support to take the war to al-Qaeda and the Taliban.[163]

Osama Bin Laden: Assassination and Counterterrorism

Even if drone strikes were put temporarily on hold due to close encounters with the Taliban's air force and bad weather,[164] Clarke, his deputy Cressey, and Black started viewing with interest the idea of weaponising the Predator. General John P. Jumper, then in charge of Air Combat Command, was put to work to develop this new capability.[165] This development encountered bureaucratic opposition and legal obstacles.[166]

The Pentagon was uninterested in weaponising the drone. If an operation had to be carried out, the Pentagon preferred that it be done with cruise missiles.[167] This option, however, had been ruled out. The Navy had been successful in obtaining the withdrawal of submarines from the Persian Gulf.[168] Institutional and cultural factors also influenced the Pentagon's stance.[169] The Air Force's cult of the fighter pilot meant that the idea of missions carried out by pilot-less drones was met with scepticism.[170] Senior leadership of the CIA was also unenthusiastic.[171] As to international legal concerns, a weaponised drone – or so it was initially thought – risked violating the US government's obligations under the Intermediate Nuclear Forces Treaty, which prohibited the United States from acquiring long-range cruise missiles. This concern was quickly set aside after a legal review, and it did not obstruct the Predator's development or deployment.[172]

While the technology itself and the fitting of the right missiles posed problems, the main hurdle remained concerns about the chain of command. Who had the right to order a strike? Who was supposed to pull the trigger? Tenet was sceptical it should be the CIA. 'Are America's leaders comfortable with the CIA doing this outside of normal military command and control?' When Charles Allen, the CIA's Assistant Director for collection, and A. B. Krongard, the Agency's number three, told Tenet they would be happy to pull the trigger, he shot them down, telling them they did not have the authority.[173] These questions remained on the agenda towards the end of the Clinton Administration.

In December, Berger asked Tenet to prepare a new memorandum on how the Agency would behave and what it would need if there were no constraints. The so-called Blue Sky memo concluded that there was no easy solution to the problem of al-Qaeda and recommended that operations be stepped up. Measures from the weaponisation of the Predator to stronger links with local allies and regional secret services featured in the recommendations.[174] On 29 December, Clarke finalised a document called 'Strategy for Eliminating the Threat from the Jihadist Network of al-Qida [*sic*]: Status and Prospects'. Building on the Blue Sky memo, Clarke advocated for a ramped-up approach to covert operations, including the use of armed Predators, expanded support for the Northern Alliance, and potential overt US military action.[175] Part of the plan, Clarke recalled, was to strike at al-Qaeda as an organisation and to kill its leaders without necessarily creating an ever-expanding 'hit list'.[176]

In the same month, some in Congress were reconsidering whether a weakening of the ban on assassination could provide an effective tool in the fight against terrorism. Congressman Barr continued his campaign against the ban and on 3 January 2001 proposed new legislation. The 'Terrorist Elimination Act of 2001' aimed at revoking obligations established by Executive Orders and at permitting US intelligence agencies and the US military to eliminate specific terrorist leaders.[177] The bill did not pass.

* * *

During the early months of the George W. Bush Administration, while some officials later denied the accusation,[178] counterterrorism took a back seat. The new team adopted a more sceptical view of the threat posed by non-state terrorist groups, preferring to focus instead on more traditional great power politics.[179] Certainly, any counterterrorism action was hampered by the decision to engage in a full policy review which moved at glacial pace.

The threat of terrorism, though, was increasing. Progress in weaponising drones also continued. On 23 January, a successful test with a Hellfire missile was carried out. Two days later, Clarke sent his 'Strategy' document to National Security Advisor Condoleezza Rice.[180] He warned that al-Qaeda was not 'some narrow, little terrorist issue' and the Administration's decision to proceed with compartmentalised policies on Central Asia risked missing the big picture. Two decisions remained pending: whether to help the Northern Alliance and whether to support Uzbekistan. Other issues included what to do with Pakistan and the Taliban, how to respond to the USS *Cole* attack, and whether to expand CIA and counterterrorism budgets and programmes. Clarke called for an urgent meeting of the principals to iron out these policy issues.[181]

In March, based on insistent requests from Clarke, Rice asked the CIA to work on a new set of authorities that would supersede the various findings and MONs of the Clinton era. The Agency prepared two documents: a broader finding that authorised the expansion of covert support for local allies, and a new MON. The MON 'included more open-ended language authorizing possible lethal action in a variety of situations'. The Agency's briefing material for Tenet made clear that the new authorities aimed at giving the CIA as much authority as permitted under the law.[182] And yet the finding (and MON), as well as the potential operations that could have gone with it, were put on hold.[183] In May, Rice and Tenet met with Clarke, Black and the chief of the Bin Laden unit. The aim was to develop a more aggressive policy towards al-Qaeda, but no major difference emerged with the policies of the Clinton era.[184]

Throughout the late spring and summer of 2001, while the CIA and the intelligence community kept raising alarms about a major potential terrorist strike, the search for better intelligence and a cleaner option against Bin Laden passed through the Predator drone. In June 2001, the Agency built a replica of Bin Laden's compound at Tarnak Farms in the Nevada desert. A Hellfire missile obliterated the compound. Cressey at the NSC was jubilant, but his satisfaction was short-lived. The Agency and the Pentagon continued to question whether weaponised drones could do the job. Tenet remained squeamish at the idea of putting the CIA in a trigger-pulling role. The Pentagon continued its bureaucratic opposition.[185] At the same time, Tenet and Black called again for the expanded covert authorities they had requested in March.[186]

Disagreements within the Administration regarding the urgency of deploying the newly weaponised drone continued.[187] Bush recalled that legal and political obstacles were not an issue. In the Administration there was an 'appetite for killing Bin Laden', albeit not to go to war against al-Qaeda.[188] Secretary of Defense Donald Rumsfeld and Secretary of State Colin Powell later made similar points. The political and legal arguments had been settled but the missing ingredient was intelligence. There was no 'opportunity to kill, capture or otherwise neutralize Osama Bin Ladin' due to a lack of 'targetable information'.[189]

While an element of post hoc rationalisation is perhaps present in these recollections, in the early summer of 2001, meetings had started to assess whether to use the armed Predator and what type of intelligence was needed for a strike. Everyone agreed to strike at Bin Laden in clear-cut circumstances. More reticence emerged in situations in which the intelligence did not make clear who was surrounding him. As Predator historian Richard Whittle put it, though, 'despite the existence of secret presidential orders, findings, and other directives', Tenet was still unsure whether the Agency had the legal authority to strike at Bin Laden.[190]

On 1 August 2001, the issue was resolved. The Deputies Committee met and, like its predecessors in the Clinton Administration, concluded that a strike against Bin Laden did not constitute assassination and did not violate Executive Order 12333. John Bellinger, then Senior Associate Counsel to the President and Legal Adviser to the National Security Council, was heavily involved in these debates. The ban on assassination, he recalled, was a consideration, but it was concluded that the ban did not apply and that targeting Bin Laden was legitimate since it was an act of self-defence and Bin Laden was not a foreign leader.[191]

Bureaucratic rivalries over costs and uncertainty as to who had the authority to take the – now legally cleared – shot continued to stall the armed Predator's deployment.[192] The urgent meeting of principals to discuss al-Qaeda that Clarke had called for in January 2001 only occurred on 4 September. The meeting discussed and approved a draft of the presidential directive against terrorism. No final decision was taken on the deployment of the weaponised drone. State was in favour. The Pentagon and Paul Wolfowitz recommended a larger strike on Bin Laden, closer to the Reagan Administration's 1986 bombing of Libya. The armed Predator drone was considered something that would have become fully operational only in the spring of 2002. The meeting did approve expanded covert authorities for the CIA based on the documents drafted by the Agency months earlier.[193] On 10 September 2001, Hadley asked Tenet to again review the covert operation authorities of the CIA since the policy review and the presidential directive on terrorism were close to completion.

Osama Bin Laden: Assassination and Counterterrorism

One day later, the al-Qaeda attack the CIA had long dreaded came. A 'day of fire,' as Bush would later call it in his memoirs.[194]

Conclusion

Reviewing the pre-9/11 hunt for Bin Laden, the analysis above has tried to debunk the still persistent myth that the Clinton Administration only had a 'law enforcement' approach to counterterrorism.[195] Both the White House and the CIA were active against terrorism. In making this point, the analysis has decoupled two often conflated dimensions. It seems clear that the Clinton and Bush administrations did not consider the ban on assassination as an obstacle when it came to direct assassination attempts against Bin Laden. Targeting Bin Laden using US forces, cruise missiles and, eventually, drone strikes was understood as permissible. The Clinton team's internal legal review concluded that this represented an act of self-defence.[196] For these operations, much depended on the quality and timeliness of the intelligence provided and on the number of civilian casualties caused by a strike.[197]

The real controversy surrounds more indirect assassination attempts and the authorities given to the CIA when it came to operating with the tribals and Massoud's forces. Here, as in the Castro episode, the main question surrounds political control and authorisations. Enough evidence exists to show that – at least on one occasion[198] – the Agency had an unequivocal authority to kill Bin Laden. The 1998 Christmas Eve MON envisaged the killing of Bin Laden.[199] During the public 9/11 Commission hearings, Berger confirmed the point. It is true, he argued, that some of the authorities given to the CIA were 'capture or kill', but 'some of these authorities explicitly involved killing'.[200] Clarke's view was that initial qualms about violating the ban on assassination had been set aside.[201] While one needs to read between the lines, Tenet admitted as much in his memoirs when he wrote:

> *Almost all* of the 'authorities' President Clinton provided to us with regard to Bin Ladin were predicated on the planning of a capture operation. It was understood that in the context of such an operation,

329

> Bin Ladin would resist and might be killed in the ensuing battle. But the context was *almost always* to attempt to capture him first [emphasis added].[202]

The double use of 'almost' in the space of one paragraph implies that while almost all the authorities were 'capture or kill', some weren't. While only a quick public reference exists, it also seems that the authorities surrounding the Massoud collaboration were – at least in one case – clearer than previously accepted. During Berger's public hearing with the 9/11 Commission, Richard Ben-Veniste, one of the 9/11 Commission's staffers, told Berger and the Commission chairman that he had just received a document from the CIA, one that nobody else had seen yet, which 'removed ambiguity in terms of whether Mr. Massoud would be rewarded whether or not bin Ladin was killed or captured'.[203]

But were the authorities given to the CIA clear? After 9/11, US officials who had worked in the Clinton Administration stressed that their intent to kill Bin Laden was obvious. In this case, Berger and Tenet were largely on the same side of the controversy. As Berger put it:

> We gave the CIA every inch of authorization that it asked for. If there was any confusion down the ranks, it was never communicated to me nor to the President. And if any additional authority had been requested, I am convinced it would have been given immediately.

Neither Tenet nor Black, who regularly briefed the White House, ever asked for clarifications on the existing authorities.[204] Tenet admitted that he did not doubt that additional authorities would have been granted if he had requested them.[205] Bush also recalled after 9/11 that he had talked to Tenet about killing Bin Laden. Tenet had replied that it would not have made much of a difference to al-Qaeda and that they never had a shot. 'The President believed that Tenet thought he (Tenet) had authority to kill Bin Ladin.'[206]

But the picture was different for those closer to the action. Coll reported that – reflecting on this issue – Black reminded colleagues of Henry II's ambiguous request to get rid of the Archbishop of Canterbury, the episode discussed by DCI Helms with the Church

Osama Bin Laden: Assassination and Counterterrorism

Committee. According to Black, the CIA was no longer in the 'rid me of this priest' business.[207] A more explicit authorisation was needed. A generally scathing report from the Office of the Inspector General conceded that these concerns were not unfounded.[208] As Paul Pillar, Deputy Chief of the CTC in the late 1990s, recalled, the authorities were blurred: 'it was never entirely clear whether the "go order" had been given and whether it would have included lethal force'.[209]

As often the case throughout this book, the language surrounding assassination was ambiguous. Beyond language and beyond the Agency's reported unwillingness to take advantage of ambiguities,[210] a moderate consensus emerges on one point. It wasn't the ban that obstructed the hunt for Bin Laden. Multiple – still classified – legal reviews had by this stage reshaped the ban to permit counterterrorism operations. Instead, it was the lack of capabilities.[211] As the Inspector General report put it, 'the failure of the Agency's covert action against Bin Ladin lay not in the language and interpretation of its authorities, but in the limitations of its covert action capabilities'.[212] The events of 9/11 removed these remaining obstacles.

Notes

1. National Security Archives, 'Bush Administration's First Memo on al-Qaeda Declassified', 27/9/2006, available at https://nsarchive2.gwu.edu/NSAEBB/NSAEBB147/index.htm (accessed 31 October 2023). A video of the interview can be found here: https://www.youtube.com/watch?v=UVqKggHxSLk.
2. Peter Bergen, *The Rise and Fall of Osama Bin Laden* (New York: Simon & Schuster, 2021), 103.
3. Dan Kaszeta, *Toxic* (London: Bloomsbury, 2020), 199–200.
4. James Boys, *Clinton's War on Terror* (London: Lynne Rienner, 2018), 180.
5. Donna Starr-Deelen, *Presidential Policies on Terrorism* (New York: Palgrave Macmillan 2014), 86.
6. Richard Shultz, 'Showstoppers', *Washington Examiner*, 26 January 2004; Daniel Benjamin and Steven Simon, *The Age of Sacred Terror* (New York: Random House 2003), 230.

7. Presidential Decision Directive 39 – US Policy on Counterterrorism, 21/6/1995, available at https://irp.fas org/offdocs/pdd39.htm (accessed 31 October 2023).
8. Amy Zegart, *Spying Blind* (Princeton, NJ: Princeton University Press, 2007), 85.
9. Lawrence Freedman, *A Choice of Enemies* (London: Phoenix, 2008), 366.
10. Melissa Boyle Mahle, *Denial and Deception* (New York: Nation Books, 2006), 192.
11. Walter Pincus, 'Relaxed CIA Covert Action Rules Urged', *Washington Post*, 30 January 1996.
12. Richard Haas, 'Don't Hobble Intelligence Gathering', *Washington Post*, 15 February 1996.
13. US Congress, Antiterrorism and Effective Death Penalty Act of 1996, available at https://www.congress.gov/104/plaws/publ132/PLAW-104publ132.pdf (accessed 31 October 2023).
14. Benjamin and Simon, *The Age*, 243.
15. Ric Prado, *Black Ops* (New York: St. Martin's, 2022), 251.
16. Mike Hurley (former CIA and 9/11 Commission staffer), Interview with the author, 10 August 2022.
17. Michael Morell, *The Great War of Our Time* (New York: Twelve, 2015), 15.
18. Lisa Mundy, *The Sisterhood: The Secret History of the Women at CIA* (London: History Press, 2023), 171–2.
19. CIA, 'Terrorism: Historical Background of the Islamic Army', 26/11/1996, National Security Archives (NSAr), 'The Central Intelligence Agency's 9/11 File', 19 June 2012, available at https://nsarchive2.gwu.edu/NSAEBB/NSAEBB381/ pdf (accessed 31 October 2023).
20. Bergen, *The Rise*, 72.
21. Richard Clarke, *Against All Enemies* (London: Free Press, 2004), 141.
22. Jeremy Scahill, *Dirty Wars* (London: Serpent's Tail, 2013), 21.
23. Steve Coll, *Directorate S* (London: Penguin, 2019), 84; Prado, *Black Ops*, 243.
24. Mahle, *Denial*, 189.
25. Barton Gellman, 'U.S. Was Foiled Multiple Times in Efforts to Capture Bin Laden or Have Him Killed', *Washington Post*, 3 October 2001.
26. National Commission on Terrorist Attacks Upon the United States (9/11 Commission) Report, 2004, available at https://govinfo.library.unt.edu/911/report/911Report.pdf (accessed 31 October 2023), 110.
27. Steve Coll, *Ghost Wars* (London: Penguin, 2004), 323.

28. 9/11 Commission, Report, 109.
29. Bergen, *The Rise*, 87.
30. 9/11 Commission Report, 110.
31. Coll, *Ghost Wars*, 372.
32. After a walk-in at the US consulate in Karachi, Kansi was lured into Pakistan and arrested by the FBI.
33. Steve Coll, 'A Secret Hunt Unravels in Afghanistan', *Washington Post*, 22 February 2004.
34. CTC, 'DCI Talking Points Regarding Operations Against Usama Bin Ladin', 25/8/1997, National Security Archives (NSAr), 'The Central Intelligence Agency's 9/11 File', (CIA 9/11 Files), 19/6/2012, available at https://nsarchive2.gwu.edu/NSAEBB/NSAEBB381/ (accessed 31 October 2023).
35. Coll, *Ghost Wars*, 373.
36. Bergen, *The Rise*, 109.
37. Scahill, *Dirty Wars*, 16.
38. Bergen, *The Rise*, 95.
39. 9/11 Commission, Report, 111.
40. Ibid.
41. The CIA's acronym for Usama Bin Laden
42. Redacted, Email to Michael Scheuer, 5/5/1998, NSAr CIA 9/11 Files.
43. 9/11 Commission, Report, 113.
44. Christopher Fuller, *See It, Shoot It* (London: Yale University Press, 2017), 156.
45. John Rizzo, *Company Man: Thirty Years of Controversy and Crisis in the CIA* (New York: Scribe, 2014), 161.
46. 9/11 Commission, Report, 113.
47. Coll, *Ghost Wars*, 394.
48. Ibid., 378.
49. Mahle, *Denial*, 211.
50. 9/11 Commission, Report, 114.
51. Mundy, *The Sisterhood*, 169–70.
51. 9/11 Commission, Report, 113.
52. Coll, *Ghost Wars*, 395.
53. Morell, *The Great War*, 17.
54. Coll, *Ghost Wars*, 395.
55. 9/11 Commission, Report, 481.
56. Richard Clarke, *Against All Enemies* (London: Free Press, 2004), 149.
57. Presidential Decision Directive 62 – Protection against Unconventional Threats to the Homeland and Americans Overseas, 22/5/1998, Clinton Digital Library (CDL).

58. Staff Statement No. 8, 'National Policy coordination', Documents of the 9/11 Commission, 3.
59. 9/11 Commission, Report, 115.
60. FBI, 'East Africa Embassy bombings', FBI History, available at https://www.fbi.gov/history/famous-cases/east-african-embassy-bombings (accessed 31 October 2023).
61. Sandy Berger, Miller Center, Oral History Interviews, 24-25/3/2005, available at https://millercenter.org/the-presidency/presidential-oral-histories/samuel-r-berger-oral-history (accessed 31 October 2023), 68.
62. Richard Clarke, Memorandum: 'Checklist for Sandy's 1PM PC', 8/8/1998, Declassified Documents concerning Usama Bin Ladin, CDL.
63. Clarke, *Against All Enemies*, 184.
64. CIA, 'Bombings in Nairobi and Dar es Salaam-An Update', Briefing Material, 14/8/1998, NSAr, CIA and 9/11.
65. Bob Woodward and Thomas Ricks, 'CIA Trained Pakistanis to Nab Terrorist but Military Coup Put an End to 1999 Plot', *Washington Post*, 3 October 2001.
66. The Washington Post, 'Our Objective Was to Damage Their Capacity to Strike', 21 August 1998.
67. The Washington Post, 'There Can Be No Safe Haven for Terrorists', 21 August 1998.
68. Barton Gellman and Dana Priest, 'U.S. Strikes Terrorist-Linked Sites in Afghanistan, Factory in Sudan', *Washington Post*, 21 August 1998.
69. Washington Post, 'No Safe Haven'.
70. Eugene Robinson and Dana Priest, 'Reports of U.S. Strikes' Destruction Vary', *Washington Post*, 22 August 1998.
71. Ryan Hendrickson, *The Clinton Wars* (Nashville, TN: Vanderbilt University Press, 2002), 106.
72. Seymour Hersh, 'The Missiles of August', *New Yorker*, 12 October 1998.
73. 9/11 Commission, Report, 118.
74. 9/11 Commission, Staff Statement No. 6, The Military, available at https://govinfo.library.unt.edu/911/staff_statements/staff_statement_6.pdf (accessed 31 October 2023), 3.
75. Ralph Peters, 'Hard Target', *Washington Post*, 30 August 1998.
76. Paul Bremer III, 'Fight Plan for a Dirty War', *Washington Post*, 24 August 1998.
77. Paul Richter, 'Congress Ponders Whether the U.S. Should Ease Ban on Assassinations', *Los Angeles Times*, 18 September 1998.

78. Tim Weiner, 'Rethinking the Ban on Political Assassinations', *New York Times*, 30 August 1998.
79. Congressional Press Release, 'Barr Calls for End to Assassination Ban', 25 August 1998.
80. Steve Coll, Zoom interview with the author, 22 February 2021.
81. Barton Gellman, 'U.S. Was Foiled Multiple Times in Efforts to Capture Bin Laden or Have Him Killed', *Washington Post*, 3 October 2001.
82. James Risen, 'U.S. Pursued Secret Efforts to Catch or Kill bin Laden', *New York Times*, 30 September 2001.
83. Paul Richter, 'White House Justifies Option of Lethal Force', *Los Angeles Times*, 29 October 1998.
84. James Risen, 'Bin Laden Was Target of Afghan Raid, U.S. Confirms', *New York Times*, 14 November 1998.
85. See Brian Rappert and Chandré Gould, *The Dis-Eases of Secrecy* (Johannesburg: Jacana, 2017), 13; Andris Banka and Adam Quinn, 'Killing Norms Softly: US Targeted Killing, Quasi-secrecy and the Assassination Ban', *Security Studies*, 27.4 (2018), 673.
86. Risen, 'Bin Laden Was Target of Afghan Raid'.
87. Rizzo, *Company Man*, 162.
88. 9/11 Commission, 8th Hearing, 'Counterterrorism Policy', 23-24/3/2004, Washington, DC, available at https://govinfo.library.unt.edu/911/hearings/hearing8.htm (accessed 1 November 2023), 82.
89. 9/11 Commission, Report, 126–7.
90. Hurley, Interview with the author.
91. Coll, *Ghost Wars*, 421.
92. Clarke, *Against All Enemies*, 185.
93. Ibid., 198; 9/11 Commission, Report, 120.
94. Mail, Richard Clarke to Steven Simon, 8/9/1998, Declassified Document Concerning Tarnak Farm, CDL.
95. Presumably the tribals.
96. Anonymous, Memorandum, 'Subject: Further operations available against Usama Bin Ladin', 18/11/1998, NSAr, CIA documents on 9/11.
97. CIA, Talking Points, '[Excised] Options for Attacking the Usama Bin Ladin Problem', 24/11/1998, NSAr, CIA documents on 9/11.
98. Bergen, *The Rise*, 125; 9/11 Commission, Staff Statements, Statement 10, 'The Performance of the Intelligence Community', available at https://govinfo.library.unt.edu/911/staff_statements/staff_statement_11.pdf (accessed 1 November 2023), 10.
99. 9/11 Commission, Staff Statement, Statement 10, 10.

100. Office of the Inspector General, Report on CIA Accountability regarding findings and conclusions of the report of the Joint Inquiry into intelligence community activities before and after the terrorist attacks of September 11, 2001 (IG Report on CIA), June 2005, CIA CREST, DOC_0006184107, x–xi.
101. 9/11 Commission, Report, 130.
102. Glenn Kessler, 'Bill Clinton and the Missed Opportunities to Kill Osama bin Laden', *Washington Post*, 16 February 2016.
103. 9/11 Commission, Report, 130.
104. Alexis Albion, Zoom interview with the author, 22 July 2022. See also Alexis Albion, 'The CIA and the 9/11 Commission Report', *Spycast*, podcast episode 500.
105. Email, [Redacted] (Schroen) to Michael Scheuer, 20/12/1998, NSAr, CIA 9/11 files.
106. Scheuer, Email to [redacted] (Schroen), 21/12/1998, NSAr, CIA 9/11 files.
107. Coll, *Ghost Wars*, 428.
108. Ibid.
109. Hugh Shelton, Clinton Presidency Project, Miller Center, Oral History Interviews, 29 May 2007, available at https://millercenter.org/the-presidency/presidential-oral-histories/henry-hugh-shelton-oral-history-chairman-joint-chiefs (accessed 1 November 2023).
110. 9/11 Commission, Report, 131.
111. Ibid., 132.
112. Coll, *Ghost Wars*, 426,
113. Rizzo, *Company Man*, 164.
114. 9/11 Commission, Report, 132.
115. Richard Clarke in *Blindspot* podcast, season 1, episode 7: Falcon Hunt, available at https://www.wnycstudios.org/podcasts/blindspot/articles/falcon-hunt (accessed 1 November 2023).
116. *Blindspot* podcast, season 1, episode 7: Falcon Hunt.
117. 9/11 Commission, Report, 133.
118. Rizzo, *Company Man*, 163.
119. 9/11 Commission, Report, 133.
120. Philip Shenon, *The Commission* (New York: Twelve, 2009), 357–8.
121. Philip Zelikow, Email exchange with the author, 11 August 2022.
122. Albion, Interview with the author.
123. 9/11 Commission, Report, 134.
124. Timothy Naftali, *Blind Spot* (New York: Basic Books, 2005), 269. See, for example, Shelton's contempt for civilian officials like Clarke, Shelton; Clinton Presidency Project, Interview, 52.

125. 9/11 Commission, Report, 137; 9/11 Commission, 8th Hearing, 124.
126. CIA, [Redacted] Talking Points: CIA Operations Against Usama Bin Ladin, 10/2/1999, NSAr, CIA 9/11 Documents.
127. Bergen, *The Rise*, 127.
128. Coll, *Ghost Wars*, 447.
129. 9/11 Commission, Report, 138.
130. *Blindspot*, episode 7.
131. 9/11 Commission, Staff Statements, Statement 6, The Military, 9.
132. 9/11 Commission, Report, 140.
133. Ibid., 142.
134. Coll, *Ghost Wars*, 443.
135. Bob Woodward and Thomas Ricks, 'CIA Trained Pakistanis to Nab Terrorist but Military Coup Put an End to 1999 Plot', *Washington Post*, 3 October 2001.
136. 9/11 Commission, Report, 126.
137. Rizzo, *Company Man*, 164.
138. 9/11 Commission, Report, 139; Zelikow, Email exchange.
139. Hank Crumpton, *The Art of Intelligence* (New York: Penguin, 2012), 135.
140. Coll, *Ghost Wars*, 466.
141. CIA, 'DCI UBL Update', 12/111999, NSAr, CIA 9/11 Documents.
142. Newsweek Staff, 'Undone by Destiny', *Newsweek*, 7 March 2004, available at https://www.newsweek.com/undone-destiny-123857 (accessed 1 November 2023).
143. Hurley, Interview with the author.
144. 9/11 Commission, Staff Statement 7, Intelligence Policy, available at https://govinfo.library.unt.edu/911/staff_statements/staff_statement_7.pdf (accessed 1 November 2023), 9.
145. Coll, *Ghost Wars*, 492.
146. 9/11 Commission, Report, 505.
147. Coll, *Ghost Wars*, 492–3.
148. 9/11 Commission, Report, 506.
149. Newsweek, 'Undone by Destiny'.
150. FBI History, 'Millennium Plot/Ahmed Ressam', available at https://www.fbi.gov/history/famous-cases/millennium-plot-ahmed-ressam (accessed 1 November 2023); Bruce Riedel, *Deadly Embrace* (Washington, DC: Brookings Institution Press, 2011), 57.
151. Coll, *Ghost Wars*, 527.
152. Richard Whittle, *Predator* (New York: Henry Holt, 2014).
153. Michael Boyle, *The Drone Age* (Oxford: Oxford University Press, 2020), 64–5.

154. Clarke in 9/11 Commission, 8th Hearing, Formulation and Conduct of US counterterrorism policy, Part 2, 24/3/2004, 151.
155. Samuel Berger, Memorandum to the President, 'Improving intelligence collection on Usama Bin Laden', undated, Declassified Documents concerning the 9/11 Commission Report, CDL.
156. 9/11 Commission, Report, 189.
157. Scahill, *Dirty Wars*, 17.
158. Boyle, *Drone Age*, 65; Clarke, *Against All Enemies*, 221.
159. Clarke, 9/11 Commission, 8th Hearing, Part 2, 24/3/2004, 151.
160. Robert Grenier, *88 Days to Kandahar* (New York: Simon & Schuster, 2015), 58.
161. 9/11 Commission, Staff Statement 8, National Policy coordination, 8.
162. Clarke to Cressey, 25/10/2000, Declassified documents concerning the 9/11 Commission Report, CDL.
163. Boys, *Clinton's War*, 188; Coll, *Ghost Wars*, 538.
164. Clarke, *Against All Enemies*, 221.
165. Whittle, *Predator*, 163.
166. James Boys, 'Predator's Progress: The Bureaucratic Challenges to the Clinton Administration's Development and Deployment of Unmanned Aerial Vehicles (1993–2001)', *Intelligence and National Security*, 38.4 (2022), doi: 10.1080/02684527.2022.2134364.
167. Benjamin and Simon, *The Age*, 345.
168. Clarke, *Against All Enemies*, 221.
169. Caitlin Lee, 'The Role of Culture in Military Innovation Studies: Lessons Learned from the US Air Force's Adoption of the Predator Drone, 1993–1997', *Journal of Strategic Studies*, 46.1 (2019), doi: 10.1080/01402390.2019.1668272.
170. Dana Priest, Phone interview with the author, 13 September 2022.
171. Clarke, *Against All Enemies*, 222.
172. Coll, *Ghost Wars*, 532.
173. 9/11 Commission, Report, 211; George Tenet, *At the Center of the Storm: My Years at the CIA* (New York: HarperCollins, 2007), 160.
174. Cofer Black in 9/11 Commission, 10th Hearing, 'Law enforcement and the intelligence community', Pt. 1, 13/4/2004, 100.
175. Richard Clarke, 'A Strategy for Eliminating the Threat from the Jihadist Networks of al Qida: Status and Prospects', NSAr, 'Bush Administration's First Memo on al-Qaeda Declassified', December 2000, available at https://nsarchive2.gwu.edu/NSAEBB/NSAEBB147/clarke%20attachment.pdf (accessed 1 November 2023).
176. Scahill, *Dirty Wars*, 7.
177. Leigh Mollo, 'The United States and Assassination Policy: Diluting the Absolute', thesis, Naval Postgraduate School, 2003, 20.

178. Colin Powell in 9/11 Commission, 8th Hearing, Part 1, 23/3/2004, 52. Memorandum for the Record, 'Commission Meeting with the President and Vice President of the United States 29/4/2004', Undated, available at https://www.archives.gov/files/declassification/iscap/pdf/2012-163-doc-1-release-material.pdf (accessed 1 November 2023) 10.
179. Scahill, *Dirty Wars*, 13.
180. Whittle, *Predator*, 187.
181. Richard Clarke, 'Presidential Policy Initiative/Review – the Al-Qida Network', Memorandum for Condoleezza Rice, 25/1/2001, NSAr, 'Bush Administration'.
182. 9/11 Commission, Report, 211.
183. Tenet, *At the Center*, 143.
184. Scahill, *Dirty Wars*, 17.
185. Peter Bergen, *The Longest War* (New York: Free Press, 2011), 45.
186. Tenet, *At the Center*, 154.
187. 9/11 Commission, Staff Statement 7, Intelligence Policy, 6.
188. 9/11 Commission, Report, 209.
189. 9/11 Commission, 8th Hearing, Part 2, 56.
190. Whittle, *Predator*; Fuller, *See It, Shoot It*, 168
191. John Bellinger III, Interview with the author, Washington, DC, 2 August 2016.
192. 9/11 Commission, Report, 212.
193. Whittle, *Predator*, 225.
194. George W. Bush, *Decision Points* (New York: Virgin Books, 2010), 126.
195. This myth persists in publications sympathetic to the Agency. Toby Harnden, *First Casualty* (London: Welbeck, 2022), 18–20.
196. 9/11 Commission, 8th Hearing, Part 1, 23/3/2004, 124.
197. Tenet, *At the Center*, 109.
198. Question marks remain surrounding the MON authorising the downing of Bin Laden's airplanes and surrounding the still secret July 1999 covert operation.
199. Email, Mike Hurley to Richard Ben-Veniste, 30/7/2011, available at https://cryptome.org/2013/05/guccifer-hurley.pdf (accessed 1 November 2023).
200. Berger in 9/11 Commission, 8th Hearing, Part 2, 99.
201. Clarke, *Against All Enemies*, 204.
202. Tenet, *At the Center*, 109.
203. 9/11 Commission, 8th Hearing, Part 1: Intelligence Policy and National Policy coordination, 87.
204. 9/11 Commission, 8th Hearing, Part 1, 75, 86.

205. 9/11 Commission, 8th Hearing, Part 2, 24/3/2004, 28.
206. Memorandum for the Record, 'Commission Meeting with the President and Vice President of the United States 29 April 2004, 9:25–12:40', undated, available at https://www.archives.gov/files/declassification/iscap/pdf/2012-163-doc-1-release-material.pdf (accessed 1 November 2023), 12.
207. Coll, *Ghost Wars*, 468.
208. IG, CIA Report, 354.
209. Paul Pillar, Skype interview with the author, 5 August 2016; Chris Woods, *Sudden Justice* (London: Hurst, 2015), 48.
210. IG, CIA Report, xxi.
211. 9/11 Commission, 8th Hearing, Part 2, 45; Rizzo, *Company Man*, 165.
212. IG, CIA Report, xxi.

Conclusion: Assassination, 'Targeted Killings' and the Ban since 9/11

On the evening of 9/11, Bush addressed a shocked nation.[1] After his address, the President chaired a meeting with select officials from the National Security Council. This would become his 'war cabinet'. Bush stressed that it was time for self-defence, to bring the fight to both terrorists and those who harboured them. On 14 September, the bipartisan support for the Administration was encapsulated in the almost unanimous[2] vote for an Authorization for the Use of Military Force (AUMF). The President was authorised:

> To use all necessary and appropriate force against those nations, organizations, or *persons* he determines planned, authorized, committed, or aided the terrorist attacks that occurred on September 11, 2001, or harbored such organizations or persons in order to prevent any future acts of international terrorism. [emphasis added][3]

On 15 and 16 September, key members of the Administration met at Camp David. Tenet took the lead in defining the Administration's response to the terrorist attacks. The DCI presented a broad plan called 'Going to War', an expanded version of the plan the CIA had prepared for its Blue Sky memo in the final days of the Clinton Administration. Tenet's plan had two main components. The first was a targeted effort to take the war to al-Qaeda and the Taliban in Afghanistan. Here, the CIA would be working with the Northern Alliance, now without its leader Massoud who had been killed by al-Qaeda operatives two days before 9/11. US Special Forces would also join the fight. The second component was a far-reaching plan for global covert operations against terrorist groups. The draft of a new Memorandum of Notification radically expanded the authorities of the CIA.[4] The CIA would be given the authority to capture and detain terrorists and terrorist suspects, but it would also be given the authority to use lethal covert action worldwide.[5]

On the evening of the 16th, seething with anger, Cheney gave an interview to NBC *Meet the Press* directly from the White House. He warned that the Administration would soon have to work on the 'dark side' in its war against terrorism.[6] On the 17th, Bush signed the MON Tenet had proposed at Camp David. As the CIA's John Rizzo recalled, the MON was several pages long:

> It was the most comprehensive, most ambitious, most aggressive, and most risky Finding or MON I was ever involved in. One short paragraph authorized the capture and detention of Al Qaeda terrorists, another authorized taking lethal action against them. The language was stark and simple.[7]

The CIA was empowered to kill members of al-Qaeda and other terrorist groups worldwide.[8] Decisions regarding who to kill were delegated to the CIA itself, initially to Director Tenet, but eventually to the Directorate of Operations, and/or to Cofer Black, head of CTC.[9]

One day later, on 18 September, Bush signed the AUMF into law. The Authorisation's distinction between organisations and persons was understood as a green light for the targeting and killing of terrorists and individuals (suspected to be) affiliated with al-Qaeda and/or other terrorist groups.[10] As a report for Congress later concluded, 'the breadth' of the authority was considered 'sufficient . . . to encompass actions that might otherwise be prohibited under the assassination ban'.[11]

On the 20th, in an address to Congress, Bush called for a global 'war on terror', one starting with al-Qaeda but not ending there.[12] When completed, the presidential directive on counterterrorism that had been in the works since before 9/11 called for the 'elimination of all terrorist organizations, networks, finances, and their access to WMD'.[13] With the AUMF, the Administration's 'war on terror' framework, the new authorities for the CIA, the expansive view of presidential power held by lawyers and key officials within the Administration,[14] and Congress's post-9/11 complacency (and complicity), a new era had begun; an era of global war. As Mark Mazzetti wrote, in this process, a new 'military-intelligence complex' emerged, one that 'short-circuited' normal mechanisms for how the US government went to war and how it decided who lived and who died.[15]

As this book has shown, this development had been long in the making. Starting in the Reagan era, the US government had worked to set (domestic) legal and political precedents for the killing of terrorists and terrorist suspects. By 9/11, counterterrorism had been effectively removed from the remit of the ban. Killing terrorists – for the US government – did not amount to assassination. The attacks and the reaction that followed helped the US government remove any lingering bureaucratic, legal and material obstacles. The US government was involved in a global war; individuals killed were victims of this war, not of assassination. The US government's language also reflected this shift. 'Assassination' was largely removed from the vernacular of US foreign policy and replaced by a more surgical and sterile euphemism, 'targeted killings'. As General Michael Hayden, CIA Director for part of the war on terror, argued, 'no one in government discusses targeted killings in terms of assassination'.[16]

The story of the rise, institutionalisation and expansion of targeted killings, including via drones, has been covered extensively elsewhere. Targeted killings were deployed primarily against terrorist groups and suspected individual terrorists and, hence, are beyond the remit of this book.[17] The brief account that follows can only represent a potted history, identifying a few points of controversy at the intersection of targeted killing, assassination and the ban since 9/11.

* * *

Under the Bush Administration, targeted killings initially took place within active battlefields such as Afghanistan. Outside declared battlefields, the 17 September finding permitted the CIA to deploy 'lethal action' worldwide. As it had done in the past, the

US government at times outsourced the act of killing to local actors and contractors. In an initiative that – according to intelligence historian John Prados – represented an effort to revive ZRRIFLE and 'executive action'[18] – the Agency developed an 'assassination squad'. Project Cannonball was devised by Jose Rodriguez at the National Clandestine Service (formerly Directorate of Operations). The project was approved by Cheney who worked to keep it hidden from Congress.[19] The squad was initially led by the controversial Ric Prado, Casey's loyal Cold Warrior who had been involved in the early fight against al-Qaeda.[20] Cannonball was eventually transferred to the contractor Blackwater when Prado and Black joined the outfit.[21]

In early October, at the start of the Afghanistan campaign, the CIA provided information to target Mullah Omar, the leader of the Taliban. After consultation among US officials, including the President, and to the dismay of some in the CIA, General Tommy Franks, in charge of the US Central Command, hesitated. In a repeat of the Clinton era, concerns surrounding civilian casualties and the chances of hitting a mosque stopped the strike. When Franks decided to hit the mosque, Omar was no longer there.[22]

In March 2002, the Department of Justice's Office of Legal Counsel issued a still classified memorandum reviewing the meaning of the ban on assassination contained in Executive Order 12333. It confirmed precedents established before and immediately after 9/11.[23] According to Richard Armitage, at the time Colin Powell's deputy at the State Department, an additional memorandum specifically authorised the use of drones for targeted killings.[24]

The new global reach of the CIA's drones was showcased in November 2002, when the first drone strike outside active battlefields in Yemen killed Qaed Salim Sinan al-Harethi, responsible for the USS *Cole* bombing, and Ahmed Hijazi (Kamal Derwish), an American citizen who was travelling with him. The strike was a defining moment for the conduct of US targeted killings and for the future of the ban on assassination. As to the latter, it crystallised legal precedents that we have observed throughout this book. Administration officials dismissed criticisms coming from several quarters, including the UN, that the strike amounted to extrajudicial killing.[25] National Security Advisor Condoleezza Rice argued that the United States was in a new kind of war and the killing of

Conclusion

an American citizen raised no issues of constitutional powers since the President had given 'broad authorities' to 'US officials in a variety of circumstances to do what they need to do to protect the country'.[26] As to the former, it signalled that the US government considered itself free to operate in a global battlefield.[27] Now, it also had the technology and capabilities at its disposal to do so.[28] The sprawling campaign of targeted killings came to entail commando raids, drone strikes, and, at times, surreptitious techniques like car bombs. These operations were conducted unilaterally, or in collaboration with US allies and their intelligence services.[29]

* * *

In early October 2002, with rumours of war against Iraq spreading in Washington, White House spokesman Ari Fleischer discussed with the press the potential costs of a new conflict. 'The cost of one bullet,' he added, 'if the Iraqi people take it on themselves, is substantially less than that.'[30] Fleischer wasn't alone. Secretary of Defense Donald Rumsfeld told the House Armed Service Committee that Saddam was free to leave the country. 'Another way to do it,' he added, 'would be to persuade enough people in Iraq the world would be a lot better world if that regime weren't there and they decided to change the regime.'[31] At a time when the CIA was revamping its effort in Iraq and with war preparations under way, this was clearly a request for a 'silver bullet' option. In rhetoric not dissimilar to that used by officials in the George H. W. Bush Administration, Fleischer and Rumsfeld were asking the Iraqi people and the Iraqi military to take it upon themselves to remove Saddam.

As the war approached, the CIA struggled to satisfy the White House's requests for evidence surrounding Iraqi WMDs. One of the Agency's main problems was the lack of assets in Iraq. Almost overnight, this seemed to change. The Agency's Iraq Operations Group suddenly recruited a group of informants codenamed ROCKSTARS. The ROCKSTARS seemed too good to be true and they probably were.[32] Two days before the invasion was scheduled to start, they told their Agency handlers that Saddam – and potentially his much-hated sons – would be staying at a compound named Dora Farms. Bush took a page from his father's bombing

345

campaign against Iraq and made the targeting of Saddam personally the first objective of the war. As the bombing went underway, investigative journalist Bob Woodward reported, 'Tenet called the situation room: "Tell the president we got the son of a bitch." They had not.'[33] With the war authorised by Congress, as in the Gulf War, the killing of Saddam – in charge of the Iraqi military – would not have been considered an assassination, even under the stringent requirements of the Church Committee.

And yet, the Administration did not refrain from engaging in assassination. Having failed to kill Saddam, in the early days of the Iraq war, the CIA's paramilitary teams, in collaboration with Special Forces, started to target Iraq's political elites and Saddam's loyalists. The CIA, the NSA and foreign intelligence services, investigative journalist Dana Priest reported, worked together to identify 'leadership targets', their homes, offices and regular locations.[34] This was a clear-cut campaign of assassination against political figures for political reasons, but in the emerging Iraqi chaos, it went largely unnoticed.

Furthermore, through its war on terror framework and self-defence justification, the Bush Administration was also able to justify its involvement in the killing of guerrilla leaders far removed from the battlefields of Iraq and Afghanistan. For example, it provided Colombia with 'a $30,000 GPS guidance kit' to turn 'a less-than-accurate 500-pound gravity bomb into a highly accurate smart bomb'. This technology was used by Colombian forces in the controversial, trans-border killing of Raul Reyes, leader of the FARC (Revolutionary Armed Forces of Colombia), while he was stationed in Ecuador. The FARC clearly qualified as an 'insurgent force', in the words of the Church Committee, or as a well-structured and well-financed organisation, in the words of Hays Parks's Memorandum of Law on assassination. The Administration dismissed these criticisms. The operation only involved the CIA indirectly, and it was conducted in self-defence.[35]

During the Bush years, the 'ban on assassination' was largely absent from domestic public discussion. When legislative efforts were made regarding the ban, they followed the example set by Bob Barr (R-GA) with his 'Terrorist Elimination Act' of 2001. In a case of validity contestation, challenging the appropriateness of the ban, Barr's argument entailed that, due to the ban, the US

Conclusion

government had often relied on large(r) deployments of military force in the attempt to kill a single individual. Assassination should be used 'sparingly' but should be available in the US government's arsenal. In January 2003 a new version of the bill was proposed by Terry Everett (R-Alabama) but did not pass.[36]

* * *

Scholars and investigative journalists have detailed the geographical and numerical expansion of drone strikes and targeted killings under Barack Obama. Victims included terrorists, suspected terrorists, those who behaved like terrorists or simply happened to live around suspected terrorists, those who succoured suspected terrorists, as well as scores of civilian casualties caught in the crossfire.[37] In 2011, having accumulated evidence of Bin Laden's presence in a compound in Abbottabad, Pakistan, the Administration engaged in a lengthy legal review to justify the strike. Lawyers from the CIA, the NSC, the Pentagon and the Joint Chiefs of Staff took part. Among other decisions, the review concluded that Obama was authorised to order a kill mission. They also concluded that the breach of Pakistani sovereignty could be justified through the 'unable or unwilling formula'.[38] According to the formula, the US government could deploy force in the territory of another state if it deemed its government unable or unwilling to act against terrorists.[39] The raid – labelled a 'kill or capture operation' – was conducted by Navy SEALs under the control of CIA Director Leon Panetta. The blending of JSOC and the CIA, as well as of their different authorities,[40] showed the extent of the evolution of the US government's targeted killing machinery.[41] Furthermore, US officials's admissions before the raid made clear that the 'kill or capture' label was perfunctory. There was no plausible scenario in which Bin Laden would have been captured.[42]

One of the largest controversies of the Obama era – certainly among those that touched upon the ban on assassination – surrounded the Administration's decision to kill the radical cleric and US citizen Anwar al-Awlaki. In an effort to legitimate the Administration's decision, several officials, including Harold Koh, the legal adviser to the State Department and Attorney General Eric Holder, stressed that targeted killings did not amount to assassination.

They were legitimate uses of force in self-defence against targets that posed an imminent threat and, hence, they did not violate the ban on assassination.[43]

These public engagements reflected a series of internal legal opinions that reviewed the permissibility of targeting al-Awlaki. In February 2010, Acting Assistant Attorney General David Barron reviewed whether the targeting of al-Awlaki represented a violation of the ban on assassination. The memorandum restated the text of the ban. Based on precedents set since the 1980s and reviewed in this book, Barron's conclusion was unequivocal: 'Consistent with the assassination ban in Executive Order 12333 [redacted] killings in self-defence are not assassination.'[44] Within the Administration, a White Paper, later leaked to the press, provided the legal rationale for the targeting of al-Awlaki. It restated the conclusion reached by Barron: 'Targeting a member of an enemy force who poses an imminent threat of violent attack to the United States is not unlawful. It is a lawful act of national self defense,' and thus does not violate the ban on assassination.[45] The White Paper went further. It redefined the meaning of imminence. In what amounted to little more than a linguistic sleight of hand,[46] imminence no longer meant temporally immediate. Instead, it referred to a more uncertain decisional standard which included calculations of available windows of opportunity, costs and benefits, and chances of forestalling future harms.[47] This redefinition built upon precedents set since the 1980s but expanded even further the reach of the US government. Al-Awlaki was killed in a drone strike in November 2011.

At the time of al-Awlaki's killing, some tried to revamp the ban on assassination and legislate a new limited prohibition. Democrat Dennis Kucinich introduced Bill HR 6010 to prohibit the extrajudicial killing of US citizens. The bill defined an extrajudicial killing as 'a premeditated and intentional use of lethal force against a United States citizen'. It also provided for three exceptions: the use of lethal force after a trial, the use of lethal force in the context of active hostilities against a citizen participating in hostile acts, and the use of force by law enforcement personnel in circumstances including self-defence.[48] The bill was introduced to the House and referred to various subcommittees but did not go any further. As in previous decades, the regulation of the power to kill remained within the executive, as reflected in a series of more restrictive presidential directives that regulated – and somewhat constrained – drone strikes in Obama's second term.[49] Most of these rules – contained within the Executive – did not survive the advent of the Trump Administration.[50]

* * *

While the evidence is scarce, it seems that – towards the end of the Obama Administration and then again under Trump – the US government also considered the assassination of a foreign head of state. As tensions with North Korea escalated during the Obama Administration, John Brennan, then CIA Director, reportedly started to consider plans for the 'indirect assassination' of Kim Jong Un, for 'man change' as opposed to regime change.[51]

The US military developed multiple contingency plans for a conflict with North Korea. Under the Trump Administration, with the conflict seemingly ready to escalate, rumours started spreading about OPLAN5015. The plan remains classified, but details have emerged. The plan is thought to entail 'guerrilla warfare, with special forces assassinations and targeted attacks on key facilities'.[52] Even more importantly, and in a return to the Dora Farms strike, the plan envisages the bombing of leadership targets with a 30,000-pound massive ordnance penetrator, to destroy possible underground bunkers.[53] An anonymous South Korean top military official told the press that the plan entailed nothing less than the 'preemptive "decapitation" of North Korean leader Kim Jong-un'.[54] This component was confirmed when North Korea hacked the South Korean military network and – allegedly – obtained copies of the joint US–South Korea war plans, including 5015, in September 2016.[55] Such a strike would have conformed to the modus operandi used by the United States against foreign officials, both in discrete uses of force and at the start of broader confrontations.

A few months later, North Korean officials denounced an alleged CIA assassination attempt against Kim Jong Un.[56] Beyond a deluge of information, North Korean authorities provided no actual evidence. The effort was likely aimed at distracting from North Korea's earlier assassination of Kim Jong Nam, brother of Kim Jong Un, killed with VX nerve agent at Kuala Lumpur International Airport.[57] Nothing came of the confrontation with North Korea.

Trump visited the country and, in a typically Trumpian twist, later declared to have 'fallen in love' with the North Korean leader.[58]

In April 2017, Trump also considered the assassination of Syrian president Bashar al-Assad, in the aftermath of a Syrian chemical weapons attack on civilians during the then raging civil war. Trump reportedly called Secretary of Defense General James Mattis. 'Let's fucking kill him! Let's go in. Let's kill the fucking lot of them,' Trump told the General, according to investigative reporter Bob Woodward.[59] Mattis refused the President's request, something Trump later bemoaned on Fox and Friends. As we saw at the start of the book, while the killing of Assad was shelved, under Trump the technology and justifications that had long characterised the killing of terrorists were deployed to kill a state official, General Qassem Soleimani.

* * *

Under President Joe Biden, the pandemic, the domestic crisis and the war in Ukraine meant that targeted killings took a back seat.[60] A new policy, not too dissimilar from the Obama-era guidelines, emerged only in October 2022.[61] With the war in Ukraine taking over the front pages, some within the United States called for assassination as a method to ease the crisis. In the spring of 2022, Lindsey Graham, the Republican senator from South Carolina, blamed Biden for the violence in Ukraine. Putin, or so he argued, had concluded that Biden was weak, and he could get away with anything. The only solution, Graham told the Fox News audience, was the assassination of Putin. 'Is there a Brutus in Russia? Is there a more successful Col. Stauffenberg in the Russian military?' 'The only way this ends,' he continued, 'is for somebody in Russia to take this guy out! You would be doing your country a great service and the world a great service.'[62] Senator Marco Rubio of Florida hinted at a similar solution: 'Oh, wouldn't it be great if someone internally just took this guy out and eliminated him,' he stated, before adding that this, of course, was not US official policy.[63]

In a repeat of the 'silver bullet' rhetoric heard during the confrontations with Noriega and Saddam, the two senators were calling on the Russian military and others close to the Russian leader to pull

Conclusion

the trigger. Jen Psaki, then White House press secretary, was quick to deny that any of the senators' comments found support in the White House. 'That is not the position of the U.S. government and certainly not a statement you'll hear from – coming from the mouth of – anybody working for the administration,' she stated.[64] A few days later, though, in an impromptu closure to his speech on the allied effort in support of Ukraine, the President concluded: 'For God's sake, this man cannot remain in power.'[65]

Biden's bluster aside, Psaki's comment was both correct and largely expected. It was expected as, in the long history of assassination, the US government has always denied its involvement in assassination and, especially, that such involvement was official policy. It was correct because, except for a (possible) early plot against Stalin, the US government has traditionally targeted leaders who have presented an easier target than Putin. It is to a summary of the book findings that we finally turn.

Assassination before the Ban

Methods and US Government Responsibility

Starting in the early Cold War, the US government used a plethora of methods to assassinate foreign leaders and officials. As detailed in the introduction, these methods can be understood along a continuum from more direct to less direct. Assassination plots were – at times – as simple as the delivery of poison. Equally direct was the use of Agency assets to engineer accidents. The evidence surrounding the *Kashmir Princess* accident (the plane crash aimed at killing Chinese Premier Zhou Enlai) remains inconclusive. The Agency, though, was certainly open to the possibility of causing a plane crash, as the plot against Raul Castro demonstrates. Similarly, individuals or small groups of assets were given the task of assassinating foreign officials. Devlin hoped that some of his assets could kill Lumumba during his house arrest. Headquarters also provided handpicked agents, such as QJWIN and WIROGUE. Moving towards more indirect methods, the Agency and other branches of government trained, financed and provided intelligence to small groups such as Cuban exiles, in the hope that they could mount successful assassination attempts.

More often, the US government and the CIA acted more indirectly. Here, they nurtured and instigated local actors. They took advantage of or redirected their pre-existing grievances and/or their plotting against foreign leaders and officials. In these cases, assassination – albeit as part of a broad arsenal of covert activities – represented a (relatively) common and (relatively) successful method of engineering covert regime change.[66] As one would expect, though, the extent of the US government's control over local actors, its awareness of (and support for) assassination, and, hence, its culpability varied and are – at times – the object of extensive debate.

In the case of Lumumba, the US government – and its allies – played a prominent role in initiating the plotting and in maintaining the pressure on Congolese authorities. They also worked to guarantee the eventual elimination of Lumumba. In the case of Trujillo, US responsibility included but was not limited to the provision of weapons. The US government was aware of and supportive of the dissidents' goal of assassinating Trujillo. CIA officials were involved in discussing assassination options (from poison pills to car accidents). They reviewed and assessed assassination plans, recommending ideal locations for the placement of explosives.

In the case of Diem, assassination was understood from the start as a likely outcome of a military coup; in some cases, it also appeared as an acceptable policy. The US government worked twice to foster a military coup. As in the case of Trujillo, it provided extensive material, financial and political support to the South Vietnamese generals. It exercised pressure for a coup and it created a system of sanctions and incentives. While US support for a coup was made conditional on certain political moves, the survival and safety of Diem was never a requirement. The proximity of Ambassador Lodge, of the CIA's Lucien Conein and other US officials to the plotters suggests that the US government's role went beyond the simple creation of conducive conditions. US officials also snubbed a last-minute opportunity to save Diem.

A similar situation emerged in the case of Schneider. The plotting of the Chilean military had – in part – a momentum of its own,[67] but US officials were aware of the role played by Schneider in obstructing a coup. The risk that the removal of Schneider might lead to bloodshed was well understood. As in the case of Lumumba, as less drastic options to remove the main obstacle to a coup fizzled out, the US government adopted harsher measures and closer collaboration with the military. The White House and the CIA, especially through Track II, continued to exercise pressure and to provide material support including weapons to the plotting military officials. The White House also continued to follow with interest Track II even after one coup attempt was halted.

Overall, except – it seems – for Gottlieb's poisoned handkerchief, none of the early Cold War plots explored in Chapter 1 succeeded. The plots against Fidel Castro represent a long history of failure, at times farcical, at times tragic. The plots against Lumumba, Trujillo, Diem and Schneider were all ultimately successful. While it is true that the US government never physically pulled the trigger, it was involved in all of them, and – often – played a dominant role.

Constraints on Assassination

In these early plots, no explicit obstacles to assassination emerged. Assassination was viewed as an acceptable – if at times unsavoury – foreign policy practice. At various stages, the US government established units tasked with the conduct of assassination, from Program Branch 7, to the 'Health Alteration Committee' and 'Executive Action'. No external oversight obstructed the conduct of assassination. Congress was generally absent, if not willing to spur the executive forward. Until the 1970s, limited media revelations regarding the US government's involvement in assassination emerged, for example stories on the CIA and Castro authored by Drew Pearson and Jack Anderson. While in one case these led to internal investigations (the CIA Inspector General reports), they did not engender public outcry nor Congressional measures to curtail such practices.

Internally, while some legal instruments were available, they were generally overlooked. As Lawrence Houston, General Counsel of the CIA from its founding to 1973, testified, he was never consulted on assassination plans.[68] Legality was not a factor in deciding whether to become involved in assassination.[69] Only in the late 1960s and early 1970s, pressured by public controversy, especially surrounding the Phoenix Program, did the CIA approve internal directives prohibiting assassination.

What obstacles did exist had to do more with the moral qualms and/or opposition to assassination for strategic reasons of the individuals involved. Moral qualms – when they emerged – seemed to surround more surreptitious methods of assassination, such as poison, but they quickly dissipated as the role of the United States government became more indirect. The CIA's Justin O'Donnell's cognitive dissonance between professing a moral opposition to directly poisoning Lumumba while wholeheartedly embracing a plot that would deliver Lumumba to his enemies is perhaps the best example. More indirect and 'cleaner' methods permitted US officials to morally distance themselves from the actions they were fostering.[70] Often, by the time any opposition emerged – as in the cases of Raul Castro, Trujillo and Diem – the train, so to speak, had already left the station. The US government and the CIA had already created the conditions and put into action mechanisms that made assassination (almost) inevitable. The last-minute telegrams expressing opposition to assassination, like the effort to purge the historical record of references to assassination encountered throughout the book, had more to do with a concern for the reputation of the United States and of the government officials involved than with moral opprobrium at assassination. The same is true of the language used to discuss assassination.

Language and Political Control of Assassination

In its investigation, the Church Committee report highlighted the pervasiveness of ambiguity, euphemisms, omissions and circumlocutory language. As we have seen, assassination did feature in the language of policymaking, but these techniques served multiple functions, including the shielding of the President's and of the US government's role in the plots.[71] And yet, a thorough analysis of the available historical record has generally permitted us to arrive at more ambitious conclusions than those reached by the Church Committee.

In the case of Lumumba, Eisenhower is likely to have ordered the assassination of the Congolese prime minister and, when his

Conclusion

National Security Advisor Gordon Gray reported Ike's requests for 'straightforward action', this included assassination. In the case of Castro, the sheer amount of evidence points – at a minimum – to President Kennedy's awareness of assassination plots against Castro. At least in one case, the Hemingway shrine episode, the evidence in unequivocal. The President was in attendance when assassination was discussed. Perhaps his awareness extended to plots involving the Mafia; certainly that of his brother did.

In the case of Trujillo, while no explicit discussion of assassination with the President is available, Henry Dearborn's communications certainly reached the White House – where Richard Goodwin read them – and the State Department. If Dearborn is to be believed, the President was fully aware of his views and of the US role in the assassination, as he confirmed in a letter to Church unearthed for this book. In the case of Diem, President Kennedy was famously shocked by the way Diem and his brother were killed. The shock at the nature of the assassination might well have been true. From the start of the crisis in South Vietnam, though, Kennedy had considered assassination a possible outcome of a coup.[72] No effort was made to stop the coup, nor to save Diem.

The Nixon White House was certainly heavily involved in the effort to prevent Allende's election and – later – his confirmation. Nixon asked to be kept informed of developments in Chile. A White House document from Alexander Haig – unearthed during research for this book – shows that the White House and Kissinger remained involved in the plotting even after the alleged cut-off date of 15 October 1970. The aim was not to stop the plotting, but to increase the chances of success when a coup did come.

One of the envisaged outcomes of the post-Watergate era and of the 'season of inquiry' was precisely to put an end to the era of ambiguity, plausible deniability and assassination. The December 1974 Hughes–Ryan amendment aimed at undermining the doctrine of plausible deniability and at putting the President more explicitly in charge of covert operations.[73] The Church Committee's investigations of assassination and the recommendation contained in its Interim Report called for a ban on assassination as an un-American foreign policy practice.

Over time, US (legal) scholars and US officials have worked to reinterpret the work of the Church Committee in the realm of assassination. They have tended to suggest that the Interim Report and its recommendations were not as restrictive as initially thought.[74] A deep dive into the work of the committee has permitted us to reach different conclusions. The Interim Report explored direct and indirect, successful and unsuccessful assassination plots. It proposed a law banning assassination. This law would have applied to assassinations and assassination attempts against foreign officials, including state leaders, state officials and leaders of political movements. The committee made a distinction between plots directly instigated by the US government and the US government's involvement in coups, but still called for a careful consideration of the risk of assassination before becoming involved in a coup. The prohibition – the committee made clear – would not apply in the case of a declared war or a use of force pursuant to the War Powers Resolution. More generally, the committee agreed that the prohibition could be suspended only in the most extreme situations of national emergency. In other cases, a threat to the United States and its interests was not sufficient to nullify the prohibition. Doing so would have meant that the United States was adopting the standards of totalitarians.[75]

The committee's efforts were thwarted by the Ford Administration's Executive Order 11905. The prohibition on assassination remained under the control of the executive. In this sense, the 'season of inquiry' did represent a watershed moment, but it did not stop the US government's involvement in assassination. The difference is more subtle. The ban changed the way in which the US government became involved in assassinations and the way in which it talked about assassination.

Assassination after the Ban

In line with existing scholarship, the analysis has understood the ban on assassination as a 'norm' that informed and – to an extent – shaped US foreign policy behaviour. The nature of the norm – ambiguous and contained solely within an Executive Order – meant

Conclusion

that the prohibition was more likely to be contested. Over time, contestation came from within and without the administrations in power. It addressed the meaning of the norm (what did assassination mean? what degree of control and involvement was necessary for a violation of the ban? how explicit did US intent need to be?) and the remit of the norm (should the ban prohibit the US government's involvement in coup? should counterterrorism sit outside the remit of the norm?). As contestation progressed, it also challenged the validity of the norm, that is, its strategic value (is the ban hindering US policymakers and the intelligence community?) and its moral appropriateness (shouldn't assassination – a more precise tool – be preferred to more indiscriminate ones like bombing?).[76] This process of contestation often resulted in making available policy options that were previously understood as prohibited.

The second part of the book has developed along two parallel planes. On one level, the analysis traced the US government's continued involvement in direct and indirect assassination plots. On another level, it has followed the politics of assassination and the ban, the processes through which the ban was discussed, reinterpreted, contested and eventually eroded.

Assassination Targets and the Politics of Assassination

As to the targets of assassination, these tracked the evolution of US foreign policy from a narrow(er) focus on the Cold War to the emergence of new enemies – drug lords, leaders of 'rogue' states and terrorists – towards the end of the Cold War and in its aftermath. As to the methods of assassination, in this second phase, the US government relied primarily on two. First, assassination and assassination plots emerged in the context of coup plotting. As it had done in the pre-1970s phase, the US government continued to support groups that intended to overthrow foreign leaders, from Qaddafi to Saddam. More often, the US government adopted direct methods. It started to rely on superior military technology, in particular, precision bombing and the targeting of command-and-control facilities, of infrastructure and of sites connected to foreign leaders (from tents to residences). These methods could only be deployed to the extent that they could be justified internally and – at times – publicly as available and legitimate policy

357

options, outside the remit of the ban and, hence, as something other than assassination.

Under Reagan, spearheaded by CIA Director William Casey and the Agency's legal counsel Stanley Sporkin, the US government started contesting the ban. Among the many justifications, it developed one surrounding 'intent'. This view played on (and exploited) the distinction identified by the Church Committee between direct instigation and more indirect roles. Despite opposition from within the Agency, the 'intent' argument permitted the Agency to become involved in third parties' actions that amounted to assassination if the US government had no explicit control on these actors and as long as no explicit directive or demonstration of intent emerged. As the confrontation with Qaddafi escalated, the Reagan Administration adopted the same justification to support groups that aimed to overthrow the Libyan dictator.

In the realm of counterterrorism, the Reagan Administration established political and legal precedents that have informed US counterterrorism policy ever since. Casey and Secretary of State George Shultz argued for a more aggressive posture against individual terrorists, terrorist groups, and states supporting terrorism. The rhetoric of pre-emption, the official call in National Security Decision Directive 138 for the 'neutralization' of terrorists, and internal legal opinions helped in removing counterterrorism from the remit of the ban. The opposition of US officials, including the CIA's John McMahon, meant that this was not a foregone or natural conclusion. Sporkin's view that terrorists could be targeted in self-defence prevailed. The ban on assassination, the Administration concluded, did not apply to counterterrorism. It only protected heads of state.

When the confrontation with a head of state escalated, the ban was once again set aside. Operation El Dorado Canyon was understood by some at the time, and by most since, as an attempt to kill Libyan leader Muhammar Qaddafi. The Administration developed a new set of legal justifications for the operation. These contested the meaning of the ban and its remit. A killing was not assassination if it occurred in self-defence, even if the target was a head of state. Furthermore, Qaddafi's status as 'head of state' did not guarantee him immunity if he was present at a legitimate military target. Reviewing the case at the time, legal scholar Bert Brandenburg

Conclusion

concluded: 'if the ban cannot survive attempts to carve out exceptions for foreign leaders who are particularly despised by the United States, its practical value approaches worthlessness'.[77]

The ban did survive, but so did US assassination policy. The Qaddafi case showed that – in the confrontation with foreign leaders – the US government no longer needed the surreptitious use of poison. If its support for coups and coup plotters failed to achieve the desired objective, the US government could always rely on (overt) military force, including aerial bombing.

The confrontation with Manuel Noriega permitted the Administration of George H. W. Bush to consolidate some of the precedents developed in the Reagan years. The failed Giroldi coup engendered a new round of contestation; this time a more assertive Congress took part. A new form of validity contestation raised questions as to whether the ban on assassination unduly constrained the conduct of US foreign policy. The Bush Administration and the CIA took advantage of this more permissive political environment to reshape the ban. William Barr's legal opinion and CIA Director William Webster's engagement with Congress resulted in increased latitude for the CIA's involvement in coups. In a throwback to Casey's 'intent' argument, the CIA was permitted to become more explicitly involved in coups and coup plotting if no explicit plan and no explicit directive to assassinate emerged.

As the Gulf War got under way, the first Bush Administration conducted targeted air strikes against Saddam Hussein personally. Having failed to dislodge Saddam, in the aftermath of the conflict the Administration developed a 'lethal finding' for the CIA, worked to foster coups, and supported the Iraqi opposition in its effort to get rid of Saddam. Various coup options were considered. The Administration's preference was for a 'palace coup' or a 'silver bullet' coup; both entailed the assassination of Saddam, a conclusion that key members of the Administration acknowledged and welcomed.

The Clinton Administration – while often understood as a low point in the recent history of the CIA – continued an overt and covert confrontation with Saddam. The 'lethal finding' seemingly remained on the books and the CIA expanded its presence in Iraq and its support for the Iraqi opposition and Kurdish groups in the north. This expanded presence introduced a new coup option, a 'rolling coup'. Much controversy surrounds the coup plot concocted by Robert

Baer, Ahmad Chalabi and Wafiq al-Samarrai. A bone of contention has to do with whether the ban on assassination played a part in the collapse of plot. While the evidence is limited, the conclusion reached in this book is that this was not the case. The point is seemingly confirmed by the more explicit support the Clinton White House provided to the plot developed by the Iraqi National Accord. Had the plot succeeded it would have led to the assassination of Saddam. Similarly, more than circumstantial evidence suggests that the bombing campaign conducted against Iraq during Operation Desert Fox aimed at more than damaging Iraq's WMD facilities. It aimed at either killing Saddam directly or at causing enough havoc in the regime to convince someone to get rid of the Iraqi dictator.

The operations and debates of the pre-9/11 hunt for Bin Laden crystallised political and legal precedents that had been developing since the Reagan years. Through legal reviews, officials in the Clinton Administration confirmed that the ban on assassination did not apply to uses of force in self-defence against terrorists. The United States could rely on its military technology and on information provided by its intelligence assets to kill Bin Laden. A more ambiguous picture emerged regarding the authorities given to the CIA to conduct assassination. As the Bush Administration took power, even before 9/11 it had reached similar conclusions regarding terrorists and the ban on assassination. In the aftermath of 9/11, these conclusions, coupled with the 'global war on terror' framework and an expansive view of presidential power, ushered in the new era of now rebranded 'targeted killings'.

* * *

The ban and US assassination policy has travelled a long way – from the Congressional chambers of the Church Committee to the smouldering remains of Soleimani's SUV at Baghdad airport. All in all, as former CIA and NSC official Bruce Riedel put it,

> Instead of asking how a doctrine (a norm?) against assassination became settled, one should recognise that assassination was never regarded as unacceptable except for a brief hiatus in the Carter years. Technology and international context determined the frequency of use.[78]

Conclusion

And yet, one element has remained constant, one that has long characterised the history of the US government's involvement in assassination. The US government has always professed shock at domestic and international accusations that it has engaged in assassination. The ban – US government officials have repeated almost like an incantation – prohibits any involvement in assassination. Calls to explicitly abolish or curtail the prohibition have been set aside. But at the same time, the US government has taken the position that anything done in self-defence – against allegedly 'imminent' threats – cannot and does not amount to assassination and the ban does not apply to terrorists in any case. This is a far cry from the extreme exceptions identified by Church. The killing of Soleimani is just the latest episode in this process. As this book has shown, from last-minute telegrams and the destruction of the historical record to the reinterpretations of the ban, assassination is something the US government does not do, except when it does.

Notes

1. George W. Bush, 'Statement by the President in His Address to the Nation', 11 September 2001, available at https://georgewbush-whitehouse.archives.gov/news/releases/2001/09/20010911-16.html (accessed 1 November 2023).
2. Gillian Brockell, 'She Was the Only Member of Congress to Vote Against War in Afghanistan', *Washington Post*, 17 August 2021, available at https://www.washingtonpost.com/history/2021/08/17/barbara-lee-afghanistan-vote/ (accessed 1 November 2023).
3. Public Law 107–40, 18/9/2001, available at https://www.congress.gov/107/plaws/publ40/PLAW-107publ40.pdf (accessed 1 November 2023).
4. National Commission on Terrorist Attacks Upon the United States (9/11 Commission) Report, 2004, available at https://govinfo.library.unt.edu/911/report/911Report.pdf (accessed 1 November 2023), 330–1.
5. Bob Woodward, *Bush at War* (New York: Pocket Books, 2003), 101.
6. The White House, 'The Vice President Appears on Meet the Press with Tim Russert', 16/9/2001, transcript, available at https://georgewbush-whitehouse.archives.gov/vicepresident/news-speeches/speeches/vp20010916.html (accessed 1 November 2023).

7. John Rizzo, *Company Man: Thirty Years of Controversy and Crisis in the CIA* (New York: Scribe, 2014), 174.
8. Chris Woods, *Sudden Justice* (London: Hurst, 1025), 49.
9. George W. Bush, *Decision Points* (New York: Crown, 2010), 186.
10. Jeremy Scahill, *Dirty Wars* (London: Serpent's Tail, 2013), 19.
11. Elizabeth Bazan, 'Assassination Ban and E.O. 12333: A Brief Summary', *Congressional Research Service*, Report for Congress, 2002, 6.
12. President Bush, Address to a Joint Session of Congress, 20/9/2001, available at https://edition.cnn.com/2001/US/09/20/gen.bush.transcript/ (accessed 1 November 2023).
13. National Security Presidential Directive 9, 'Defeating the Terrorist Threat to the United States', 25/10/2001, available at https://irp.fas.org/offdocs/nspd/nspd-9.pdf (accessed 1 November 2023).
14. Charlie Savage, *Takeover* (New York: Little, Brown, 2007), 146–55.
15. Mark Mazzetti, *The Way of the Knife* (New York: Penguin, 2014), 4.
16. General Michael Hayden, Skype interview with the author, 22 August 2016.
17. See Scahill, *Dirty Wars*; Woods, *Sudden Justice*; Daniel Klaidman, *Kill or Capture* (New York: Mariner Books, 2013).
18. John Prados, *Ghosts of Langley* (New York: The New Press, 2017), 113; Steve Coll, *Directorate S* (London: Penguin, 2019), 85.
19. Coll, *Directorate S*, 85.
20. For the controversy surrounding Prado's mobster career, see Evan Wright, *How to Get Away with Murder in America* (San Francisco, CA: Byliner Originals, 2012), ebook, chapter 31, 'The Woofer and the Quiet Man'.
21. Wright, *How to Get Away*, chapter 31.
22. Coll, *Directorate S*, 69–71. Whittle provides a different narrative of the same episode. In Whittle, General Franks overrules Lieutenant General Charles Wald, in charge of the air war, and authorises an early strike. See Richard Whittle, *Predator* (New York: Henry Holt, 2014), 246–68.
23. Charlie Savage, *Power Wars* (New York: Little, Brown, 2015), 237.
24. Woods, *Sudden Justice*, 50.
25. United States Mission to Geneva, 'Inquiry from Special Rapporteur on Extrajudicial, Summary or Arbitrary Executions. Telegram to Secretary of State', 15/112002, available at https://www.aclu.org/files/dronefoia/dos/drone_dos_20110720DOS_DRONE000134.pdf (accessed 1 November 2023).
26. Scahill, *Dirty Wars*, 77.
27. Ibid.

28. Bruce Riedel, Interview with the author, 4 August 2016, Washington, DC.
29. Such as the 2008 cooperation between the CIA and Mossad in the case of Hezbollah leader Imad Mughniyeh. Adam Goldman and Helen Nakashima, 'CIA and Mossad killed senior Hezbollah figure in car bombing,' *The Washington Post*, 20 January 2015. See also Ronen Bergman, *Rise and Kill First* (New York: Random House, 2018), 597–600.
30. Walter Pincus, 'Attack May Spark Coup In Iraq, Say U.S. Analysts', *Washington Post*, 6 October 2002.
31. Pincus, 'Attack May Spark Coup'.
32. James Risen, *State of War* (New York: Pocket Books, 2006), 130–1.
33. Bob Woodward, *Fear* (New York: Simon & Schuster, 2018), 182.
34. Dana Priest, 'U.S. Teams Seek to Kill Iraqi Elite', *Washington Post*, 29 March 2003.
35. Dana Priest, 'Covert Action in Colombia', *Washington Post*, 21 December 2013.
36. Leigh Mollo, 'The United States and Assassination Policy: Diluting the Absolute', thesis, Naval Postgraduate School, 2003, 29.
37. Trevor McCrisken, 'Ten Years On: Obama's War on Terrorism in Rhetoric and Practice', *International Affairs*, 87.4 (2011), 781–801. Hugh Gusterson, 'Drone Warfare in Waziristan and the New Military Humanism,' Current Anthropology, 60, https://www.journals.uchicago.edu/doi/full/10.1086/701022, and Tara McKelvey, 'Drones kill rescuers in 'double tap', say activists,' BBC News, 22 October 2013, https://www.bbc.co.uk/news/world-us-canada-24557333.
38. Charlie Savage, 'How 4 Federal Lawyers Paved the Way to Kill Osama bin Laden', *New York Times*, 28 October 2015, available at https://www.nytimes.com/2015/10/29/us/politics/obama-legal-authorization-osama-bin-laden-raid.html (accessed 1 November 2023).
39. White House, 'Report on the Legal and Policy Frameworks Guiding the United States' Use of Military Force and Related Security Operations', December 2016, available at https://www.justsecurity.org/wp-content/uploads/2016/12/framework.Report_Final.pdf (accessed 1 November 2023); Mary Ellen O'Connell, 'Twenty Years of Drone Attacks', EJIL Talk [blog], 15 November 2022, available at https://www.ejiltalk.org/twenty-years-of-drone-attacks/ (accessed 1 November 2023).
40. Robert Chesney, 'Military-Intelligence Convergence and the Law of Title 10/Title 50 Debate', *Journal of National Security Law and Policy*, 5 (2011–12), 539; Jennifer Kibbe, 'CIA/SOF Convergence and Congressional Oversight', *Intelligence and National Security*, 38.1 (2023).
41. Mazzetti, *The Way*, chapter 7.

42. Klaidman, *Kill or Capture*, 245.
43. Harold Koh, 'The Obama Administration and International Law', *American Society of International Law*, 25 March 2010, available at https://2009-2017.state.gov/s/l/releases/remarks/139119.htm (accessed 1 November 2023); Eric Holder, 'Attorney General Eric Holder Speaks at Northwestern University School of Law', 5 March 2012, available at https://www.justice.gov/opa/speech/attorney-general-eric-holder-speaks-northwestern-university-school-law (accessed 1 November 2023).
44. David Barron, Memorandum for the Attorney General, 19/2/2010, available at https://nsarchive2.gwu.edu/NSAEBB/NSAEBB529-Anwar-al-Awlaki-File/documents/15)%20OLC%20Barron-Lederman%20February%202010%20Awlaki%20memo.pdf (accessed 1 November 2023). A later memorandum by the same author provided a more extensive legal justification but – on the ban – it reached the same conclusion, citing the Hays Parks memorandum. David Barron, Memorandum for the Attorney General, 16/7/2010, available at https://nsarchive2.gwu.edu/NSAEBB/NSAEBB529-Anwar-al-Awlaki-File/documents/16) OLC Barron-Lederman July 2010 Awlaki memo.pdf (accessed 1 November 2023).
45. Department of Justice, 'Lawfulness of a Lethal Operation Directed Against a U.S. Citizen Who Is a Senior Operational Leader of Al-Qa'ida or An Associated Force', 8/11/2011, available at https://www.justice.gov/sites/default/files/oip/legacy/2014/07/23/dept-white-paper.pdf (accessed 1 November 2023).
46. Luca Trenta, 'The Obama Administration's Conceptual Change: Imminence and the Legitimation of Targeted Killings', *European Journal of International Security*, 3.1 (2017); Noura Erakat, 'New Imminence in the Time of Obama: The Impact of Targeted Killings on the Law of Self-defense', *Arizona Law Review*, 56 (2014).
47. General Michael Hayden, Email exchange with the author, 9 September 2016.
48. H.R. 6010, 111th Congress, available at https://www.congress.gov/bill/111th-congress/house-bill/6010/text?r=28&s=1 (accessed 1 November 2023).
49. 'Procedures for approving direct action against terrorist targets located outside the United States and areas of active hostilities', 22/5/2013, available at https://www.justice.gov/oip/foia-library/procedures_for_approving_direct_action_against_terrorist_targets/download (accessed 1 November 2023).
50. Charlie Savage, 'Trump's Secret Rules for Drone Strikes Outside War Zones Are Disclosed,' *The New York Times*, 1 May 2021.
51. Woodward, *Fear*, 182.

52. Michael Peck, 'OPLAN 5015: The Secret Plan for Destroying North Korea (and Start World War III?)', *The National Interest*, 11 March 2017.
53. Woodward, *Fear*, 184.
54. Editorial Board, 'OPLAN 5015', *The Korean Times*, 7 October 2015.
55. AFP in Seoul, 'North Korea Hacked South's Secret Joint US War Plans – Reports', *The Guardian*, 10 October 2017, available at https://www.theguardian.com/world/2017/oct/10/north-korea-hacked-us-war-plans-south-korea-reports (accessed 1 November 2023).
56. Ewen MacAskill, 'North Korea Accuses CIA of Biochemical Plot to Kill Kim Jong-un', *The Guardian*, 5 May 2017.
57. Hannah Ellis-Petersen and Benjamin Haas, 'How North Korea Got Away with the Assassination of Kim Jong-nam', *The Guardian*, 1 April 2019, available at https://www.theguardian.com/world/2019/apr/01/how-north-korea-got-away-with-the-assassination-of-kim-jong-nam (accessed 9 November 2023).
58. Phil Rucker and Josh Dawsey, '"We fell in love": Trump and Kim Shower Praise, Stroke Egos on Path to Nuclear Negotiations', *Washington Post*, 25 February 2019.
59. Phil Rucker and Rober Costa, 'Bob Woodward's New Book Reveals A 'Nervous Breakdown' of Trump's Presidency', *Washington Post*, 4 September 2018; Woodward, *Fear*, chapter 18.
60. Jeremy Scahill, 'The Mysterious Case of Joe Biden and the Future of Drone Wars', *The Intercept*, 15 December 2021, available at https://theintercept.com/2021/12/15/drone-strikes-joe-biden-pentagon-kabul/ (accessed 1 November 2023).
61. Charlie Savage, 'White House Tightens Rules on Counterterrorism Drone Strikes', *New York Times*, 7 October 2022, available at https://www.nytimes.com/2022/10/07/us/politics/drone-strikes-biden-trump.html#:~:text=WASHINGTON%20—%20President%20Biden%20has%20signed,of%20warfare%2C%20according%20to%20officials (accessed 8 November 2023).
62. Justin Baragona, 'Lindsey Graham Calls for the Assassination of Vladimir Putin', *Daily Beast*, 4 March 2022, available at https://www.thedailybeast.com/lindsey-graham-calls-for-the-assassination-of-vladimir-putin (accessed 1 November 2023).
63. Craig Copetas, 'Ex-Black Ops Agent: This Is How Putin Could Meet His End', *Daily Beast*, 16 March 2022, available at https://www.thedailybeast.com/ex-black-ops-agent-explains-how-putin-could-meet-his-end (accessed 1 November 2023).
64. VOA News, 'White House Disavows Senator's Call for Assassination of Putin', *Voice of America*, 4 March 2022, available at

https://www.voanews.com/a/white-house-disavows-senator-s-call-for-assassination-of-putin-/6471280.html (accessed 1 November 2023).
65. White House, 'Remarks by President Biden on the United Efforts of the Free World to Support the People of Ukraine', 26/3/2022, available at https://www.whitehouse.gov/briefing-room/speeches-remarks/2022/03/26/remarks-by-president-biden-on-the-united-efforts-of-the-free-world-to-support-the-people-of-ukraine/ (accessed 1 November 2023).
66. This goes against the conclusion reached in Lindsey O'Rourke, *Covert Regime Change* (Ithaca, NY: Cornell University Press, 2018), 63.
67. James Lockhart, *Chile, the CIA, and the Cold War* (Edinburgh: Edinburgh University Press, 2019).
68. Lawrence Houston, Senate Select Committee to Study Governmental Operations with Respect to Intelligence Activities Testimony, 2/6/1975, Digital National Security Archives, Covert Operations II, 4–5.
69. Arturo Jimenez-Bacardi, 'From Lawless to Secret Law: The United States, the CIA and Extra-judicial Killing', in Alison Brysk and Michael Stohl (eds), *Contracting Human Rights* (Cheltenham: Edward Elgar, 2018), 127.
70. Ruth Jamieson and Kieran McEvoy, 'State Crime by Proxy and Juridical Othering', *British Journal of Criminology*, 45 (2005), 505.
71. Michael Poznansky, 'Revisiting Plausible Deniability', *Strategic Studies*, 45.4 (2022), 511–33.
72. Luke Nichter, *The Last Brahmin: Henry Cabot Lodge Jr. and the Making of the Cold War* (New Haven, CT: Yale University Press, 2020), 129.
73. Loch Johnson, *The Third Option* (Oxford: Oxford University Press, 2022), 182.
74. See Michael Schmitt, 'State-Sponsored Assassination in International and Domestic Law', *Yale Journal of International Law*, 17.2 (1992), 609–85, who argues that an imminent danger was sufficient to suspend the prohibition and that only covert assassinations were prohibited; or David Ennis, 'Preemption, Assassination, and the War on Terrorism', *Campbell Law Review*, 27.2 (2005), 253–77, who argues that the Church Committee only dealt with state leaders.
75. See Chapter 8.
76. Luca Trenta, 'Death by Reinterpretation: Dynamics of Norm Contestation and the US Ban on Assassination in the Reagan Years', *Journal of Global Security Studies*, 6.4 (2021), doi: 10.1093/jogss/ogab012.
77. Bert Brandenburg, 'The Legality of Assassination as an Aspect of Foreign Policy', *Virginia Journal of International Law*, 27.3 (1986–7), 696.
78. Bruce Riedel, Interview with the author, 4 August 2016, Washington, DC.

Resources

List of Interviews and Exchanges

Albion, Alexis, Zoom interview, 22 July 2022
Banks, William, Zoom interview, 9 September 2021
Bellinger III, John, Interview, 2 August 2016, Washington, DC
Bird, Kai, Phone interview with the author, 26 August 2022
Byman, Daniel, Zoom interview, 10 December 2021
Coll, Steve, Zoom interview, 22 February 2021
Craxi, Vittorio Michele ('Bobo', son of former Italian prime minister Bettino Craxi), Exchange with the author, 7 September 2023
Hart, Gary, Skype interview, 20 May 2016
Hayden, Michael (Gen.), Skype interview, 22 August 2016; email exchange 9 September 2016; Zoom interview, 4 January 2022
Hurley, Mike, Zoom interview, 10 August 2022
Indyk, Martin, Zoom interview, 12 October 2022
Jeffreys-Jones, Rhodri, Phone interview 17 May 2016
Kinzer, Stephen, Zoom interview, 14 February 2021
Lake, Anthony, Phone interview, 16 June 2022
McManus, Doyle, Interview 3 August 2016
Mondale, Walter, Skype interview, 26 May 2016
Nouzille, Vincent, Skype interview 2 October 2020
Pillar, Paul, Skype interview, 5 August 2016
Priest, Dana, Phone interview, 13 September 2022
Quandt, William, Interview, 19 July 2012, Charlottesville, Virginia
Riedel, Bruce, Interview, 4 August 2016, Washington, DC
Rust, William, Zoom interview, 21 April 2022
Schwarz, Frederick A. O., Phone interview, 11 May 2016
Scranton, Margaret, Zoom interview 8 December 2021
Shane, Scott, Skype interview, 3 August 2016
Siekmeier, James, Zoom interview, 9 June 2022

Vega, Bernardo, Skype interview, 5 May 2022
Weiner, Tim, Zoom interview, 3 February 2022
Whippl, Joseph, Phone interview, 19 February 2022
Wittes, Benjamin, 5 August 2016
Zelikow, Philip, Email exchange, 11 August 2022

Archives

Archivo General de la Nación, Republica Dominicana
Association for Diplomatic Studies and Training, oral history interviews
Biblioteca Nacional De Chile
CIA CREST/Reading Room
Columbia University, Oral History Research Project
Cryptocomb
Cryptome.org
Daniel Schorr, Personal Papers, Library of Congress
Digital National Security Archives
Federation of American Scientists, Intelligence Reform Program
Frank Church Papers, Albertson Library, Boise State University
George H. W. Bush Presidential Library (GHWBL)
George W. Bush White House, archived
George McTurnan Kahin Papers, Cornell University Library
Gerald Ford Presidential Library
John F. Kennedy Presidential Library and Digital Library
Lyndon Baynes Johnson Presidential Library
Mary Ferrell Foundation Archive
Miller Center, Oral History Interviews and White House Tapes
National Commission on Terrorist Attacks Upon the United States (9/11 Commission) Report, Hearings and Staff Files
National Security Archives, George Washington University
Richard Nixon Presidential Library
Ronald Reagan Presidential Library
The Black Vault
United Nations Official Documents System
US Department of State, Chile Declassification Project Collection
US Department of State, Office of the Historian, Foreign Relations of the United States volumes (FRUS)
US House of Representatives, Select Committee on Assassinations, Report, hearings, testimonies, and appendix volumes

US House of Representatives, Permanent Select Committee on Intelligence and Senate Select Committee on Intelligence, Report of the Joint Inquiry into the terrorist attacks of September 11, 2001, December 2002
US Library of Congress
US National Archives and Records Administration
US National Archives, The President John F. Kennedy Assassination Records Collection (JFKAR)
US Senate Select Committee to Study Governmental Operations with Respect to Intelligence Activities reports, addenda, hearings and testimonies
William J. Clinton Presidential Library and Digital Library
William J. Clinton Presidential History Project

Index

Afghanistan
    CIA recruitment of tribal groups, 305, 306–9, 313–14, 316–17, 329
    Mullah Omar, 344
    Predator programme, 323–4
    strikes against al-Qaeda's training camps, 291, 309–11
    US support for the mujahideen, 228–9
    US weapons supplied to, 228–31
    weaponised drones, 325–6
    see also Bin Laden, Osama
Africa
    Eurocentric racism and the newly independent African nations, 48–9
    in US foreign policy, 48, 61
    see also Congo; Lumumba, Patrice
Alawi, Iyad, 286–7
Alessandri, Jorge, 155, 157, 159
Allen, Morse, 24, 27–8, 29
Allen, Richard, 218, 231
Allende, Salvador
    US attempts to prevent the confirmation of (Track I), 155, 156, 157, 158–9, 161, 162, 163–4, 166
    US involvement in a coup to overthrow, 156–8
    victory in the 1970 election, 155, 156, 158
    see also Chile

al-Qaeda
    attack on the USS *Cole*, 323, 327, 344
    Blue Sky memo, 325–6
    Clarke's 'Strategy' document, 326–7
    the 'Millennium plot,' 323
    post-9/11 MON, 342
    threat from, 301–2
    see also Bin Laden, Osama
Anderson, Frank, 277, 280, 282
Anderson, Jack, 154, 155
Angleton, James, 183
Arbenz, Jacobo, 31, 38
Artime, Manuel, 97–8, 251
al-Assad, Bashar, 350
assassinations
    and American self-perceptions, 3, 360–1
    archival sources, 14–15
    the CIA's internal prohibition against, 182, 197
    conditions for, 4
    decision-making processes, 5, 7
    definitional debates, 200–1, 263
    definitions, 12, 20 n.53
    direct/indirect US government involvement, 5–6
    the domestic political environment, 4, 5, 7

Index

'Executive Order 12333 and Assassination' (Parks Memorandum), 264–5, 266, 292, 301
in historical records, 93, 272
history of in foreign policy, 3–4, 5, 13–14, 180, 181
imminent threat assessments, 2–3, 194, 264
as an indirect outcome of a coup, 260–2, 265, 271, 292–3, 201257
plausible deniability and, 4
politics of, 3–4, 5, 7
practices, 3, 13–14
presidential control over, 5, 6–7
quasi-secrecy, 8–9
research sources, 14–15
Rockefeller Commission's investigation into, 181–2, 184–7, 190, 200
the season of inquiry and, 181–2, 183, 200
in US foreign policy, 3
the war on drugs and, 4
the war on terror and, 4, 13–14
wartime/peacetime boundaries, 12, 198, 228, 264
see also ban on assassinations; language; targeted killings
Avrakatos, Gust, 229, 230
al-Awlaki, Anwar, 347

Baer, Robert, 282, 283, 284, 285, 286, 292
Baker, James, 7, 255, 256, 271
ban on assassination
Church Committee's call for a law prohibiting assassination, 197–9, 355–6
under the Clinton Administration, 228–9, 292, 311–13
Congressional debate over, 261–2, 265–6, 273
contestations, 8, 12, 182, 260–2, 311–12, 359

the 'contra war' against the Sandinistas and, 226–8
counterterrorism measures and, 303, 311–12, 343
covert operation reporting, 11
definitional debates, 8
Executive Order 11905, 3, 182, 199, 201, 356
Executive Order 12036, 201–2, 215, 217–18
Executive Order 12333, 218, 222, 261, 264–5, 344, 348
'Executive Order 12333 and Assassination' (Parks Memorandum), 264–5, 266, 292, 301
and the failed Iraqi uprising, 273, 275
Ford administration's publication of, 11, 182, 199
the language of assassinations and, 7–8
legal reviews, 8
as a norm, 8, 356–7
and operations against Bin Laden, 289, 301–2, 307, 311–12, 328, 329–30
Reagan's reinterpretation of, 214, 239–40, 358
redrafting of Carter's Executive Order 12036, 217–18
reinterpretation of under George W. Bush, 262–3, 264–5, 266, 346–7
and the removal of Saddam Hussein, 275–6, 288–9, 292
self-defence against terrorism and, 238, 312–13
strategic ambiguity of, 199–200, 272–3
and the supply of weapons to the mujahideen of Afghanistan, 228–31
targeted killings and, 344–5
the targeting of al-Awlaki and, 347, 348

371

Index

ban on assassination (*Cont.*)
  third-party actors and, 226, 227–8, 233
  US foreign policy and, 272–3
  US government's public position on, 3, 360–1
  US involvement in coups, 252, 254
  US involvement in coups and risk of leader's deaths, 257, 260–2, 265, 271, 292–3
  wartime/peacetime boundaries, 264
Barr, William, 262, 271, 303, 326, 347, 359
Barron, David, 348
Belgium
  Congo's independence ceremony, 46
  Lumumba's execution, 66
  military aggression in post-independent Congo, 47–8, 49–50, 51
  plans to assassinate Lumumba, 50–1, 53, 58
  support for Moise Tshombe in Katanga, 46, 48, 49, 50
  see also Congo; Lumumba, Patrice
Belin, David, 185–6, 187
Bell, Griffin, 201–2
Bennett, Donald, 167
Berger, Sandy, 290, 306, 309, 310, 313–14, 317, 318, 325
Berle, Adolphe, 122–3
Berry, Lorenzo (Wimpy), 112, 116, 119, 121
Biden, Joe, 350–1
Bin Laden, Osama
  the ban on assassinations and, 289, 301–2, 307, 311–12, 328, 329–30
  bombing of the Khowst training camp, 291, 309–11
  Clinton Administration's intent to kill, 329–31
  Clinton's hunt for, 301, 306–9, 314, 315, 318, 320, 323, 329

  direct covert operations against, 315–16
  George W. Bush's pre-9/11 operations against, 13, 327, 360
  Massoud-CIA collaboration, 321–2, 329, 330
  MON for the CIA and Massoud relationship, 321
  MON providing kill authority, 316–18
  MONs authorising capture operations, 307, 313, 316–17
  Obama's strikes against, 347
  as a potential terrorist threat, 302, 303, 304
  Predator/weaponised drones against, 323–4, 325–6, 327–8
  in Sudan, 304–5
  tribal-led capture operations, 306–9, 313–14, 316–17, 329
  US failed strike attempts against, 319–20
  US-Pakistan joint operation against, 320–1
  see also Afghanistan
biological weapons, 77; *see also* poisons
Bissell, Richard
  on Kennedy's knowledge of the Castro plots, 81
  language and plausible deniability, 67
  plot against Lumumba, 51, 56, 57, 59, 66
  plot against Qassem, 37
  plots against Castro, 77, 80, 81, 83, 88, 99–100
  plots against Sukarno, 35
  plots against Trujillo, 116, 118, 120–1, 122, 125
  testimony to the Church Committee, 196
Black, Cofer, 304, 306, 317, 319, 321, 327, 342
Blair, Tony, 289

372

Index

Boren, David, 259
Brandenburg, Bert, 359
Brennan, John, 349
Broe, William, 157, 160
Bruemmer, Russell, 262
Brundage, Fitzhugh, 5
Brzezinski, Zbigniew, 201
Buchen, Philip, 185, 191
Buckley, William, 224
Bundy, McGeorge, 87, 94, 98, 118
Burden, William, 50–1
Bureau of Narcotics and Dangerous Drugs (BNDD), 250–1
Bush, George H. W.
   attempted assassination of, 280
   conditions for regime change in Iraq, 273–4
   covert operations against Noriega, 252, 254–6, 263, 265
   on the need for a coup in Iraq, 273, 274–5
   political fallout after the failed coup against Noriega, 259
   reinterpretation of the ban on assassination, 262–3, 264–5, 266
Bush, George W.
   Authorization for the Use of Military Force (AUMF), 341, 342
   campaign of assassination in Iraq, 345–6
   counterterrorism under, 326, 342–3
   9/11, 341
   post-9/11 MON, 342
   pre-9/11 operations against Bin Laden, 13, 327, 360
   reinterpretation of the ban on assassination, 262–3, 264–5, 266, 346–7
   targeted killings, 343–4

Cabell, Charles, 76, 82
Cabral, Donald Reid, 117
Campbell, Judith, 91
Cannistraro, Vincent, 232–3
Carlucci, Frank, 219
Carter, Jimmy
   Executive Order 12036, 201–2, 217–18
   Executive Order 12333, 218
   foreign policy under, 201, 202
   observation of the 1989 Panamanian elections, 256
Casey, William
   on the assassination of Qaddafi, 235
   attitude towards the law, 216, 224
   as CIA director, 215–17
   conduct of covert operations, 215–16, 239
   counterterrorism measures, 220, 358
   influence on foreign policy, 215
   Iran-contra scandal, 226, 228, 239
   redrafting of Carter's Executive Order 12036, 217–18
   reinvigorated role for the CIA, 265
   support for the mujahideen of Afghanistan, 229, 230
Castro, Fidel
   the AMLASH (Cubela) operation against, 95–7, 98, 100
   Church Committee report on, 193–4, 195
   CIA-Mafia joint plots, 80–2, 83, 85, 91–2, 93–4, 99, 100
   CIA's long-term assassination campaign against, 75–6, 98–100, 184
   early CIA assassination plots, 77–9
   Eisenhower's knowledge of the assassination plots, 76–7, 82–3, 99–100
   executive action and plots against, 83–4, 93, 100
   Hemingway shrine plot, 90, 99
   honeytrap poison plot, 78
   impact on Trujillo's position, 111, 113, 122

Index

Castro, Fidel (*Cont.*)
  indirect assassination plots, 84–5
  Johnson-era plots, 98
  Kennedy-era plots, 83–93
  language of the plots against, 80–1, 89–90, 92–3, 98–9, 100
  NPIC-related plans against Castro, 84–5
  Operation Patty assassination plot, 87
  poison plots against, 81–2, 83, 91, 93–4
  possible chemical contaminants, 77
  in the Rockefeller Commission's investigation, 185, 187
  scuba-diving assassination plots, 94–5
  see also Cuban exiles
Castro, Raul, 4, 79, 82, 125
Central Intelligence Agency (CIA)
  (im)plausible deniability construct, 9
  during the Clinton Administration, 273, 279–80
  Cold War assassinations, 3–4, 5, 351
  compliance with the Rockefeller Commission, 184–7, 200
  continuities with wartime OOS culture, 26–7, 30, 215
  counterterrorism capabilities, 233–4
  early OPC assassination plots, 29–30
  early use of assassination, 24–5
  the 'Family Jewels,' 182, 185, 188
  glossary for covert operations, 11
  indirect involvement via third-party actors, 5–6, 38, 352
  internal prohibition on assassination, 182, 197
  mind control operations, 24, 27–9
  Program Branch 7 (P/B7), 29–30
  reinvigorated role for under Reagan, 213–15, 216, 217
  response to the Church Committee, 189
  'the spiel,' 10, 82, 123
  'A Study in Assassination' (assassination manual), 32, 38
  submissions of possible scandalous activities, 182
  targeting of Third World nations, 4, 9
  Watergate's impact on, 187–8
  see also Church Committee; covert operations
Chalabi, Ahmad, 277–9, 281–6, 287, 288, 289, 292, 360
Cheney, Dick, 183, 187, 257, 260, 272, 344
Chiang Kai Shek, 30–1, 193
Chile
  false flaggers in, 163, 165, 172
  15th October decision, 169–70, 173
  40 Committee's strategy for, 155, 158, 160, 161, 164, 168
  plausible deniability over, 158
  prevention of Allende's confirmation (Track I strategy), 155, 156, 157, 158–9, 161, 162, 163–4, 166
  Schneider's opposition to a coup, 155, 156, 157, 158, 161–2
  US creation of conditions for a military coup (Track II strategy), 155, 156–8, 160–1, 162–3, 164, 165–70, 172, 174, 352
  in US foreign policy, 156, 159
  US interference in the 1970 elections, 155
  US supply of weapons to military in, 155, 165, 166, 171, 172
  see also Allende, Salvador; Korry, Edward; Schneider, General René

374

Index

China
  Chiang Kai Shek plot, 30–1, 193
  Zhou Enlai plots, 32–4, 38, 193, 351
Christopher, Warren, 280, 285
Church, Frank, 188–9, 190
Church Committee (Senate Select Committee to Study Governmental Operations with Respect to Intelligence Activities),
  on assassination in US foreign policy, 193–7
  assessment of the Schneider assassination, 170, 173–4
  call for a law prohibiting assassination, 11, 182, 197–9, 355–6
  Chiang Kai Shek plot, 193
  CIA release of documents to, 189–90
  definition of a 'foreign official,' 198
  Ford administration's attempt to undermine, 181–2, 200
  Ford administration's Executive Order and, 11, 182, 199, 356
  indirect deaths of foreign officials, 194–5
  indirect US government involvement in Trujillo, Diem and Schneider, 193
  interim report into assassination plots, 182, 190–1, 355–6
  investigation into Colonel al-Mahdawi's death, 37
  investigation into Diem's assassination, 134
  investigation into Lumumba's assassination, 66–7, 193, 195
  on the language of assassination, 195–6, 354
  on the plausible deniability doctrine, 196–7
  on plots against Castro, 193–4, 195
  Reagan Administration's attitude towards, 213, 214, 216
  release of assassination documents to, 190–1
  report on US involvement in Cold War-era assassinations, 11
  the report's publication, 192–3
  the Sukarno case, 43 n.70, 193
  testimonies to, 192
  on US involvement in coups, 194
  wartime/peacetime boundaries, 198, 228, 356
  White House manipulation of, 189, 190
  Zhou Enlai plot, 193
Clarke, Richard
  on covert operations against al-Qaeda, 326
  the hunt for Bin Laden, 304, 306, 307, 308, 309–10, 314, 316, 317, 319, 321
  Predator drones against Bin Laden, 323
  'Strategy' document on al-Qaeda, 326–7
Clarridge, Dewey, 227, 228, 233–4, 236–7, 288
Clinton, Bill
  Administration's relationship with the CIA, 273, 279–80, 359
  ban on assassinations and the removal of Saddam Hussein, 288–9
  bombing of the Iraqi intelligence headquarters, 280–1
  counterterrorism measures, 302–3, 309
  the hunt for Bin Laden, 301, 306–9, 314, 315, 318, 320, 323, 329
  impeachment trial, 291, 311
  the intent to kill Bin Laden, 329–31
  Iraq during the administration of, 273, 280
  MON providing kill authority, 317–18

375

Index

Clinton (*Cont.*)
  Presidential Decision Directives, 302, 309
  review of the ban on assassinations, 311–13
  US support for Chalabi's opposition, 281–3
Cohen, David, 303–4
Cohen, Stanley, 9, 231, 237
Cohen, William
  on the ban on assassinations, 261, 262
  on the bombing of the Khowst training camp, 310
  covert operations against Noriega, 259–60
  the hunt for Bin Laden, 314
  strikes in Iraq, 291
Colby, William
  on the call for a law prohibiting assassination, 198
  the Church Committee and, 189, 190
  on the CIA's involvement in illegal activities, 180–1, 182, 183, 184, 185
  meeting with Seymour Hersh, 183
  on US supply of weapons, 194
  Zhou Enlai plots, 32, 33
Cold War
  assassinations during, 3–4, 5, 351
  Bandung Conference, 33, 34
  Chiang Kai Shek plot, 30–1
  Cold War dynamics, 10, 25–6
  constraints on assassination, 353–4
  Jacobo Arbenz plot, 31, 38
  language of assassinations, 7, 10, 38
  plausible deniability, 10
  regime change, 35–7, 38–9
  Stalin plot, 31
  Sukarno plot, 34
  targeting of leaders of non-aligned countries, 4, 10, 33–5
  US assassination methods and responsibility, 352
  Zhou Enlai plots, 32–4, 38, 193, 351
Coll, Steve, 229, 305, 307, 316, 322
Colombia, 346
Colson, Charles, 154
Conein, Lucien
  oversight of the November 1963 coup, 140, 141, 142, 143, 144–7, 148, 352
  the summer 1963 attempted coup, 134–5, 137, 138
Congo
  Belgian presence in, post-independence, 47–8, 49–50, 65
  Cold War lens applied to, 48
  independence, 45, 47
  Kasavubu-led vote of no confidence in Lumumba, 54, 55
  Mobutu's US-backed coup, 55–6
  secession of Katanga, 46, 48, 49, 50, 51–2, 53
  the UN and the removal of Belgian troops, 48, 49–50, 51
  US policy on, 48
  see also Kasavubu, Joseph; Lumumba, Patrice; Mobutu, Joseph
Congress
  Anti-terrorism and Effective Death Penalty Act of 1996, 303
  attempted law on the prohibition of assassinations, 200–1
  Congressional notification, 3
  Congressional oversight, 7, 215
  debate on the ban, 273
  hearings after the failed Giroldi coup, 259–60, 359
  investigation into the CIA's wrongdoings, 188–9
  Iraq Liberation Act (ILA), 289, 290
  'National Intelligence Reorganization and Reform Act,' 201
  refusal to support the July 1988 Panama coup, 254, 259–60

Index

reinterpretation of the ban on assassination, 261–2, 265–6
Cordier, Andrew, 54–5
counterterrorism
 aggressive and lethal covert operations against terrorists, 221, 222–3, 224
 the ban on assassinations and, 303, 311–12, 343
 the Beirut bombings in 1983, 219–20
 the CIA's capabilities, 233–4
 CIA's virtual tracking station, 303–4
 under the Clinton Administration, 302–3, 309
 under George W. Bush, 326, 342–3
 National Security Decision Directives under Reagan, 219, 221, 222, 224, 234, 358
 the NSC's role in, 220–1
 as outside WPR requirements, 237–9
 pre-emptive self-defence strikes, 237–8, 264, 265, 266, 303, 310–11, 312–13
 Presidential Decision Directives, 302, 309
 under the Reagan Administration, 214, 219, 220, 358
Counter-Terrorism Group (CTG), 1
Counter-Terrorist Security Group (CSG), 309
covert operations
 under 55412 Special Group, 52–3, 55, 77
 under Casey as CIA director, 215–16, 239
 during the Cold War, 25–6
 Doolittle report, 26
 false flaggers, 163, 165, 172
 40 Committee, 155, 158, 160, 161, 164, 168
 Intelligence Support Activity (ISA), 220

International Activities Division (IAD), 227
 1974 Hughes-Ryan amendment, 11, 188, 355
 the 'plumbers,' 154, 250, 251
 proposed outlaw of, 188
 Special Group Augmented (SGA), 89, 90, 92–3, 99
 US involvement in coups, 194, 201
Cressey, Robert, 324, 325
Cuba
 Bay of Pigs invasion, 85, 86, 122, 285
 CIA contingency plans, post-Castro, 79, 87–8
 covert war and overthrow of Castro, 76–7
 Guantanamo base, 86
 Operation Mongoose, 89–91, 100
 support for Noriega, 255
 in US foreign policy, 111
 see also Castro, Fidel
Cuban exiles
 Artime's brigade (Project AMWORLD), 97–8
 CIA's long-term assassination campaigns and, 75, 76
 liaison with Trujillo's forces, 76
 NPIC-related plans against Castro, 84–5
 Operation Patty, 86, 87
 post-Bay of Pigs invasion, 86
 Sturgis and Operation 40, 78
 US-backed assassination mission, 78–9
 use of the Guantanamo base, 86–7
Cubela, Rolando, 95–6, 97, 100

Davis, Arthur, 254
Dearborn, Henry
 contacts with dissident groups, 112, 114–15, 119, 120
 Kennedy's knowledge of the assassination plot, 126, 354

377

Index

Dearborn (*Cont.*)
  on need for action against Trujillo, 114, 115, 121, 123, 124–5, 126
  US supply of weapons to the dissidents, 110, 114, 116, 119, 121, 122
decision-making processes
  and the evolution of assassination plots, 5
  new legal interpretations of the ban, 8
  presidential control over, 5, 6–7
  quasi-secrecy, 8–9
DeGraffenreid, Ken, 217
Delvalle, Eric, 253–4
Deutch, John, 287, 303, 306
Devine, Frank, 115, 116, 120, 123, 125
Devlin, Larry
  assassination plot against Lumumba, 47, 53, 55–6, 57–9, 66, 84
  as Chief of Station in Congo, 49
  the communist threat in Congo, 51, 52
  Congo and the new Kennedy administration, 64–5
  contacts with Mobutu, 60
  Lumumba's escape and recapture by his enemies, 61–5, 66
Diaz, Juan Tomas, 112
Diem, Ngo Dinh
  army crackdown on the Buddhist monks, 135–6
  Church Committee report on, 193
  the coup of November 1963, 140–6
  future after the possible summer 1963 coup, 137–9
  killing of, 133–4, 146, 147
  language of assassination, 134
  language of possible assassination of, 141–3, 149
  Minh's coup d'etat against, 133
  request for departure from Vietnam, 145–6
  as a staunch US ally, 134
  US knowledge of the possible summer coup/assassination, 135–7
  US relations with, post-attempted coup, 139–40
  US stance on the Buddhist's demands, 135
  US stance on the possible assassination of, 141–2, 352, 354
  US's unwillingness to safeguard, post-coup, 133–4, 352
Dillon, Douglas, 51, 52, 187
domestic law
  drafting of presidential findings, 11
  legal reviews of the ban, 8
  legal work, 8, 239–40
  legalisation of covert operations, 11–12
Dominican Republic
  Castro and the Cuban situation, 111, 113, 122
  dissident assassination plot against Trujillo, 117, 118–26, 127
  Kennedy's knowledge of the Trujillo plots, 118, 126, 354
  in US foreign policy, 118
  US retreat from Trujillo assassination policy, 124–5
  US transfer of weapons to the dissidents, 110, 114, 115, 116–17, 118, 119–20, 121–3, 124–5, 126, 352
  US-backed regime change, 112–13
  see also Trujillo, Rafael
Don, Tran Van, 140, 143, 145, 146, 148
Donovan, William, 215
Douglas-Home, Alec, 58
drones
  government use of for assassinations, 5
  Hellfire missiles, 326, 327
  Predator drones against Bin Laden, 323–4

Index

Predator programme, 343
strikes under Obama, 347–8
targeted killings policy, 13–14, 343, 344
weaponised drones, 325–6, 327–8
Dugan, Mike, 272
Dulles, Allen
Abdul Karim Qassem plot, 36
on the Castro regime, 76
Kennedy's knowledge of the Castro plots, 81, 100
plot against Lumumba, 47, 51, 52, 53, 55, 57, 66
plots against Castro, 77, 80, 82–3, 99, 100
plots against Trujillo, 113
Stalin plot, 31
Zhou Enlai plot, 34

Edwards, Augustin, 158, 159
Edwards, Sheffield, 27–9, 80, 81, 86, 92, 99
Egypt, 36, 231, 233
Ehrlichman, John, 250
Eisenhower, Dwight
assassination order against Lumumba, 47, 52, 53, 55, 56, 57, 66–7, 196, 354
necessity of unsavoury measures, 26
plots against Castro, 76–7, 82–3, 99–100
plots against Trujillo, 111, 115, 116, 126
Elder, William, 90, 99
Esterline, Jake, 77

Fadlallah, Mohammed Hussein, 220, 224–5, 230, 239
Farland, Robert, 112, 113, 114
FBI (Federal Bureau of Investigation), 82, 85–6, 87, 91
Fields, Glen, 57
Fitzgerald, Desmond, 94, 95, 96–7
Fleischer, Ari, 345

Ford, Gerald
on the call for a law prohibiting assassination, 198–9
the Church Committee's assassination interim report, 191–2
Executive Order 11905, 11, 182, 199, 200, 356
Ford administration's attempt to undermine the Church Committee, 181–2, 200
investigation into the CIA's wrongdoings, 180, 184–5
foreign policy
assassinations's history in, 3–4, 5
the ban on assassinations's influence on, 8, 272–3
under the Carter Administration, 201, 202
Casey as CIA Director and, 215
Chile in, 156
Church Committee report on assassination in, 193–7
on Congo/Africa, 48, 61
on Cuba, 98, 111
on the Dominican Republic, 118
international terrorism in, 213
on South Vietnam, 134
Forrestal, Michael, 136, 138
Fortier, Donald, 232–3
Fredman, Johnathan, 202
Frei, Eduardo
conditions for a military coup (Track II strategy), 162–3, 168
firing of Admiral Porta, 168, 171
on Schneider's opposition to a coup, 158
support for the assassination of Schneider, 164–5
US attempts to prevent the confirmation of Allende (Track I), 155, 156, 157, 163–4
US support a coup to prevent Allende's confirmation, 160–1, 162

379

Index

Galindez, Jesus de, 111
Geyer, Georgie Anne, 226
Giancana, Sam, 80, 81–2, 86, 91, 192
Giroldi, Moises, 256–8, 359
Gonzales, Alonzo, 86–7
Goodwin, Richard, 88, 123–5
Gordon, John, 86, 87
Gore, Al, 280, 285, 289
Gottlieb, Sidney
    as the CIA's 'poisoner in chief,' 29
    Mahdawi poisoned handkerchief, 37, 38, 352
    poison plot against Lumumba, 56–7, 59, 66
    poison plots against Castro, 91, 95
    the Sukarno plot, 34, 35
Gray, Gordon, 52–3, 55, 67, 82–3, 196
Gray, Marvin, 185, 187
Great Britain, 36, 58, 63
Gregg, Donald, 217
Grenier, Robert, 323
Großklaus, Mathias, 13–14
Gruffydd Jones, Branwen, 14
Guatemala, 31, 38
Guevara, Che, 79, 82
Gunn, Edward, 154

Haass, Richard, 277–8, 303
Haig, Alexander, 162, 169, 170, 213, 231
Halpern, Sam, 83, 94, 97
Hammarskjöld, Dag, 48, 50, 54, 60–1, 181
Harvey, William, 83–4, 91, 93, 99, 272
Hayden, Michael, 343
Hecksher, Henry, 157, 166, 168
Helms, Richard
    and the ban on assassinations, 181
    on a coup in Chile, 158, 159–60, 164, 170, 172
    investigation into the CIA's wrongdoings, 184
    plots against Castro, 88–9, 93, 96, 99
    testimony to the Church Committee, 196, 330–1
    testimony to the Rockefeller Commission, 186
Hemingway, Mary, 90, 99
Herrera Hassan, Eduardo, 252–3
Hersh, Seymour, 183, 236, 291
Herter, Christian, 51, 76–7, 113
Hezbollah, 219–20
Hilsman, Roger, 136, 139
Holman, Ned, 117
Hoover, J. Edgar, 82, 86, 91, 100
Houston, Lawrence, 91, 92, 94, 197, 353–4
Hunt, E. Howard, 154, 251
Hurley, Mike, 314
Hussein, Saddam
    assassination of within US military strategy, 271–2, 359
    ban on assassinations and the removal of, 275–6, 288–9, 292
    failed Jabr coup, 278
    George W. Bush's campaign of assassination, 345–6
    Operation Desert Fox, 266, 290–1, 293, 360
    plot against Abdul Karim Qassem, 36–7
    propaganda campaigns against, 278, 279
    US desire for the assassination of, post-Gulf War, 275–7, 278, 293
    see also Iraq
hypnosis, 24, 27

Ileo, Joseph, 54
Indyk, Martin, 282, 283, 285, 290
Ingersoll, John, 250
Inman, John, 216, 217
international law, 3, 13, 265, 266
International Telephone & Telegraph Corporation (ITT), 155

380

Index

Iraq
  the Badr Brigades uprising, 283–6
  the ban on assassinations and the failed uprising, 273, 275
  bombing of the Iraqi intelligence headquarters, 280–1
  during the Clinton Administration, 273
  failed uprising against Saddam, 273, 274–5
  George W. Bush's campaign of assassination, 345–6
  invasion of Kuwait, 271, 273
  Jordan-based coup, 286–7
  no-fly zones, 275, 279, 280
  regime change (1959), 36
  sanctions against, 275, 276, 280, 290
  US conditions for regime change in, 273–4
  US hopes for a 'silver bullet' option, 273, 274, 276, 282, 293, 345, 359
  US military strategy, 271–2
  US support for Chalabi's opposition and the INC, 277–9, 281–6, 287, 288, 289, 292, 360
  weapons inspections, 275, 280, 290
  weapons of mass destruction (WMDs), 273, 277–8, 286, 288, 290–1, 345
  see also Hussein, Saddam
Iraq Liberation Act (ILA), 289, 290
Iraqi National Accord (INA), 286–7
Iraqi National Congress (INC), 277–9, 281–6, 287, 288, 289
Israel, 236
Izaguirre de la Riva, Alfredo, 86

Jabr, Saad, 278
Jacobsen, Annie, 17 n.14
Jennings, Peter, 276
Johnson, Alexis, 160, 165
Johnson, Loch, 188, 190
Johnson, Lyndon B., 98
Johnson, Robert, 52, 67

Kamel, Huseein, 286–7
Kansi, Mir Aimal, 305
Karamessines, Tom, 160, 168–9, 170, 173
Kasavubu, Joseph
  Mobutu's coup, 55–6, 60
  plan to overthrow Lumumba, 54–5
  as President of Congo, 45
  relations with the UN, 60–1
  request for Soviet assistance, 49, 50
  request for Western assistance, 47, 48
  support for Mobutu, 60
Kendall, Donald, 158, 159
Kennedy, John
  affair with Judith Campbell, 91
  assassination, 97
  CIA contingency plans, post-Castro, 87–8
  election, 61, 63
  executive action capability against Castro, 100
  plots against Castro, 81, 88, 100
  plots against Trujillo, 111, 116–26, 354
  policy towards Lumumba, 64–5
  on the possible coup and assassinations of Diem and Nhu, 135–9, 140–2, 147
  reaction to the deaths of Diem and Nhu, 147, 354
  Special Group Augmented (SGA), 89
Kennedy, Robert
  Balletti wiretap case, 87
  briefings on CIA-Mafia plots, 91–2, 99, 100
  meeting with Cubela, 96
  Operation Mongoose, 89–91, 100
  plots against Castro, 88, 94, 100, 184
Kettani, Ben Hammou, 55, 62

381

Index

Khamenei, Ayatollah Ali, 1, 2
Kim Jong Un, 349–50
King, J. C., 76, 77
Kirkpatrick, John, 227
Kissinger, Henry
  on the call for a law prohibiting assassination, 198
  compliance with the Church Committee, 190–1
  on a coup in Chile, 157, 158, 160, 164, 165, 167, 169, 170
  Executive Order 11905, 200
  on the 'Family Jewels,' 182
  investigation into the CIA's wrongdoings, 183–4
  relationship with William Colby, 183
Koch, Noel, 219, 220
Korry, Edward
  on a possible coup to overthrow Allende, 157–8, 165
  prevention of Allende's confirmation (Track I strategy), 156, 157, 158–9, 160–2
  on Schneider's opposition to a coup, 161–2
Krogh, Egil, 250

Laden, Osama bin *see* Bin Laden, Osama
Lake, Anthony, 280, 282, 285, 287, 303–4
language
  around the removal of Saddam Hussein, 292
  of assassinations, 5, 7
  and the authorisation to kill Bin Laden, 329–31
  and the ban on assassinations, 7
  of Carter's Executive Order 12036, 201–2, 217
  Church Committee report on, 195–6, 354
  CIA glossary for covert operations, 11

  of the Cold War, 7, 10, 38
  definitional debates, 8, 263
  of the Lumumba assassination plot, 47, 52–3, 55, 56, 57, 66–7, 354
  'neutralization' euphemism, 181, 221, 226–7, 228, 239, 358
  plausible deniability and, 67
  of the plots against Castro, 80–1, 89–90, 92–3, 98–9, 100
  of the plots against Trujillo, 110, 115, 123–4, 127, 354
  on the possible assassination of Diem, 134, 141–3, 149
  presidential deniability and, 196
  'the spiel,' 10, 82, 123
  targeted killing euphemism, 343
Lansdale, Edward, 89–91, 93, 140–1
Lazarus, Artie, 30, 33
Lebanon
  CIA training of intelligence teams, 223, 224
  targeting of Sheikh Fadlallah, 220, 224–5, 230, 239
Libya, 231, 232, 233
  see also Qaddafi, Muhammar
Liddy, Gordon, 154, 251
Lockhart, James, 171
Lodge, Henry Cabot, 133–4, 135–6, 139, 140, 144, 352
Lord, Winston, 159
Lorenz, Marita, 78
Lovell, Stanley, 25
Lubis, Zulkifli, 34–5
Lugar, Richard, 275, 289
Lumumba, Patrice
  anti-colonial struggle, 46
  Church Committee report on, 66–7, 193, 195
  as a communist and Soviet ally, 46, 49, 51, 52
  Congo independence speech, 45
  early career, 45–6
  Eisenhower's assassination order, 47, 52, 53, 55, 56, 57, 66–7, 196

382

Index

election as prime minister, 46
escape, re-capture and execution, 61–6
under house arrest, 56, 59, 60, 61
military reforms, 47
poison plot, 56–8, 59
relations with the UN, 54–5, 60–1
request for Western assistance, 47–8, 49
third-party actors mobilised against, 58–60, 63–4, 84, 352
US assessment of the leadership of, 48–9
US calls for the overthrow of, 50–1, 52–6
visit to the US, 51
see also Congo

MacMaster, Bruce, 163
Mafia
  Balletti wiretap FBI investigation, 82, 85–6, 87, 91
  in Cuba, 80
  joint CIA-Mafia plots against Castro, 75, 80–2, 83, 85, 91–2, 93–4, 99, 100
  Sturgis and Operation 40, 78
Maguire, John, 224
al-Mahdawi, Fahdil Abbas, 37
Maheu, Robert
  Balletti wiretap case, 82, 86–7
  CIA plots against Sukarno, 35, 80
  CIA-backed assassination plot against Castro, 75
  involvement with Trujillo, 111
  joint CIA-Mafia plots against Castro, 80–2, 83, 85, 91–2, 93–4, 99, 100
Manchurian candidates, 24–5, 28
Mankel, Jose Marie Andre (QJWIN-1)
  plot against Lumumba, 59–60, 61–2, 63, 64, 67, 84, 351
  plots against Castro, 84
Mann, Thomas, 115, 116

Marik, Warren, 282, 283, 288
Martinez Nunez, Jose Raul, 79
Massoud, Ahmed Shah, 315, 321–2, 329, 330
McCone, John, 88, 91, 93, 98, 99, 141
McMahon, John, 216, 221, 223, 229, 230, 358
McNamarra, Robert, 136, 139–40, 186
Meese, Edwin, 218
Memorandum of Notifications (MONs)
  authorising capture operations for Bin Laden, 307, 313, 316–17
  CIA and Massoud relationship, 321
  post-9/11, 342
  providing kill authority for Bin Laden, 316–18
mind control operations, 24–5, 26, 27–9
Minh, Duong Van, 133–4, 140, 141; *see also* Diem, Ngo Dinh; South Vietnam
Mitchell, John, 159
Mobutu, Joseph
  Agency support, 60
  assassination plot against Lumumba, 55
  attack on Kasai, 53–4
  as chief of staff, 47
  and Lumumba's escape, 61–2
  relations with the CIA, 49
  UN support for, 54–5, 62
  US-backed coup, 55–6
Mondale, Walter, 185, 195, 202, 226
morality/ethics
  of Cold War-era assassination, 354
  of direct vs indirect approaches, 59, 66
  of mind control experiments, 24, 29
Moss, Randy, 312
Murray, William, 79
Musawi, Hussein, 220

Index

Nasser, Gamal Abdel, 36
Nhu, Ngo Dinh
   army crackdown on the Buddhist monks, 135
   contact with North Vietnam, 140
   future after the attempted summer coup, 137–9
   killing of, 133–4, 146, 147
   Minh's coup d'etat, 144–5
   US knowledge of the possible summer coup/assassination, 135
Nicaragua
   the CIA-trained Contras, 225–6, 251
   the Contras manual and the ban on assassinations, 226–8
Nichter, Luke, 138, 146, 148
Nitze, Paul, 31
Nixon, Richard
   Anderson's investigations into, 154
   covert operations against Noriega, 250–1, 252
   on the need to assassinate Saddam Hussein, 276
   order for the instigation of a coup in Chile, 159–60, 167
   personal interest in the situation in Chile, 158, 159, 166, 169
   the war on drugs, 250
   Watergate, 182, 251
Nkrumah, Kwame, 45
Noriega, Manuel
   covert operations under George H. W. Bush, 252, 254–6, 263, 265
   covert operations under Nixon, 250–1, 252
   covert operations under Reagan, 251–5, 265
   the Giroldi coup, 256–8, 359
   relationship with the CIA, 251
   risk of assassination during US-backed coups, 254
   snatch operation against, 255–6

North, Oliver
   the 'contra war' against the Sandinistas, 226, 251
   hard-line policies, 221
   Lebanese CIA-trained hit teams, 223, 224
   on Qaddafi's threat, 235–6
North Korea, 349–50

Obama, Barack, 347–8, 349
O'Connell, James, 80, 85
O'Connell, Jeff, 308
O'Donnell, Justin, 59–60, 61, 66, 195, 354
Omar, Mullah, 344
Ossa, Ricardo, 160
Owen, Robert Edward, 116

Panama
   Bush-era involvement in coups, 252
   contestations over the ban on assassinations, post-failed coup, 260–5
   Eric Delvalle and coup plots, 253–4
   the Giroldi coup, 256–8, 359
   as a global drug hub, 250
   1989 elections, 255, 256
   US support for a coup, 252, 253
   see also Noriega, Manuel
Parks, Hays, 264–5, 266, 301
Parrott, Thomas, 82, 87–8, 116
Pash, Boris, 29–30
Pawley, William, 76, 112
Perry, William, 285
Phillips, David Attlee, 160, 194
Phillips, Rufus, 136
plausible deniability
   as an assassination condition, 4
   the attack Sheikh Fadlallah, 220, 224–5, 230, 239
   in the Chilean coup strategy, 158
   Church Committee report on, 196–7

Index

during the Cold War, 10
the 'contra war' against the Sandinistas and, 227
of the coup in Vietnam, 142–3
(im)plausible deniability construct, 9, 148
interpretive denial, 9, 231, 237
language and, 67
1974 Hughes-Ryan amendment, 11, 188, 355
presidential deniability, 196
in the Soleimani case, 4
'the spiel,' 10, 82, 123
tribal-led capture operations of Bin Laden, 307–8
US support and third-party actors/intermediaries, 5–6
use of false flaggers, 163, 165
poisons
  CIA collaboration with the military, 25, 29
  as a direct government method, 38
  early CIA assassination plots, 29–30, 34
  Health Alteration Committee (HAC), 37, 38
  plot against Abdul Karim Qassem, 37
  poison plots against Castro, 78, 81–2, 83, 91, 93–4, 95
  against Sukarno, 35
  use against Lumumba, 56–8, 59
politics
  of assassinations, 7
  of the Cold War plots, 38
  domestic political environment, 4, 5, 7
  domestic politics and the hunt for Bin Laden, 323
Porta, Fernando, 168, 171
Powell, Colin, 257, 258, 280–1, 327, 344
Powers, Thomas, 10, 25, 82, 123, 174
Prado, Ric, 215, 304, 344
Prados, John, 81, 344
Prats, Carlos, 159
Priest, Dana, 346
Prouty, Fletcher, 78
Psaki, Jen, 351
Putin, Vladimir, 350–1

Qaddafi, Muhammar
  arming of anti-Qaddafi groups, 233
  campaign of assassination against, 214, 231, 232, 235–7, 289
  FLOWER plan, 232–3, 240
  Operation El Dorado Canyon, 235–7, 239, 358–9
  propaganda campaign against, 232
  US support for a coups against, 231–2
Qassem, Abdul Karim, 36–7

racism
  intelligence collection and analysis, 4
  leader assessment criteria, 9–10, 48–9, 51
Reagan, Ronald
  counterterrorism measures, 214, 219, 220, 358
  covert operations against Noriega, 251–5, 265
  focus on international terrorism, 213
  foreign policy on Libya, 231, 233
  legal work, 239–40
  National Security Decision Directives, 219, 221, 222, 224, 234, 358
  reinterpretation of the ban on assassination, 214, 239–40, 358
  the reinvigorated CIA under, 213, 214–15, 216, 217
  second 1984 presidential debate, 226
  support for the mujahideen, 228–9
  the war on drugs, 251–2
  see also Qaddafi, Muhammar
Reed, Lear, 112, 114

Index

regime change
  assassination as a tool for, 4
  during the Cold War, 35–7, 38–9
  Dominican Republic, 112–13
  in Indonesia, 35
  in Iraq (1959), 36–7
  in Syria, 36
  see also Dominican Republic;
    South Vietnam
Reno, Janet, 308, 317
Rice, Condoleezza, 326, 344–5
Richardson, John, 139, 140, 142–3
Richter, Steve, 281–2, 286, 287
Riedel, Bruce, 360
Risen, James, 313
Rizzo, John, 11, 313, 317, 321, 342
Rockefeller, Nelson, 185, 187
Rockefeller Commission, 181–2,
  184–7, 190, 200, 214
Rodriguez, Felix, 84–5, 97
Rodriguez, Pablo, 165
Roosevelt, Cornelius, 81
Rosselli, Johnny, 78, 80, 81, 91, 192
Rubottom, Roy, 113, 115
Rumsfeld, Donald, 183, 327, 345
Rusk, Dean, 118, 135, 136, 139, 141
Russia, 350–1

Samarrai, Wafiq, 283, 285–6, 292, 293
Sanchez, Nestor, 96, 97
Saudi Arabia, 224–5
Scheuer, Michael, 304, 305, 306–7,
  315, 316, 317, 318, 319
Schlesinger, James, 182
Schneider, René
  assassination as a possible outcome
    for, 155, 166, 173, 174, 352–3
  assassinations plots against, 159,
    164–5
  Church Committee report on, 193
  opposition to a coup, 155, 156,
    157, 158, 161–2
  US collaboration in the kidnap
    plot, 155, 165, 166, 167, 168,
    171–2, 174

Schorr, Daniel, 180, 181
Schroen, Gary, 307, 308, 315, 316,
  318
Schwarzkopf, Norman, 274
Schweizer, Peter, 229
Scowcroft, Brent, 271, 272, 274,
  276
Severo Cabral, Angel, 121, 126
Sforza, Anthony, 163
Shelton, Hugh, 310
Shimon, Joseph, 75
Shultz, George
  as a Casey ally, 217, 221
  on Operation El Dorado Canyon,
    237
  on Qadcafi's threat, 234
  on US counterterrorism measures,
    220, 221, 358
  US policy on Noriega, 254–5
Smathers, George, 112
Smith, David, 141
Smith, Joseph, 26, 31, 38, 146
Sofaer, Abraham, 237–8, 264, 265,
  266, 313
Soleimani, Qassem
  assassination, 1–2
  Bin Laden's assassination and, 13
  plausible deniability, 4
  US justification for the killing, 2–3,
    350
South Vietnam
  army crackdown on the Buddhist
    monks, 135, 136
  Civil Operations and Rural
    Development Support (CORDS),
    181
  Conein's liaison with Minh's coup,
    144–6
  indirect US government
    involvement, 147–8
  Lodge's policy on, 140, 144
  November 1963 coup, 149
  Phoenix Program, 21 n.62, 181,
    226, 227, 354
  in US foreign policy, 134, 139–40

386

Index

US knowledge of the possible summer coup, 135–7
US plausible deniability over, 142–3, 148
US stance on Diem's possible assassination, 141–2, 352, 354
US support for the November 1963 coup, 133–4, 140, 141–3, 144–7, 180–1
US support for the summer 1963 coup, 137–9
Soviet Union (USSR), 49; *see also* Cold War
Specter, Arlen, 289
Sporkin, Stanley, 216, 224, 240
Stalin, Joseph, 31
state-sponsored terrorism
  the 'contra war' against the Sandinistas and, 226–7
  term, 213
Sturgis, Frank (Fiorini), 77–8
Sudan, 232, 239, 291, 304–5, 310
Sukarno
  assassination plots against, 34–5
  Church Committee report on, 43 n.70, 193
  CIA campaign to discredit, 35, 80
Syria, 36, 219–20
Szulc, Tad, 88

targeted killings
  the ban on assassinations and, 344–5
  against Bin Laden, 347
  under the Bush Administration, 343–4
  drones, 344
  as a euphemism for assassinations, 343
  under the Obama Administration, 347–8
  Project Cannonball, 344
  use of drones, 13–14, 343
Taylor, Maxwell, 85–6, 89, 139–40, 147

Tenet, George
  the ban on assassinations and Bin Laden, 329–30
  Blue Sky memo, 325–6
  covert operation authorities of the CIA, 328
  hunt for Bin Laden, 306, 308–10, 314, 315, 316, 318, 319, 321, 322, 325, 327
  9/11 response, 341
  operations against Saddam Hussein, 282, 287, 346
terrorism
  al-Qaeda's threat, 301–2
  attacks at Vienna and Rome airports, 233
  the Embassy bombings, 309, 310
  hijacking of a TWA flight, 233, 236
  in Reagan's foreign policy, 180
  West Berlin club bombing, 235
  see also Bin Laden, Osama; counterterrorism; state-sponsored terrorism
third-party actors
  assassinations by and the ban on, 226, 227–8, 233
  during the Cold War, 351–2
  indirect US government involvement, 5–6, 38, 352
  Lebanese, CIA-trained hit teams, 223–4
  plausible deniability and, 5–6
  plot against Lumumba, 58–60, 63–4, 84, 351, 352
  plots against Castro, 84
  Sukarno plot, 34–5
  Zhou Enlai plots, 32–4
Thomas, Evan, 87, 100
Thomas, Frank, 116
Thurman, Maxwell, 257
Timberlake, Clare, 47–8, 50, 53, 54
Tirado, Hugo, 171
Torrijos, Omar, 250–1
Tower, John, 189, 190

387

Index

Trafficante, Santo, 81, 85
Trujillo, Rafael
  alliance with the CIA, 31
  Church Committee report on, 193
  Eisenhower-era plot against, 111, 112–16, 126
  Kennedy-era plot against, 111, 116–26
  kidnap of Jesus de Galindez, 111
  killed while visiting a mistress, 111, 125–6
  language of the plots against, 110, 115, 123–4, 127, 354
  the Rockefeller Commission's investigation and, 185, 187
  as a staunch US ally, 110–11
  US direct involvement with the local plotters, 6
  US operational proposal against, 116, 117, 118–26, 127
  US-backed invasion of Cuba, 76
  see also Dominican Republic
Trump, Donald
  assassination of Soleimani, 1–3, 350
  Bashar al-Assad as a possible target, 350
  Kim Jong Un as a possible target, 349–50
Truscott, Lucien, 34
Tsang, Steve, 33
Tshombe, Moise, 46, 48, 49, 50
Turner, Stansfield, 202, 215, 217
Tweedy, Bronson, 55, 56, 57, 58–9, 66
Tzitzichvili, David (WIROGUE-1), 63–4, 65

United Nations (UN)
  involvement in Congo, 48, 49–50, 51, 54–5, 60–1
  sanctions against Iraq, 275
  UN Charter, Article 51, 3

Vaky, Viron, 159
Valenzuela, Camilo, 157, 158, 164–5, 169, 171, 172, 174
Varona, Tony, 81, 85, 91
Viaux, Roberto, 155, 156, 160, 165, 166–9, 171, 172–4
Vicini, Gianni, 116, 117, 121

Walker, William, 252–3
war on drugs, 4, 250, 251–2
war on terrorism, 4, 13–14
Watergate, 187–8
weapons
  aerial bombings, 12
  for AMLASH (Cubela), 97, 98
  arming of anti-Qaddafi groups, 233
  in the Church Committee report, 194
  for the Dominican dissidents, 110, 114, 115, 116–17, 118, 119–20, 121–3, 124–5, 126, 352
  drugs and poisons, 25, 28, 29
  hypnosis as, 24, 27
  mind control operations, 24–5, 26, 27–9
  precision bombing, 5
  US supply to Chile, 155, 165, 166, 171, 172
  US support for the mujahideen, 228–31
  see also drones
Weatherby, William, 95–6
Webster, William, 7, 240, 252, 254, 260–1, 276, 359
Weinberger, Caspar, 221, 237
Wimert, Paul, 163, 164, 167, 171, 172
Wisner, Frank, 30, 31, 34
Woodward, Bob, 3, 346, 350
Woolsey, James, 280, 281, 288

Zelikow, Philip, 318
Zhou Enlai, 32–4, 38, 193, 351

Printed and bound by CPI Group (UK) Ltd, Croydon, CR0 4YY
20/01/2025
01822670-0007